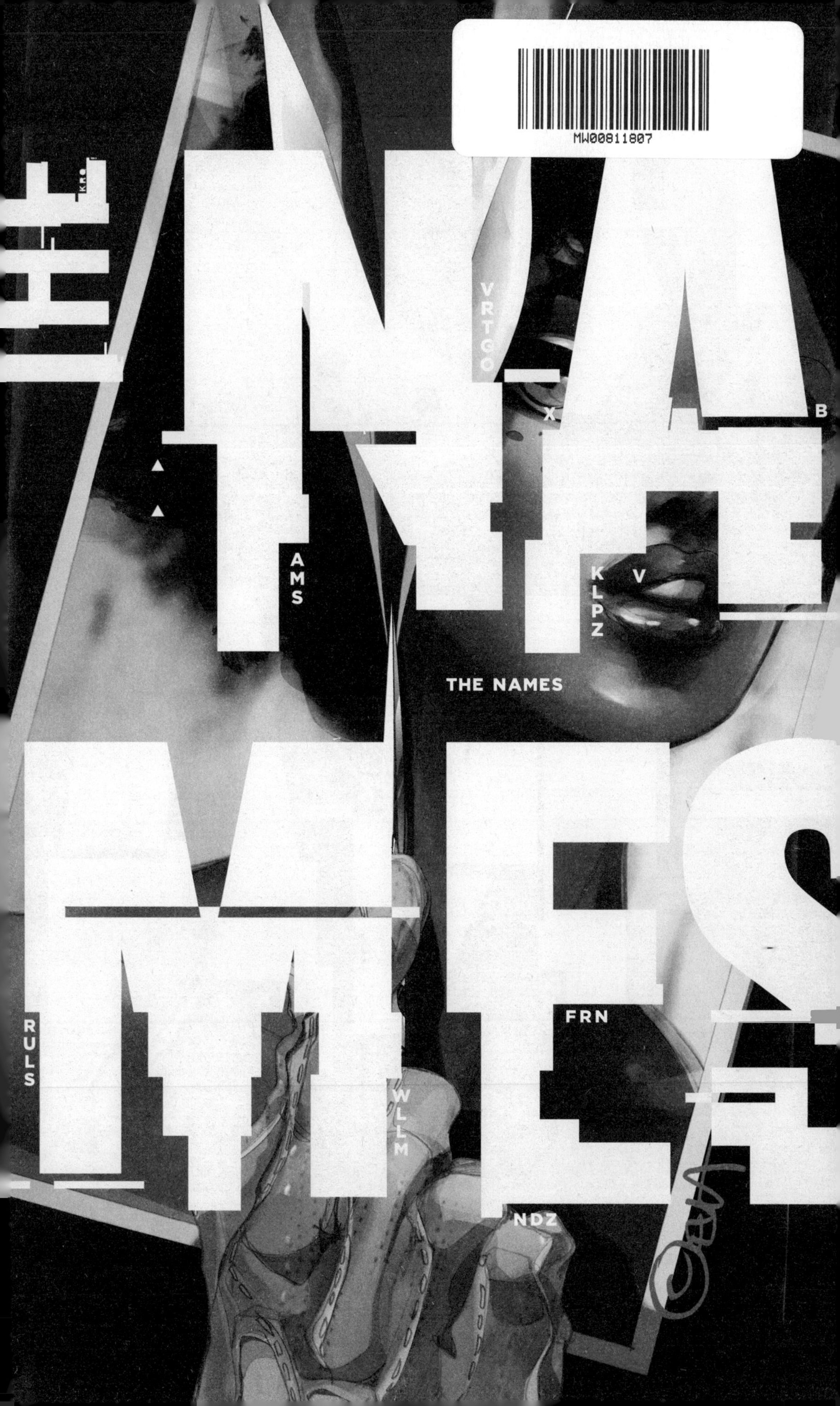
THE NAMES
VRTGO
X
B
AMS
K V
KLPZ
THE NAMES
RULS
FRN
WLLM
NDZ

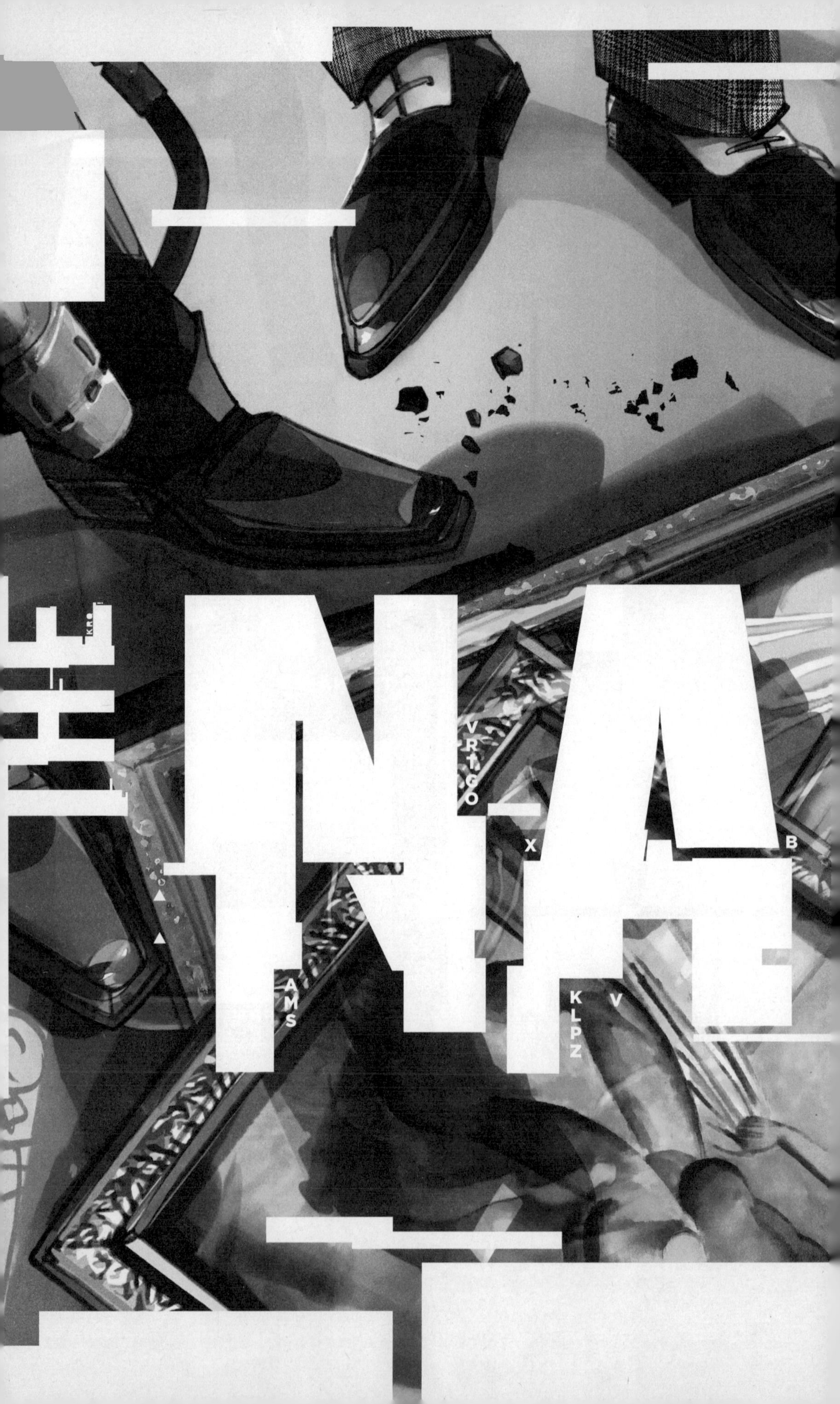
THE
NA
VRTGO
X
B
AMS
K
V
KLPZ

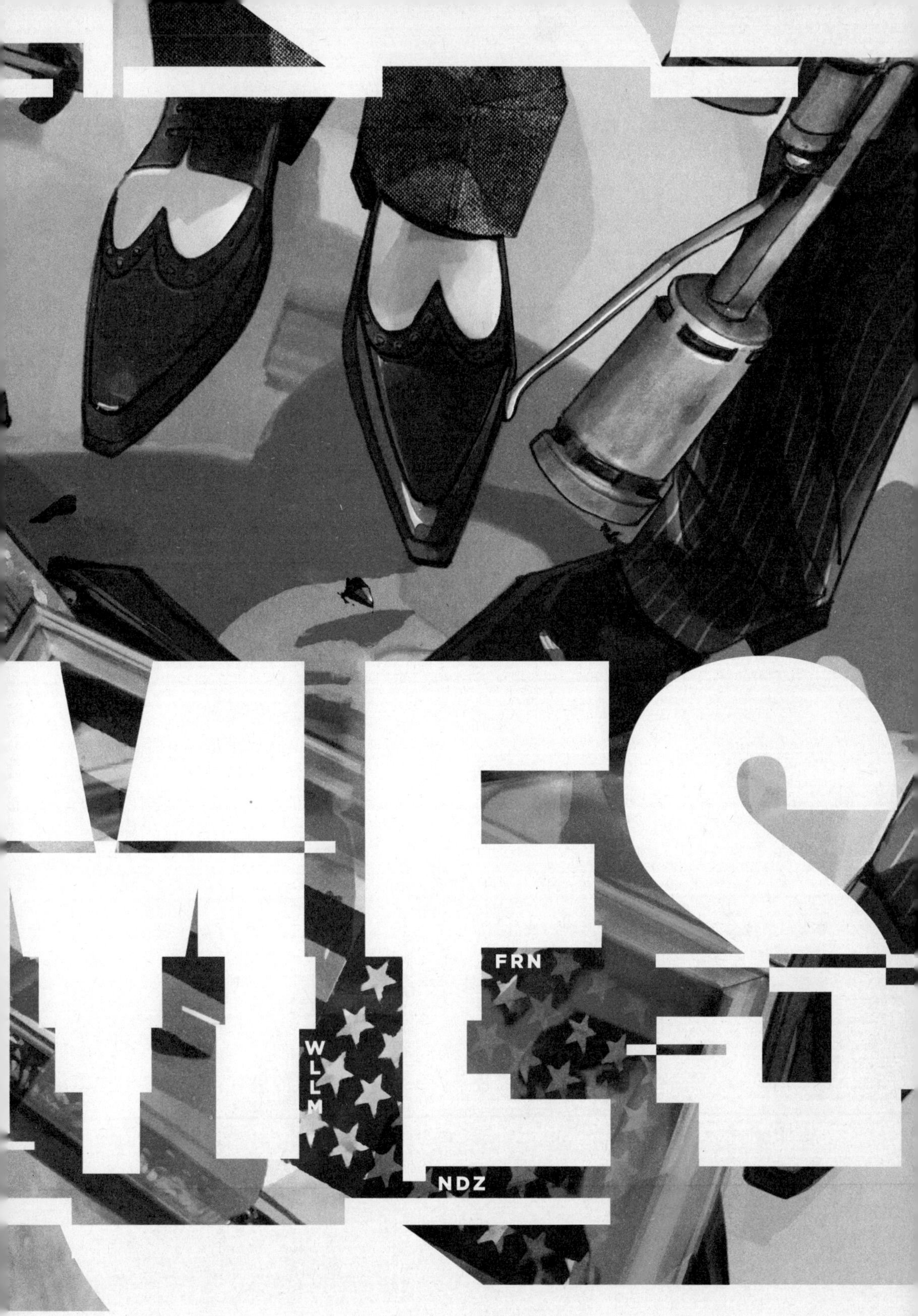
FRN
WLLM
NDZ

Script by Peter Milligan   Art by Leandro Fernandez
Color by Cris Peter   Letters by Carlos M. Mangual
Cover Art and Original Series Covers by Celia Calle
THE NAMES created by Peter Milligan and Leandro Fernandez

Will Dennis Editor – Original Series
Greg Lockard Associate Editor – Original Series
Jeb Woodard Group Editor – Collected Editions
Scott Nybakken Editor
Louis Prandi Publication Design

Shelly Bond VP & Executive Editor – Vertigo

Diane Nelson President
Dan DiDio and Jim Lee Co-Publishers
Geoff Johns Chief Creative Officer
Amit Desai Senior VP – Marketing & Global Franchise Management
Nairi Gardiner Senior VP – Finance
Sam Ades VP – Digital Marketing
Bobbie Chase VP – Talent Development
Mark Chiarello Senior VP – Art, Design & Collected Editions
John Cunningham VP – Content Strategy
Anne DePies VP – Strategy Planning & Reporting
Don Falletti VP – Manufacturing Operations
Lawrence Ganem VP – Editorial Administration & Talent Relations
Alison Gill Senior VP – Manufacturing & Operations
Hank Kanalz Senior VP – Editorial Strategy & Administration
Jay Kogan VP – Legal Affairs
Derek Maddalena Senior VP – Sales & Business Development
Dan Miron VP – Sales Planning & Trade Development
Nick Napolitano VP – Manufacturing Administration
Carol Roeder VP – Marketing
Eddie Scannell VP – Mass Account & Digital Sales
Susan Sheppard VP – Business Affairs
Courtney Simmons Senior VP – Publicity & Communications
Jim (Ski) Sokolowski VP – Comic Book Specialty & Newsstand Sales

Library of Congress Cataloging-in-
Publication Data

Milligan, Peter.
    The Names / Peter Milligan, writer;
Leandro Fernandez, artist.
        pages cm
    ISBN 978-1-4012-5243-4
(paperback)
    1. International finance—Comic
books, strips, etc. 2. Murder—Comic
books, strips, etc. 3. Graphic
novels. I. Fernandez, Leandro,
illustrator. II. Title.
    PN6737.M536N36 2015
    741.5'942—dc23

2015008053

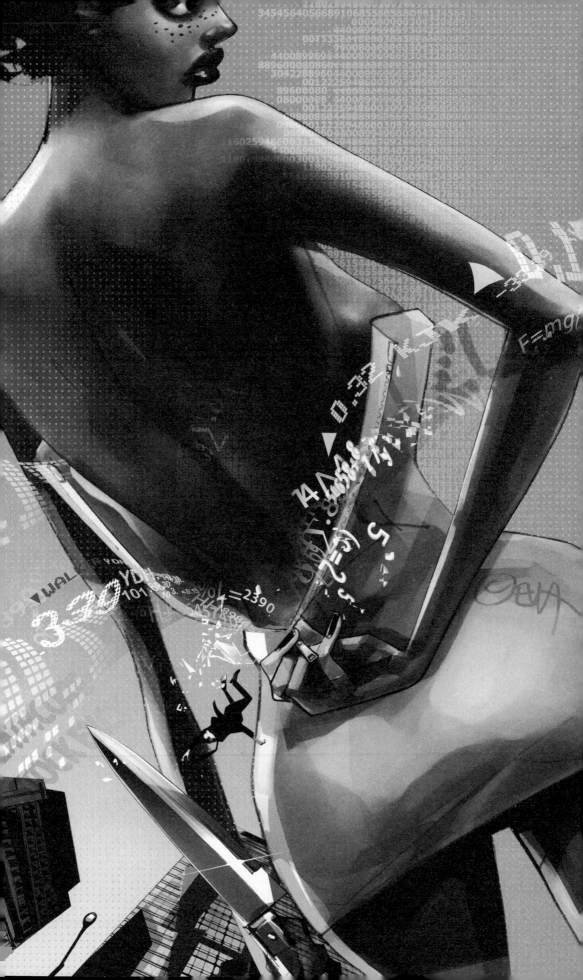

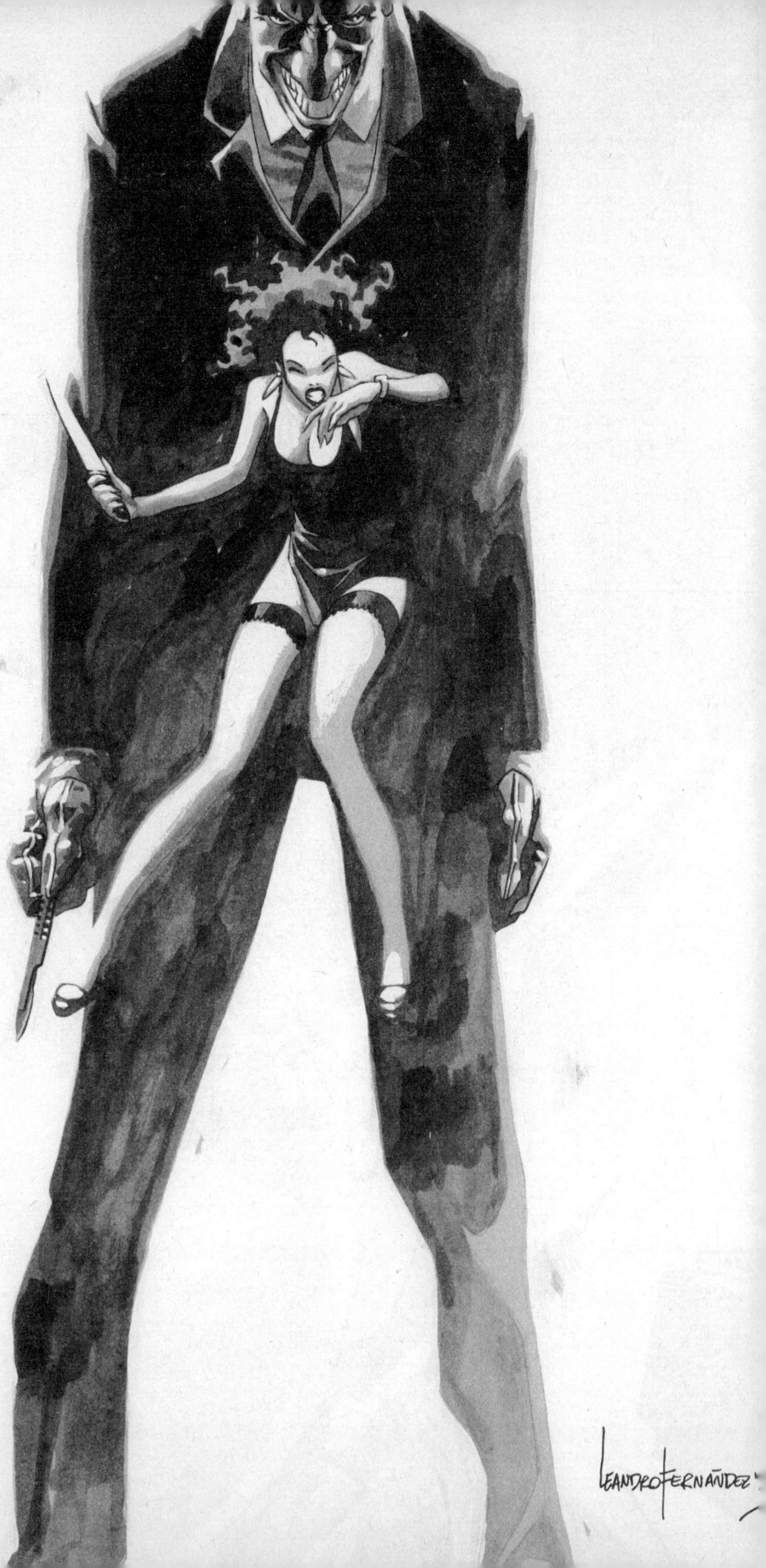
LEANDRO FERNÁNDEZ

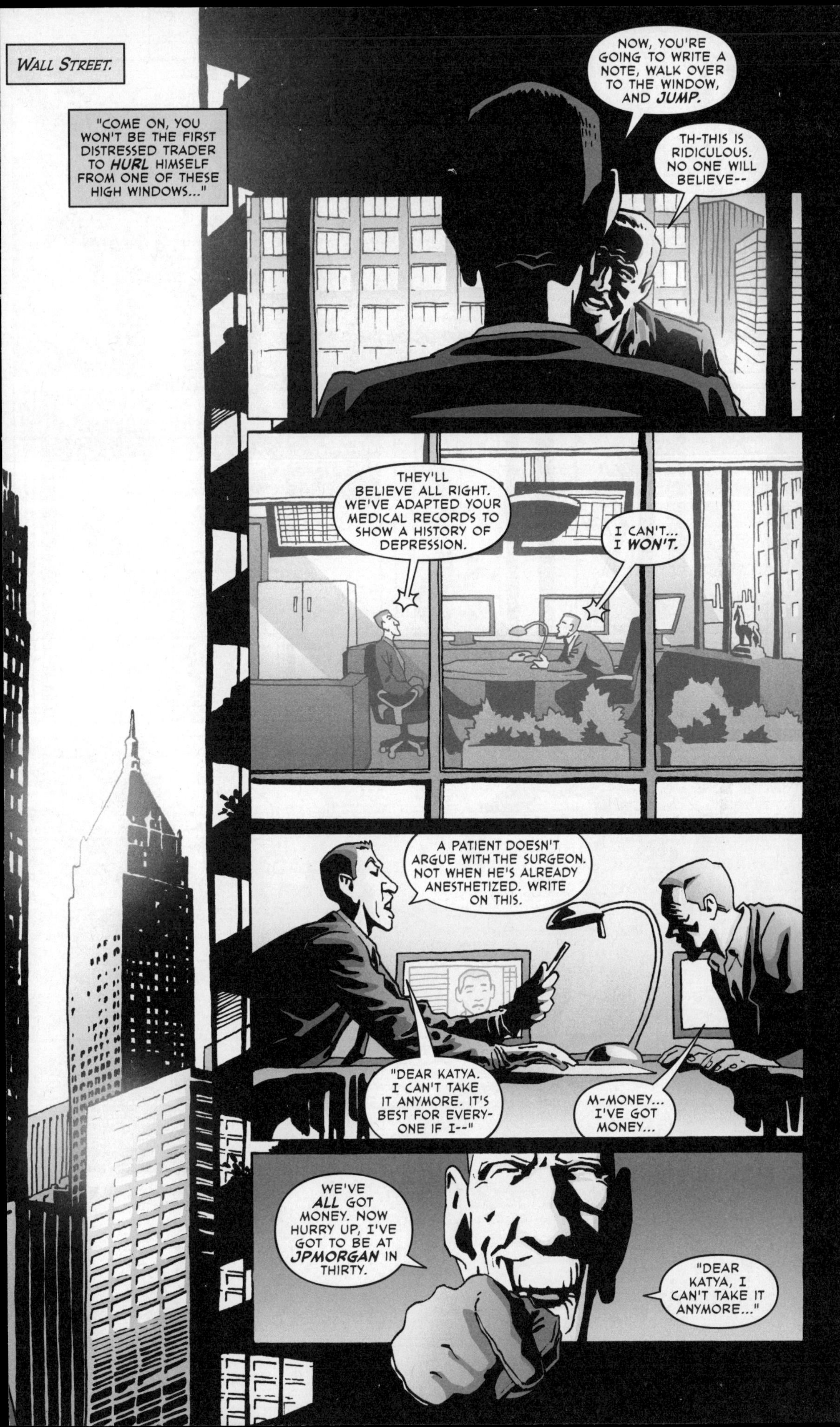

WALL STREET.
"COME ON, YOU WON'T BE THE FIRST DISTRESSED TRADER TO HURL HIMSELF FROM ONE OF THESE HIGH WINDOWS..."
NOW, YOU'RE GOING TO WRITE A NOTE, WALK OVER TO THE WINDOW, AND JUMP.
TH-THIS IS RIDICULOUS. NO ONE WILL BELIEVE--
THEY'LL BELIEVE ALL RIGHT. WE'VE ADAPTED YOUR MEDICAL RECORDS TO SHOW A HISTORY OF DEPRESSION.
I CAN'T... I WON'T.
A PATIENT DOESN'T ARGUE WITH THE SURGEON. NOT WHEN HE'S ALREADY ANESTHETIZED. WRITE ON THIS.
"DEAR KATYA. I CAN'T TAKE IT ANYMORE. IT'S BEST FOR EVERY-ONE IF I--"
M-MONEY... I'VE GOT MONEY...
WE'VE ALL GOT MONEY. NOW HURRY UP, I'VE GOT TO BE AT JPMORGAN IN THIRTY.
"DEAR KATYA, I CAN'T TAKE IT ANYMORE..."

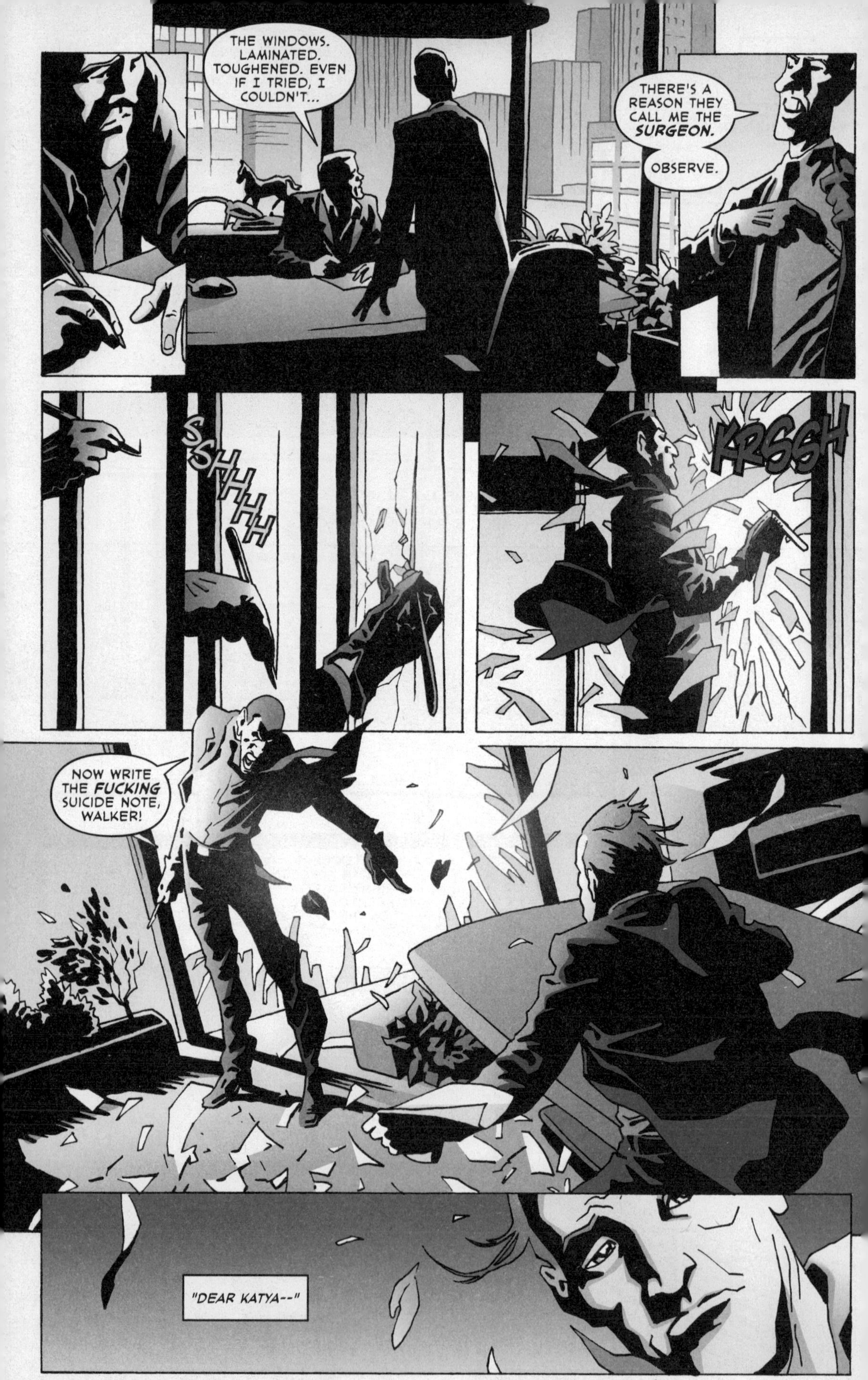
THE WINDOWS. LAMINATED. TOUGHENED. EVEN IF I TRIED, I COULDN'T...
THERE'S A REASON THEY CALL ME THE SURGEON.
OBSERVE.
SSHHHH
KRSSH
NOW WRITE THE FUCKING SUICIDE NOTE, WALKER!
"DEAR KATYA--"

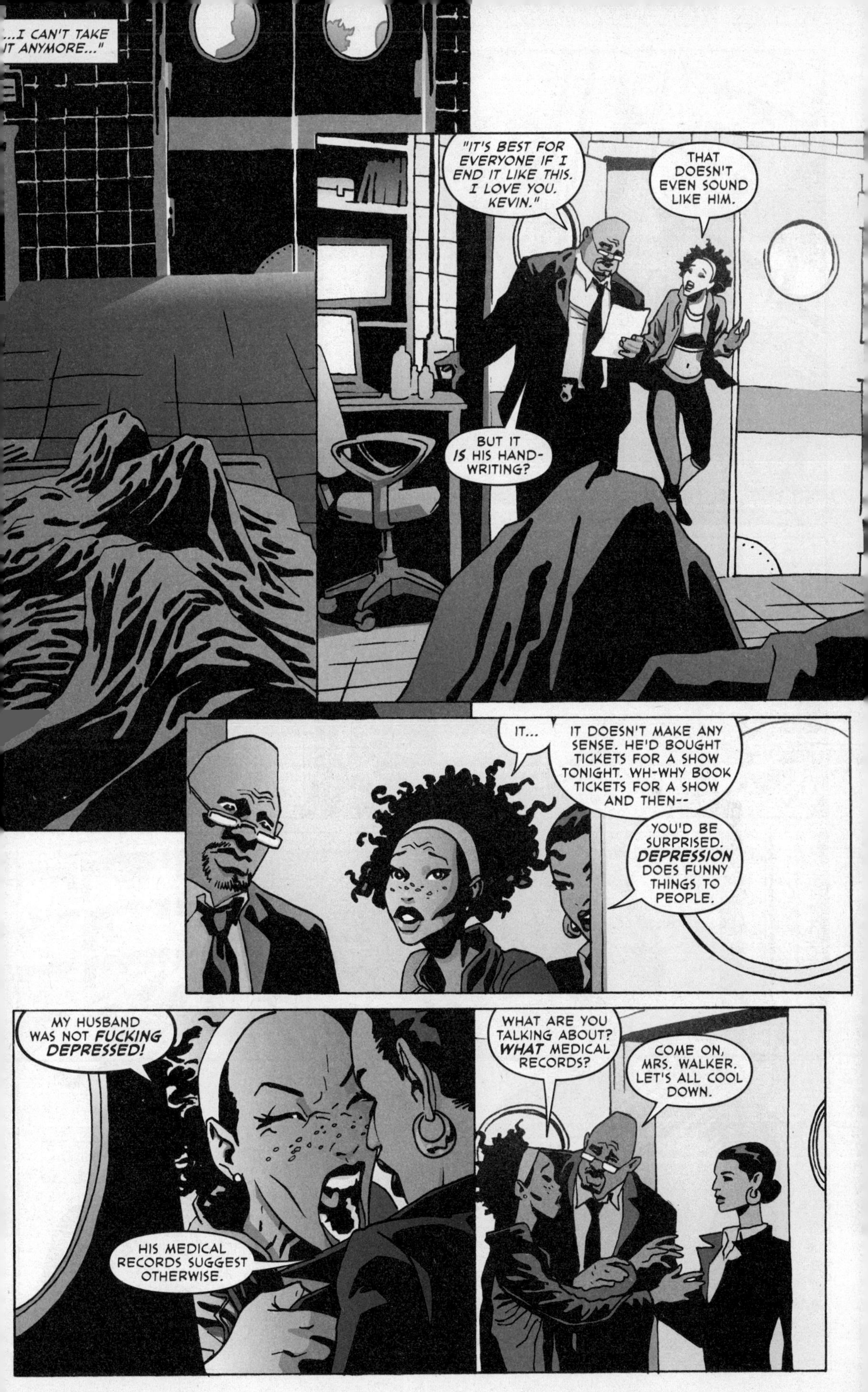
...I CAN'T TAKE IT ANYMORE..."
"IT'S BEST FOR EVERYONE IF I END IT LIKE THIS. I LOVE YOU. KEVIN."
THAT DOESN'T EVEN SOUND LIKE HIM.
BUT IT *IS* HIS HAND-WRITING?
IT...
IT DOESN'T MAKE ANY SENSE. HE'D BOUGHT TICKETS FOR A SHOW TONIGHT. WH-WHY BOOK TICKETS FOR A SHOW AND THEN--
YOU'D BE SURPRISED. ***DEPRESSION*** DOES FUNNY THINGS TO PEOPLE.
MY HUSBAND WAS NOT ***FUCKING DEPRESSED!***
HIS MEDICAL RECORDS SUGGEST OTHERWISE.
WHAT ARE YOU TALKING ABOUT? ***WHAT*** MEDICAL RECORDS?
COME ON, MRS. WALKER. LET'S ALL COOL DOWN.

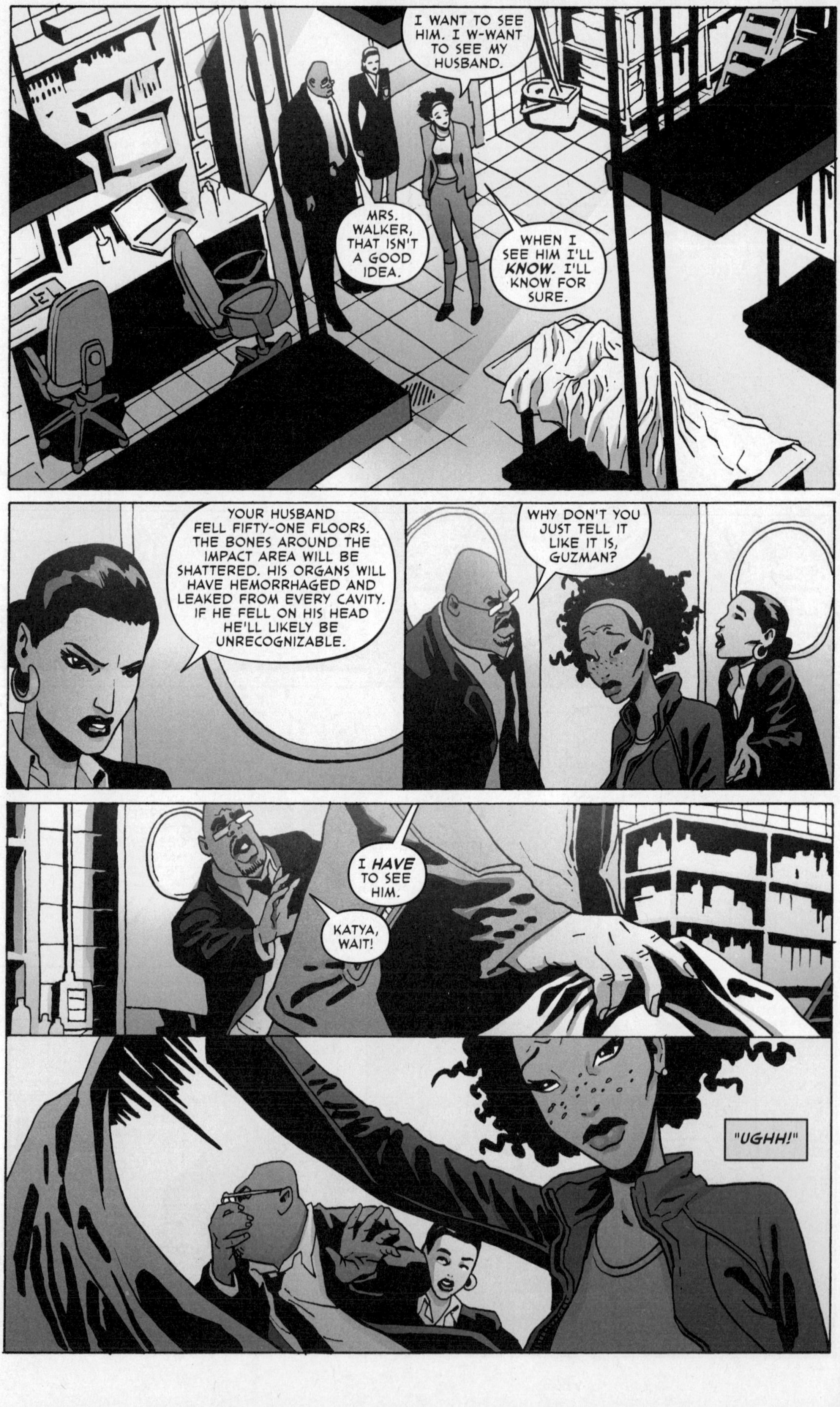
I WANT TO SEE HIM. I W-WANT TO SEE MY HUSBAND.
MRS. WALKER, THAT ISN'T A GOOD IDEA.
WHEN I SEE HIM I'LL *KNOW.* I'LL KNOW FOR SURE.
YOUR HUSBAND FELL FIFTY-ONE FLOORS. THE BONES AROUND THE IMPACT AREA WILL BE SHATTERED. HIS ORGANS WILL HAVE HEMORRHAGED AND LEAKED FROM EVERY CAVITY. IF HE FELL ON HIS HEAD HE'LL LIKELY BE UNRECOGNIZABLE.
WHY DON'T YOU JUST TELL IT LIKE IT IS, GUZMAN?
I *HAVE* TO SEE HIM.
KATYA, WAIT!
"UGHH!"

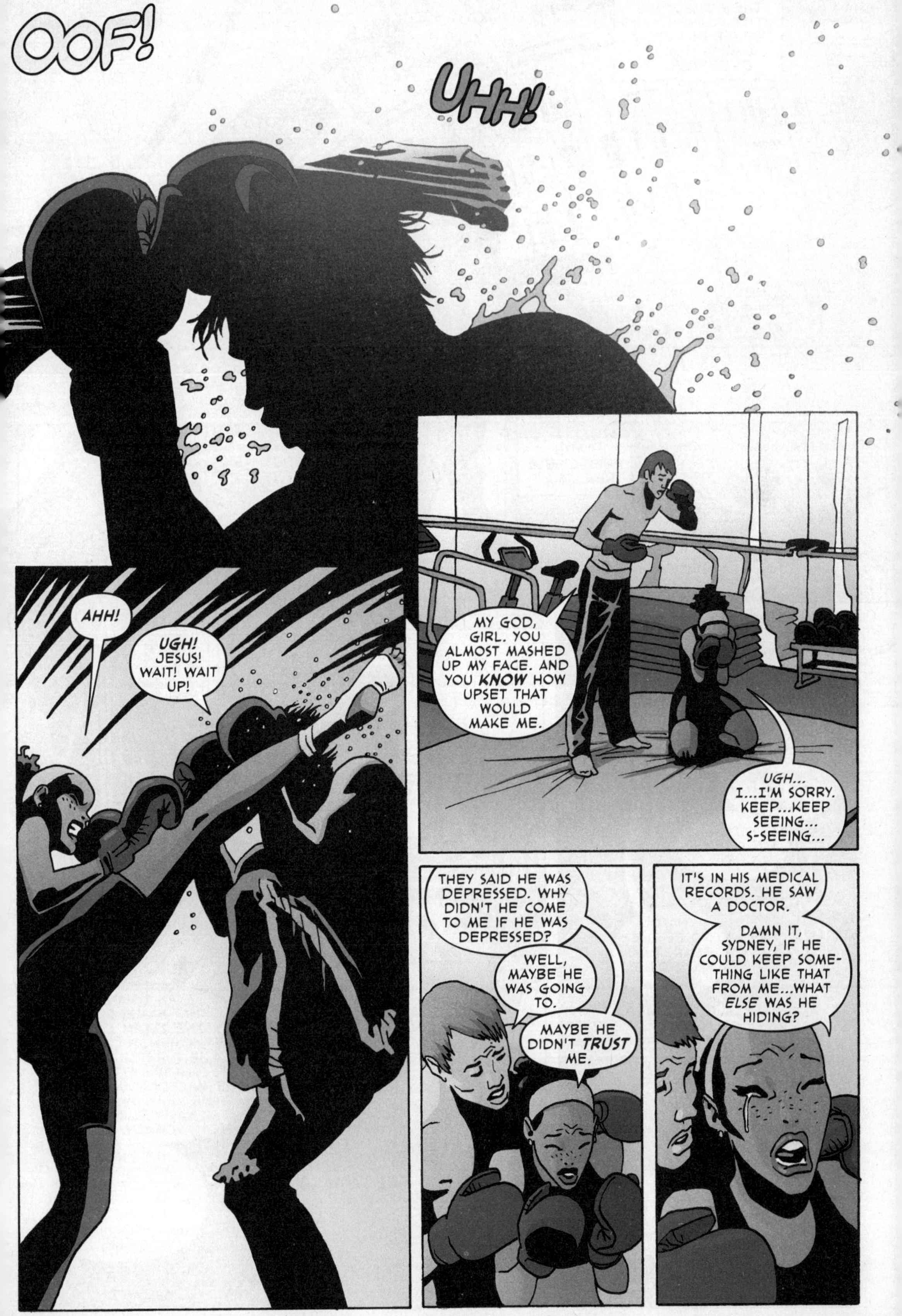

OOF!
UHH!
AHH!
UGH! JESUS! WAIT! WAIT UP!
MY GOD, GIRL. YOU ALMOST MASHED UP MY FACE. AND YOU KNOW HOW UPSET THAT WOULD MAKE ME.
UGH... I...I'M SORRY. KEEP...KEEP SEEING... S-SEEING...
THEY SAID HE WAS DEPRESSED. WHY DIDN'T HE COME TO ME IF HE WAS DEPRESSED?
WELL, MAYBE HE WAS GOING TO.
MAYBE HE DIDN'T TRUST ME.
IT'S IN HIS MEDICAL RECORDS. HE SAW A DOCTOR.
DAMN IT, SYDNEY, IF HE COULD KEEP SOME-THING LIKE THAT FROM ME...WHAT ELSE WAS HE HIDING?

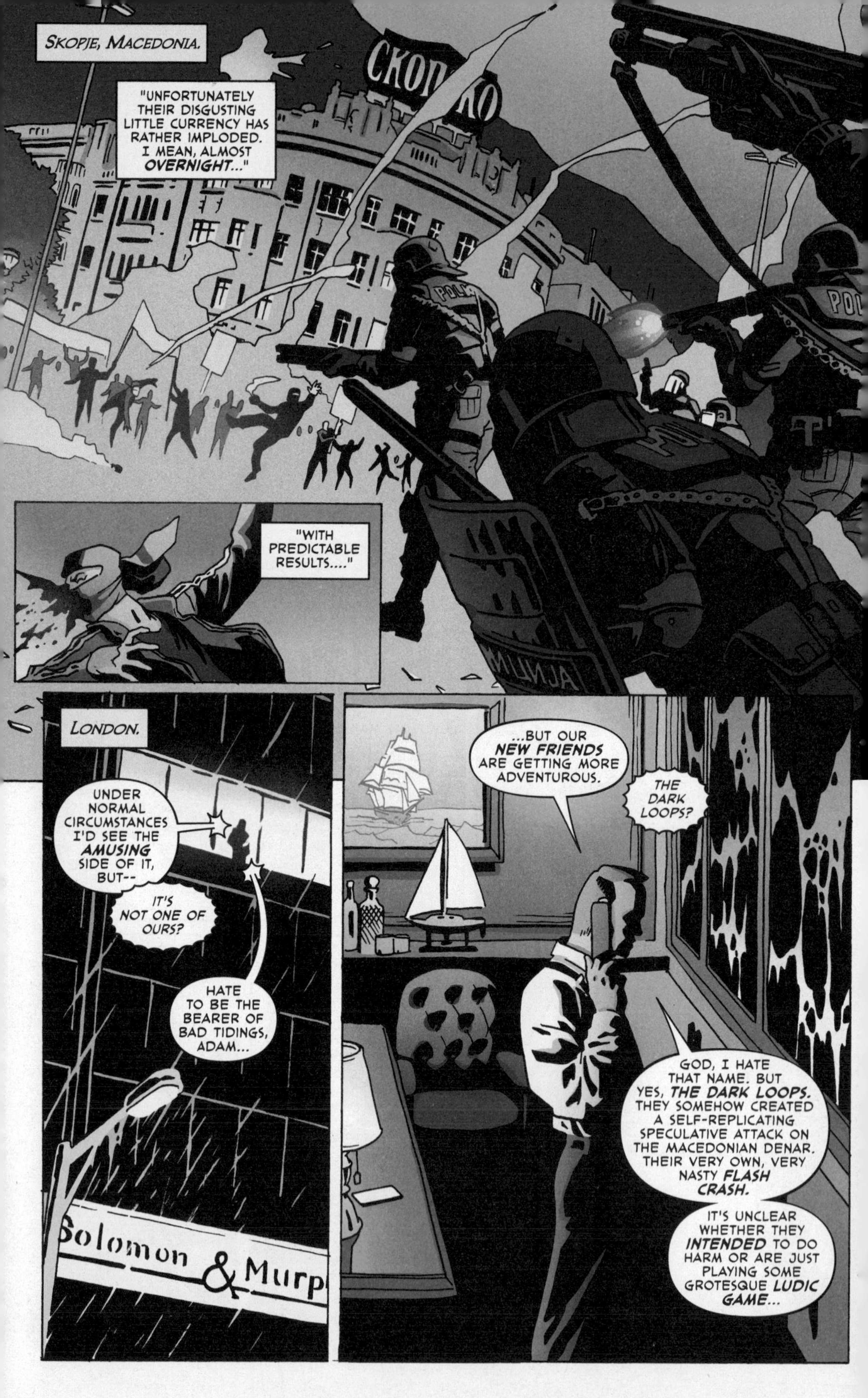
SKOPJE, MACEDONIA.
"UNFORTUNATELY THEIR DISGUSTING LITTLE CURRENCY HAS RATHER IMPLODED. I MEAN, ALMOST OVERNIGHT..."
"WITH PREDICTABLE RESULTS...."
LONDON.
UNDER NORMAL CIRCUMSTANCES I'D SEE THE AMUSING SIDE OF IT, BUT--
IT'S NOT ONE OF OURS?
HATE TO BE THE BEARER OF BAD TIDINGS, ADAM...
Solomon & Murp
...BUT OUR NEW FRIENDS ARE GETTING MORE ADVENTUROUS.
THE DARK LOOPS?
GOD, I HATE THAT NAME. BUT YES, THE DARK LOOPS. THEY SOMEHOW CREATED A SELF-REPLICATING SPECULATIVE ATTACK ON THE MACEDONIAN DENAR. THEIR VERY OWN, VERY NASTY FLASH CRASH.
IT'S UNCLEAR WHETHER THEY INTENDED TO DO HARM OR ARE JUST PLAYING SOME GROTESQUE LUDIC GAME...

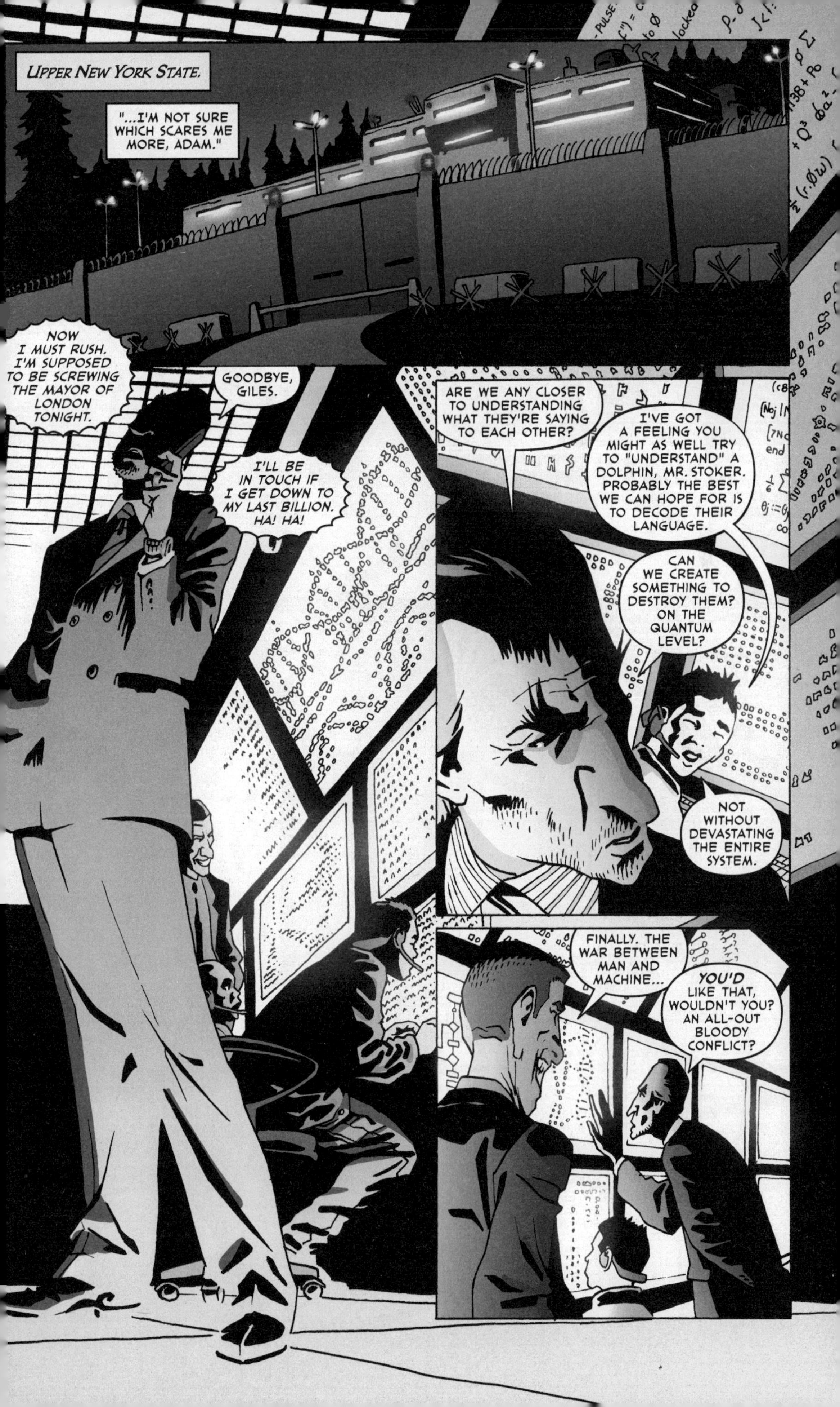
UPPER NEW YORK STATE.
"...I'M NOT SURE WHICH SCARES ME MORE, ADAM."
NOW I MUST RUSH. I'M SUPPOSED TO BE SCREWING THE MAYOR OF LONDON TONIGHT.
GOODBYE, GILES.
I'LL BE IN TOUCH IF I GET DOWN TO MY LAST BILLION. HA! HA!
ARE WE ANY CLOSER TO UNDERSTANDING WHAT THEY'RE SAYING TO EACH OTHER?
I'VE GOT A FEELING YOU MIGHT AS WELL TRY TO "UNDERSTAND" A DOLPHIN, MR. STOKER. PROBABLY THE BEST WE CAN HOPE FOR IS TO DECODE THEIR LANGUAGE.
CAN WE CREATE SOMETHING TO DESTROY THEM? ON THE QUANTUM LEVEL?
NOT WITHOUT DEVASTATING THE ENTIRE SYSTEM.
FINALLY. THE WAR BETWEEN MAN AND MACHINE...
YOU'D LIKE THAT, WOULDN'T YOU? AN ALL-OUT BLOODY CONFLICT?

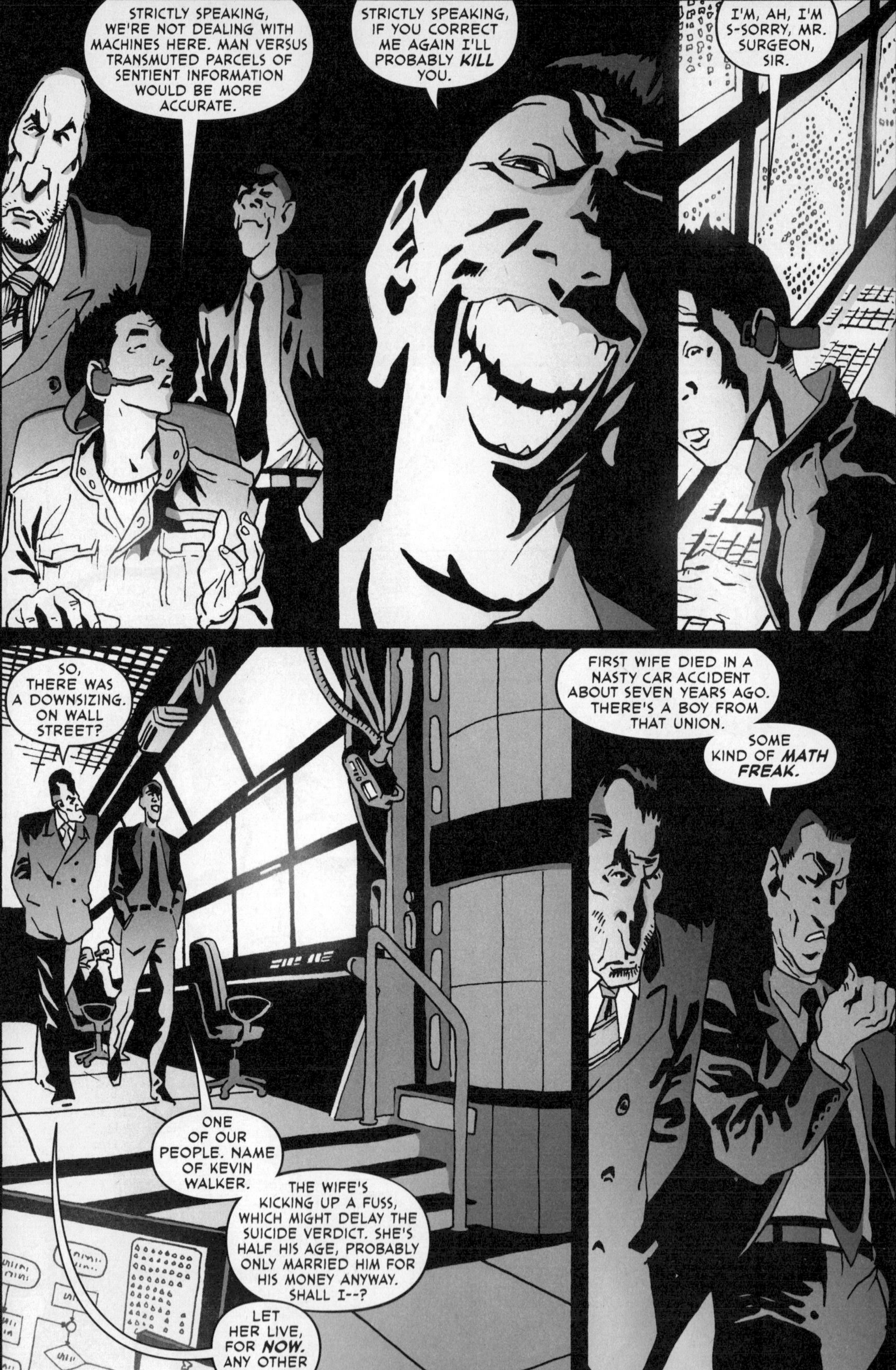
STRICTLY SPEAKING, WE'RE NOT DEALING WITH MACHINES HERE. MAN VERSUS TRANSMUTED PARCELS OF SENTIENT INFORMATION WOULD BE MORE ACCURATE.
STRICTLY SPEAKING, IF YOU CORRECT ME AGAIN I'LL PROBABLY KILL YOU.
I'M, AH, I'M S-SORRY, MR. SURGEON, SIR.
SO, THERE WAS A DOWNSIZING. ON WALL STREET?
ONE OF OUR PEOPLE. NAME OF KEVIN WALKER.
THE WIFE'S KICKING UP A FUSS, WHICH MIGHT DELAY THE SUICIDE VERDICT. SHE'S HALF HIS AGE, PROBABLY ONLY MARRIED HIM FOR HIS MONEY ANYWAY. SHALL I--?
LET HER LIVE, FOR NOW. ANY OTHER FAMILY?
FIRST WIFE DIED IN A NASTY CAR ACCIDENT ABOUT SEVEN YEARS AGO. THERE'S A BOY FROM THAT UNION.
SOME KIND OF MATH FREAK.

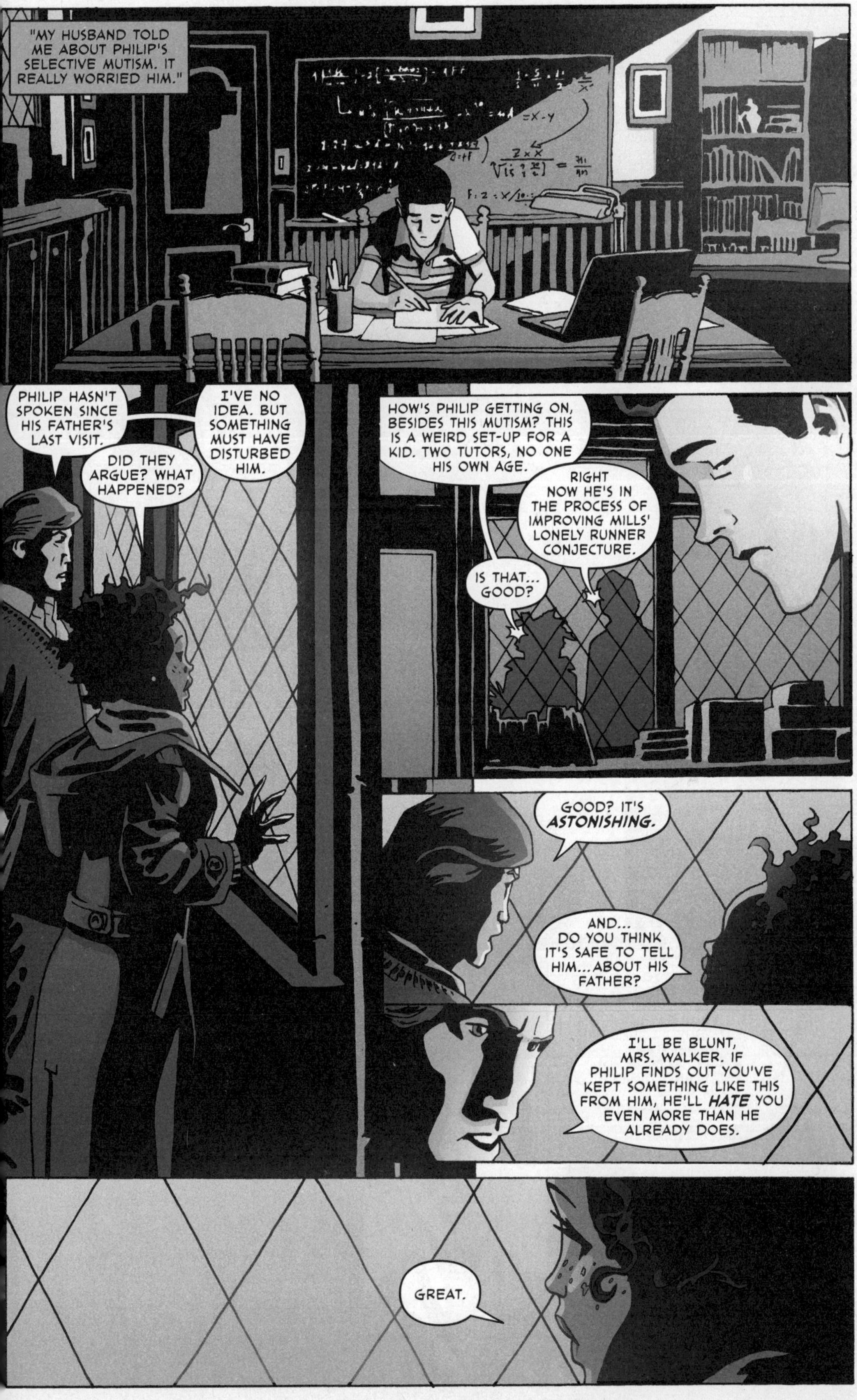
"MY HUSBAND TOLD ME ABOUT PHILIP'S SELECTIVE MUTISM. IT REALLY WORRIED HIM."
PHILIP HASN'T SPOKEN SINCE HIS FATHER'S LAST VISIT.
DID THEY ARGUE? WHAT HAPPENED?
I'VE NO IDEA. BUT SOMETHING MUST HAVE DISTURBED HIM.
HOW'S PHILIP GETTING ON, BESIDES THIS MUTISM? THIS IS A WEIRD SET-UP FOR A KID. TWO TUTORS, NO ONE HIS OWN AGE.
RIGHT NOW HE'S IN THE PROCESS OF IMPROVING MILLS' LONELY RUNNER CONJECTURE.
IS THAT... GOOD?
GOOD? IT'S ASTONISHING.
AND... DO YOU THINK IT'S SAFE TO TELL HIM... ABOUT HIS FATHER?
I'LL BE BLUNT, MRS. WALKER. IF PHILIP FINDS OUT YOU'VE KEPT SOMETHING LIKE THIS FROM HIM, HE'LL HATE YOU EVEN MORE THAN HE ALREADY DOES.
GREAT.

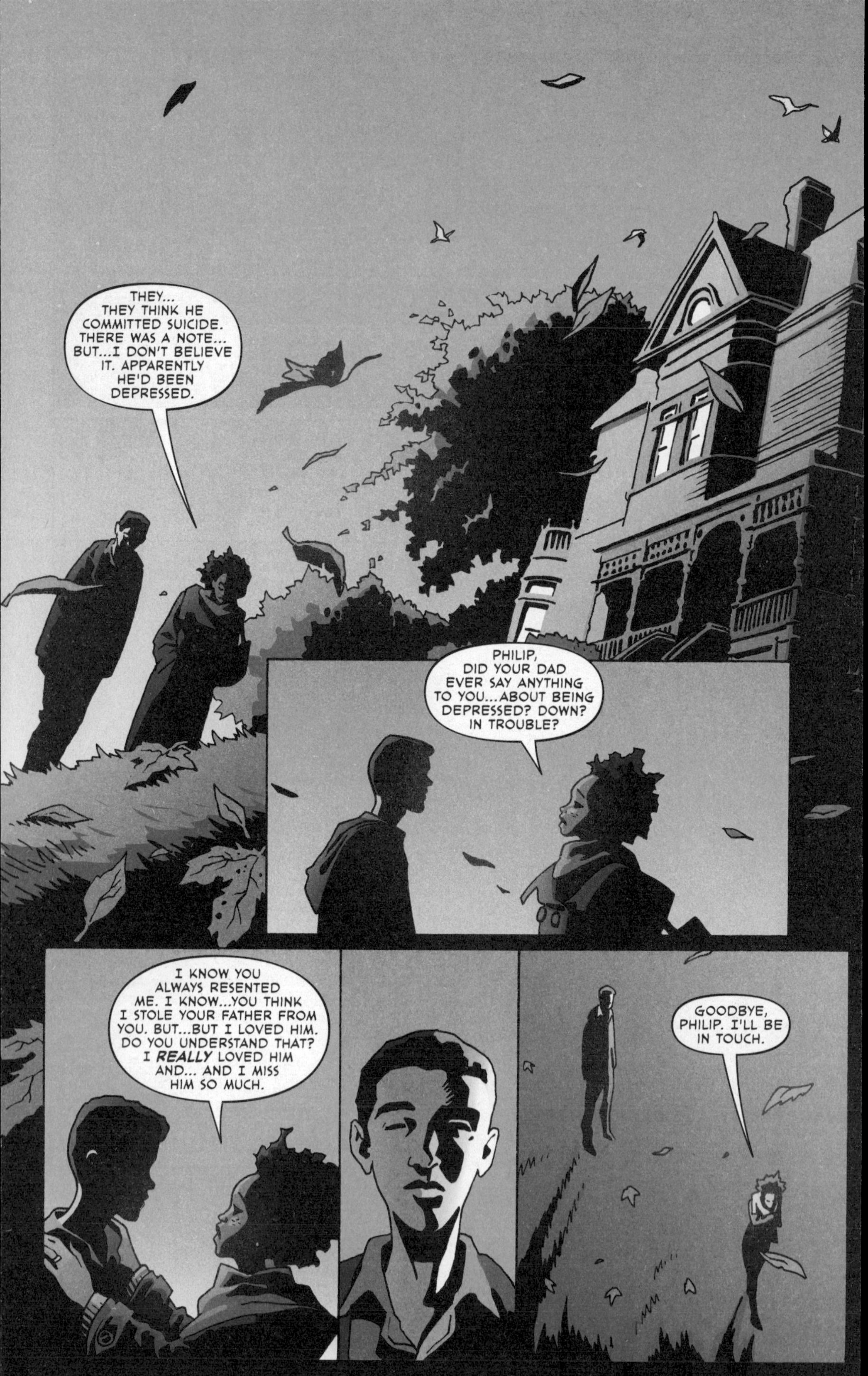
THEY... THEY THINK HE COMMITTED SUICIDE. THERE WAS A NOTE... BUT...I DON'T BELIEVE IT. APPARENTLY HE'D BEEN DEPRESSED.
PHILIP, DID YOUR DAD EVER SAY ANYTHING TO YOU...ABOUT BEING DEPRESSED? DOWN? IN TROUBLE?
I KNOW YOU ALWAYS RESENTED ME. I KNOW...YOU THINK I STOLE YOUR FATHER FROM YOU. BUT...BUT I LOVED HIM. DO YOU UNDERSTAND THAT? I REALLY LOVED HIM AND... AND I MISS HIM SO MUCH.
GOODBYE, PHILIP. I'LL BE IN TOUCH.

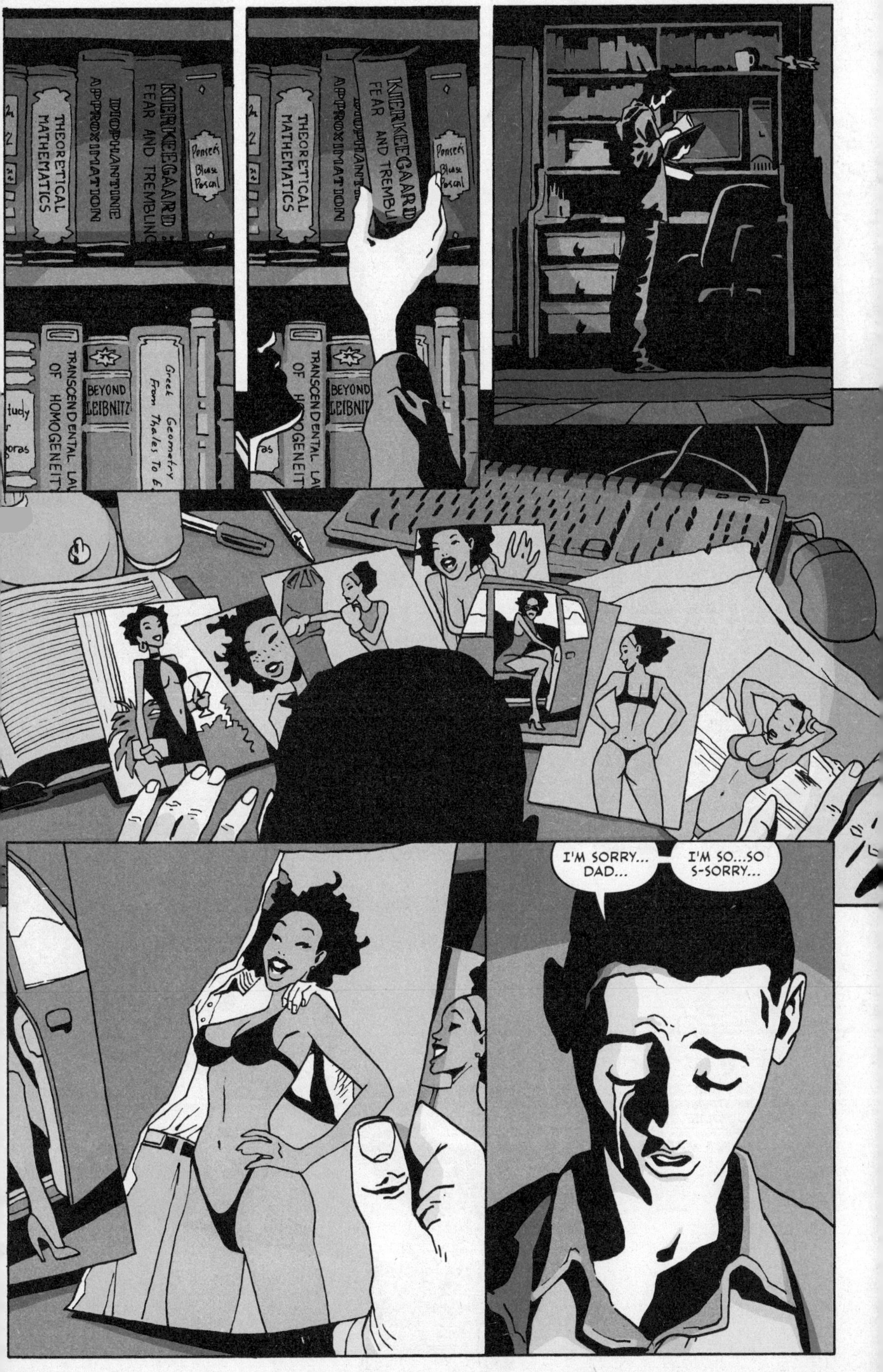
KIERKEGAARD
FEAR AND TREMBLING
DIOPHANTINE
APPROXIMATION
THEORETICAL
MATHEMATICS
Pensees
Blaise
Pascal
TRANSCENDENTAL LAW
OF HOMOGENEITY
BEYOND
LEIBNITZ
Greek Geometry
From Thales To E
I'M SORRY... DAD...
I'M SO...SO S-SORRY...

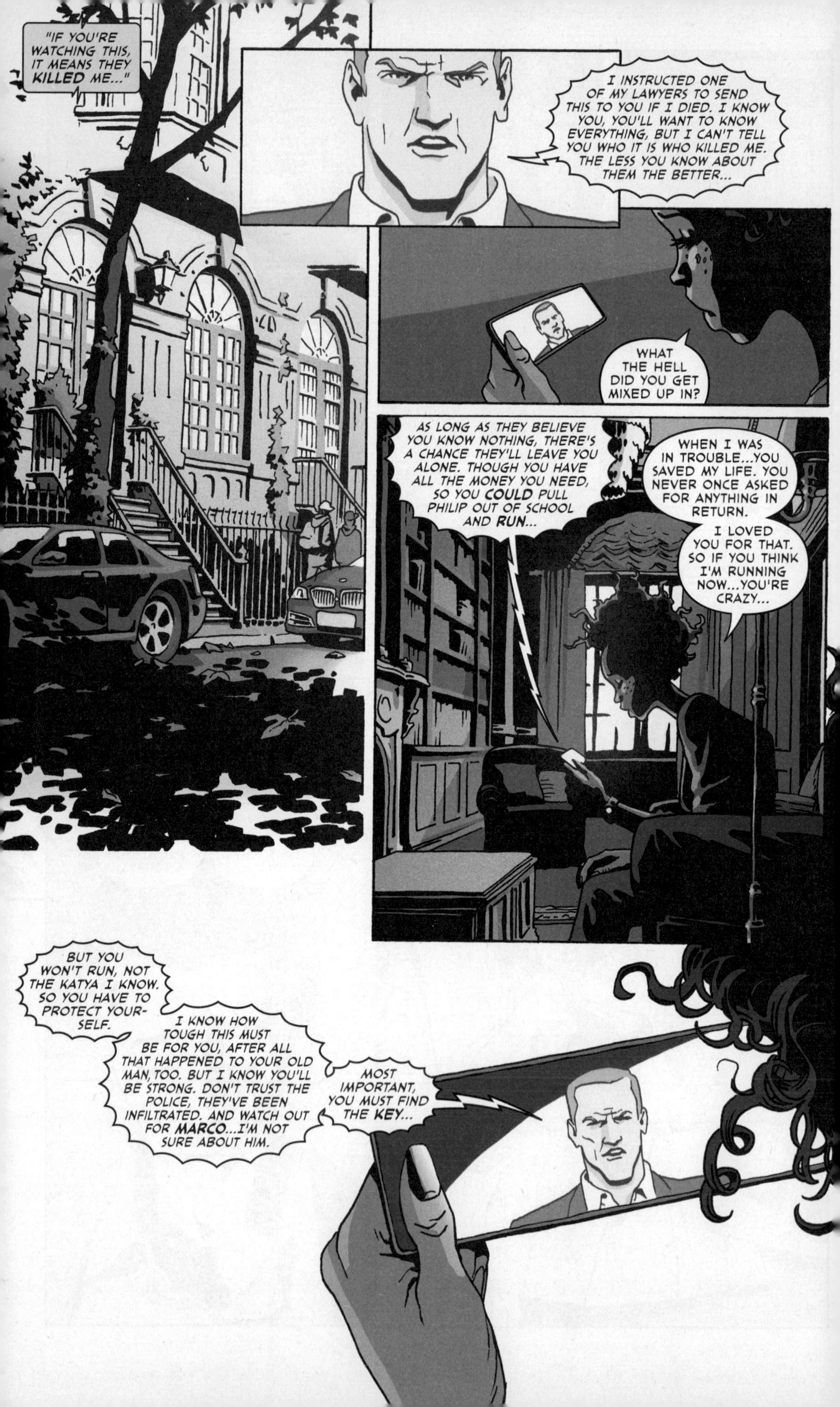
"IF YOU'RE WATCHING THIS, IT MEANS THEY KILLED ME..."
I INSTRUCTED ONE OF MY LAWYERS TO SEND THIS TO YOU IF I DIED. I KNOW YOU, YOU'LL WANT TO KNOW EVERYTHING, BUT I CAN'T TELL YOU WHO IT IS WHO KILLED ME. THE LESS YOU KNOW ABOUT THEM THE BETTER...
WHAT THE HELL DID YOU GET MIXED UP IN?
AS LONG AS THEY BELIEVE YOU KNOW NOTHING, THERE'S A CHANCE THEY'LL LEAVE YOU ALONE. THOUGH YOU HAVE ALL THE MONEY YOU NEED, SO YOU COULD PULL PHILIP OUT OF SCHOOL AND RUN...
WHEN I WAS IN TROUBLE...YOU SAVED MY LIFE. YOU NEVER ONCE ASKED FOR ANYTHING IN RETURN.
I LOVED YOU FOR THAT. SO IF YOU THINK I'M RUNNING NOW...YOU'RE CRAZY...
BUT YOU WON'T RUN, NOT THE KATYA I KNOW. SO YOU HAVE TO PROTECT YOURSELF.
I KNOW HOW TOUGH THIS MUST BE FOR YOU, AFTER ALL THAT HAPPENED TO YOUR OLD MAN, TOO. BUT I KNOW YOU'LL BE STRONG. DON'T TRUST THE POLICE, THEY'VE BEEN INFILTRATED. AND WATCH OUT FOR MARCO...I'M NOT SURE ABOUT HIM.
MOST IMPORTANT, YOU MUST FIND THE KEY...

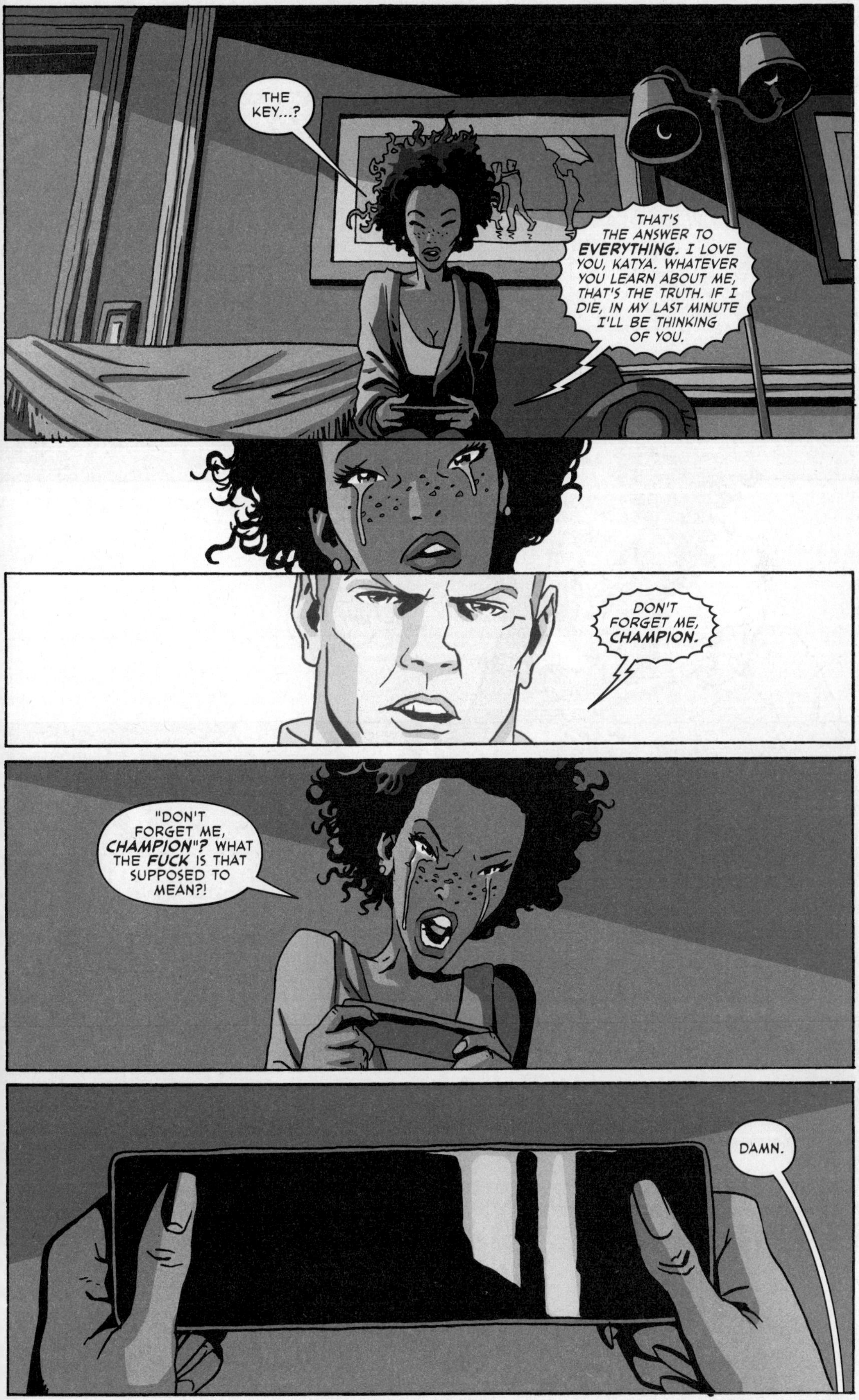
THE KEY...?
THAT'S THE ANSWER TO **EVERYTHING.** I LOVE YOU, KATYA. WHATEVER YOU LEARN ABOUT ME, THAT'S THE TRUTH. IF I DIE, IN MY LAST MINUTE I'LL BE THINKING OF YOU.
DON'T FORGET ME, **CHAMPION.**
"DON'T FORGET ME, ***CHAMPION***"? WHAT THE ***FUCK*** IS THAT SUPPOSED TO MEAN?!
DAMN.

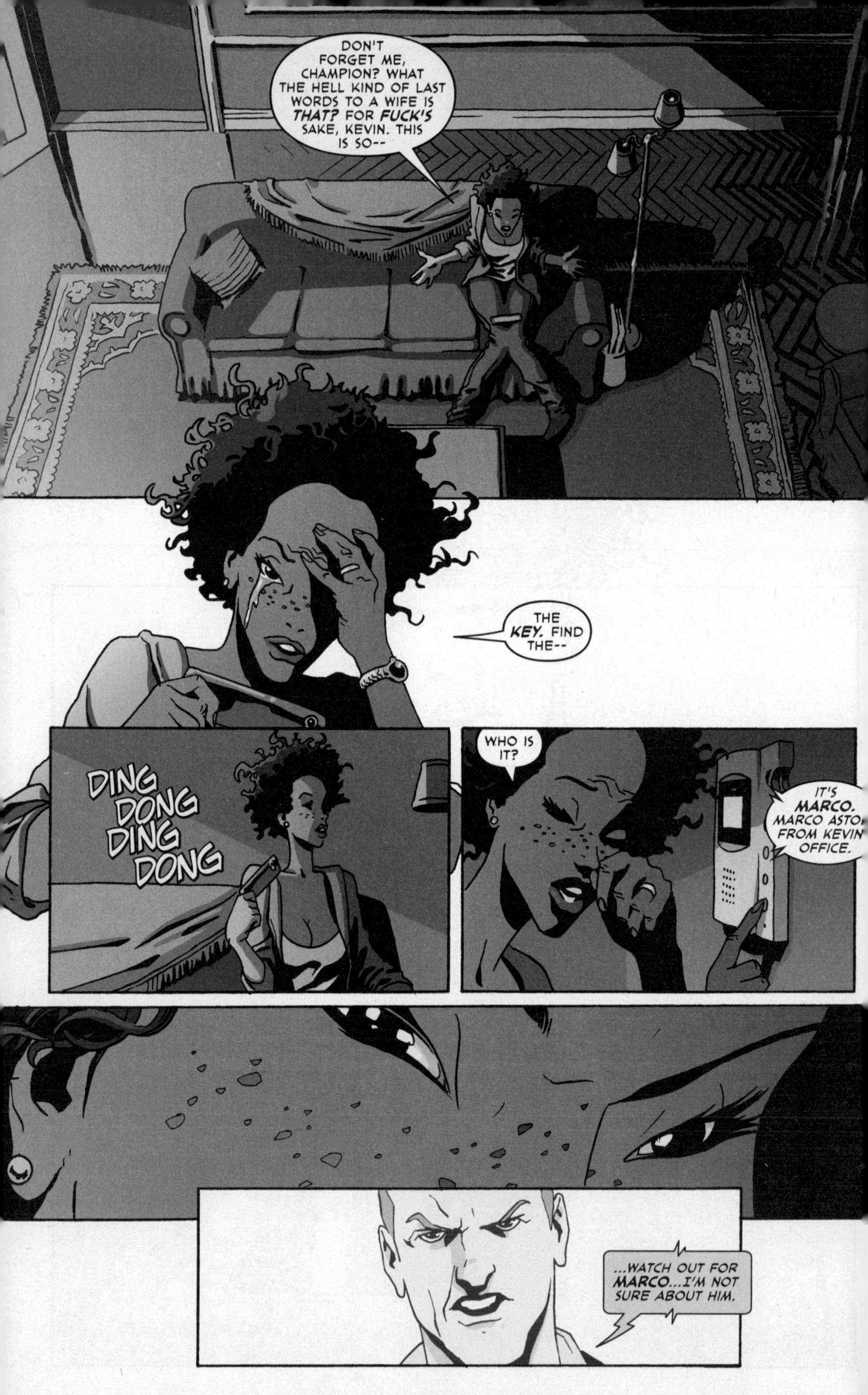
DON'T FORGET ME, CHAMPION? WHAT THE HELL KIND OF LAST WORDS TO A WIFE IS THAT? FOR FUCK'S SAKE, KEVIN. THIS IS SO--
THE KEY. FIND THE--
DING DONG DING DONG
WHO IS IT?
IT'S MARCO. MARCO ASTO FROM KEVIN OFFICE.
...WATCH OUT FOR MARCO...I'M NOT SURE ABOUT HIM.

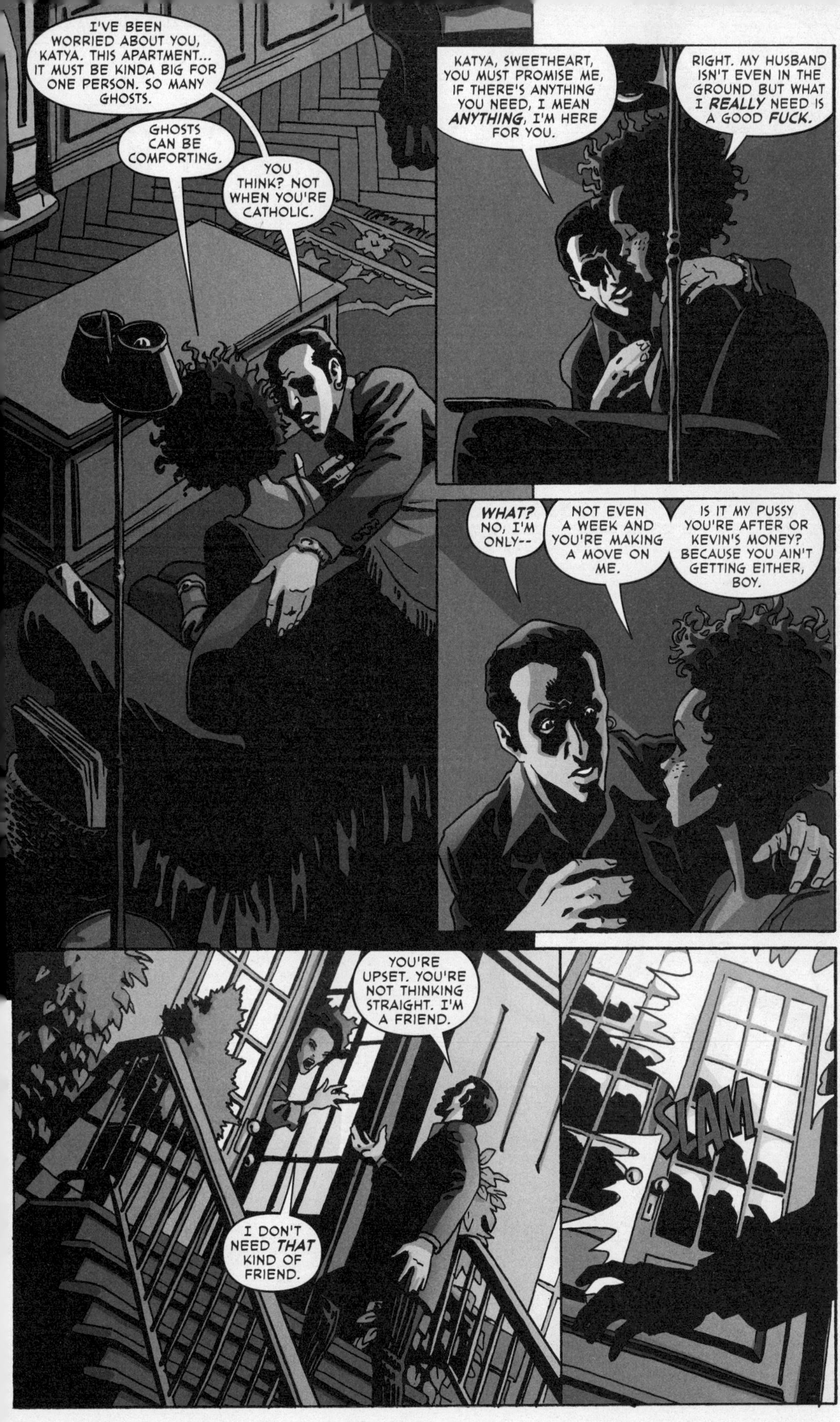
I'VE BEEN WORRIED ABOUT YOU, KATYA. THIS APARTMENT... IT MUST BE KINDA BIG FOR ONE PERSON. SO MANY GHOSTS.
GHOSTS CAN BE COMFORTING.
YOU THINK? NOT WHEN YOU'RE CATHOLIC.
KATYA, SWEETHEART, YOU MUST PROMISE ME, IF THERE'S ANYTHING YOU NEED, I MEAN ANYTHING, I'M HERE FOR YOU.
RIGHT. MY HUSBAND ISN'T EVEN IN THE GROUND BUT WHAT I REALLY NEED IS A GOOD FUCK.
WHAT? NO, I'M ONLY--
NOT EVEN A WEEK AND YOU'RE MAKING A MOVE ON ME.
IS IT MY PUSSY YOU'RE AFTER OR KEVIN'S MONEY? BECAUSE YOU AIN'T GETTING EITHER, BOY.
YOU'RE UPSET. YOU'RE NOT THINKING STRAIGHT. I'M A FRIEND.
I DON'T NEED THAT KIND OF FRIEND.
SLAM

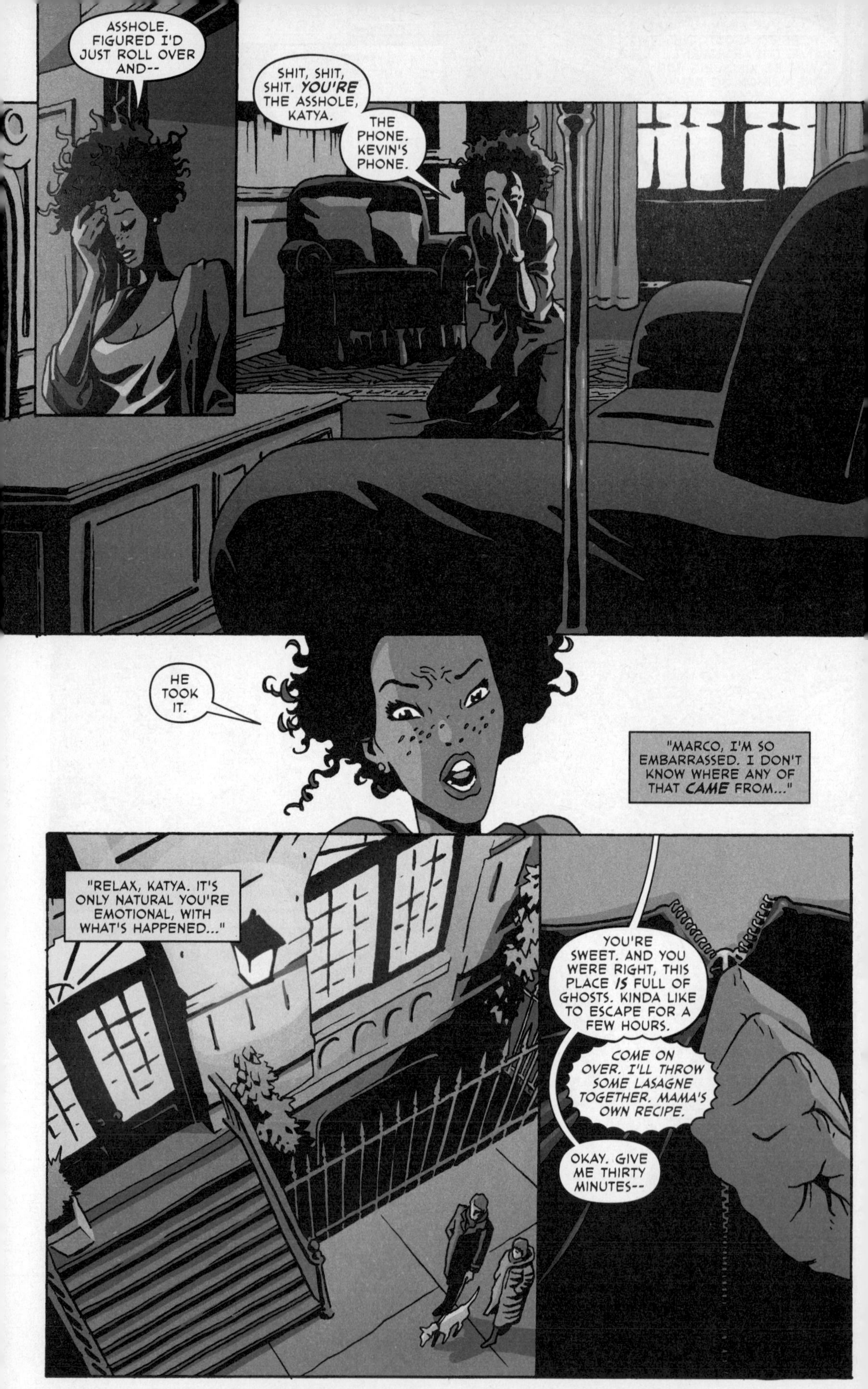
ASSHOLE. FIGURED I'D JUST ROLL OVER AND--
SHIT, SHIT, SHIT. *YOU'RE* THE ASSHOLE, KATYA.
THE PHONE. KEVIN'S PHONE.
HE TOOK IT.
"MARCO, I'M SO EMBARRASSED. I DON'T KNOW WHERE ANY OF THAT *CAME* FROM..."
"RELAX, KATYA. IT'S ONLY NATURAL YOU'RE EMOTIONAL, WITH WHAT'S HAPPENED..."
YOU'RE SWEET. AND YOU WERE RIGHT, THIS PLACE *IS* FULL OF GHOSTS. KINDA LIKE TO ESCAPE FOR A FEW HOURS.
COME ON OVER. I'LL THROW SOME LASAGNE TOGETHER. MAMA'S OWN RECIPE.
OKAY. GIVE ME THIRTY MINUTES--

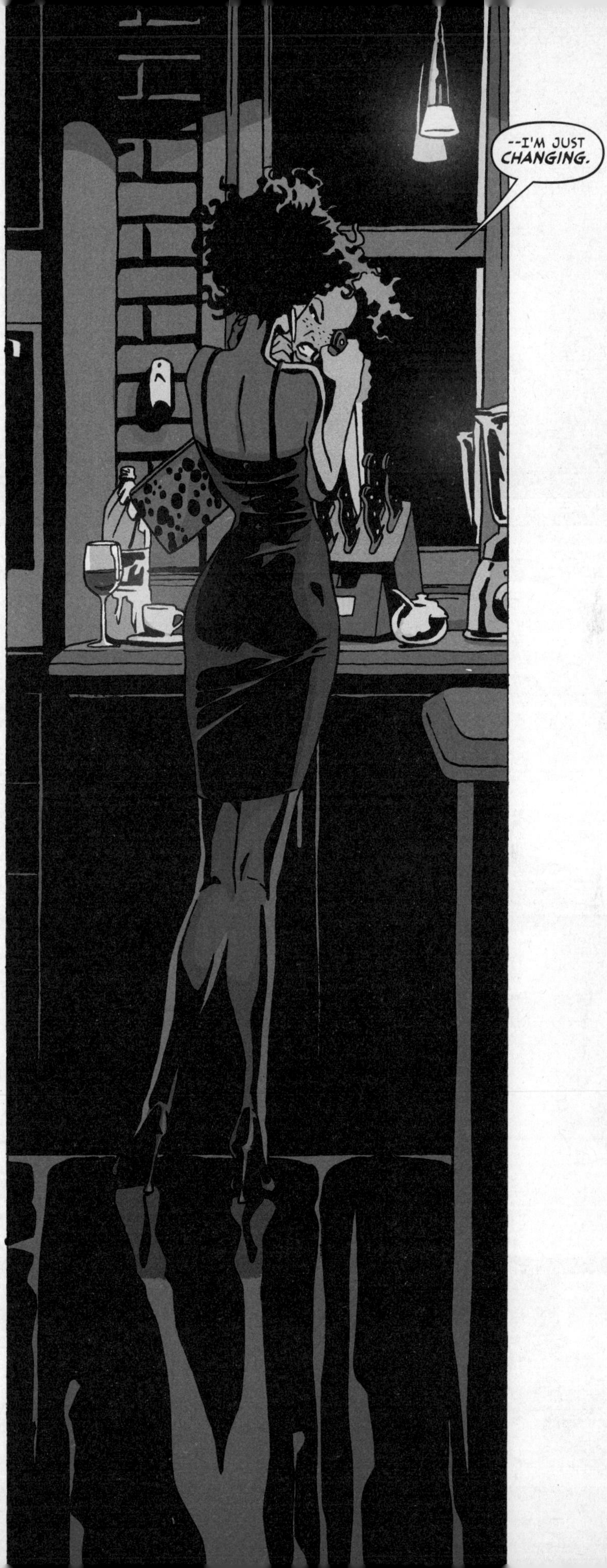
--I'M JUST CHANGING.

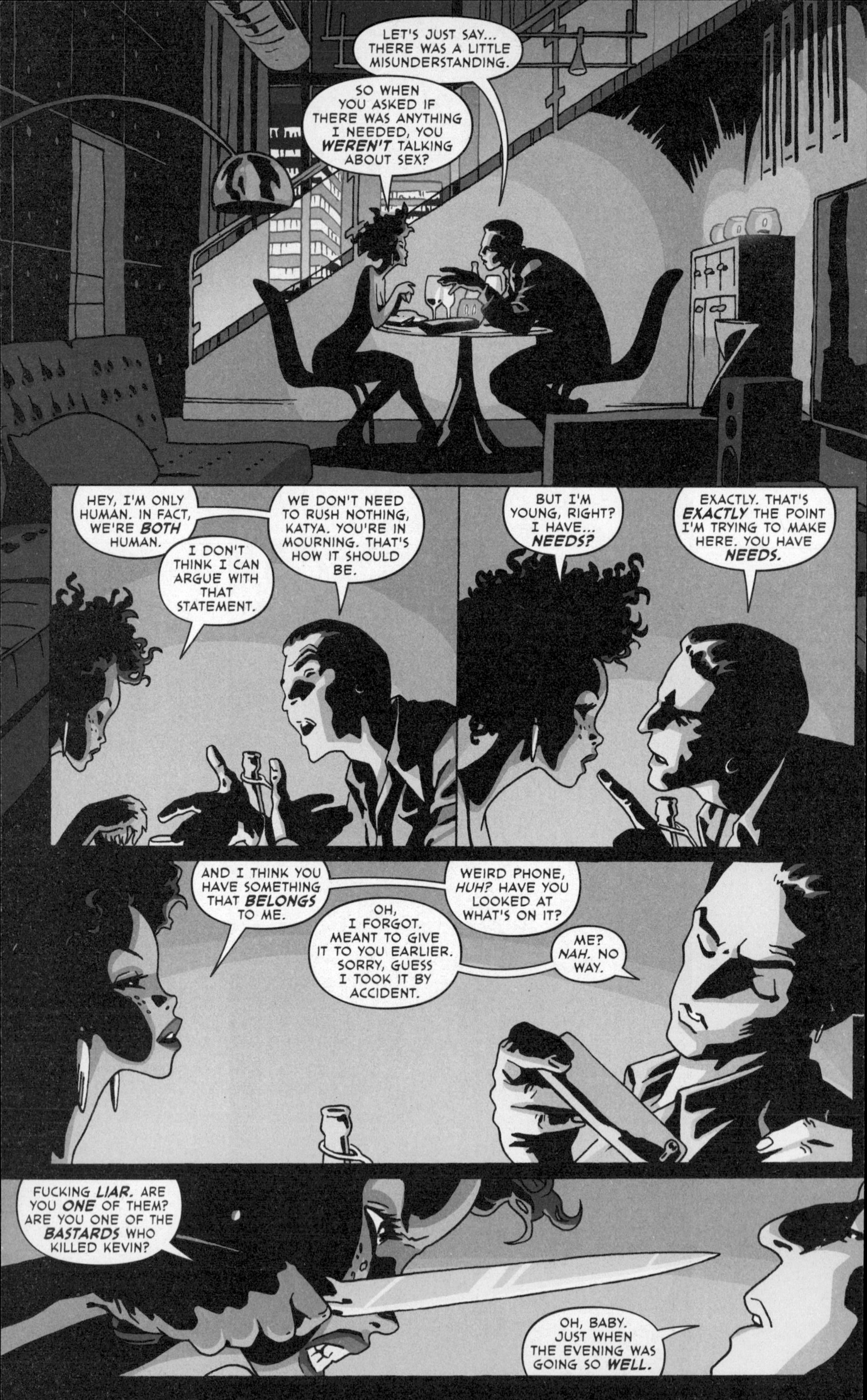

LET'S JUST SAY... THERE WAS A LITTLE MISUNDERSTANDING.
SO WHEN YOU ASKED IF THERE WAS ANYTHING I NEEDED, YOU *WEREN'T* TALKING ABOUT SEX?
HEY, I'M ONLY HUMAN. IN FACT, WE'RE *BOTH* HUMAN.
I DON'T THINK I CAN ARGUE WITH THAT STATEMENT.
WE DON'T NEED TO RUSH NOTHING, KATYA. YOU'RE IN MOURNING. THAT'S HOW IT SHOULD BE.
BUT I'M YOUNG, RIGHT? I HAVE... *NEEDS?*
EXACTLY. THAT'S *EXACTLY* THE POINT I'M TRYING TO MAKE HERE. YOU HAVE *NEEDS.*
AND I THINK YOU HAVE SOMETHING THAT *BELONGS* TO ME.
OH, I FORGOT. MEANT TO GIVE IT TO YOU EARLIER. SORRY, GUESS I TOOK IT BY ACCIDENT.
WEIRD PHONE, *HUH?* HAVE YOU LOOKED AT WHAT'S ON IT?
ME? *NAH.* NO WAY.
FUCKING *LIAR.* ARE YOU *ONE* OF THEM? ARE YOU ONE OF THE *BASTARDS* WHO KILLED KEVIN?
OH, BABY. JUST WHEN THE EVENING WAS GOING SO *WELL.*

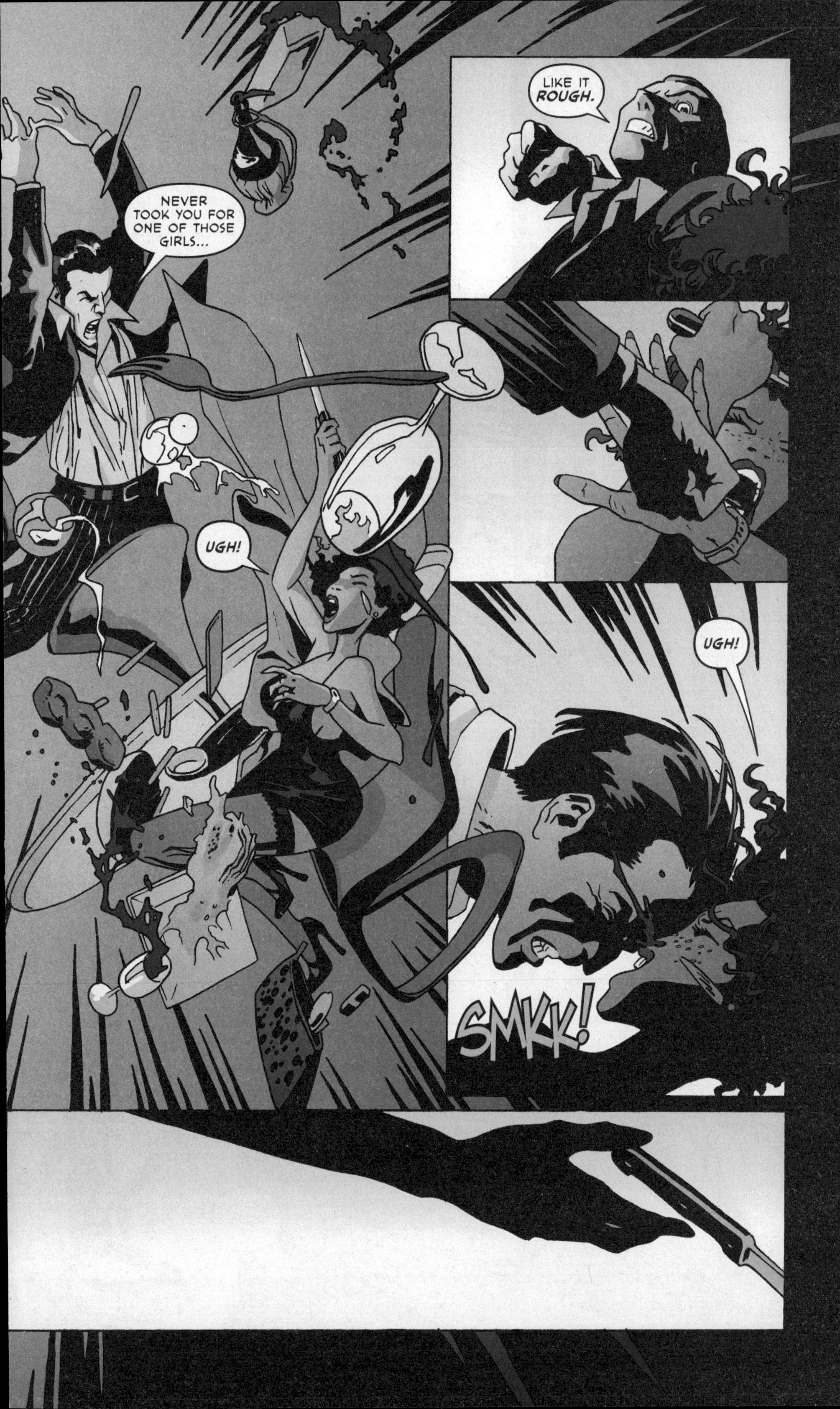
NEVER TOOK YOU FOR ONE OF THOSE GIRLS...
LIKE IT ROUGH.
UGH!
UGH!
SMKK!

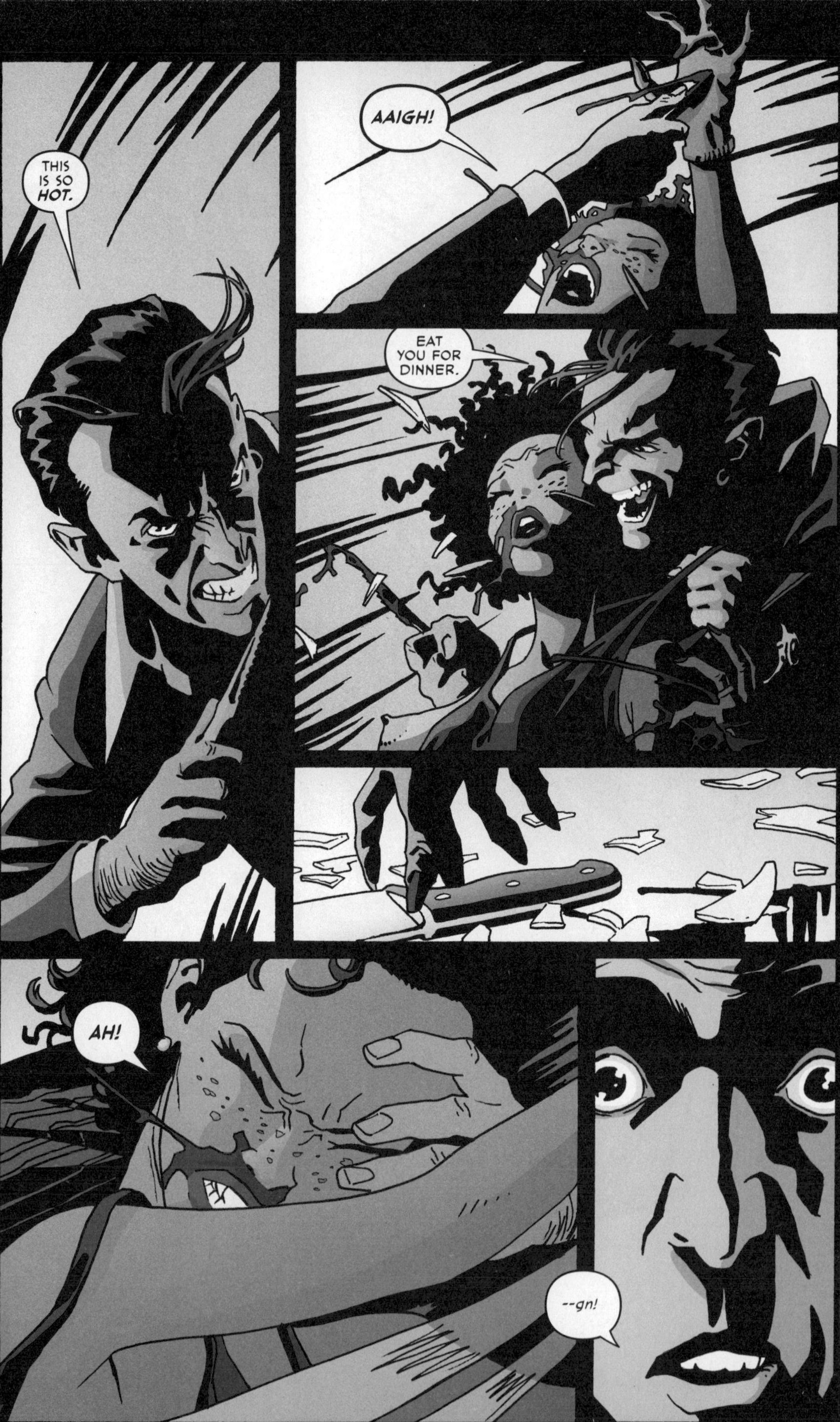
THIS IS SO HOT.
AAIGH!
EAT YOU FOR DINNER.
AH!
--gn!

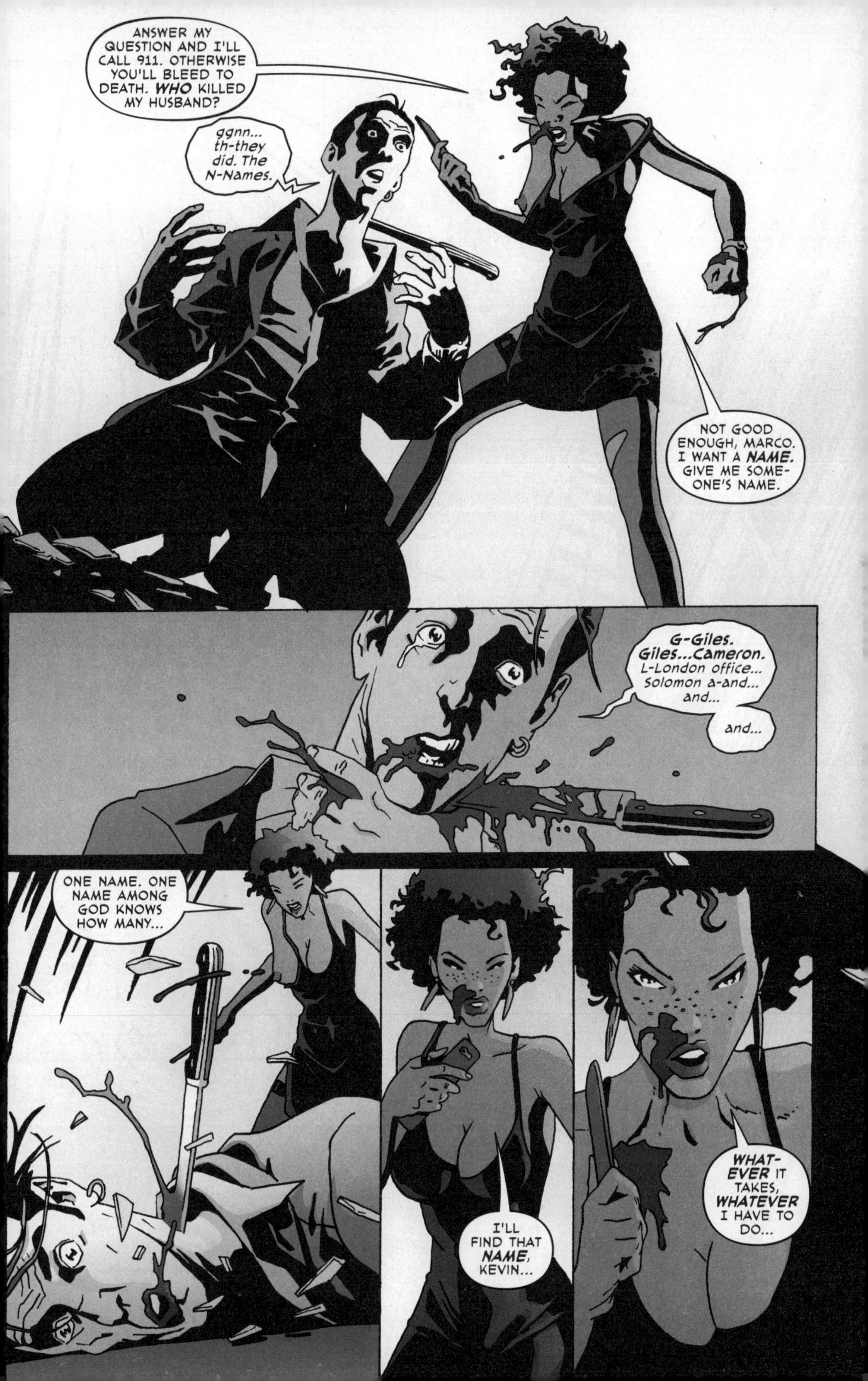
ANSWER MY QUESTION AND I'LL CALL 911. OTHERWISE YOU'LL BLEED TO DEATH. WHO KILLED MY HUSBAND?
ggnn... th-they did. The N-Names.
NOT GOOD ENOUGH, MARCO. I WANT A NAME. GIVE ME SOME-ONE'S NAME.
G-Giles. Giles...Cameron. L-London office... Solomon a-and... and...
and...
ONE NAME. ONE NAME AMONG GOD KNOWS HOW MANY...
I'LL FIND THAT NAME, KEVIN...
WHAT-EVER IT TAKES, WHATEVER I HAVE TO DO...

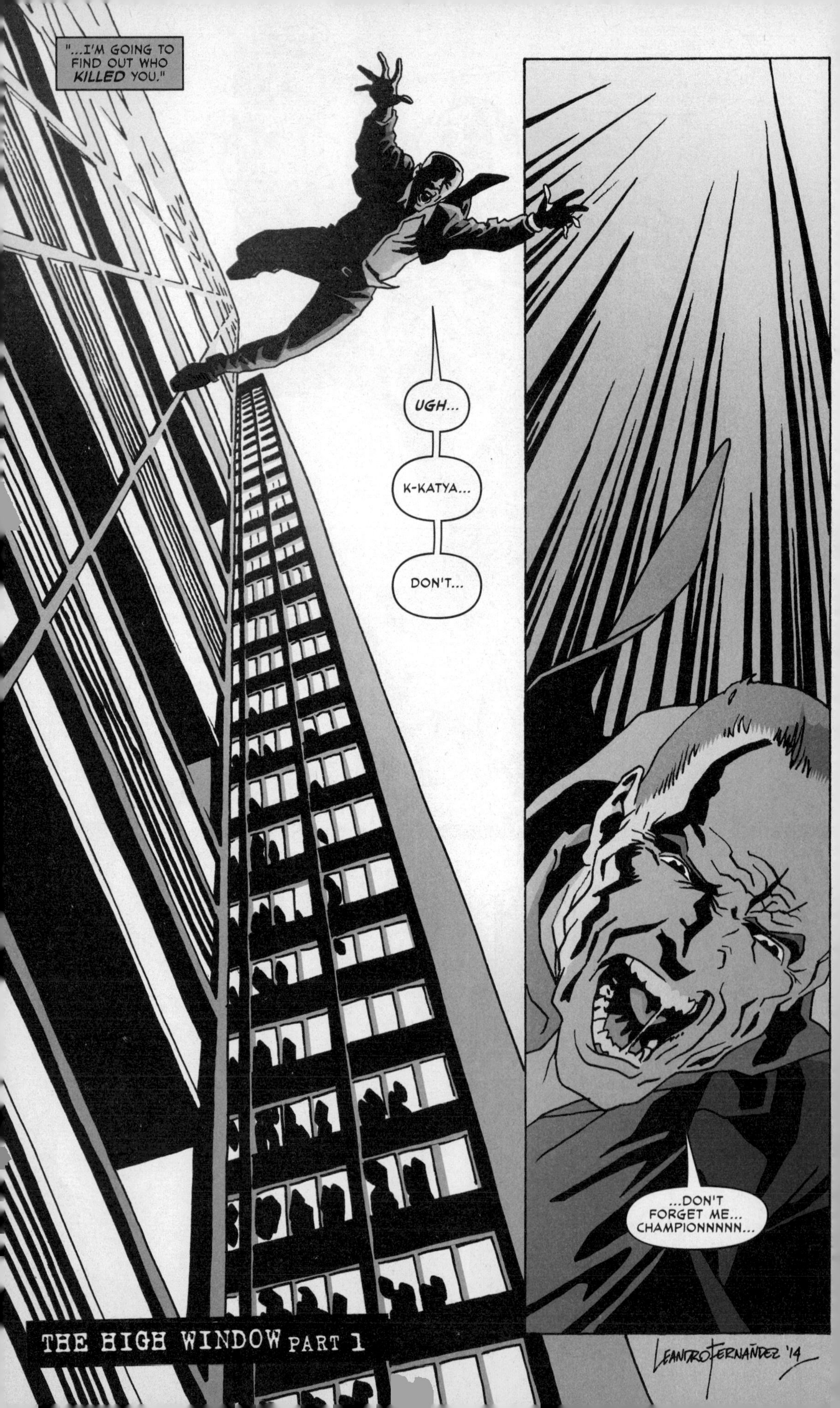
"...I'M GOING TO FIND OUT WHO KILLED YOU."
UGH...
K-KATYA...
DON'T...
...DON'T FORGET ME... CHAMPIONNNNN...
THE HIGH WINDOW PART 1
LEANDRO FERNÁNDEZ '14

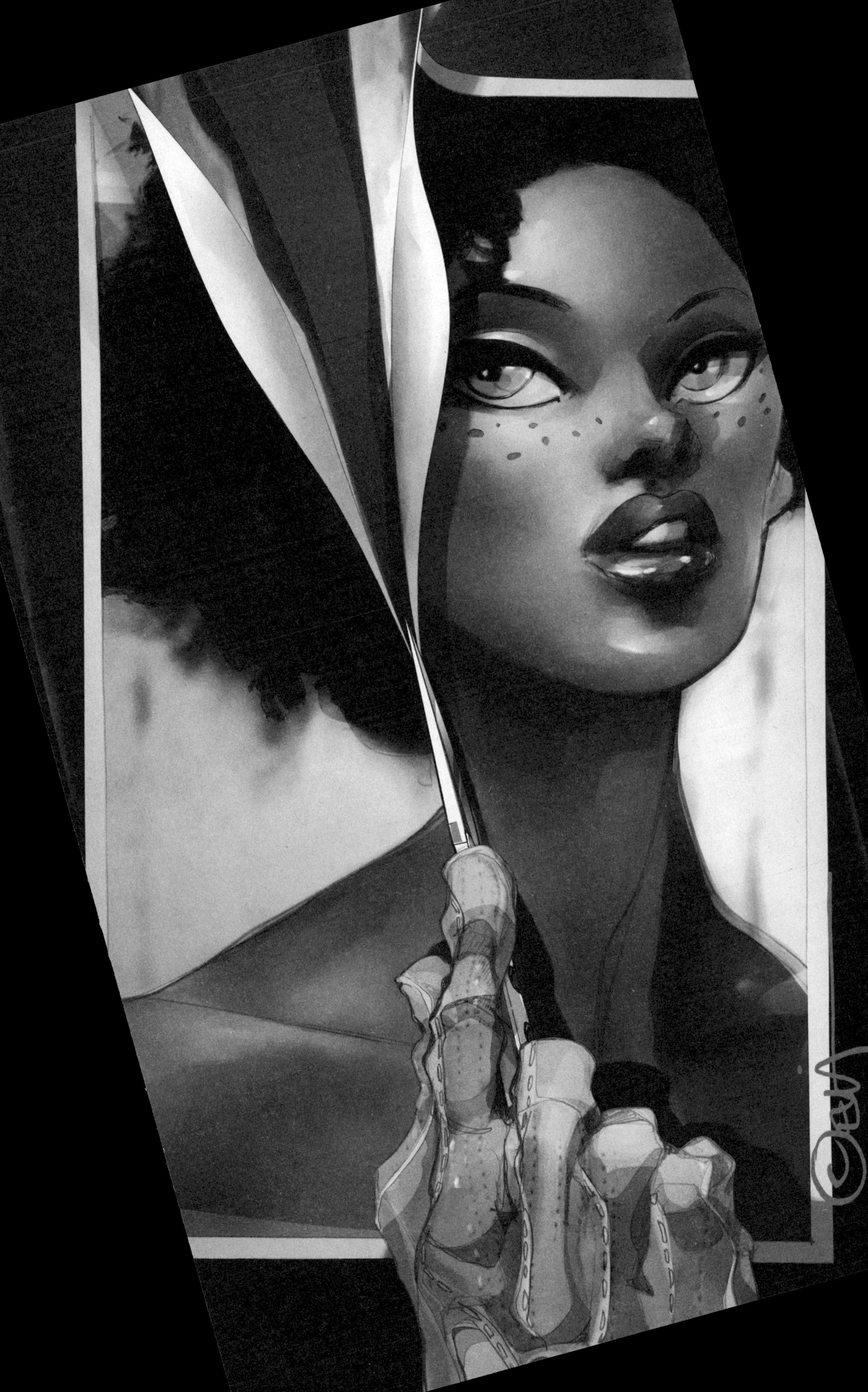

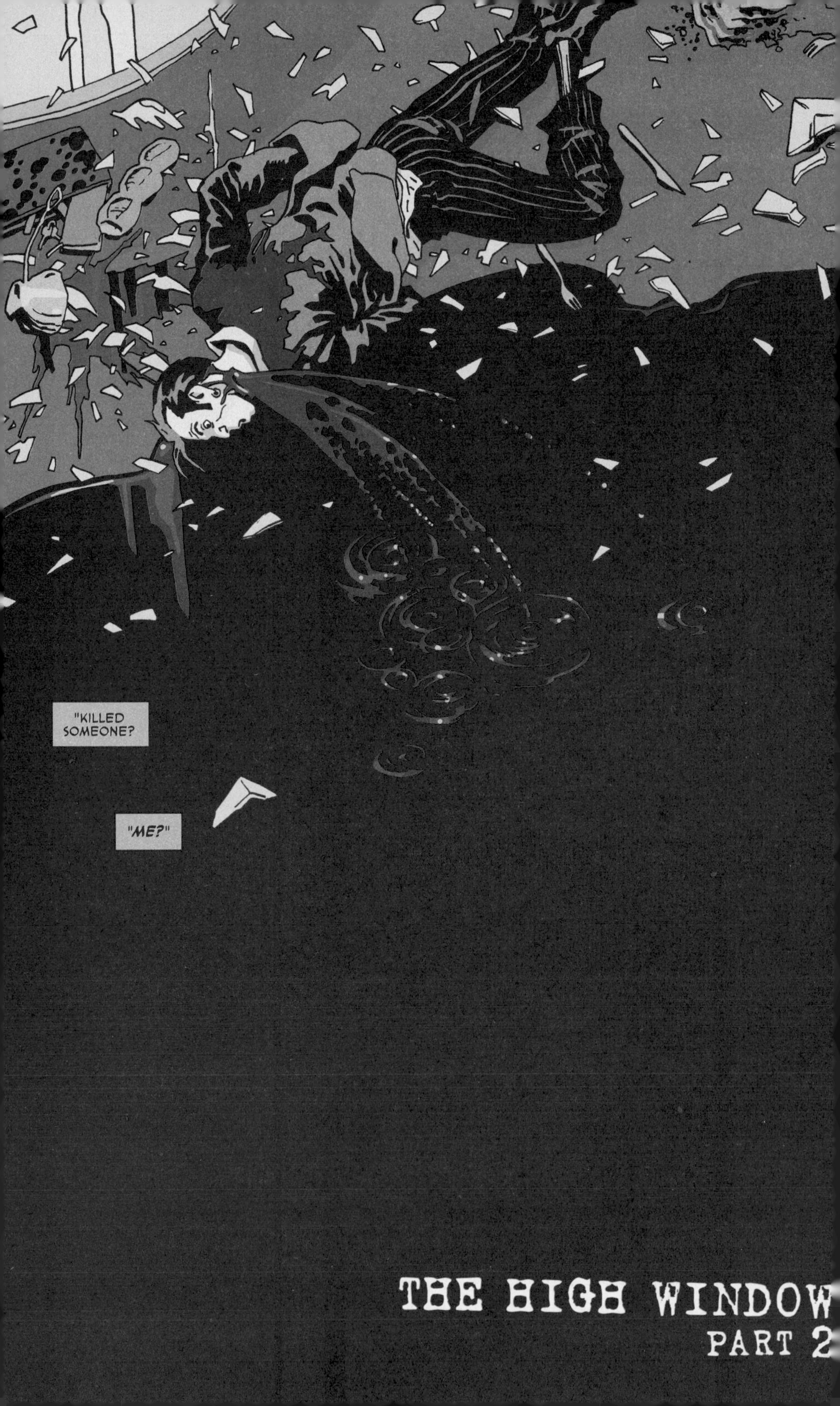
"KILLED SOMEONE?
"ME?"
THE HIGH WINDOW
PART 2

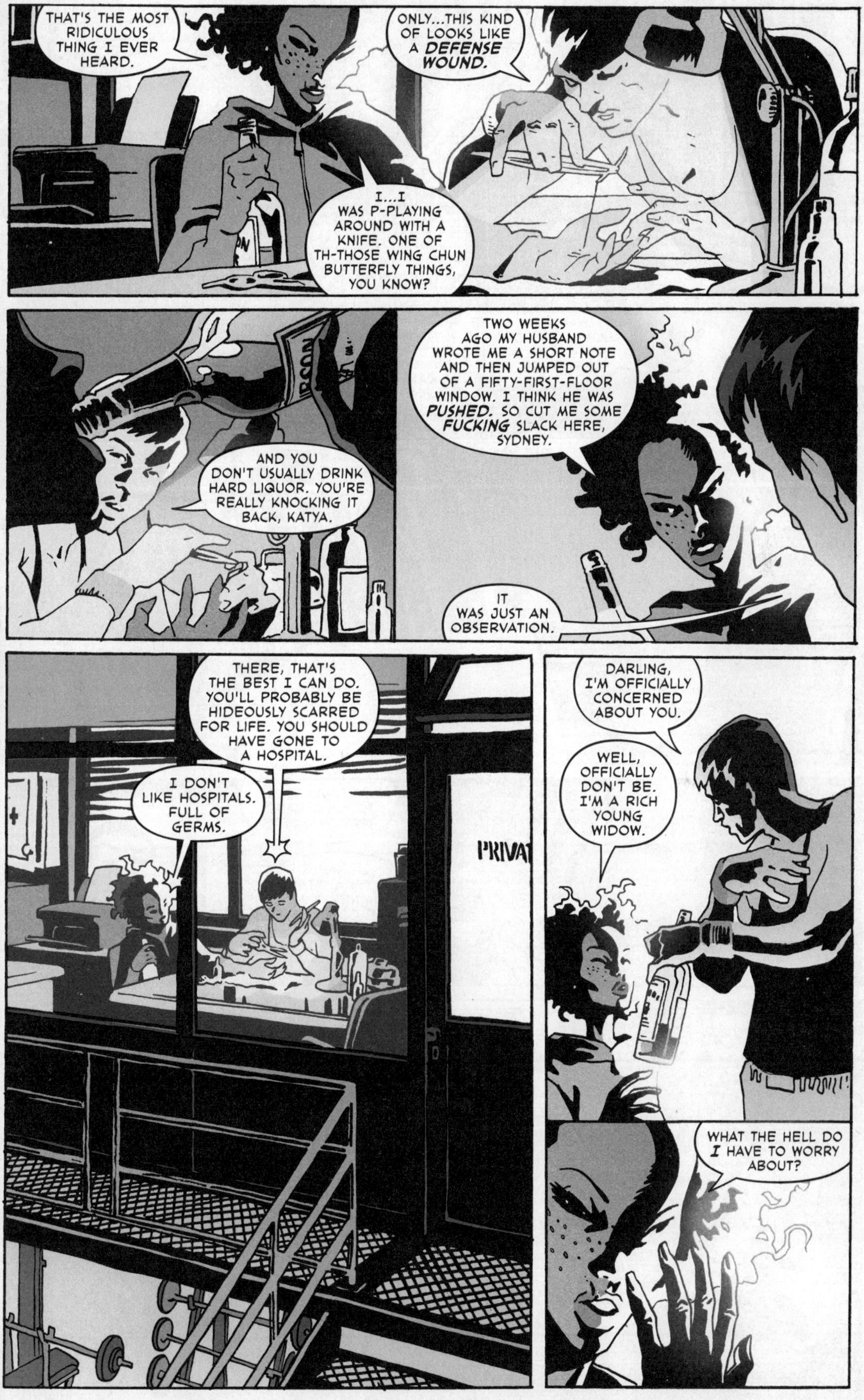
THAT'S THE MOST RIDICULOUS THING I EVER HEARD.
ONLY...THIS KIND OF LOOKS LIKE A *DEFENSE WOUND.*
I...I WAS P-PLAYING AROUND WITH A KNIFE. ONE OF TH-THOSE WING CHUN BUTTERFLY THINGS, YOU KNOW?
AND YOU DON'T USUALLY DRINK HARD LIQUOR. YOU'RE REALLY KNOCKING IT BACK, KATYA.
TWO WEEKS AGO MY HUSBAND WROTE ME A SHORT NOTE AND THEN JUMPED OUT OF A FIFTY-FIRST-FLOOR WINDOW. I THINK HE WAS *PUSHED.* SO CUT ME SOME *FUCKING* SLACK HERE, SYDNEY.
IT WAS JUST AN OBSERVATION.
THERE, THAT'S THE BEST I CAN DO. YOU'LL PROBABLY BE HIDEOUSLY SCARRED FOR LIFE. YOU SHOULD HAVE GONE TO A HOSPITAL.
I DON'T LIKE HOSPITALS. FULL OF GERMS.
PRIVAT
DARLING, I'M OFFICIALLY CONCERNED ABOUT YOU.
WELL, OFFICIALLY DON'T BE. I'M A RICH YOUNG WIDOW.
WHAT THE HELL DO *I* HAVE TO WORRY ABOUT?

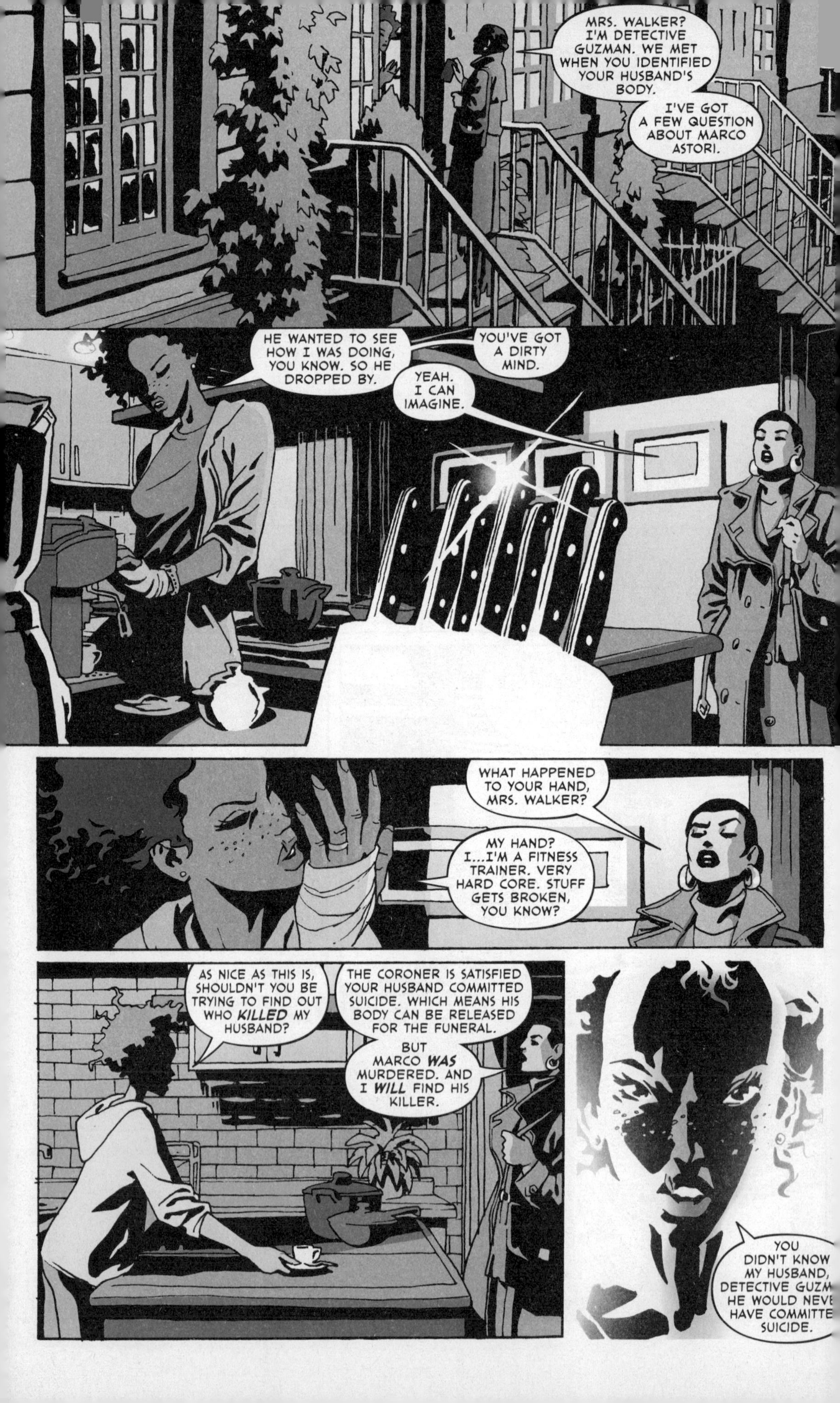
MRS. WALKER? I'M DETECTIVE GUZMAN. WE MET WHEN YOU IDENTIFIED YOUR HUSBAND'S BODY.
I'VE GOT A FEW QUESTION ABOUT MARCO ASTORI.
HE WANTED TO SEE HOW I WAS DOING, YOU KNOW. SO HE DROPPED BY.
YEAH. I CAN IMAGINE.
YOU'VE GOT A DIRTY MIND.
WHAT HAPPENED TO YOUR HAND, MRS. WALKER?
MY HAND? I...I'M A FITNESS TRAINER. VERY HARD CORE. STUFF GETS BROKEN, YOU KNOW?
AS NICE AS THIS IS, SHOULDN'T YOU BE TRYING TO FIND OUT WHO KILLED MY HUSBAND?
THE CORONER IS SATISFIED YOUR HUSBAND COMMITTED SUICIDE. WHICH MEANS HIS BODY CAN BE RELEASED FOR THE FUNERAL.
BUT MARCO WAS MURDERED. AND I WILL FIND HIS KILLER.
YOU DIDN'T KNOW MY HUSBAND, DETECTIVE GUZM HE WOULD NEVE HAVE COMMITTE SUICIDE.

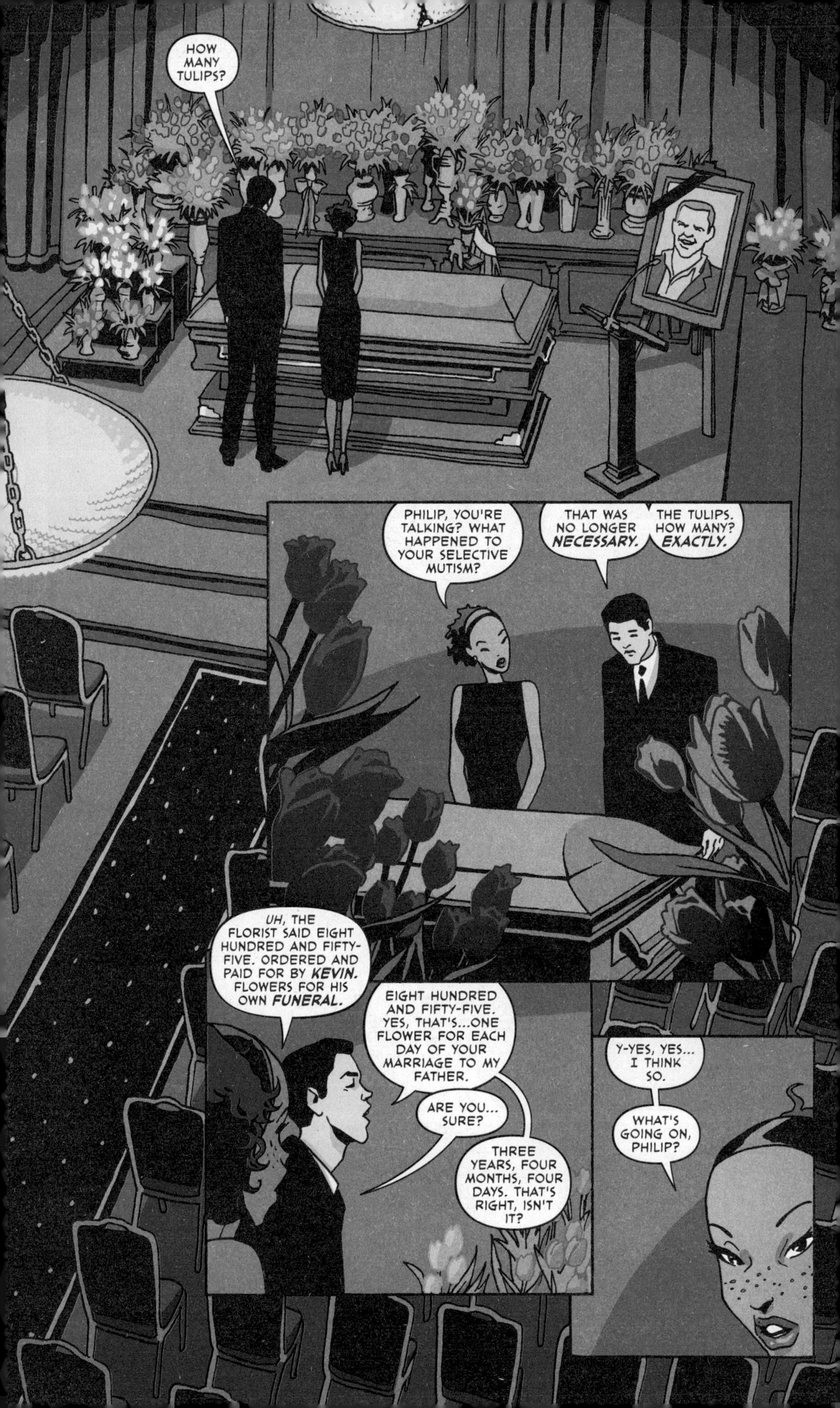
HOW MANY TULIPS?
PHILIP, YOU'RE TALKING? WHAT HAPPENED TO YOUR SELECTIVE MUTISM?
THAT WAS NO LONGER *NECESSARY.*
THE TULIPS. HOW MANY? *EXACTLY.*
UH, THE FLORIST SAID EIGHT HUNDRED AND FIFTY-FIVE. ORDERED AND PAID FOR BY *KEVIN.* FLOWERS FOR HIS OWN *FUNERAL.*
EIGHT HUNDRED AND FIFTY-FIVE. YES, THAT'S...ONE FLOWER FOR EACH DAY OF YOUR MARRIAGE TO MY FATHER.
ARE YOU... SURE?
THREE YEARS, FOUR MONTHS, FOUR DAYS. THAT'S RIGHT, ISN'T IT?
Y-YES, YES... I THINK SO.
WHAT'S GOING ON, PHILIP?

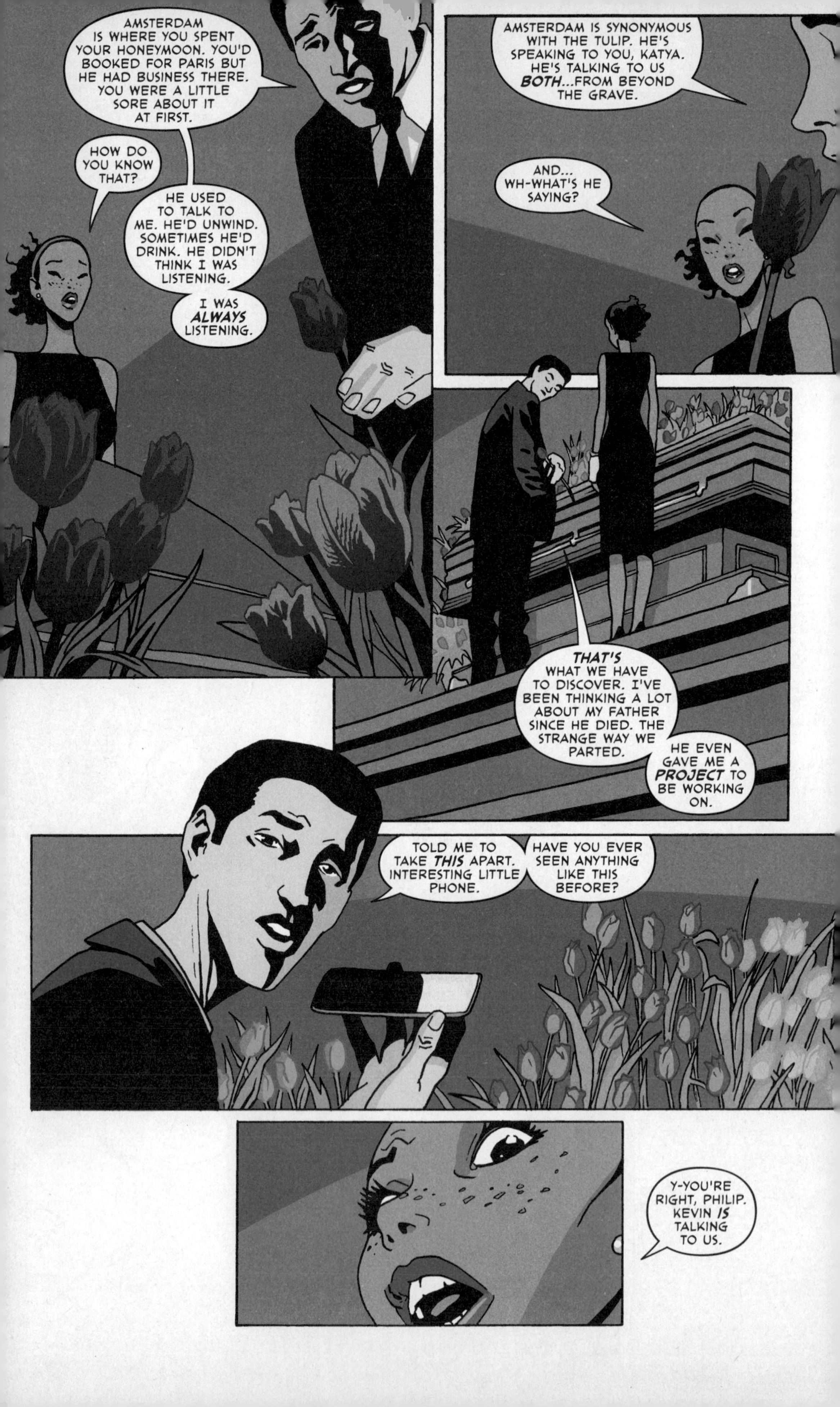

AMSTERDAM IS WHERE YOU SPENT YOUR HONEYMOON. YOU'D BOOKED FOR PARIS BUT HE HAD BUSINESS THERE. YOU WERE A LITTLE SORE ABOUT IT AT FIRST.
HOW DO YOU KNOW THAT?
HE USED TO TALK TO ME. HE'D UNWIND. SOMETIMES HE'D DRINK. HE DIDN'T THINK I WAS LISTENING.
I WAS ALWAYS LISTENING.
AMSTERDAM IS SYNONYMOUS WITH THE TULIP. HE'S SPEAKING TO YOU, KATYA. HE'S TALKING TO US BOTH...FROM BEYOND THE GRAVE.
AND... WH-WHAT'S HE SAYING?
THAT'S WHAT WE HAVE TO DISCOVER. I'VE BEEN THINKING A LOT ABOUT MY FATHER SINCE HE DIED. THE STRANGE WAY WE PARTED.
HE EVEN GAVE ME A PROJECT TO BE WORKING ON.
TOLD ME TO TAKE THIS APART. INTERESTING LITTLE PHONE.
HAVE YOU EVER SEEN ANYTHING LIKE THIS BEFORE?
Y-YOU'RE RIGHT, PHILIP. KEVIN IS TALKING TO US.

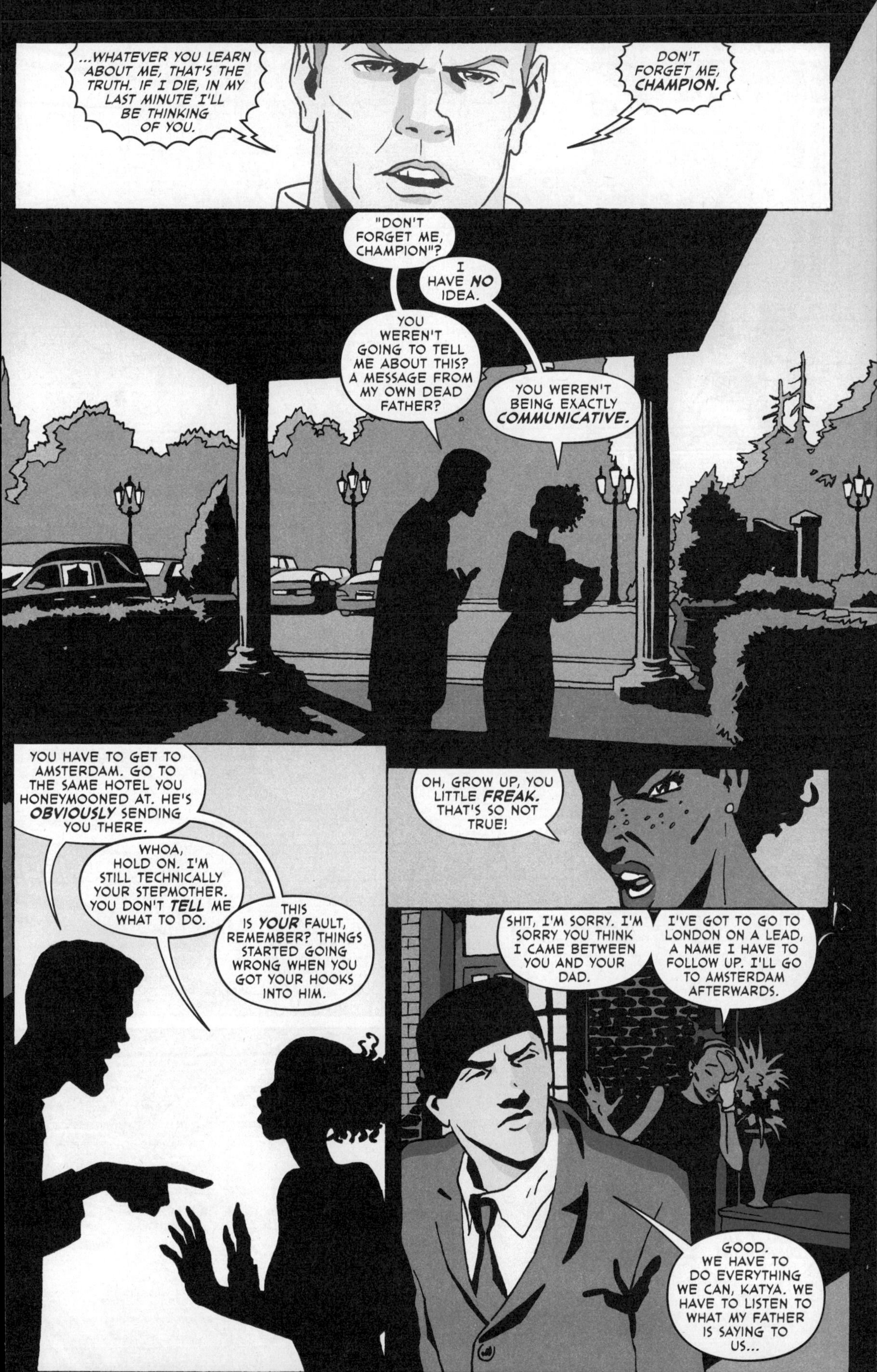
...WHATEVER YOU LEARN ABOUT ME, THAT'S THE TRUTH. IF I DIE, IN MY LAST MINUTE I'LL BE THINKING OF YOU.
DON'T FORGET ME, CHAMPION.
"DON'T FORGET ME, CHAMPION"?
I HAVE NO IDEA.
YOU WEREN'T GOING TO TELL ME ABOUT THIS? A MESSAGE FROM MY OWN DEAD FATHER?
YOU WEREN'T BEING EXACTLY COMMUNICATIVE.
YOU HAVE TO GET TO AMSTERDAM. GO TO THE SAME HOTEL YOU HONEYMOONED AT. HE'S OBVIOUSLY SENDING YOU THERE.
WHOA, HOLD ON. I'M STILL TECHNICALLY YOUR STEPMOTHER. YOU DON'T TELL ME WHAT TO DO.
THIS IS YOUR FAULT, REMEMBER? THINGS STARTED GOING WRONG WHEN YOU GOT YOUR HOOKS INTO HIM.
OH, GROW UP, YOU LITTLE FREAK. THAT'S SO NOT TRUE!
SHIT, I'M SORRY. I'M SORRY YOU THINK I CAME BETWEEN YOU AND YOUR DAD.
I'VE GOT TO GO TO LONDON ON A LEAD, A NAME I HAVE TO FOLLOW UP. I'LL GO TO AMSTERDAM AFTERWARDS.
GOOD. WE HAVE TO DO EVERYTHING WE CAN, KATYA. WE HAVE TO LISTEN TO WHAT MY FATHER IS SAYING TO US...

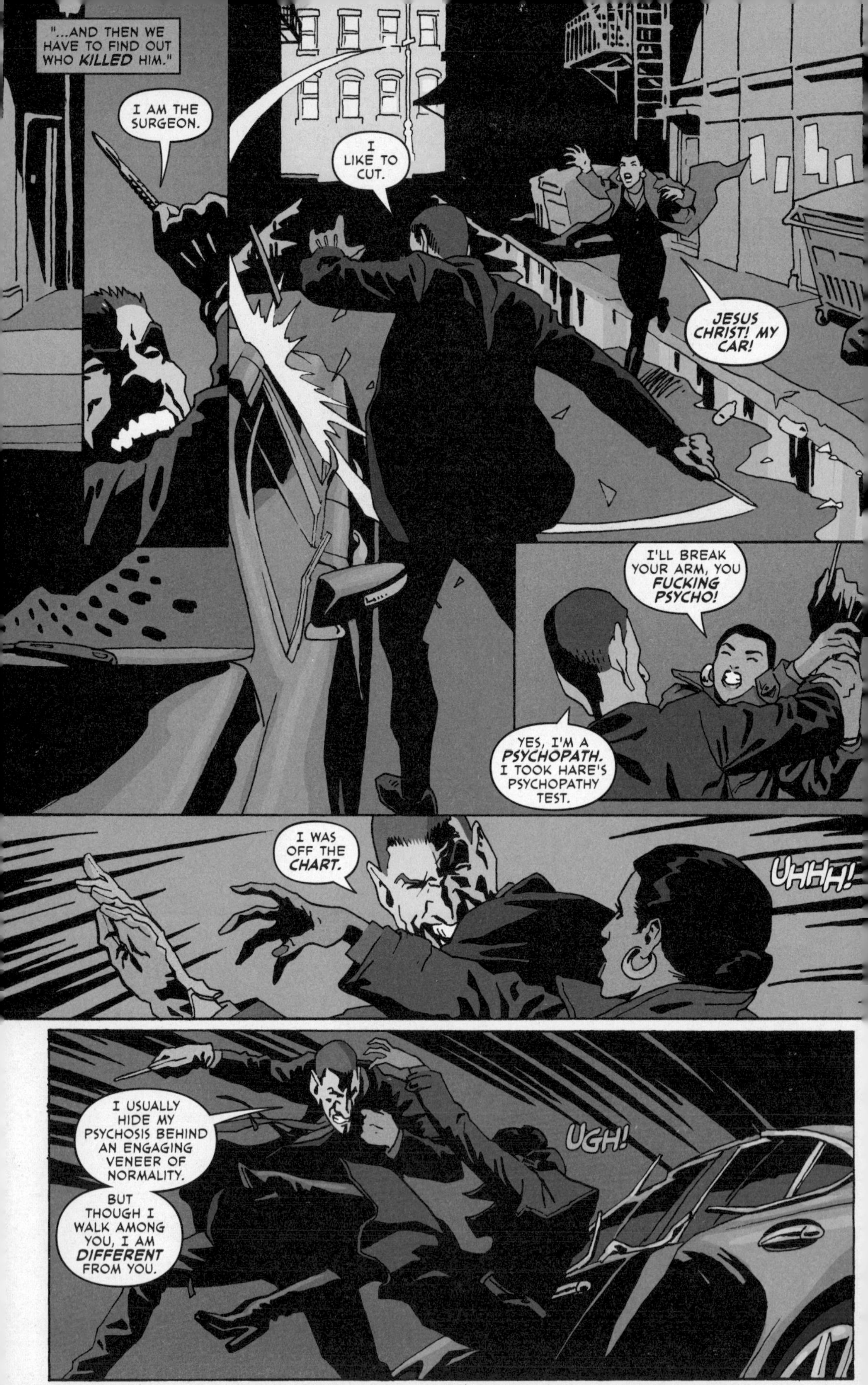
"...AND THEN WE HAVE TO FIND OUT WHO KILLED HIM."
I AM THE SURGEON.
I LIKE TO CUT.
JESUS CHRIST! MY CAR!
I'LL BREAK YOUR ARM, YOU FUCKING PSYCHO!
YES, I'M A PSYCHOPATH. I TOOK HARE'S PSYCHOPATHY TEST.
I WAS OFF THE CHART.
UHHH!
I USUALLY HIDE MY PSYCHOSIS BEHIND AN ENGAGING VENEER OF NORMALITY.
BUT THOUGH I WALK AMONG YOU, I AM DIFFERENT FROM YOU.
UGH!

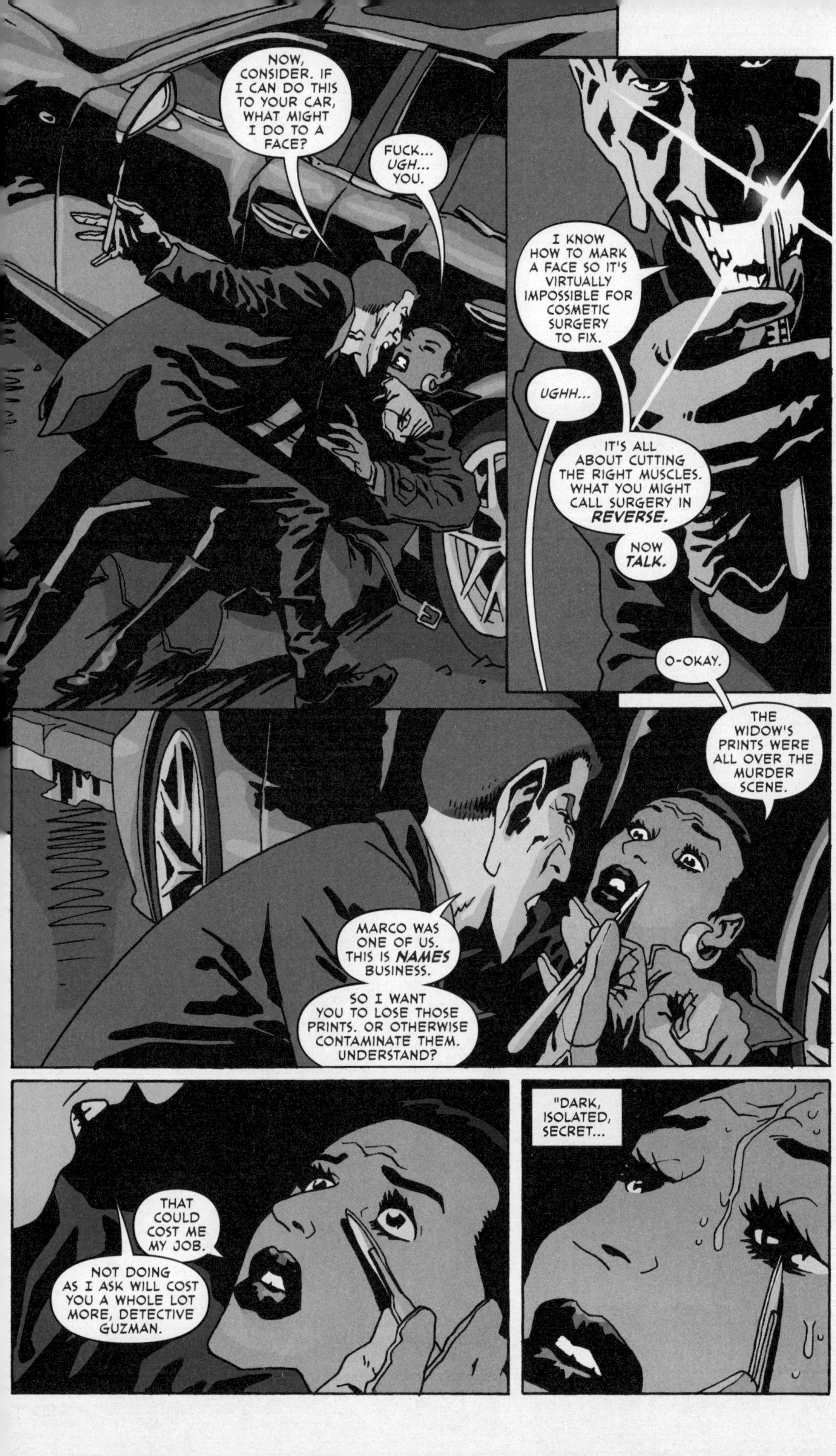
NOW, CONSIDER. IF I CAN DO THIS TO YOUR CAR, WHAT MIGHT I DO TO A FACE?
FUCK... UGH... YOU.
I KNOW HOW TO MARK A FACE SO IT'S VIRTUALLY IMPOSSIBLE FOR COSMETIC SURGERY TO FIX.
UGHH...
IT'S ALL ABOUT CUTTING THE RIGHT MUSCLES. WHAT YOU MIGHT CALL SURGERY IN REVERSE.
NOW TALK.
O-OKAY.
THE WIDOW'S PRINTS WERE ALL OVER THE MURDER SCENE.
MARCO WAS ONE OF US. THIS IS NAMES BUSINESS.
SO I WANT YOU TO LOSE THOSE PRINTS. OR OTHERWISE CONTAMINATE THEM. UNDERSTAND?
THAT COULD COST ME MY JOB.
NOT DOING AS I ASK WILL COST YOU A WHOLE LOT MORE, DETECTIVE GUZMAN.
"DARK, ISOLATED, SECRET...

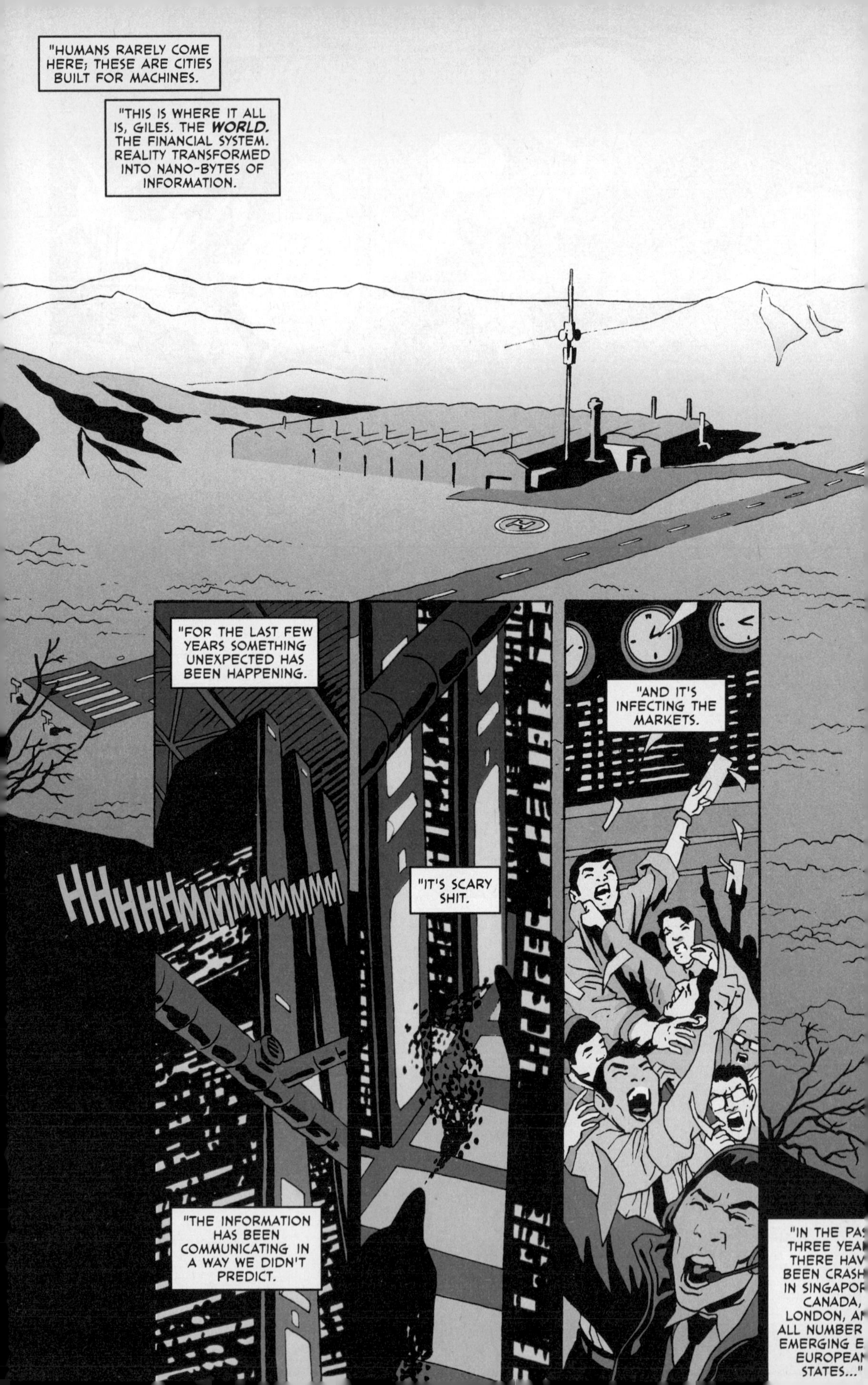
"HUMANS RARELY COME HERE; THESE ARE CITIES BUILT FOR MACHINES.
"THIS IS WHERE IT ALL IS, GILES. THE *WORLD.* THE FINANCIAL SYSTEM. REALITY TRANSFORMED INTO NANO-BYTES OF INFORMATION.
"FOR THE LAST FEW YEARS SOMETHING UNEXPECTED HAS BEEN HAPPENING.
HHHHHMMMMMMMMM
"IT'S SCARY SHIT.
"THE INFORMATION HAS BEEN COMMUNICATING IN A WAY WE DIDN'T PREDICT.
"AND IT'S INFECTING THE MARKETS.
"IN THE PAS THREE YEA THERE HAV BEEN CRASH IN SINGAPOR CANADA, LONDON, A ALL NUMBER EMERGING E EUROPEA STATES..."

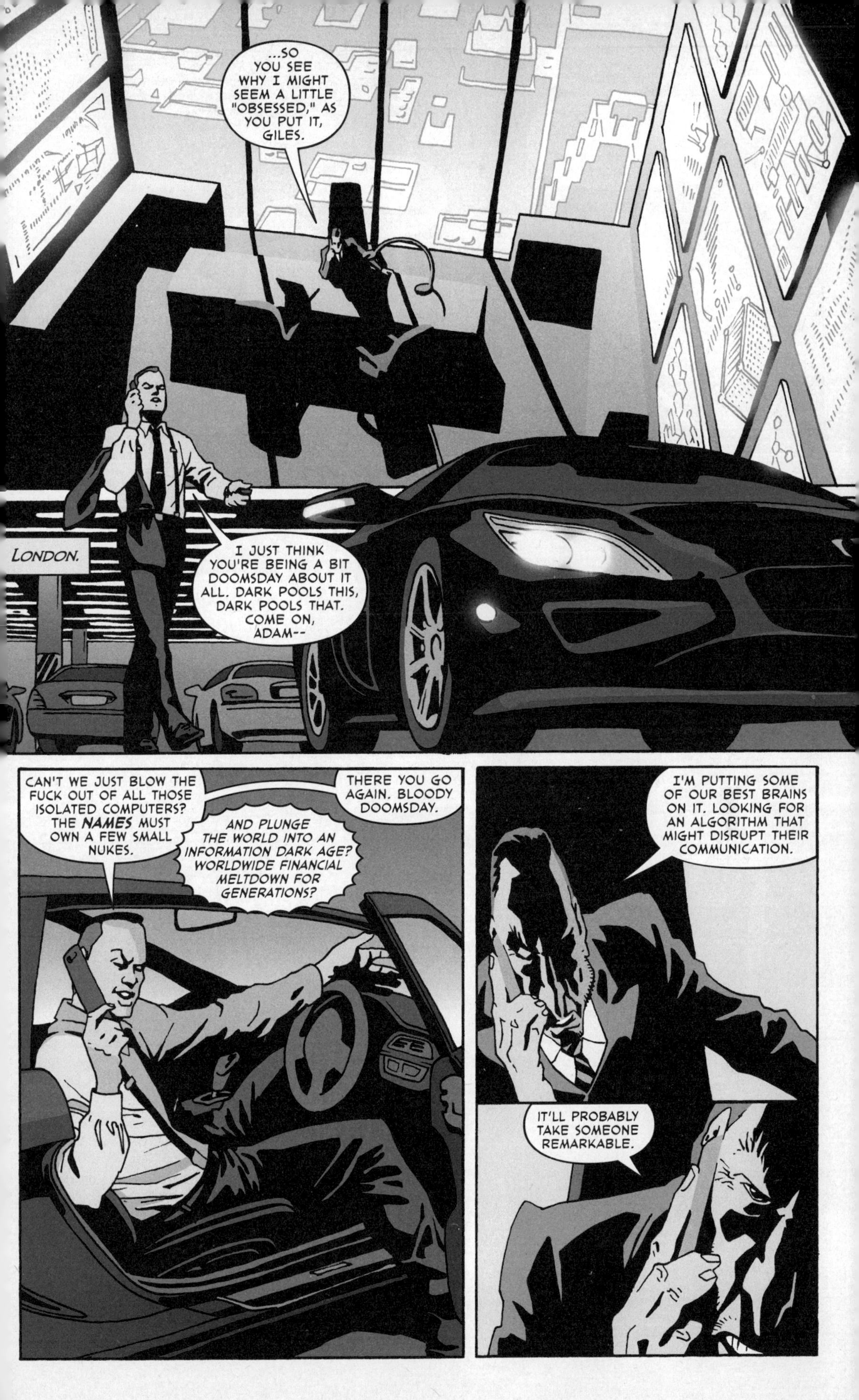
...SO YOU SEE WHY I MIGHT SEEM A LITTLE "OBSESSED," AS YOU PUT IT, GILES.
LONDON.
I JUST THINK YOU'RE BEING A BIT DOOMSDAY ABOUT IT ALL. DARK POOLS THIS, DARK POOLS THAT. COME ON, ADAM--
CAN'T WE JUST BLOW THE FUCK OUT OF ALL THOSE ISOLATED COMPUTERS? THE NAMES MUST OWN A FEW SMALL NUKES.
AND PLUNGE THE WORLD INTO AN INFORMATION DARK AGE? WORLDWIDE FINANCIAL MELTDOWN FOR GENERATIONS?
THERE YOU GO AGAIN. BLOODY DOOMSDAY.
I'M PUTTING SOME OF OUR BEST BRAINS ON IT. LOOKING FOR AN ALGORITHM THAT MIGHT DISRUPT THEIR COMMUNICATION.
IT'LL PROBABLY TAKE SOMEONE REMARKABLE.

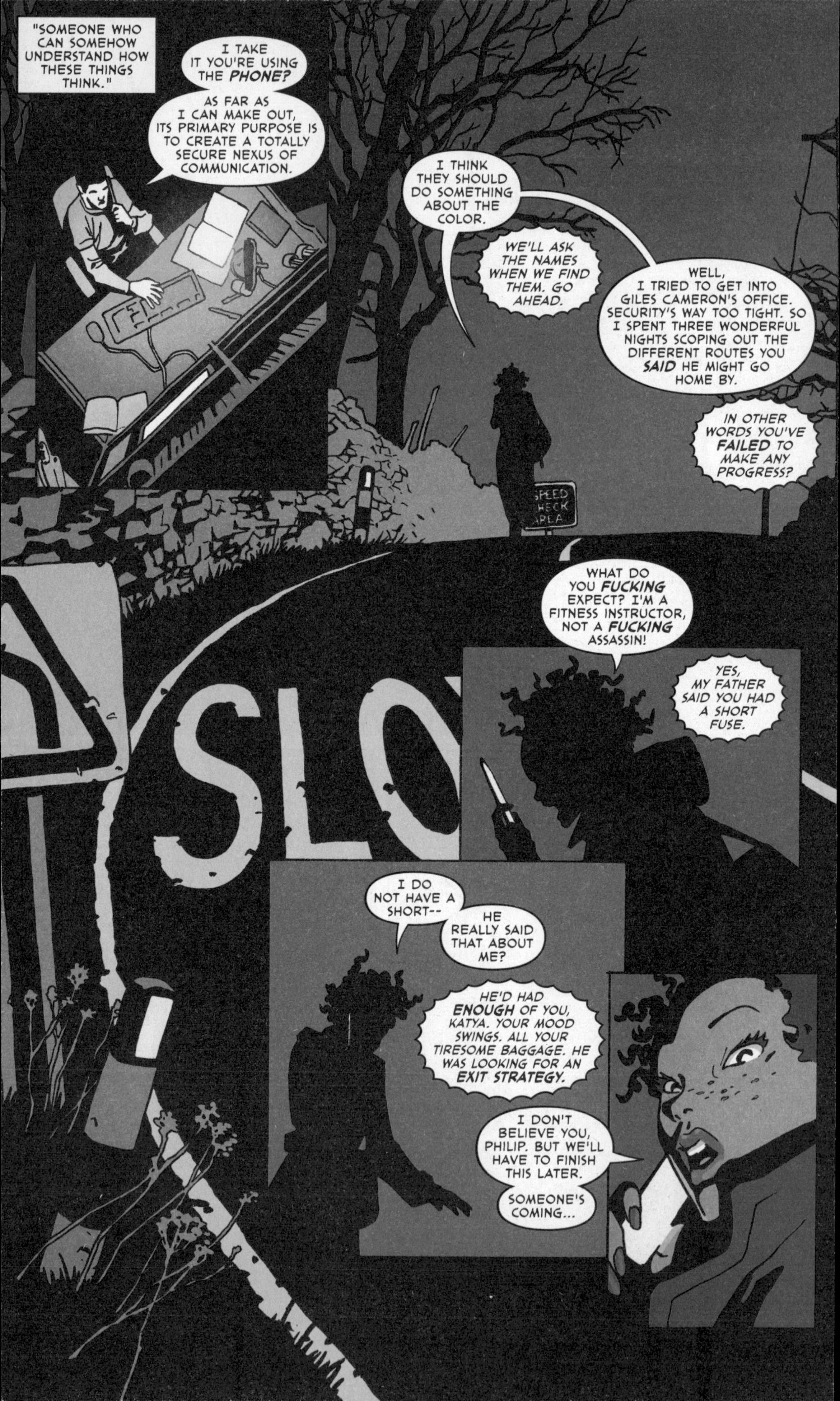
"SOMEONE WHO CAN SOMEHOW UNDERSTAND HOW THESE THINGS THINK."
I TAKE IT YOU'RE USING THE PHONE?
AS FAR AS I CAN MAKE OUT, ITS PRIMARY PURPOSE IS TO CREATE A TOTALLY SECURE NEXUS OF COMMUNICATION.
I THINK THEY SHOULD DO SOMETHING ABOUT THE COLOR.
WE'LL ASK THE NAMES WHEN WE FIND THEM. GO AHEAD.
WELL, I TRIED TO GET INTO GILES CAMERON'S OFFICE. SECURITY'S WAY TOO TIGHT. SO I SPENT THREE WONDERFUL NIGHTS SCOPING OUT THE DIFFERENT ROUTES YOU SAID HE MIGHT GO HOME BY.
IN OTHER WORDS YOU'VE FAILED TO MAKE ANY PROGRESS?
SPEED CHECK AREA
WHAT DO YOU FUCKING EXPECT? I'M A FITNESS INSTRUCTOR, NOT A FUCKING ASSASSIN!
YES, MY FATHER SAID YOU HAD A SHORT FUSE.
SLO
I DO NOT HAVE A SHORT--
HE REALLY SAID THAT ABOUT ME?
HE'D HAD ENOUGH OF YOU, KATYA. YOUR MOOD SWINGS. ALL YOUR TIRESOME BAGGAGE. HE WAS LOOKING FOR AN EXIT STRATEGY.
I DON'T BELIEVE YOU, PHILIP. BUT WE'LL HAVE TO FINISH THIS LATER.
SOMEONE'S COMING...

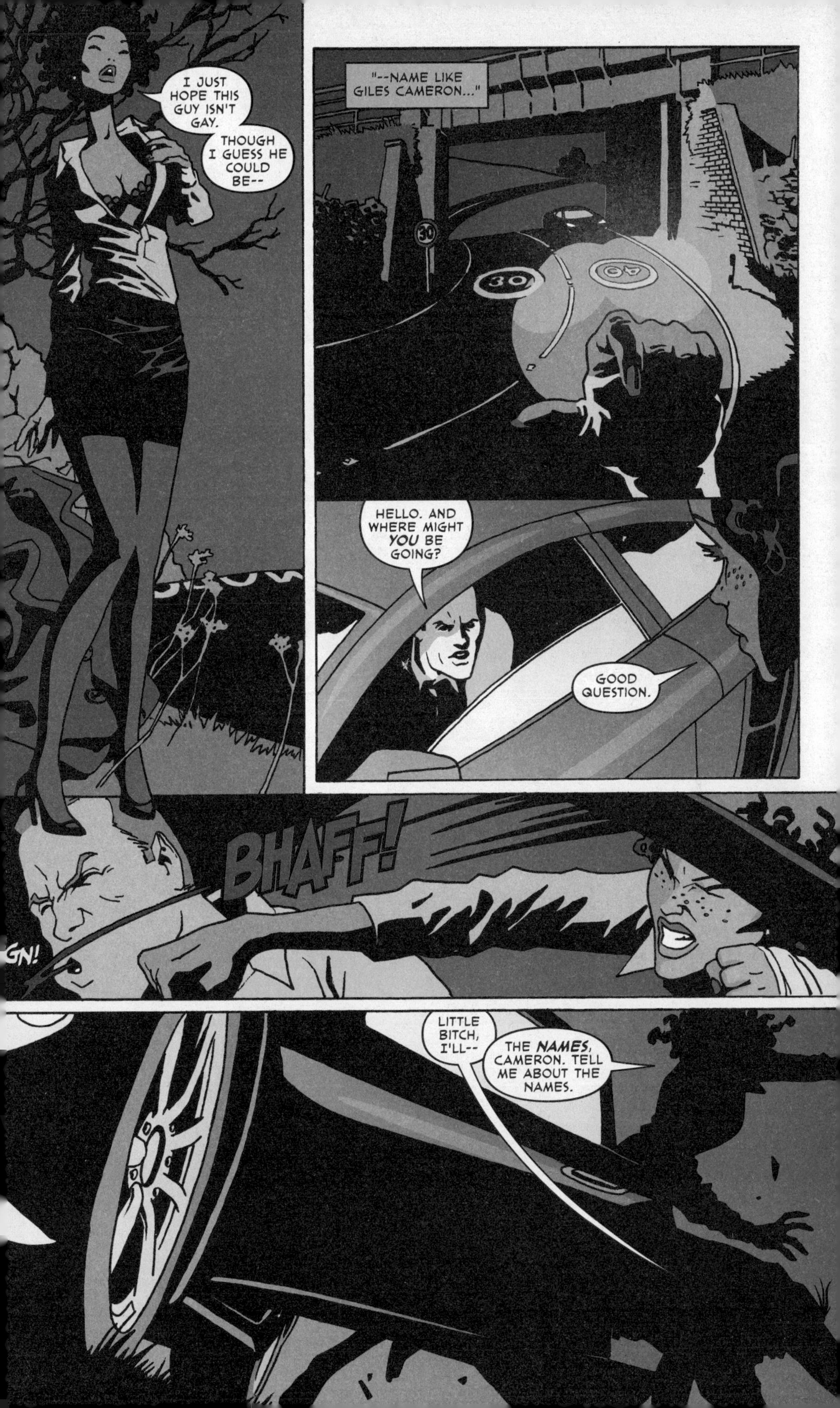
I JUST HOPE THIS GUY ISN'T GAY.
THOUGH I GUESS HE COULD BE--
"--NAME LIKE GILES CAMERON..."
HELLO. AND WHERE MIGHT *YOU* BE GOING?
GOOD QUESTION.
BHAFF!
GN!
LITTLE BITCH, I'LL--
THE ***NAMES***, CAMERON. TELL ME ABOUT THE NAMES.

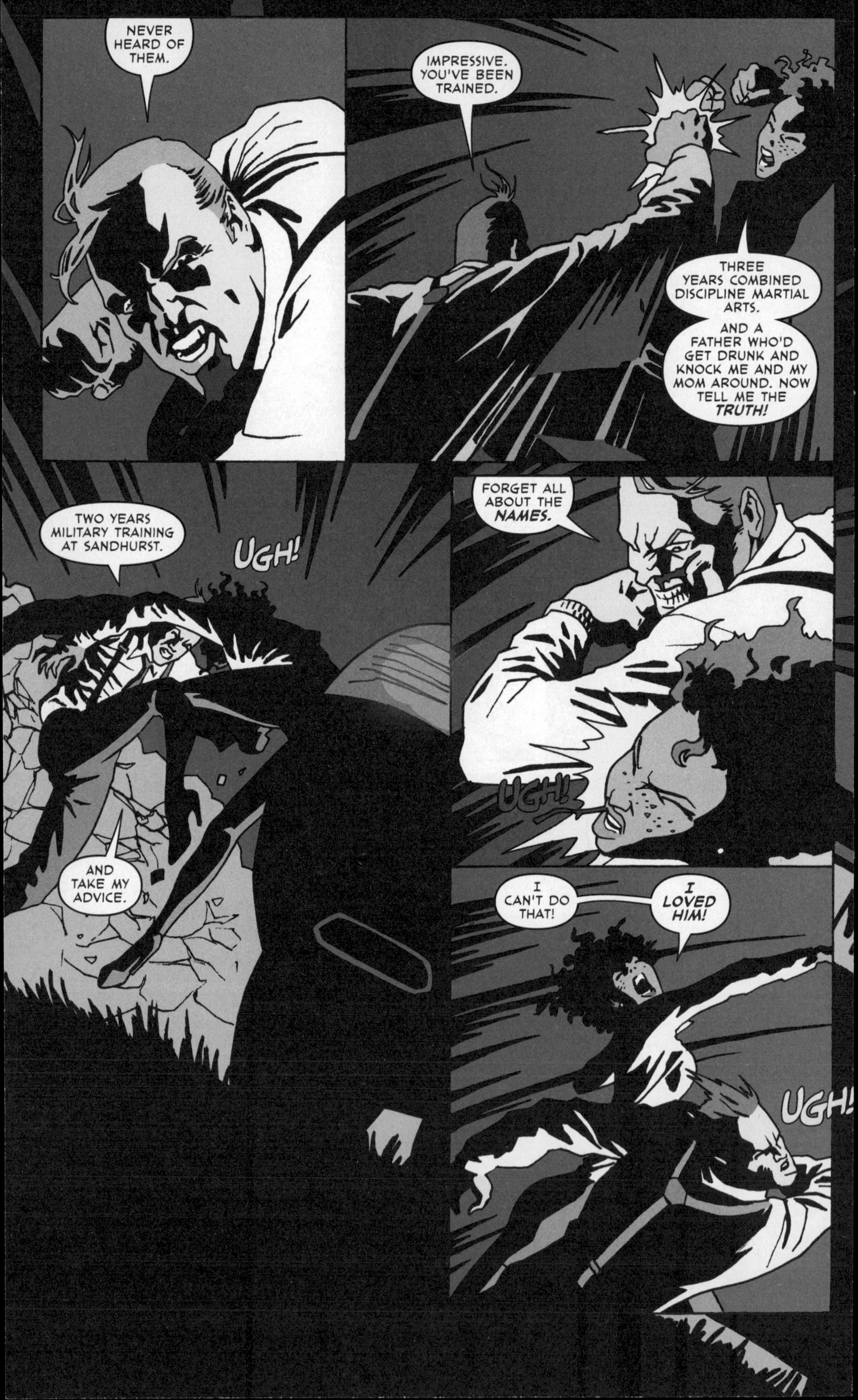
NEVER HEARD OF THEM.
IMPRESSIVE. YOU'VE BEEN TRAINED.
THREE YEARS COMBINED DISCIPLINE MARTIAL ARTS.
AND A FATHER WHO'D GET DRUNK AND KNOCK ME AND MY MOM AROUND. NOW TELL ME THE TRUTH!
TWO YEARS MILITARY TRAINING AT SANDHURST.
UGH!
AND TAKE MY ADVICE.
FORGET ALL ABOUT THE NAMES.
UGH!
I CAN'T DO THAT!
I LOVED HIM!
UGH!

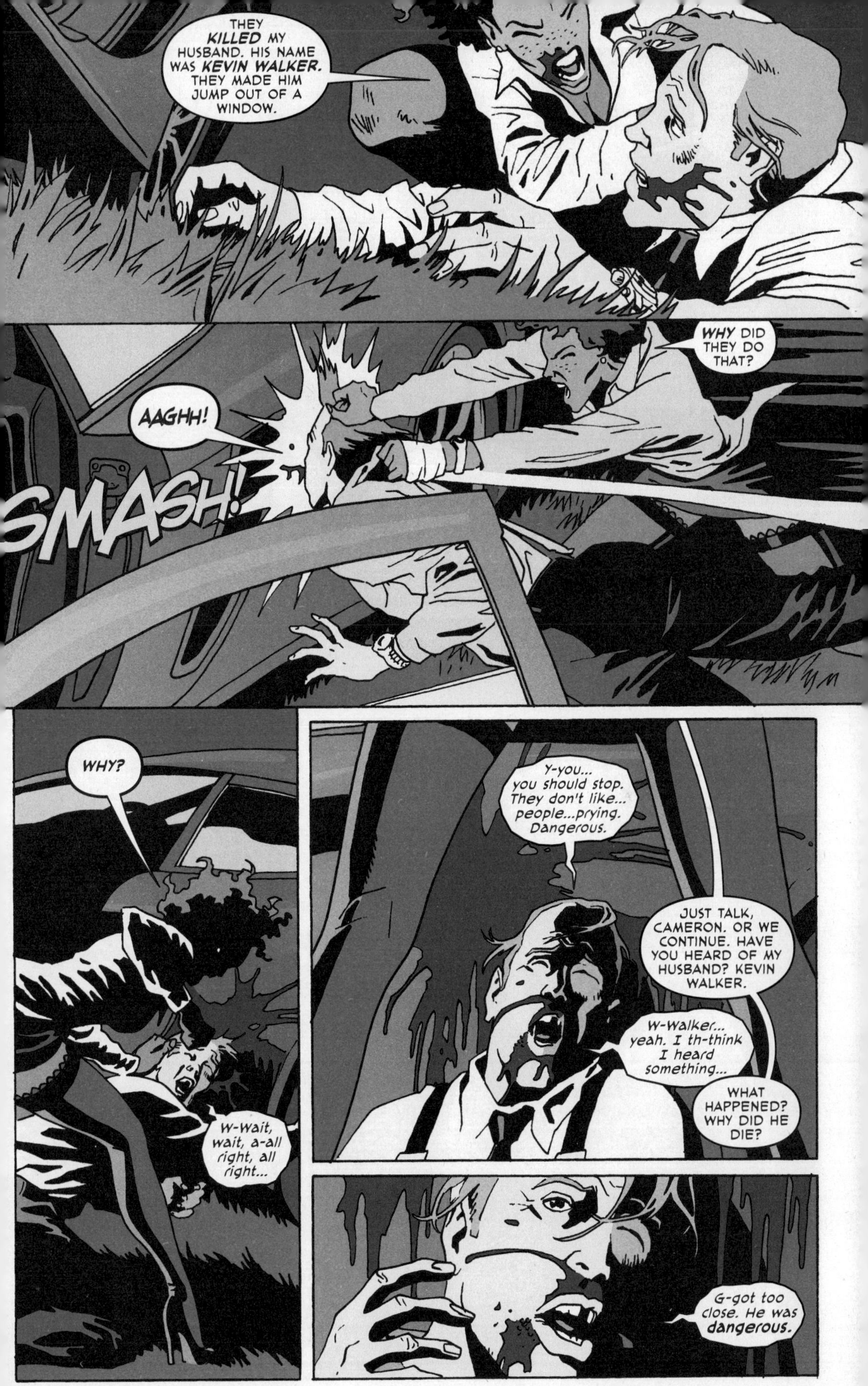
THEY KILLED MY HUSBAND. HIS NAME WAS KEVIN WALKER. THEY MADE HIM JUMP OUT OF A WINDOW.
WHY DID THEY DO THAT?
AAGHH!
SMASH!
WHY?
W-Wait, wait, a-all right, all right...
Y-you... you should stop. They don't like... people...prying. Dangerous.
JUST TALK, CAMERON. OR WE CONTINUE. HAVE YOU HEARD OF MY HUSBAND? KEVIN WALKER.
W-Walker... yeah. I th-think I heard something...
WHAT HAPPENED? WHY DID HE DIE?
G-got too close. He was dangerous.

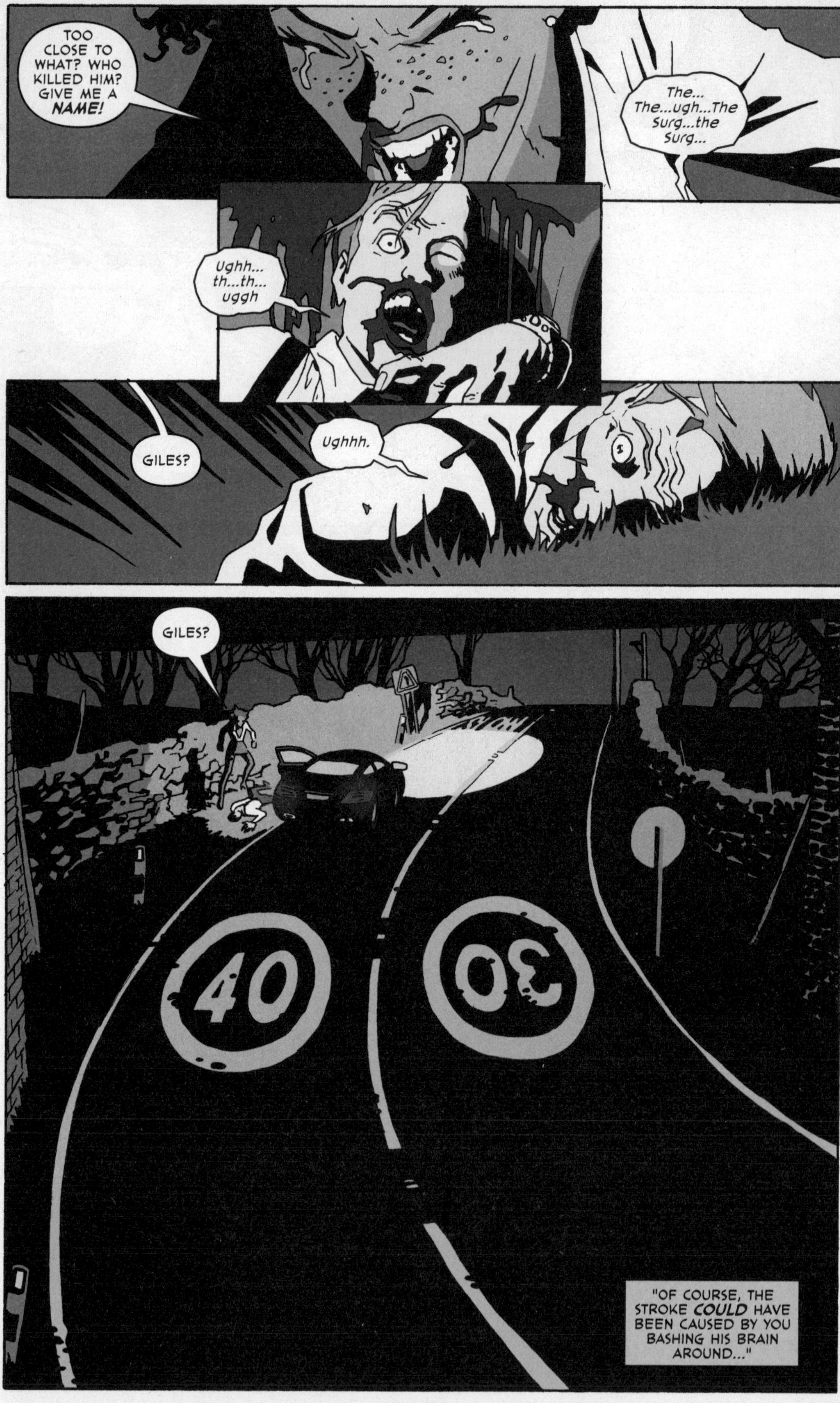
TOO CLOSE TO WHAT? WHO KILLED HIM? GIVE ME A **NAME!**
The... The...ugh...The Surg...the Surg...
Ughh... th...th... uggh
GILES?
Ughhh.
GILES?
"OF COURSE, THE STROKE **COULD** HAVE BEEN CAUSED BY YOU BASHING HIS BRAIN AROUND..."

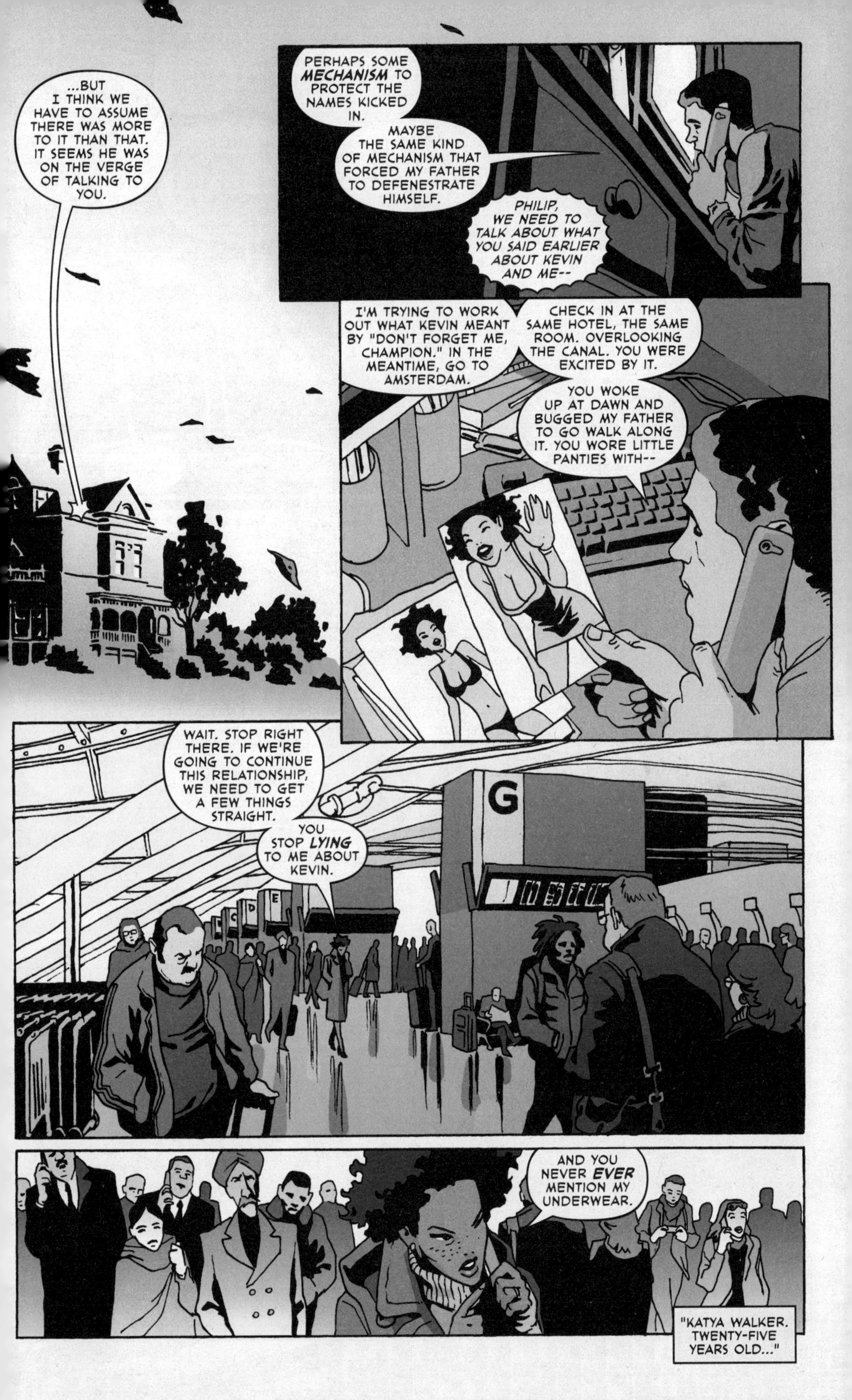
...BUT I THINK WE HAVE TO ASSUME THERE WAS MORE TO IT THAN THAT. IT SEEMS HE WAS ON THE VERGE OF TALKING TO YOU.
PERHAPS SOME *MECHANISM* TO PROTECT THE NAMES KICKED IN.
MAYBE THE SAME KIND OF MECHANISM THAT FORCED MY FATHER TO DEFENESTRATE HIMSELF.
PHILIP, WE NEED TO TALK ABOUT WHAT YOU SAID EARLIER ABOUT KEVIN AND ME--
I'M TRYING TO WORK OUT WHAT KEVIN MEANT BY "DON'T FORGET ME, CHAMPION." IN THE MEANTIME, GO TO AMSTERDAM.
CHECK IN AT THE SAME HOTEL, THE SAME ROOM. OVERLOOKING THE CANAL. YOU WERE EXCITED BY IT.
YOU WOKE UP AT DAWN AND BUGGED MY FATHER TO GO WALK ALONG IT. YOU WORE LITTLE PANTIES WITH--
WAIT. STOP RIGHT THERE. IF WE'RE GOING TO CONTINUE THIS RELATIONSHIP, WE NEED TO GET A FEW THINGS STRAIGHT.
YOU STOP *LYING* TO ME ABOUT KEVIN.
G
AND YOU NEVER *EVER* MENTION MY UNDERWEAR.
"KATYA WALKER. TWENTY-FIVE YEARS OLD..."

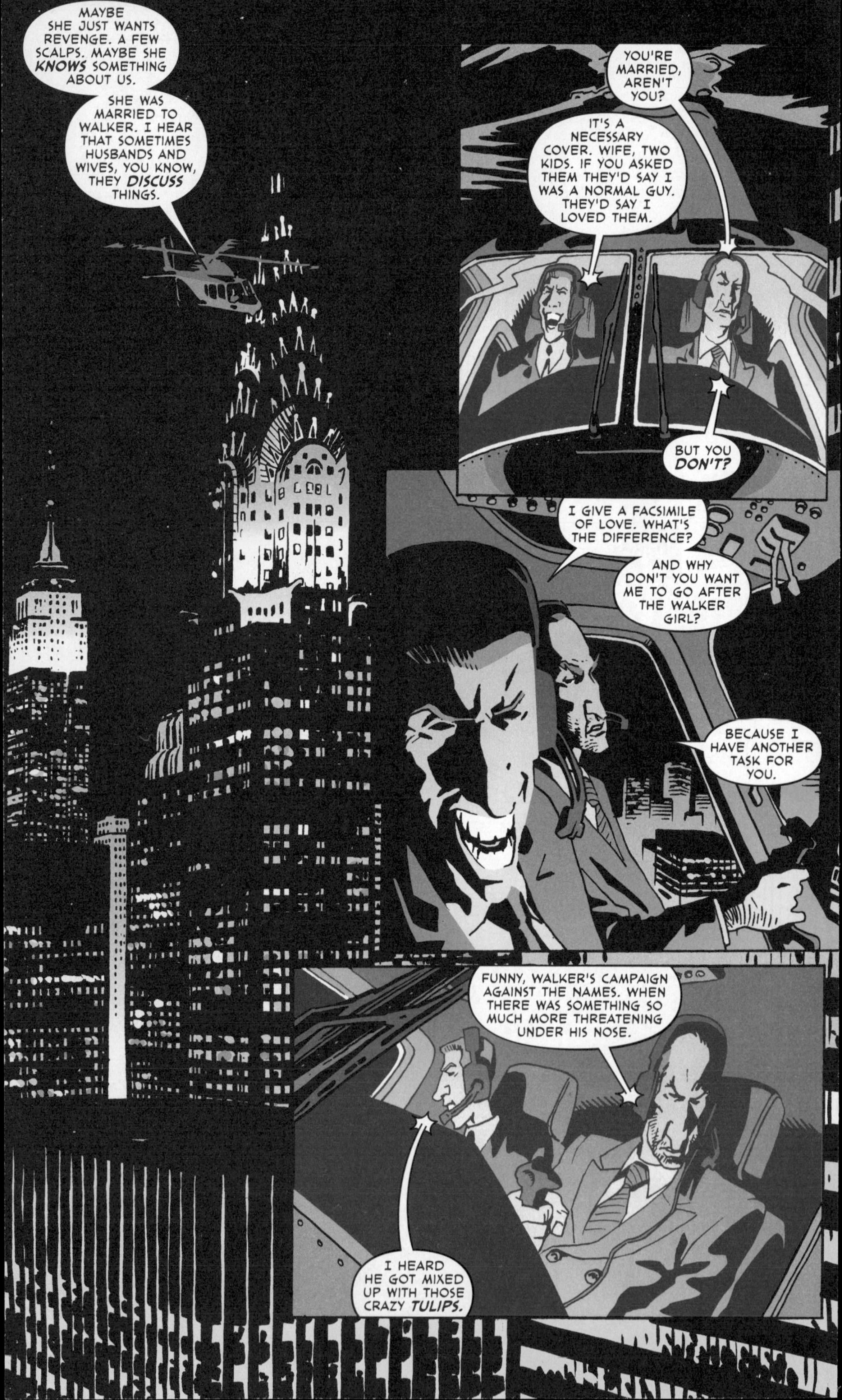
MAYBE SHE JUST WANTS REVENGE. A FEW SCALPS. MAYBE SHE KNOWS SOMETHING ABOUT US.
SHE WAS MARRIED TO WALKER. I HEAR THAT SOMETIMES HUSBANDS AND WIVES, YOU KNOW, THEY DISCUSS THINGS.
YOU'RE MARRIED, AREN'T YOU?
IT'S A NECESSARY COVER. WIFE, TWO KIDS. IF YOU ASKED THEM THEY'D SAY I WAS A NORMAL GUY. THEY'D SAY I LOVED THEM.
BUT YOU DON'T?
I GIVE A FACSIMILE OF LOVE. WHAT'S THE DIFFERENCE?
AND WHY DON'T YOU WANT ME TO GO AFTER THE WALKER GIRL?
BECAUSE I HAVE ANOTHER TASK FOR YOU.
FUNNY, WALKER'S CAMPAIGN AGAINST THE NAMES. WHEN THERE WAS SOMETHING SO MUCH MORE THREATENING UNDER HIS NOSE.
I HEARD HE GOT MIXED UP WITH THOSE CRAZY TULIPS.

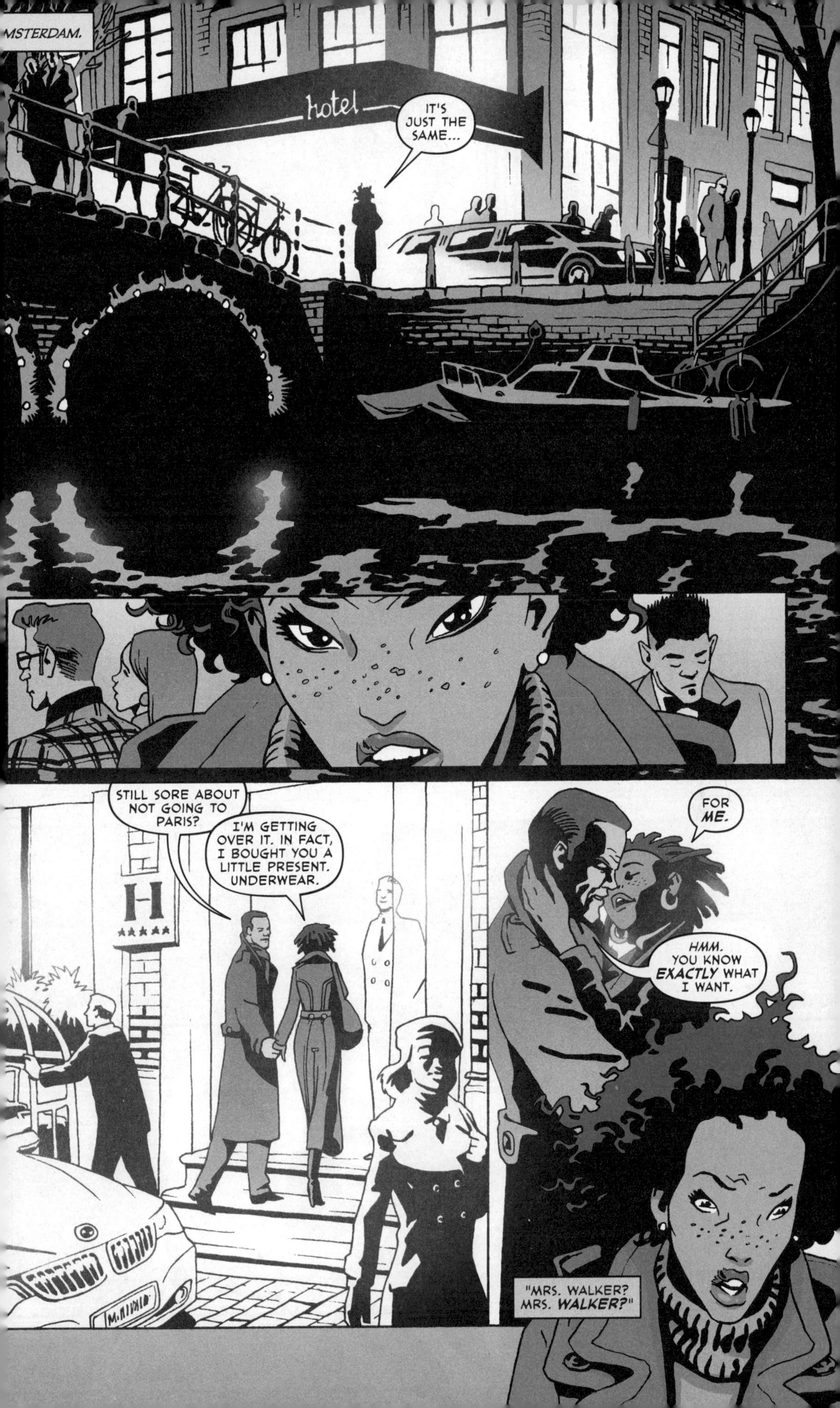
MSTERDAM.
hotel
IT'S JUST THE SAME...
STILL SORE ABOUT NOT GOING TO PARIS?
I'M GETTING OVER IT. IN FACT, I BOUGHT YOU A LITTLE PRESENT. UNDERWEAR.
H
FOR ME.
HMM. YOU KNOW EXACTLY WHAT I WANT.
"MRS. WALKER? MRS. WALKER?"

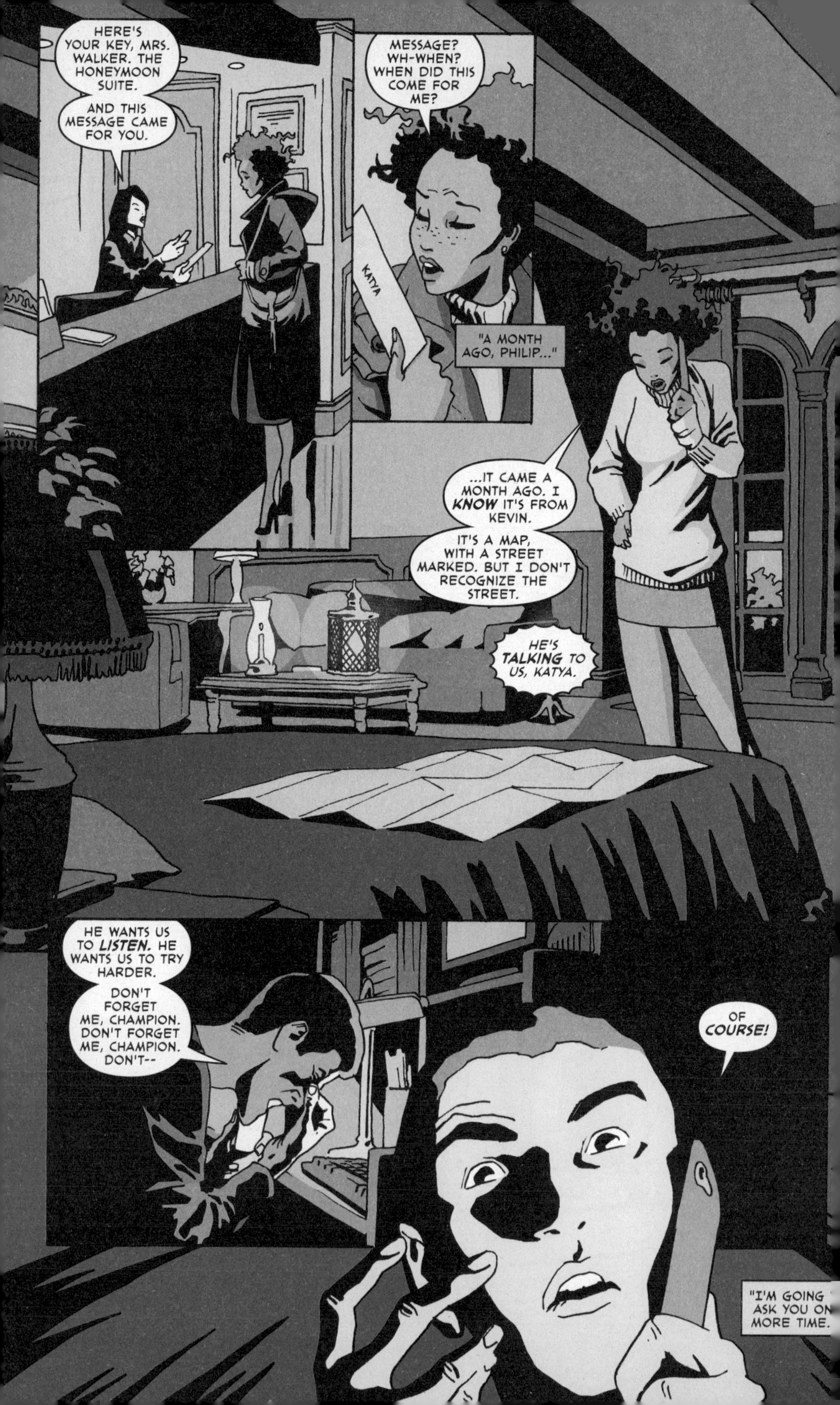
HERE'S YOUR KEY, MRS. WALKER. THE HONEYMOON SUITE.
AND THIS MESSAGE CAME FOR YOU.
MESSAGE? WH-WHEN? WHEN DID THIS COME FOR ME?
KATYA
"A MONTH AGO, PHILIP..."
...IT CAME A MONTH AGO. I *KNOW* IT'S FROM KEVIN.
IT'S A MAP, WITH A STREET MARKED. BUT I DON'T RECOGNIZE THE STREET.
HE'S *TALKING* TO US, KATYA.
HE WANTS US TO *LISTEN.* HE WANTS US TO TRY HARDER.
DON'T FORGET ME, CHAMPION. DON'T FORGET ME, CHAMPION. DON'T--
OF *COURSE!*
"I'M GOING ASK YOU ON MORE TIME.

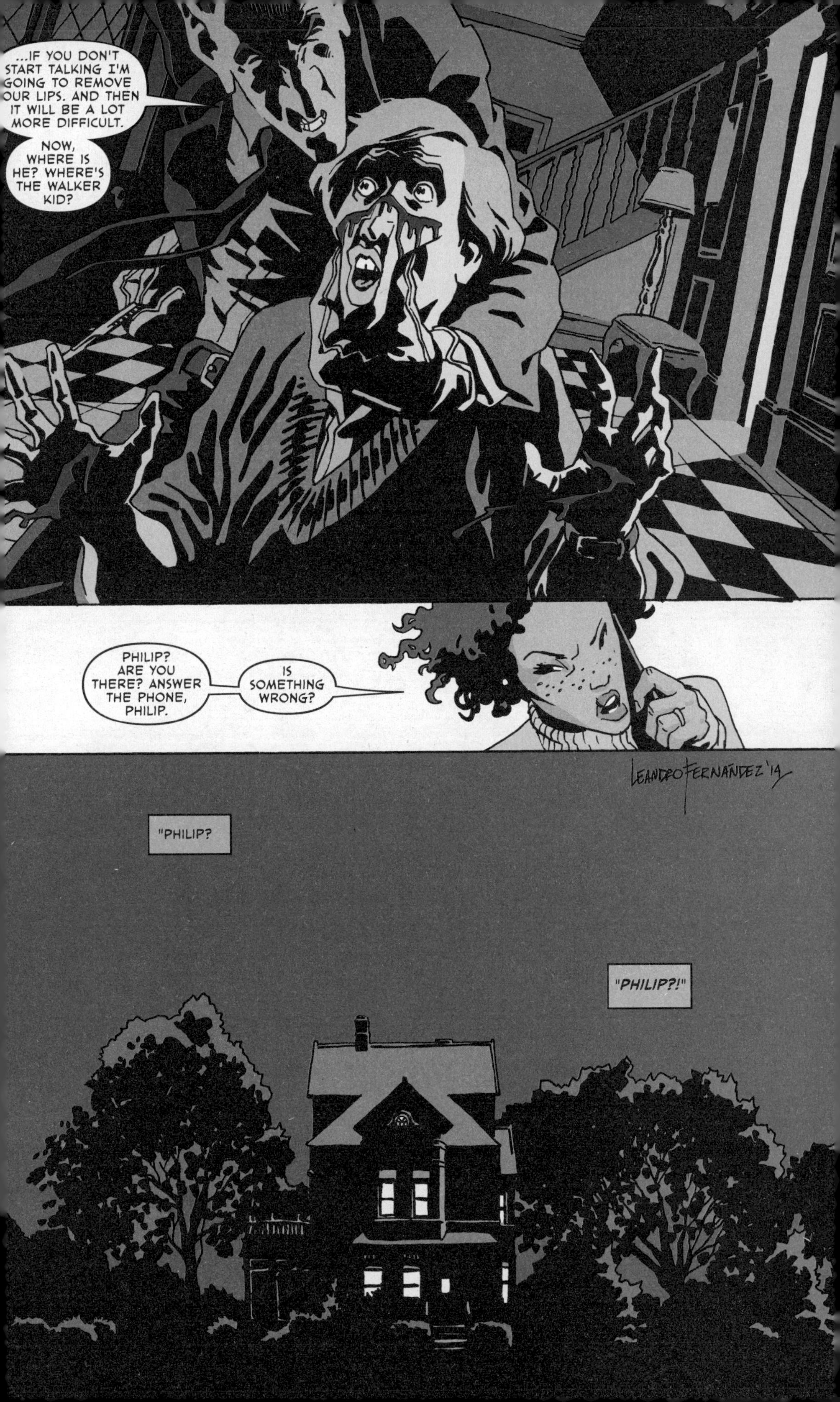
...IF YOU DON'T START TALKING I'M GOING TO REMOVE OUR LIPS. AND THEN IT WILL BE A LOT MORE DIFFICULT.
NOW, WHERE IS HE? WHERE'S THE WALKER KID?
PHILIP? ARE YOU THERE? ANSWER THE PHONE, PHILIP.
IS SOMETHING WRONG?
LEANDRO FERNÁNDEZ '14
"PHILIP?
"PHILIP?!"

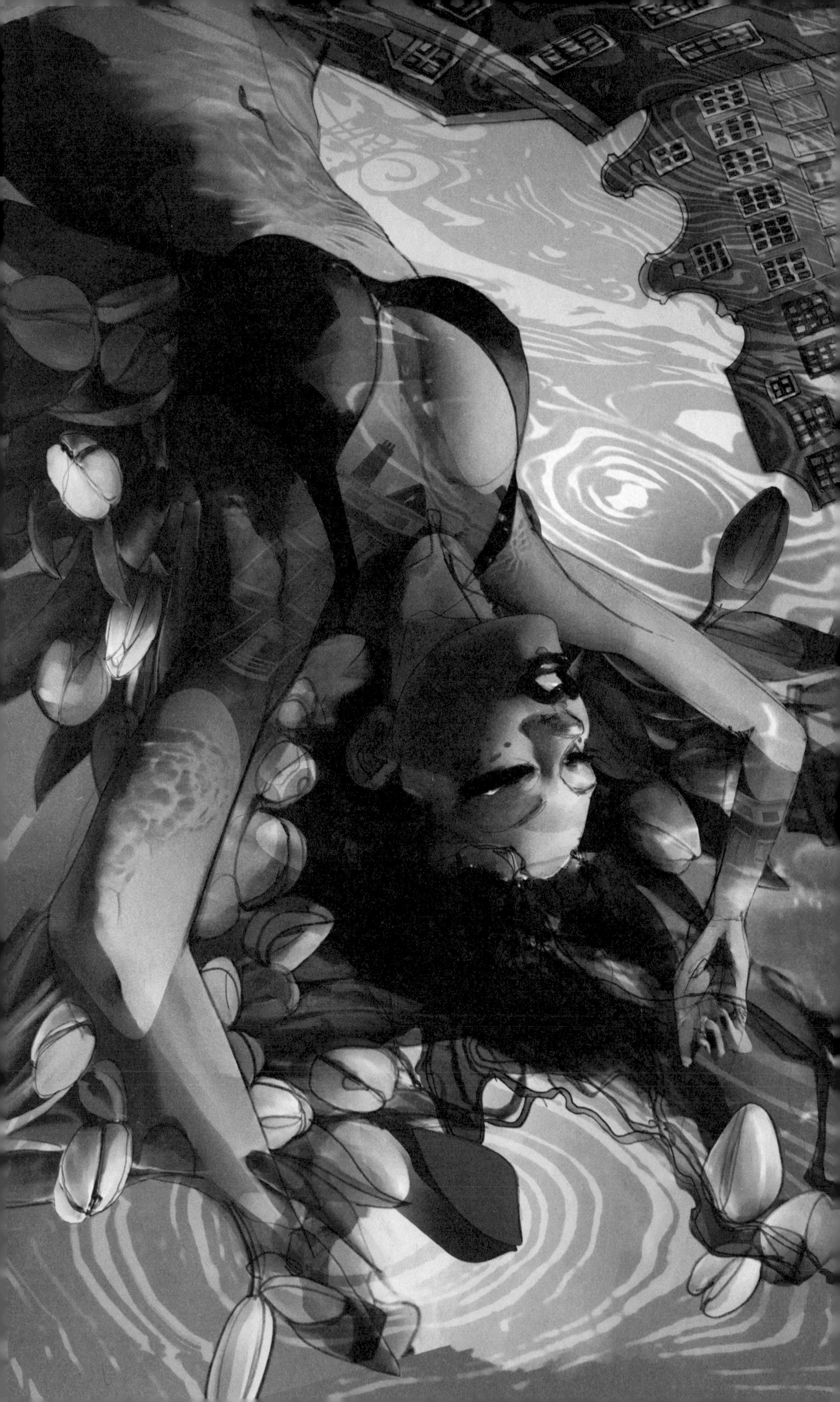

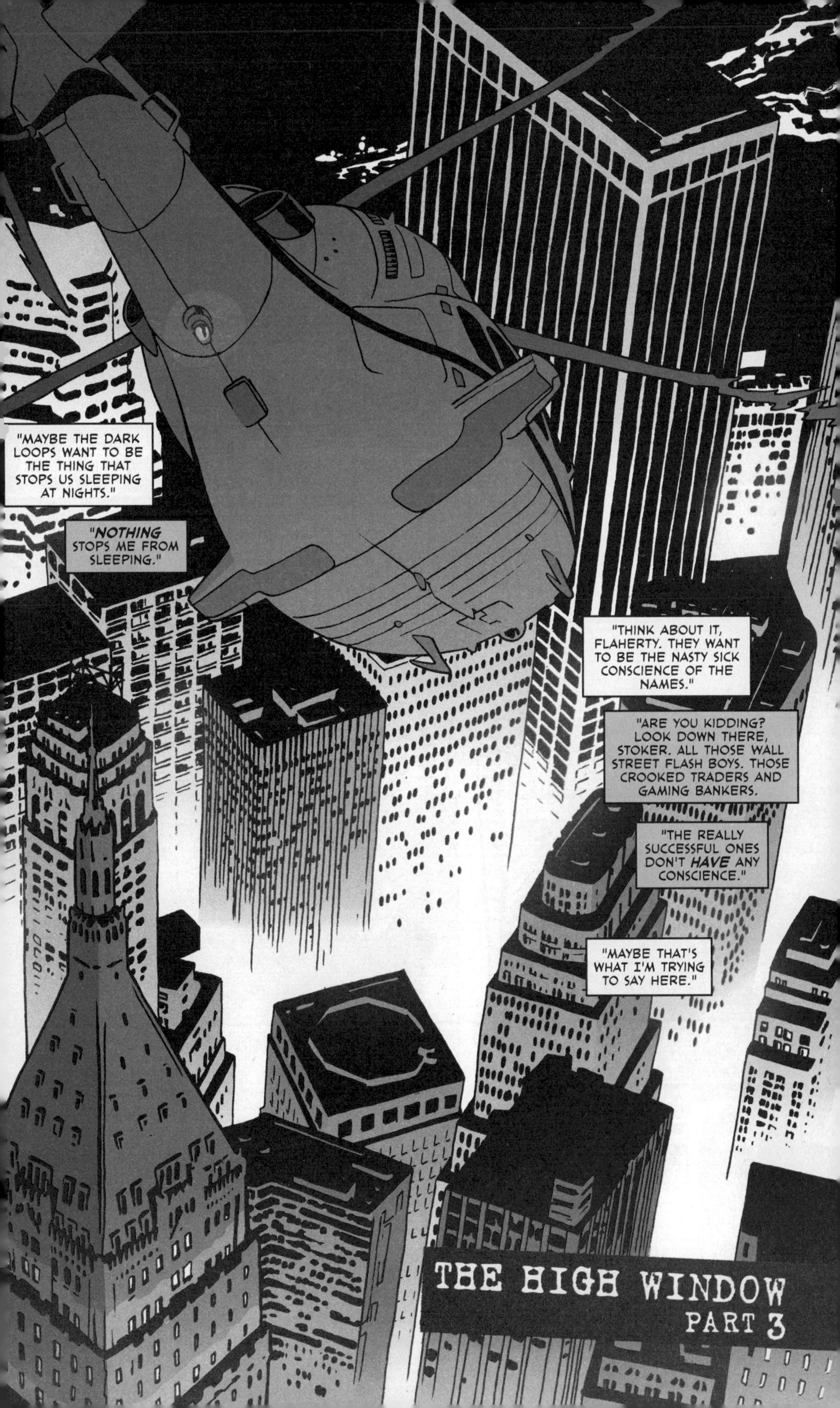
"MAYBE THE DARK LOOPS WANT TO BE THE THING THAT STOPS US SLEEPING AT NIGHTS."
"*NOTHING* STOPS ME FROM SLEEPING."
"THINK ABOUT IT, FLAHERTY. THEY WANT TO BE THE NASTY SICK CONSCIENCE OF THE NAMES."
"ARE YOU KIDDING? LOOK DOWN THERE, STOKER. ALL THOSE WALL STREET FLASH BOYS. THOSE CROOKED TRADERS AND GAMING BANKERS.
"THE REALLY SUCCESSFUL ONES DON'T *HAVE* ANY CONSCIENCE."
"MAYBE THAT'S WHAT I'M TRYING TO SAY HERE."
THE HIGH WINDOW
PART 3

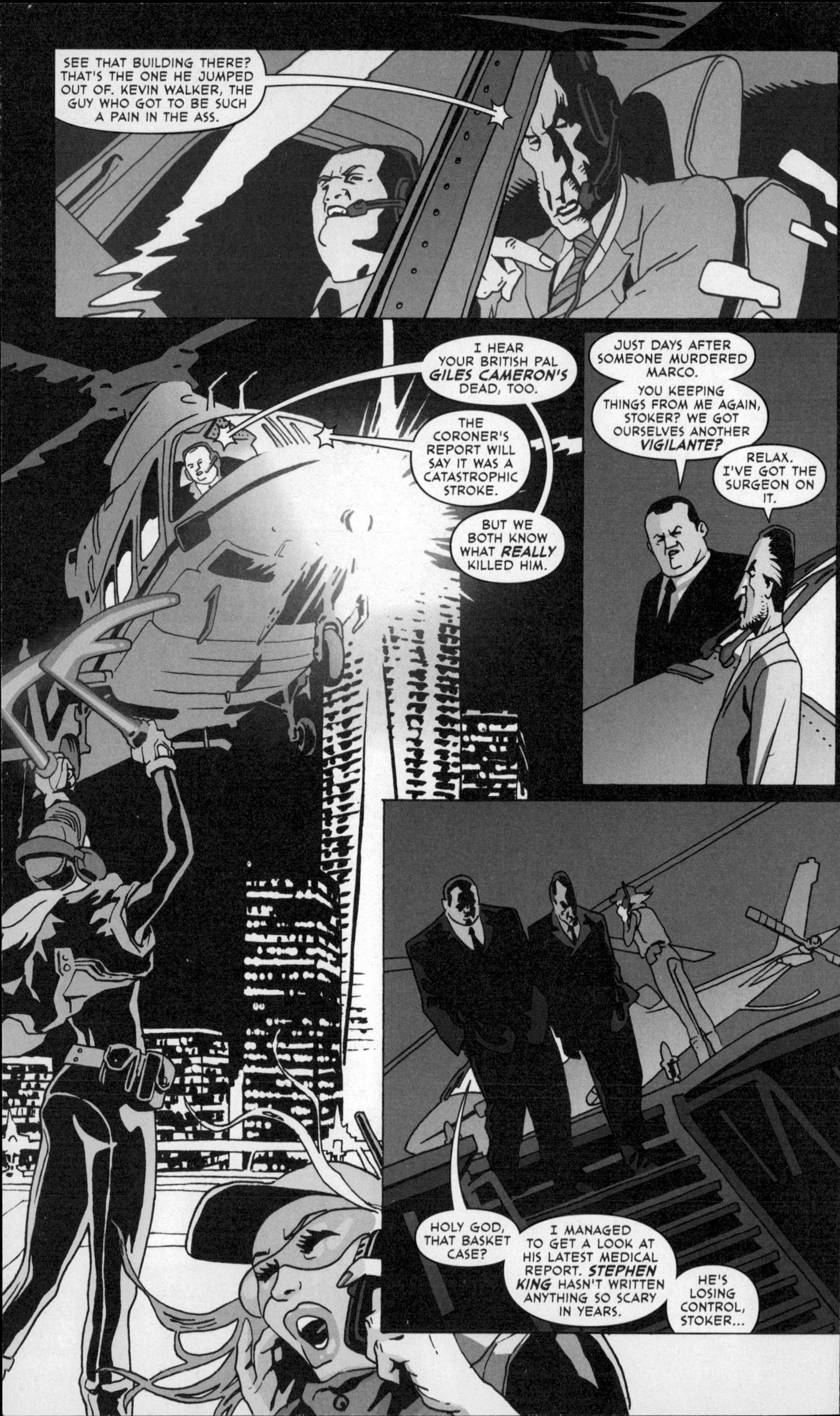
SEE THAT BUILDING THERE? THAT'S THE ONE HE JUMPED OUT OF. KEVIN WALKER, THE GUY WHO GOT TO BE SUCH A PAIN IN THE ASS.
I HEAR YOUR BRITISH PAL GILES CAMERON'S DEAD, TOO.
THE CORONER'S REPORT WILL SAY IT WAS A CATASTROPHIC STROKE.
BUT WE BOTH KNOW WHAT REALLY KILLED HIM.
JUST DAYS AFTER SOMEONE MURDERED MARCO.
YOU KEEPING THINGS FROM ME AGAIN, STOKER? WE GOT OURSELVES ANOTHER VIGILANTE?
RELAX. I'VE GOT THE SURGEON ON IT.
HOLY GOD, THAT BASKET CASE?
I MANAGED TO GET A LOOK AT HIS LATEST MEDICAL REPORT. STEPHEN KING HASN'T WRITTEN ANYTHING SO SCARY IN YEARS.
HE'S LOSING CONTROL, STOKER...

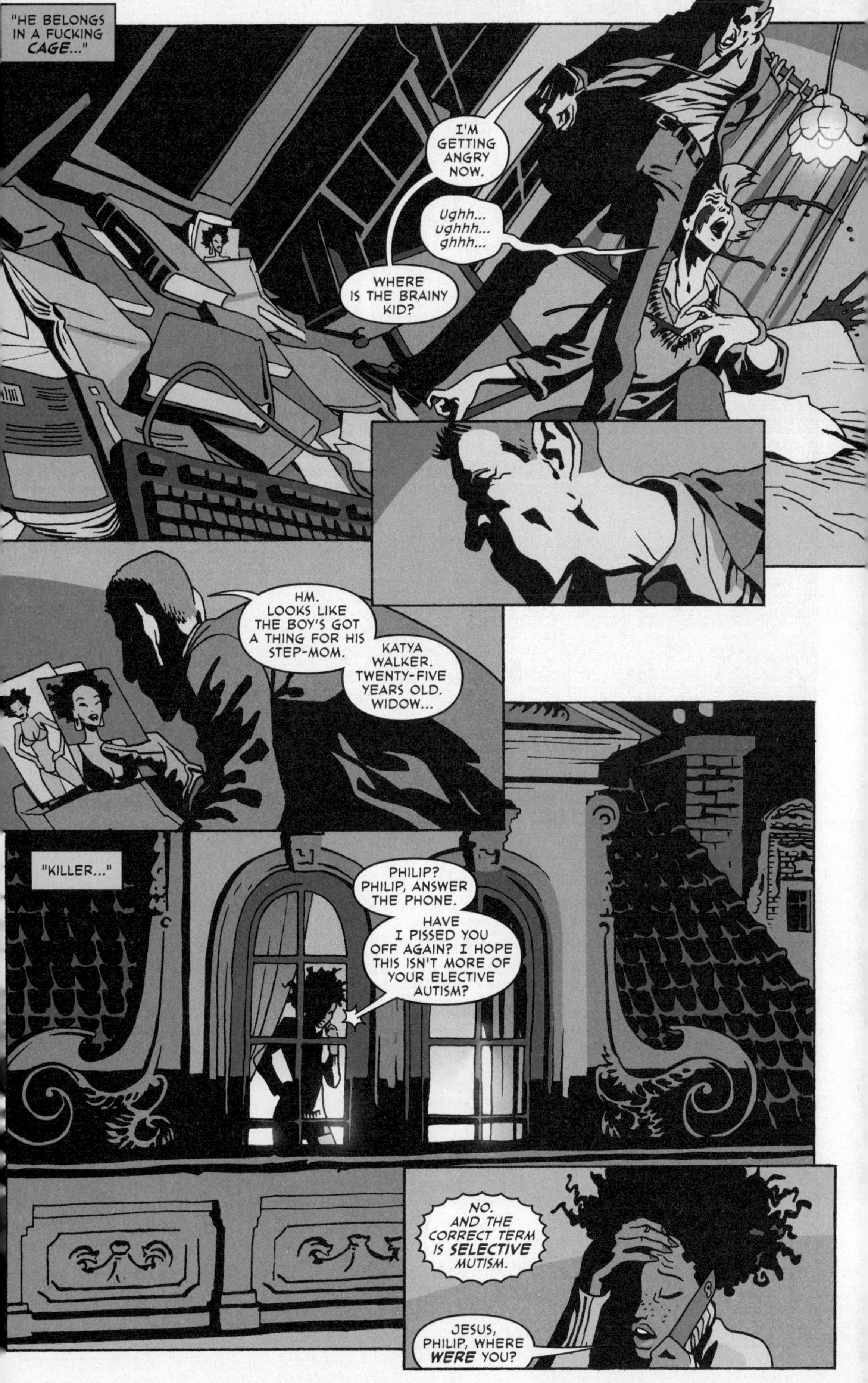
"HE BELONGS IN A FUCKING *CAGE*..."
I'M GETTING ANGRY NOW.
Ughh... ughhh... ghhh...
WHERE IS THE BRAINY KID?
HM. LOOKS LIKE THE BOY'S GOT A THING FOR HIS STEP-MOM.
KATYA WALKER. TWENTY-FIVE YEARS OLD. WIDOW...
"KILLER..."
PHILIP? PHILIP, ANSWER THE PHONE.
HAVE I PISSED YOU OFF AGAIN? I HOPE THIS ISN'T MORE OF YOUR ELECTIVE AUTISM?
NO. AND THE CORRECT TERM IS **SELECTIVE** MUTISM.
JESUS, PHILIP, WHERE ***WERE*** YOU?

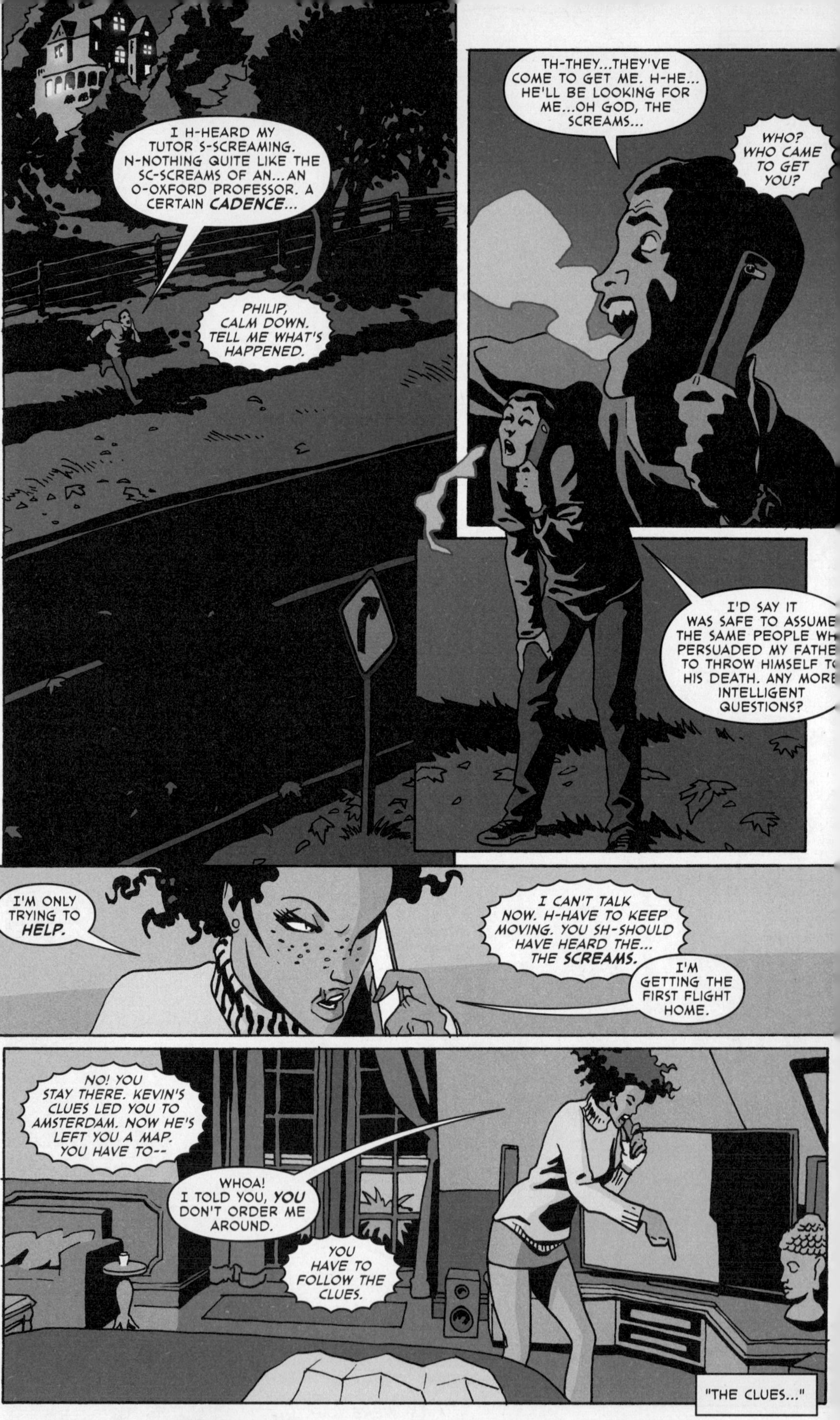
I H-HEARD MY TUTOR S-SCREAMING. N-NOTHING QUITE LIKE THE SC-SCREAMS OF AN...AN O-OXFORD PROFESSOR. A CERTAIN CADENCE...
PHILIP, CALM DOWN. TELL ME WHAT'S HAPPENED.
TH-THEY...THEY'VE COME TO GET ME. H-HE... HE'LL BE LOOKING FOR ME...OH GOD, THE SCREAMS...
WHO? WHO CAME TO GET YOU?
I'D SAY IT WAS SAFE TO ASSUME THE SAME PEOPLE WH PERSUADED MY FATHE TO THROW HIMSELF T HIS DEATH. ANY MORE INTELLIGENT QUESTIONS?
I'M ONLY TRYING TO HELP.
I CAN'T TALK NOW. H-HAVE TO KEEP MOVING. YOU SH-SHOULD HAVE HEARD THE... THE SCREAMS.
I'M GETTING THE FIRST FLIGHT HOME.
NO! YOU STAY THERE. KEVIN'S CLUES LED YOU TO AMSTERDAM. NOW HE'S LEFT YOU A MAP. YOU HAVE TO--
WHOA! I TOLD YOU, YOU DON'T ORDER ME AROUND.
YOU HAVE TO FOLLOW THE CLUES.
"THE CLUES..."

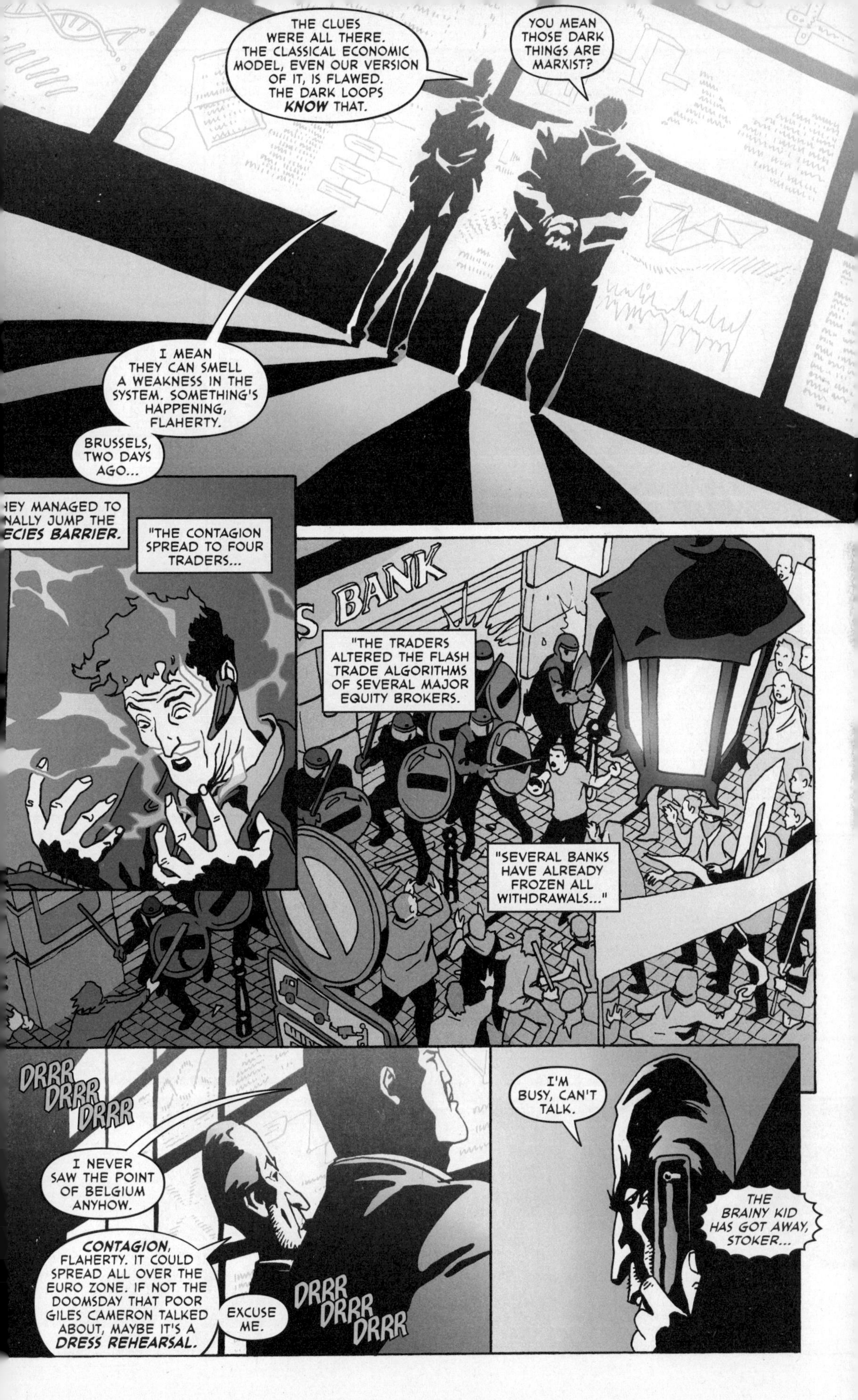
THE CLUES WERE ALL THERE. THE CLASSICAL ECONOMIC MODEL, EVEN OUR VERSION OF IT, IS FLAWED. THE DARK LOOPS KNOW THAT.
YOU MEAN THOSE DARK THINGS ARE MARXIST?
I MEAN THEY CAN SMELL A WEAKNESS IN THE SYSTEM. SOMETHING'S HAPPENING, FLAHERTY.
BRUSSELS, TWO DAYS AGO...
HEY MANAGED TO NALLY JUMP THE ECIES BARRIER.
"THE CONTAGION SPREAD TO FOUR TRADERS...
S BANK
"THE TRADERS ALTERED THE FLASH TRADE ALGORITHMS OF SEVERAL MAJOR EQUITY BROKERS.
"SEVERAL BANKS HAVE ALREADY FROZEN ALL WITHDRAWALS..."
DRRR DRRR DRRR
I NEVER SAW THE POINT OF BELGIUM ANYHOW.
CONTAGION, FLAHERTY. IT COULD SPREAD ALL OVER THE EURO ZONE. IF NOT THE DOOMSDAY THAT POOR GILES CAMERON TALKED ABOUT, MAYBE IT'S A DRESS REHEARSAL.
EXCUSE ME.
DRRR DRRR DRRR
I'M BUSY, CAN'T TALK.
THE BRAINY KID HAS GOT AWAY, STOKER...

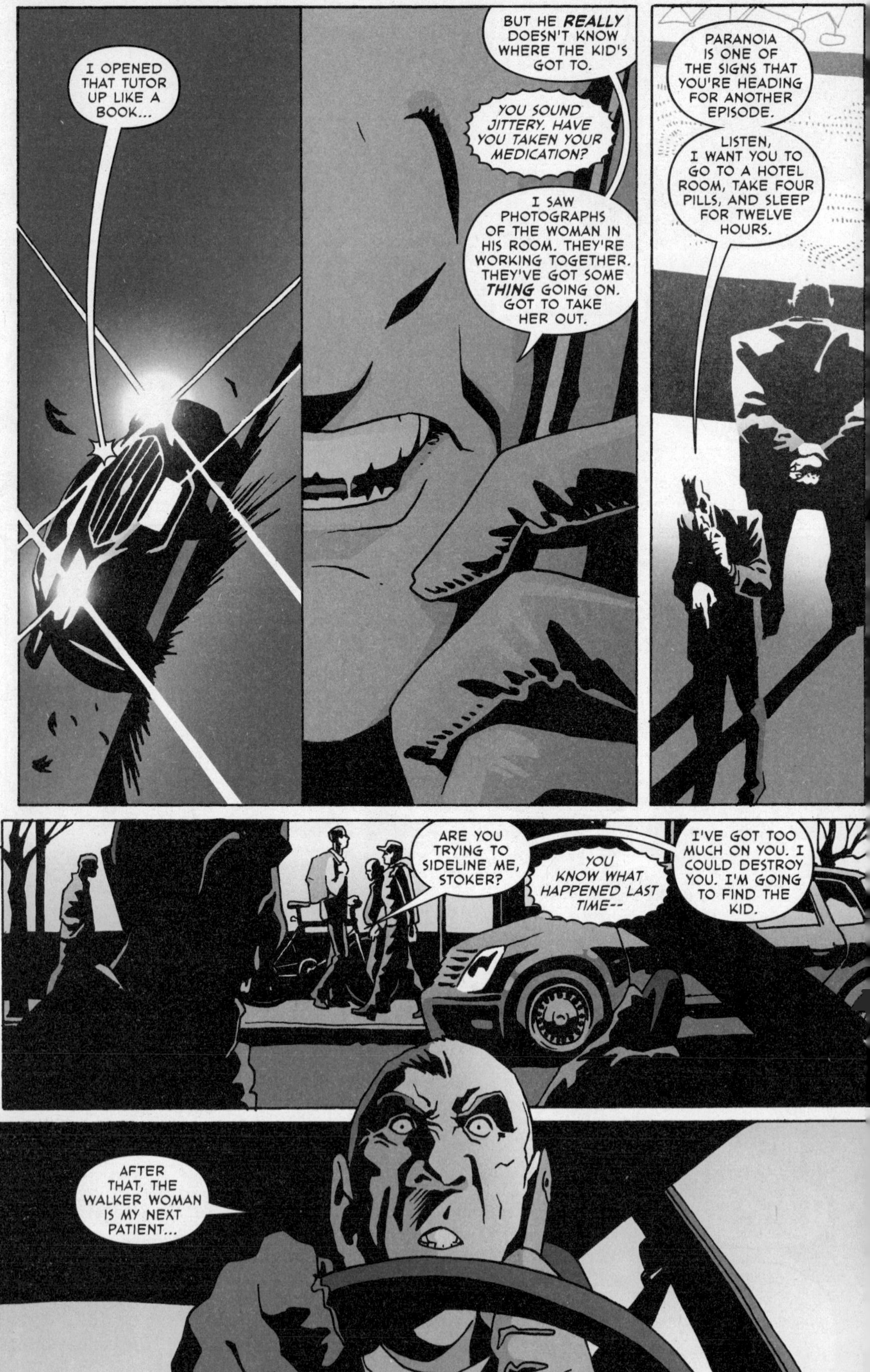
I OPENED THAT TUTOR UP LIKE A BOOK...
BUT HE REALLY DOESN'T KNOW WHERE THE KID'S GOT TO.
YOU SOUND JITTERY. HAVE YOU TAKEN YOUR MEDICATION?
I SAW PHOTOGRAPHS OF THE WOMAN IN HIS ROOM. THEY'RE WORKING TOGETHER. THEY'VE GOT SOME THING GOING ON. GOT TO TAKE HER OUT.
PARANOIA IS ONE OF THE SIGNS THAT YOU'RE HEADING FOR ANOTHER EPISODE.
LISTEN, I WANT YOU TO GO TO A HOTEL ROOM, TAKE FOUR PILLS, AND SLEEP FOR TWELVE HOURS.
ARE YOU TRYING TO SIDELINE ME, STOKER?
YOU KNOW WHAT HAPPENED LAST TIME--
I'VE GOT TOO MUCH ON YOU. I COULD DESTROY YOU. I'M GOING TO FIND THE KID.
AFTER THAT, THE WALKER WOMAN IS MY NEXT PATIENT...

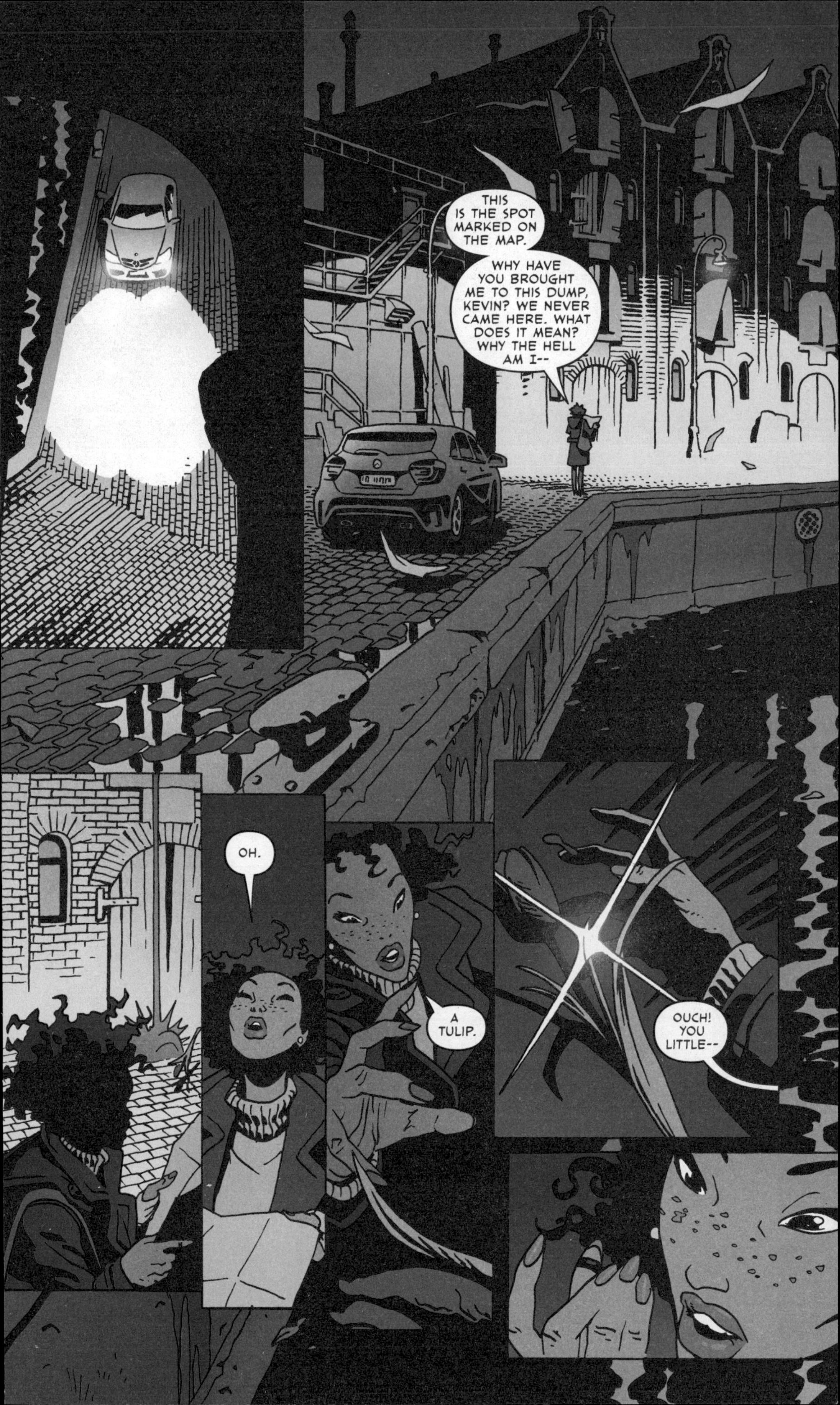
THIS IS THE SPOT MARKED ON THE MAP.
WHY HAVE YOU BROUGHT ME TO THIS DUMP, KEVIN? WE NEVER CAME HERE. WHAT DOES IT MEAN? WHY THE HELL AM I--
OH.
A TULIP.
OUCH! YOU LITTLE--

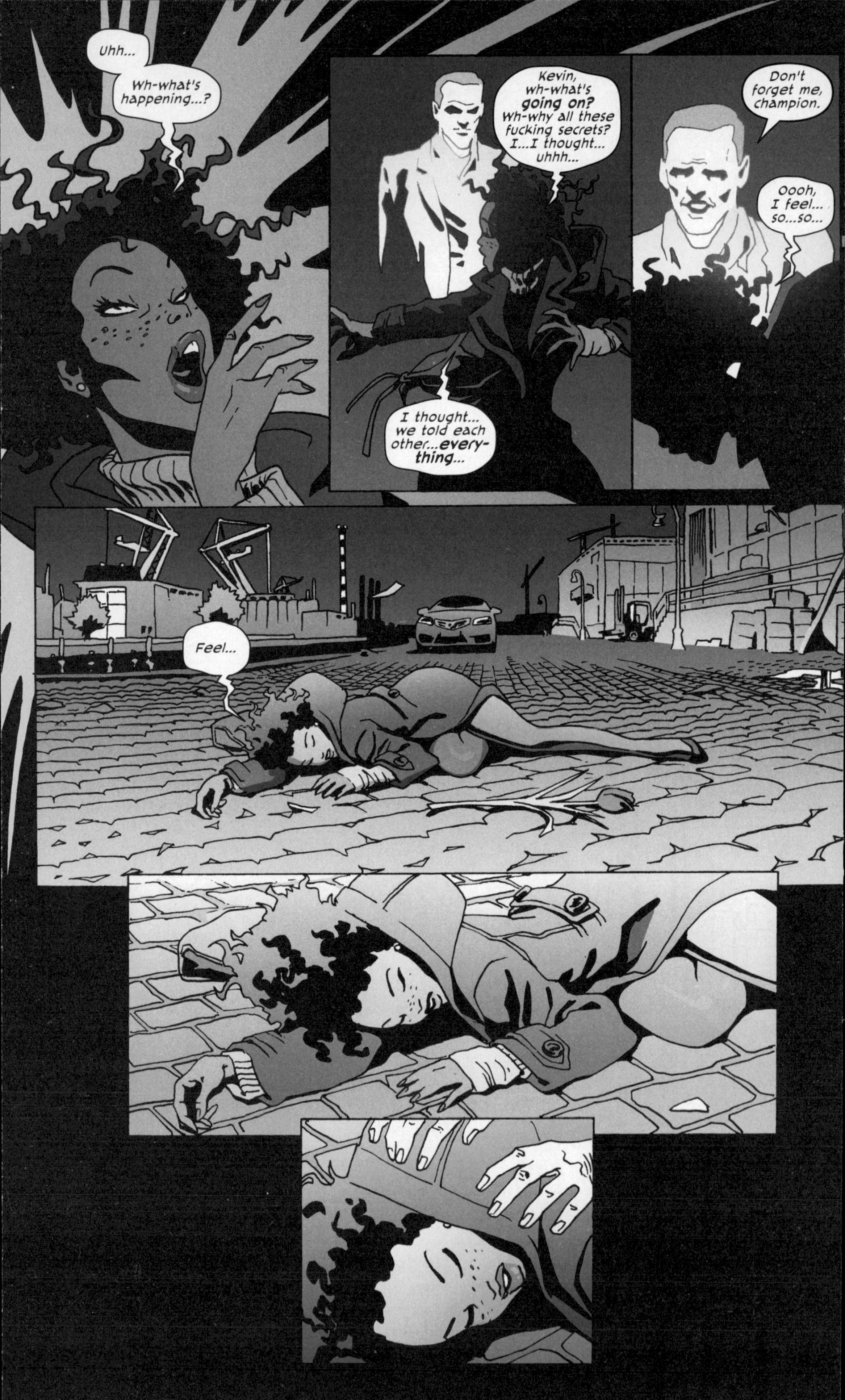
Uhh...
Wh-what's happening...?
Kevin, wh-what's going on? Wh-why all these fucking secrets? I...I thought... uhhh...
I thought... we told each other...everything...
Don't forget me, champion.
Oooh, I feel... so...so...
Feel...

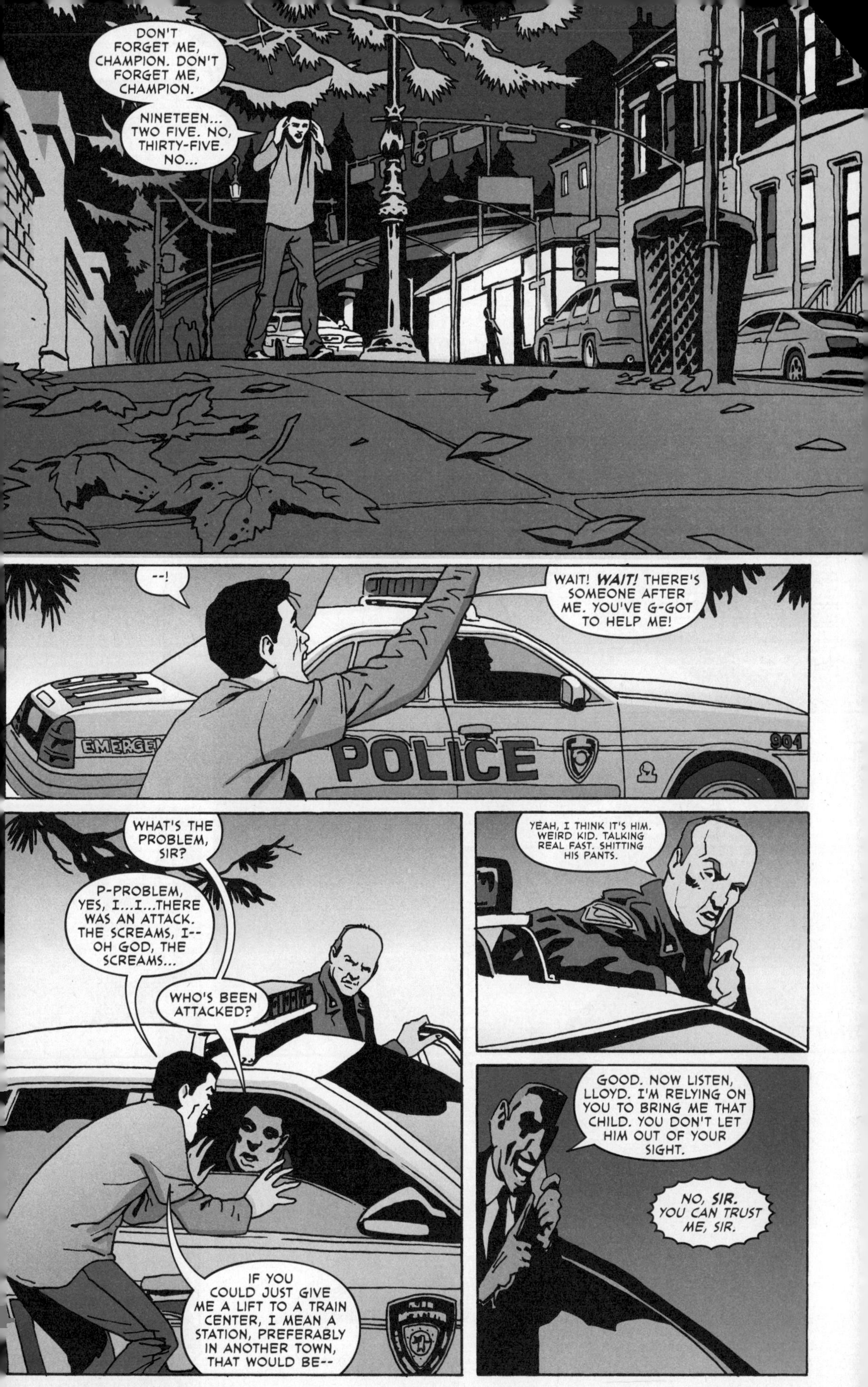
DON'T FORGET ME, CHAMPION. DON'T FORGET ME, CHAMPION.
NINETEEN... TWO FIVE. NO, THIRTY-FIVE. NO...
--!
WAIT! *WAIT!* THERE'S SOMEONE AFTER ME. YOU'VE G-GOT TO HELP ME!
EMERGEN
POLICE
904
WHAT'S THE PROBLEM, SIR?
P-PROBLEM, YES, I...I...THERE WAS AN ATTACK. THE SCREAMS, I--OH GOD, THE SCREAMS...
WHO'S BEEN ATTACKED?
IF YOU COULD JUST GIVE ME A LIFT TO A TRAIN CENTER, I MEAN A STATION, PREFERABLY IN ANOTHER TOWN, THAT WOULD BE--
YEAH, I THINK IT'S HIM. WEIRD KID. TALKING REAL FAST. SHITTING HIS PANTS.
GOOD. NOW LISTEN, LLOYD. I'M RELYING ON YOU TO BRING ME THAT CHILD. YOU DON'T LET HIM OUT OF YOUR SIGHT.
NO, SIR. YOU CAN TRUST ME, SIR.

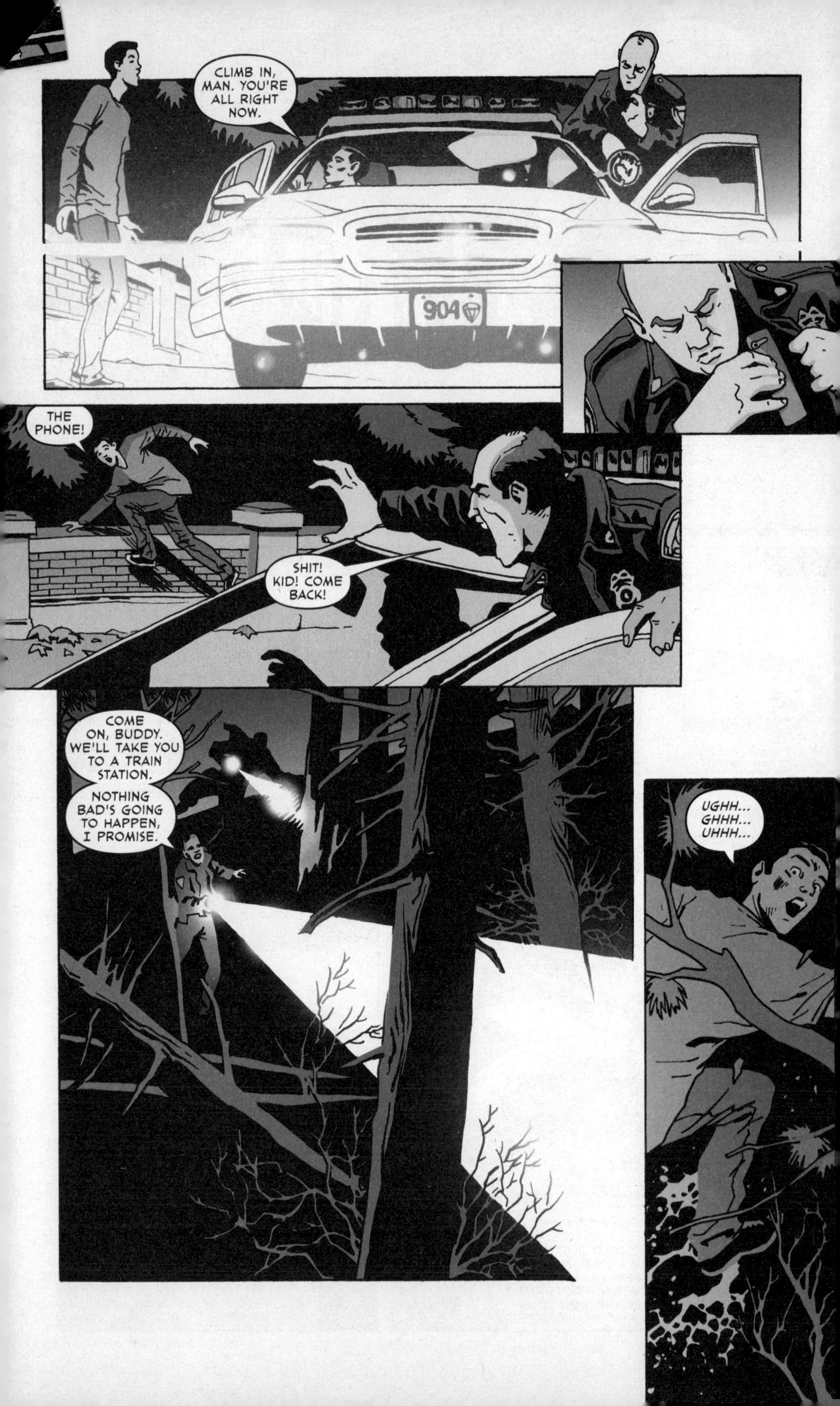
CLIMB IN, MAN. YOU'RE ALL RIGHT NOW.
904
THE PHONE!
SHIT! KID! COME BACK!
COME ON, BUDDY. WE'LL TAKE YOU TO A TRAIN STATION.
NOTHING BAD'S GOING TO HAPPEN, I PROMISE.
UGHH... GHHH... UHHH...

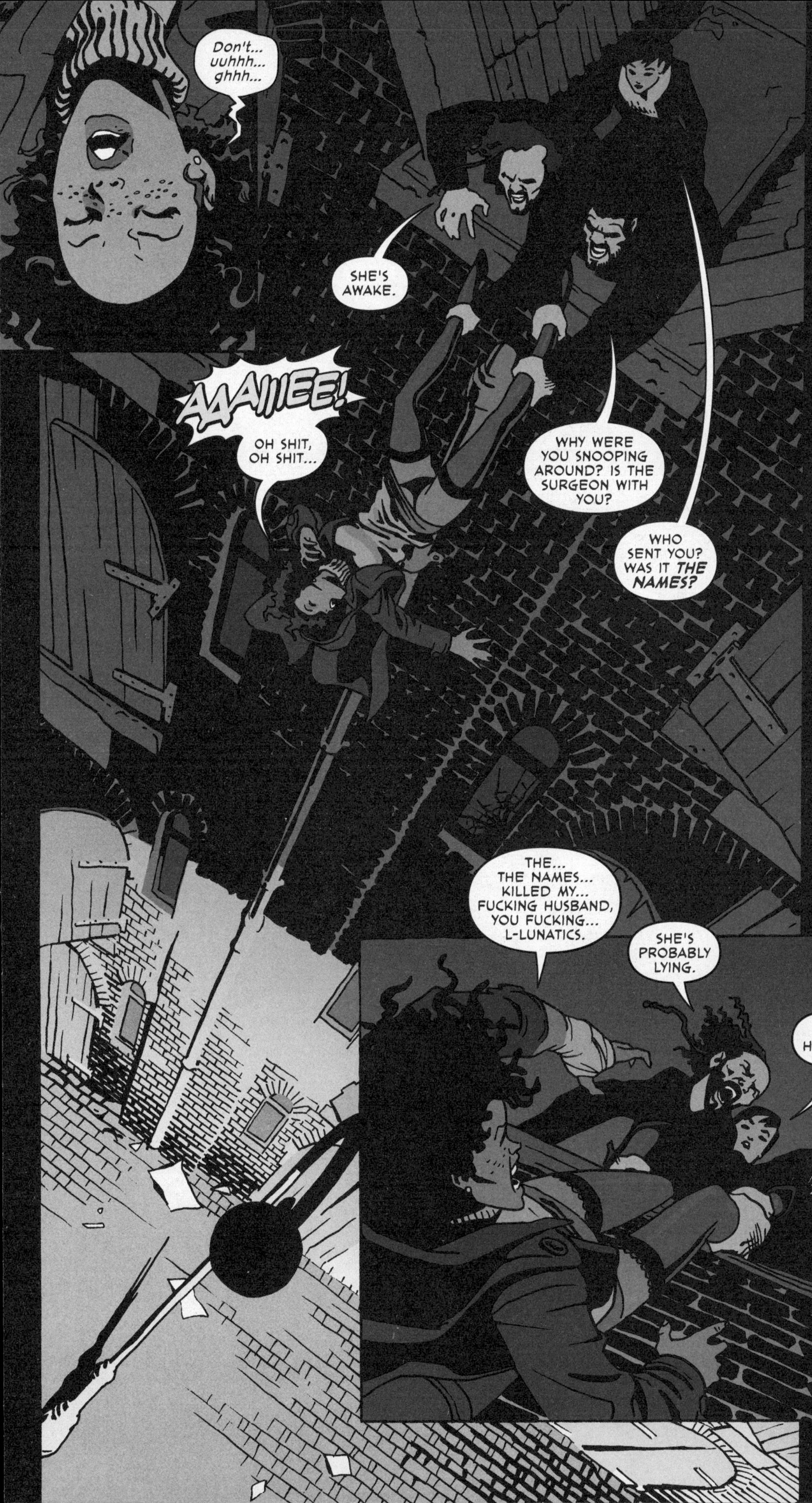
Don't... uuhhh... ghhh...
SHE'S AWAKE.
AAAIIIEEE!
OH SHIT, OH SHIT...
WHY WERE YOU SNOOPING AROUND? IS THE SURGEON WITH YOU?
WHO SENT YOU? WAS IT THE NAMES?
THE... THE NAMES... KILLED MY... FUCKING HUSBAND, YOU FUCKING... L-LUNATICS.
SHE'S PROBABLY LYING.
PULL HER UP.

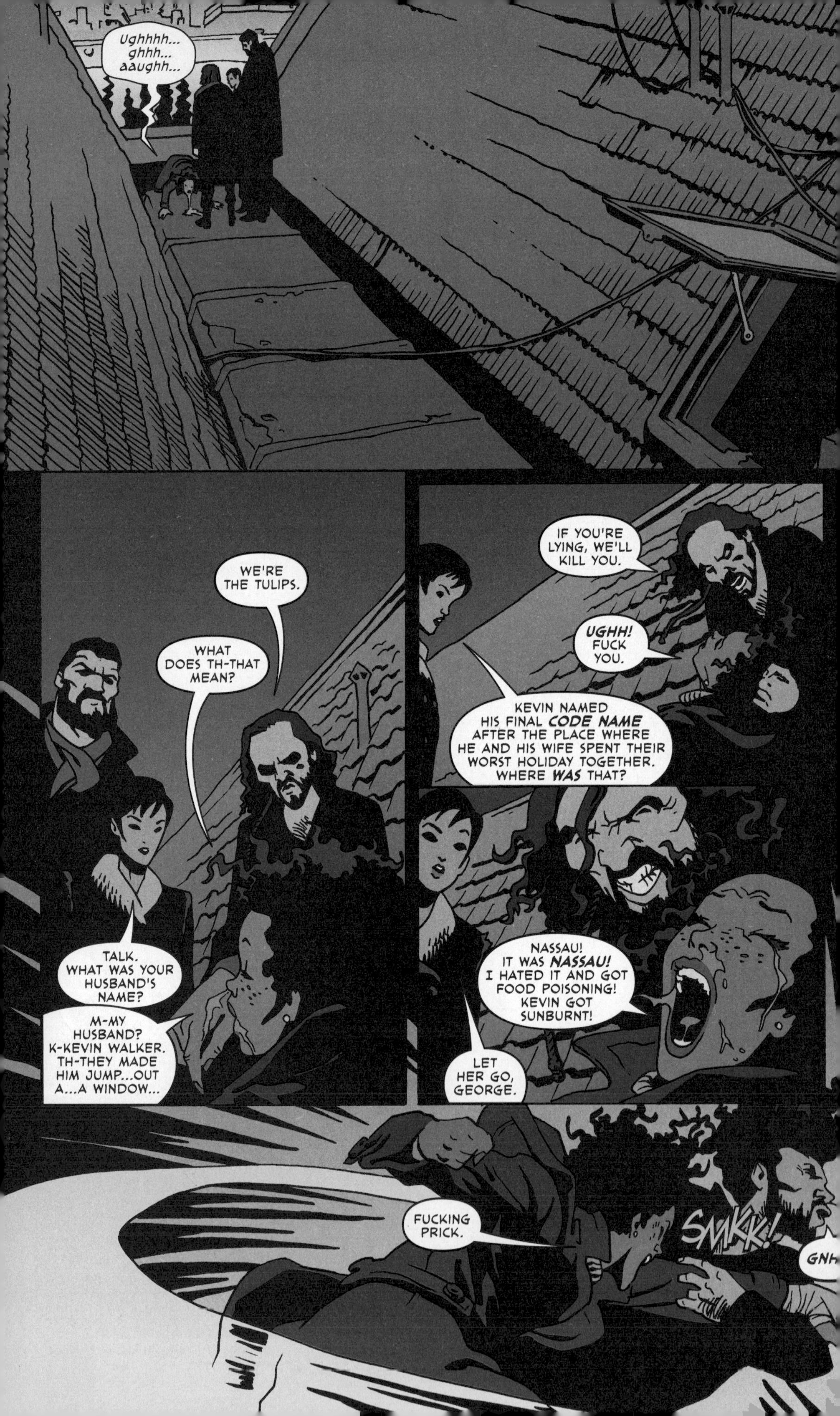
Ughhhh... ghhh... aaughh...
WE'RE THE TULIPS.
WHAT DOES TH-THAT MEAN?
TALK. WHAT WAS YOUR HUSBAND'S NAME?
M-MY HUSBAND? K-KEVIN WALKER. TH-THEY MADE HIM JUMP...OUT A...A WINDOW...
IF YOU'RE LYING, WE'LL KILL YOU.
UGHH! FUCK YOU.
KEVIN NAMED HIS FINAL CODE NAME AFTER THE PLACE WHERE HE AND HIS WIFE SPENT THEIR WORST HOLIDAY TOGETHER. WHERE WAS THAT?
NASSAU! IT WAS NASSAU! I HATED IT AND GOT FOOD POISONING! KEVIN GOT SUNBURNT!
LET HER GO, GEORGE.
FUCKING PRICK.
SNAKK!
GNH

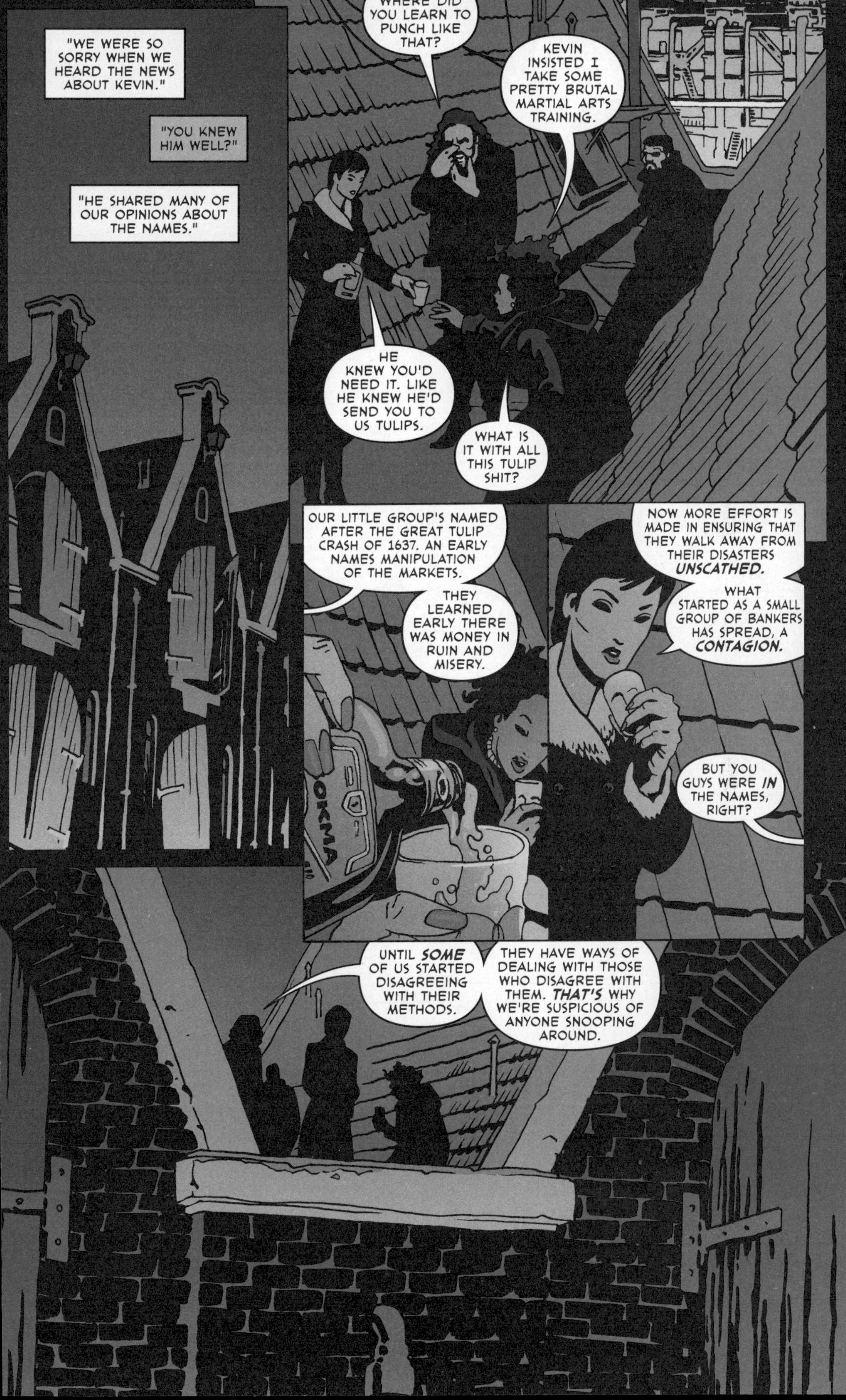
"WE WERE SO SORRY WHEN WE HEARD THE NEWS ABOUT KEVIN."
"YOU KNEW HIM WELL?"
"HE SHARED MANY OF OUR OPINIONS ABOUT THE NAMES."
WHERE DID YOU LEARN TO PUNCH LIKE THAT?
KEVIN INSISTED I TAKE SOME PRETTY BRUTAL MARTIAL ARTS TRAINING.
HE KNEW YOU'D NEED IT. LIKE HE KNEW HE'D SEND YOU TO US TULIPS.
WHAT IS IT WITH ALL THIS TULIP SHIT?
OUR LITTLE GROUP'S NAMED AFTER THE GREAT TULIP CRASH OF 1637. AN EARLY NAMES MANIPULATION OF THE MARKETS.
THEY LEARNED EARLY THERE WAS MONEY IN RUIN AND MISERY.
NOW MORE EFFORT IS MADE IN ENSURING THAT THEY WALK AWAY FROM THEIR DISASTERS *UNSCATHED.*
WHAT STARTED AS A SMALL GROUP OF BANKERS HAS SPREAD, A *CONTAGION.*
BUT YOU GUYS WERE *IN* THE NAMES, RIGHT?
UNTIL *SOME* OF US STARTED DISAGREEING WITH THEIR METHODS.
THEY HAVE WAYS OF DEALING WITH THOSE WHO DISAGREE WITH THEM. *THAT'S* WHY WE'RE SUSPICIOUS OF ANYONE SNOOPING AROUND.

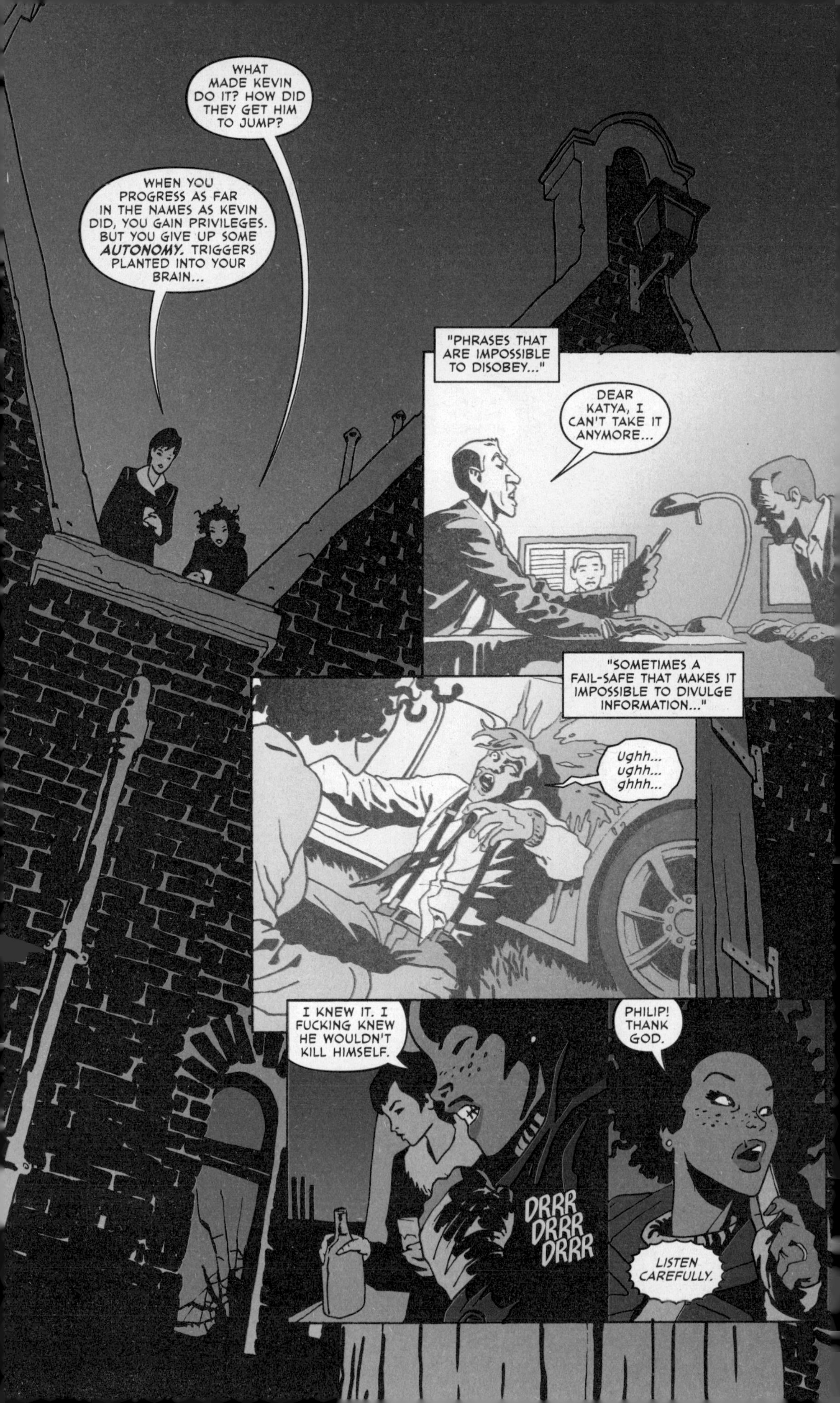
WHAT MADE KEVIN DO IT? HOW DID THEY GET HIM TO JUMP?
WHEN YOU PROGRESS AS FAR IN THE NAMES AS KEVIN DID, YOU GAIN PRIVILEGES. BUT YOU GIVE UP SOME ***AUTONOMY.*** TRIGGERS PLANTED INTO YOUR BRAIN...
"PHRASES THAT ARE IMPOSSIBLE TO DISOBEY..."
DEAR KATYA, I CAN'T TAKE IT ANYMORE...
"SOMETIMES A FAIL-SAFE THAT MAKES IT IMPOSSIBLE TO DIVULGE INFORMATION..."
Ughh... ughh... ghhh...
I KNEW IT. I FUCKING KNEW HE WOULDN'T KILL HIMSELF.
DRRR DRRR DRRR
PHILIP! THANK GOD.
LISTEN CAREFULLY.

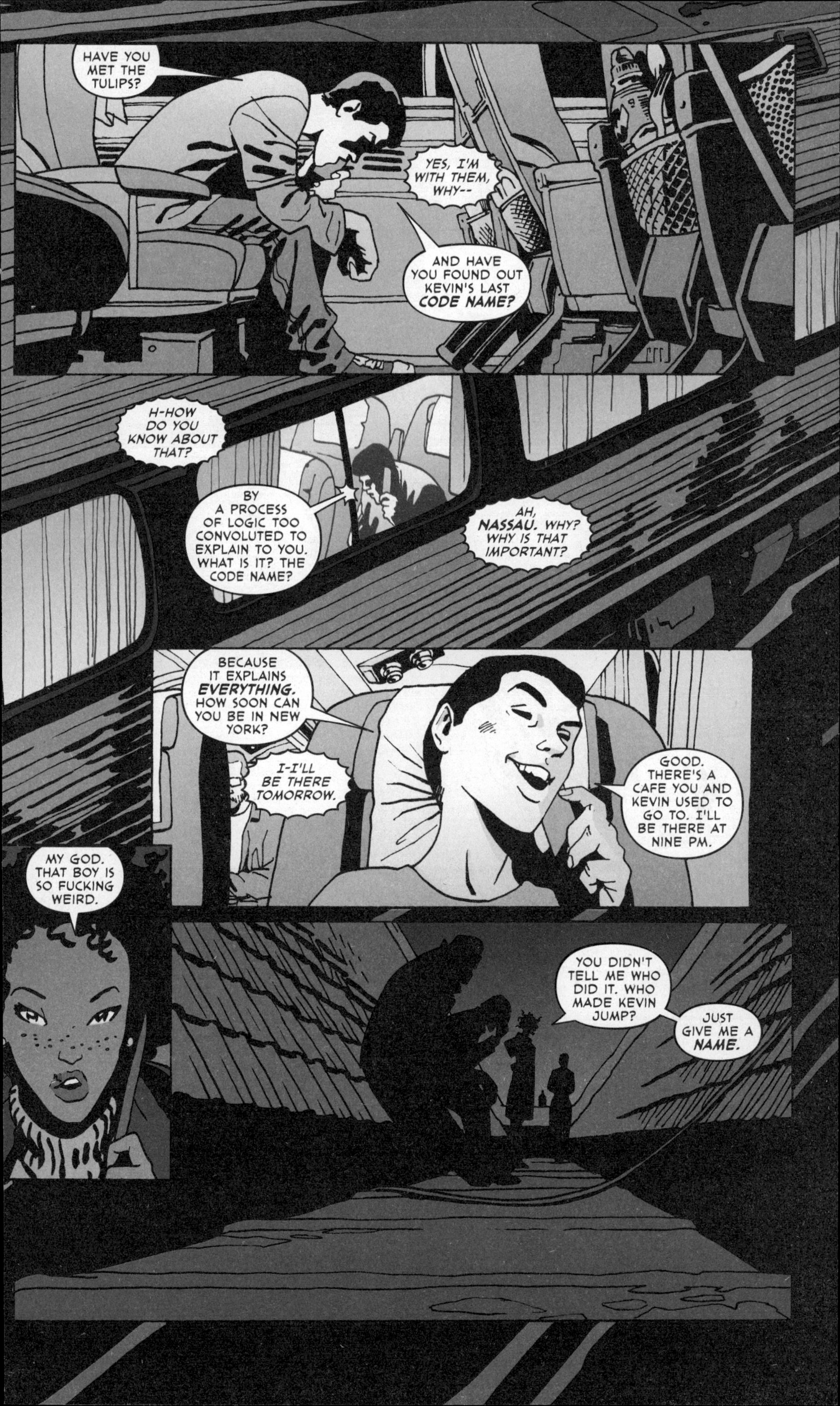
HAVE YOU MET THE TULIPS?
YES, I'M WITH THEM, WHY--
AND HAVE YOU FOUND OUT KEVIN'S LAST **CODE NAME?**
H-HOW DO YOU KNOW ABOUT THAT?
BY A PROCESS OF LOGIC TOO CONVOLUTED TO EXPLAIN TO YOU. WHAT IS IT? THE CODE NAME?
AH, **NASSAU.** WHY? WHY IS THAT IMPORTANT?
BECAUSE IT EXPLAINS **EVERYTHING.** HOW SOON CAN YOU BE IN NEW YORK?
I-I'LL BE THERE TOMORROW.
GOOD. THERE'S A CAFE YOU AND KEVIN USED TO GO TO. I'LL BE THERE AT NINE PM.
MY GOD. THAT BOY IS SO FUCKING WEIRD.
YOU DIDN'T TELL ME WHO DID IT. WHO MADE KEVIN JUMP?
JUST GIVE ME A **NAME.**

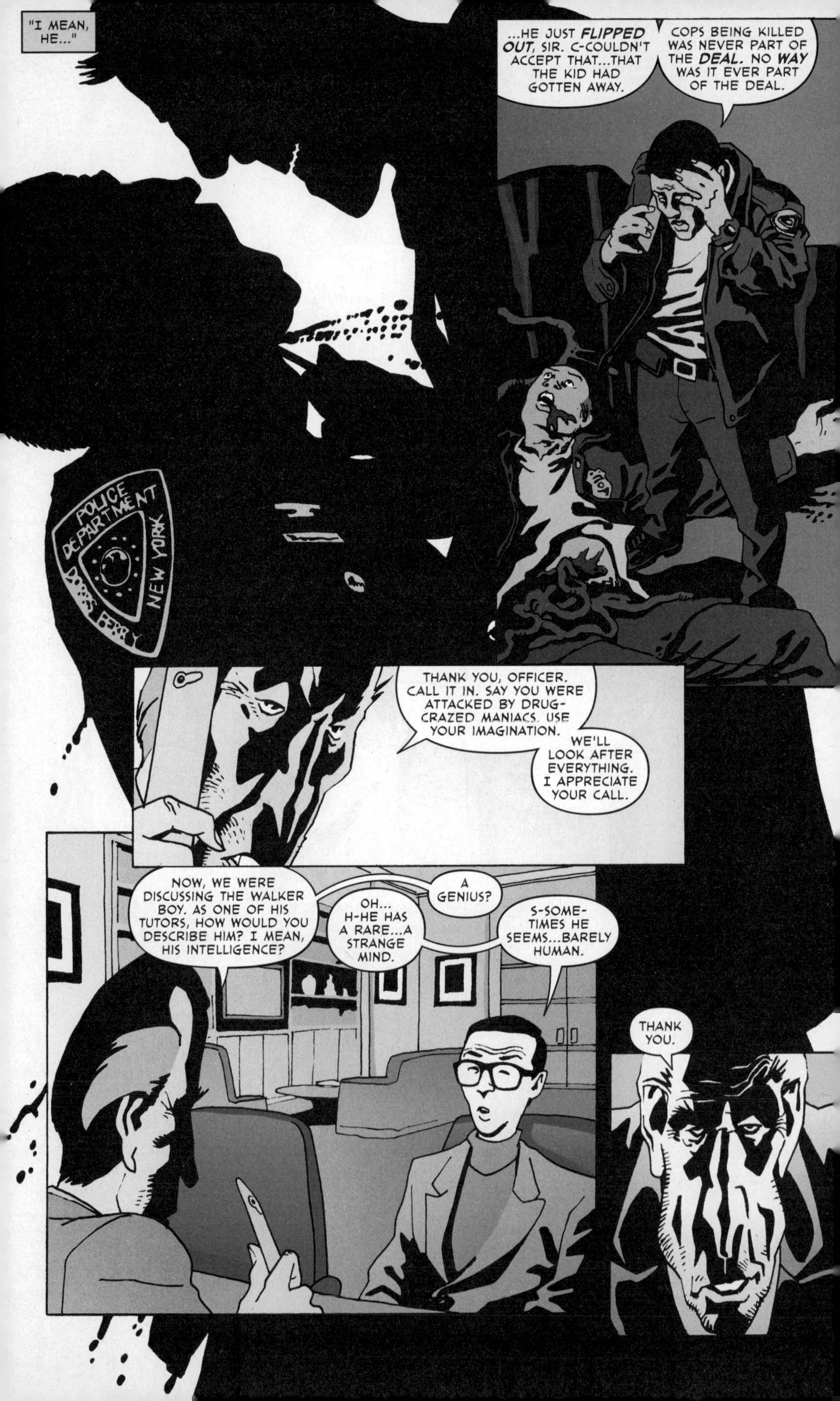
"I MEAN, HE..."
...HE JUST FLIPPED OUT, SIR. C-COULDN'T ACCEPT THAT...THAT THE KID HAD GOTTEN AWAY.
COPS BEING KILLED WAS NEVER PART OF THE DEAL. NO WAY WAS IT EVER PART OF THE DEAL.
POLICE DEPARTMENT DOBBS FERRY NEW YORK
THANK YOU, OFFICER. CALL IT IN. SAY YOU WERE ATTACKED BY DRUG-CRAZED MANIACS. USE YOUR IMAGINATION.
WE'LL LOOK AFTER EVERYTHING. I APPRECIATE YOUR CALL.
NOW, WE WERE DISCUSSING THE WALKER BOY. AS ONE OF HIS TUTORS, HOW WOULD YOU DESCRIBE HIM? I MEAN, HIS INTELLIGENCE?
OH... H-HE HAS A RARE...A STRANGE MIND.
A GENIUS?
S-SOME-TIMES HE SEEMS...BARELY HUMAN.
THANK YOU.

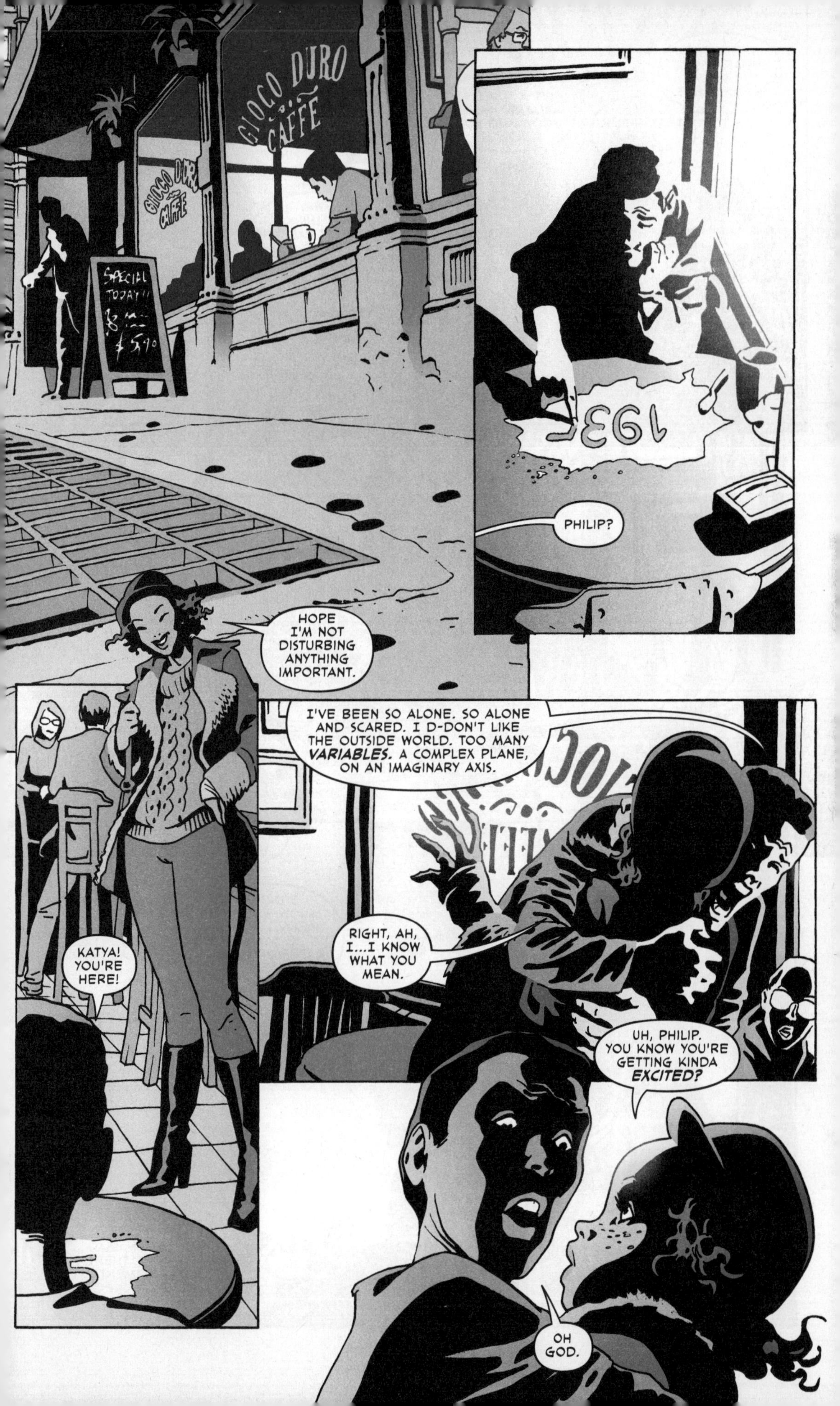

GIOCO DURO CAFFE
SPECIAL TODAY!!
$5.90
PHILIP?
HOPE I'M NOT DISTURBING ANYTHING IMPORTANT.
KATYA! YOU'RE HERE!
I'VE BEEN SO ALONE. SO ALONE AND SCARED. I D-DON'T LIKE THE OUTSIDE WORLD. TOO MANY ***VARIABLES.*** A COMPLEX PLANE, ON AN IMAGINARY AXIS.
RIGHT, AH, I...I KNOW WHAT YOU MEAN.
UH, PHILIP. YOU KNOW YOU'RE GETTING KINDA ***EXCITED?***
OH GOD.

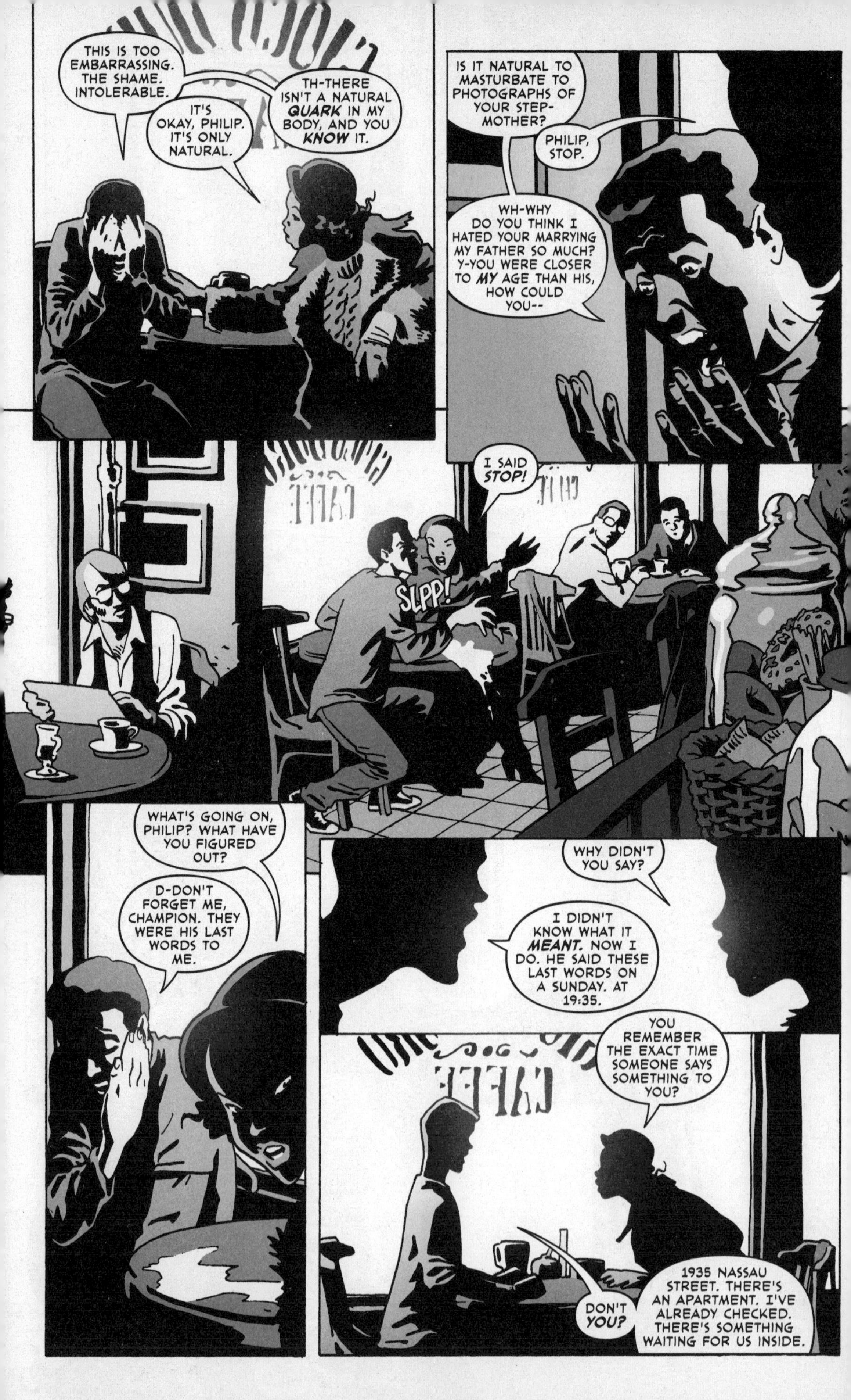
THIS IS TOO EMBARRASSING. THE SHAME. INTOLERABLE.
IT'S OKAY, PHILIP. IT'S ONLY NATURAL.
TH-THERE ISN'T A NATURAL QUARK IN MY BODY, AND YOU KNOW IT.
IS IT NATURAL TO MASTURBATE TO PHOTOGRAPHS OF YOUR STEP-MOTHER?
PHILIP, STOP.
WH-WHY DO YOU THINK I HATED YOUR MARRYING MY FATHER SO MUCH? Y-YOU WERE CLOSER TO MY AGE THAN HIS, HOW COULD YOU--
I SAID STOP!
SLPP!
WHAT'S GOING ON, PHILIP? WHAT HAVE YOU FIGURED OUT?
D-DON'T FORGET ME, CHAMPION. THEY WERE HIS LAST WORDS TO ME.
WHY DIDN'T YOU SAY?
I DIDN'T KNOW WHAT IT MEANT. NOW I DO. HE SAID THESE LAST WORDS ON A SUNDAY. AT 19:35.
YOU REMEMBER THE EXACT TIME SOMEONE SAYS SOMETHING TO YOU?
DON'T YOU?
1935 NASSAU STREET. THERE'S AN APARTMENT. I'VE ALREADY CHECKED. THERE'S SOMETHING WAITING FOR US INSIDE.

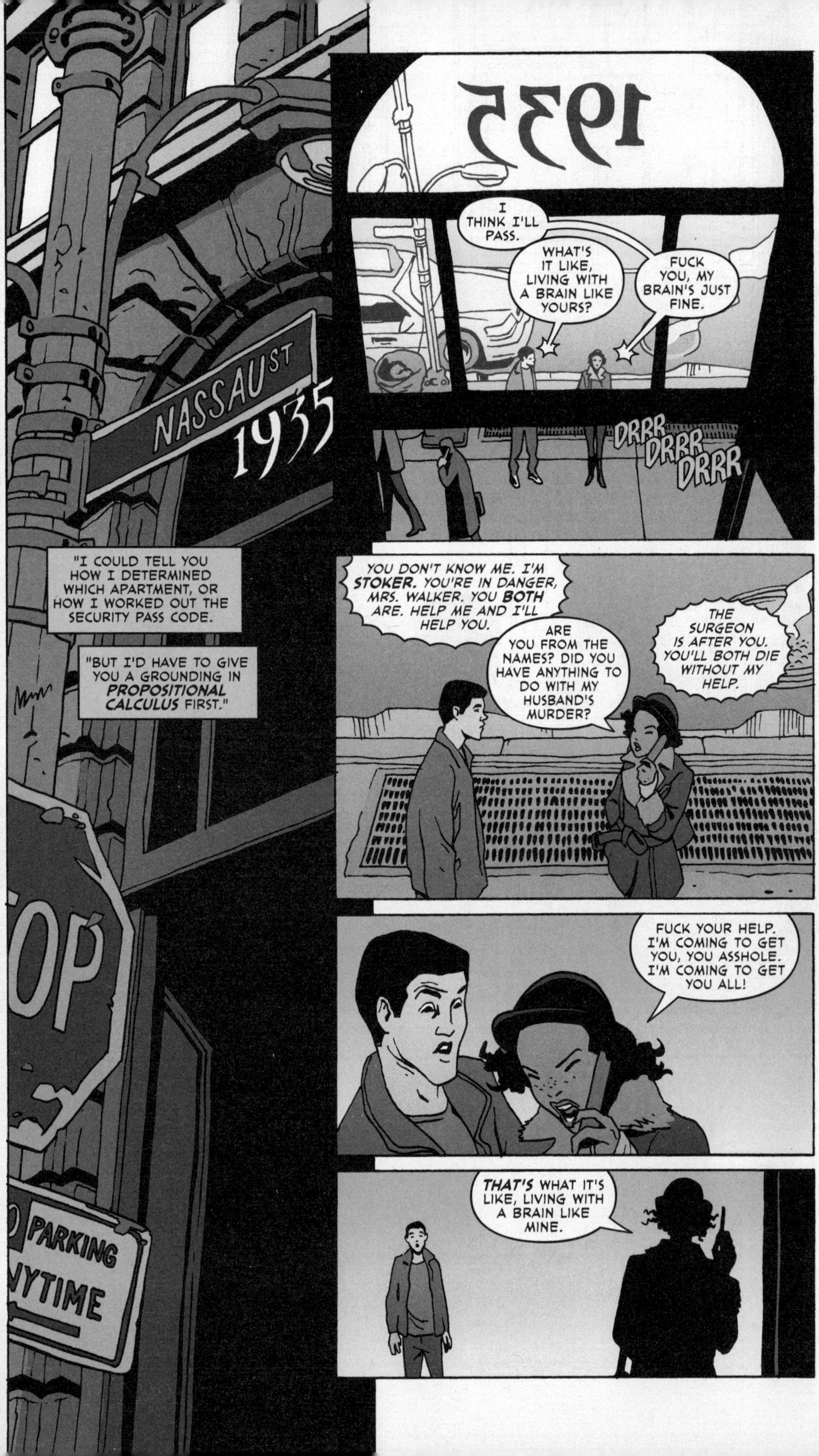
NASSAU ST
1935
"I COULD TELL YOU HOW I DETERMINED WHICH APARTMENT, OR HOW I WORKED OUT THE SECURITY PASS CODE.
"BUT I'D HAVE TO GIVE YOU A GROUNDING IN PROPOSITIONAL CALCULUS FIRST."
STOP
PARKING
NYTIME
1935
I THINK I'LL PASS.
WHAT'S IT LIKE, LIVING WITH A BRAIN LIKE YOURS?
FUCK YOU, MY BRAIN'S JUST FINE.
DRRR DRRR DRRR
YOU DON'T KNOW ME. I'M STOKER. YOU'RE IN DANGER, MRS. WALKER. YOU BOTH ARE. HELP ME AND I'LL HELP YOU.
ARE YOU FROM THE NAMES? DID YOU HAVE ANYTHING TO DO WITH MY HUSBAND'S MURDER?
THE SURGEON IS AFTER YOU. YOU'LL BOTH DIE WITHOUT MY HELP.
FUCK YOUR HELP. I'M COMING TO GET YOU, YOU ASSHOLE. I'M COMING TO GET YOU ALL!
THAT'S WHAT IT'S LIKE, LIVING WITH A BRAIN LIKE MINE.

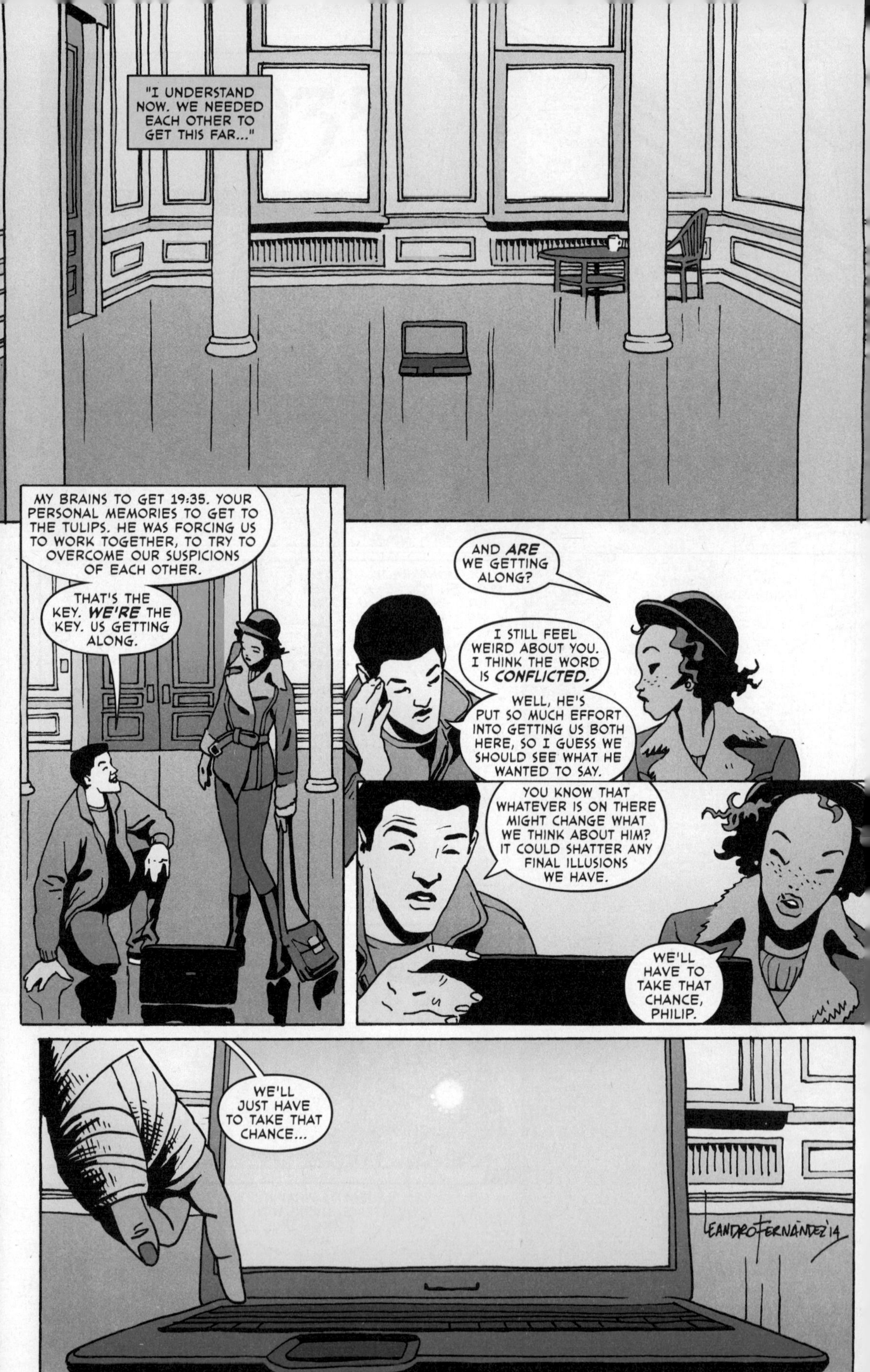
"I UNDERSTAND NOW. WE NEEDED EACH OTHER TO GET THIS FAR..."
MY BRAINS TO GET 19:35. YOUR PERSONAL MEMORIES TO GET TO THE TULIPS. HE WAS FORCING US TO WORK TOGETHER, TO TRY TO OVERCOME OUR SUSPICIONS OF EACH OTHER.
THAT'S THE KEY. WE'RE THE KEY. US GETTING ALONG.
AND ARE WE GETTING ALONG?
I STILL FEEL WEIRD ABOUT YOU. I THINK THE WORD IS CONFLICTED.
WELL, HE'S PUT SO MUCH EFFORT INTO GETTING US BOTH HERE, SO I GUESS WE SHOULD SEE WHAT HE WANTED TO SAY.
YOU KNOW THAT WHATEVER IS ON THERE MIGHT CHANGE WHAT WE THINK ABOUT HIM? IT COULD SHATTER ANY FINAL ILLUSIONS WE HAVE.
WE'LL HAVE TO TAKE THAT CHANCE, PHILIP.
WE'LL JUST HAVE TO TAKE THAT CHANCE...
LEANDRO FERNÁNDEZ '14

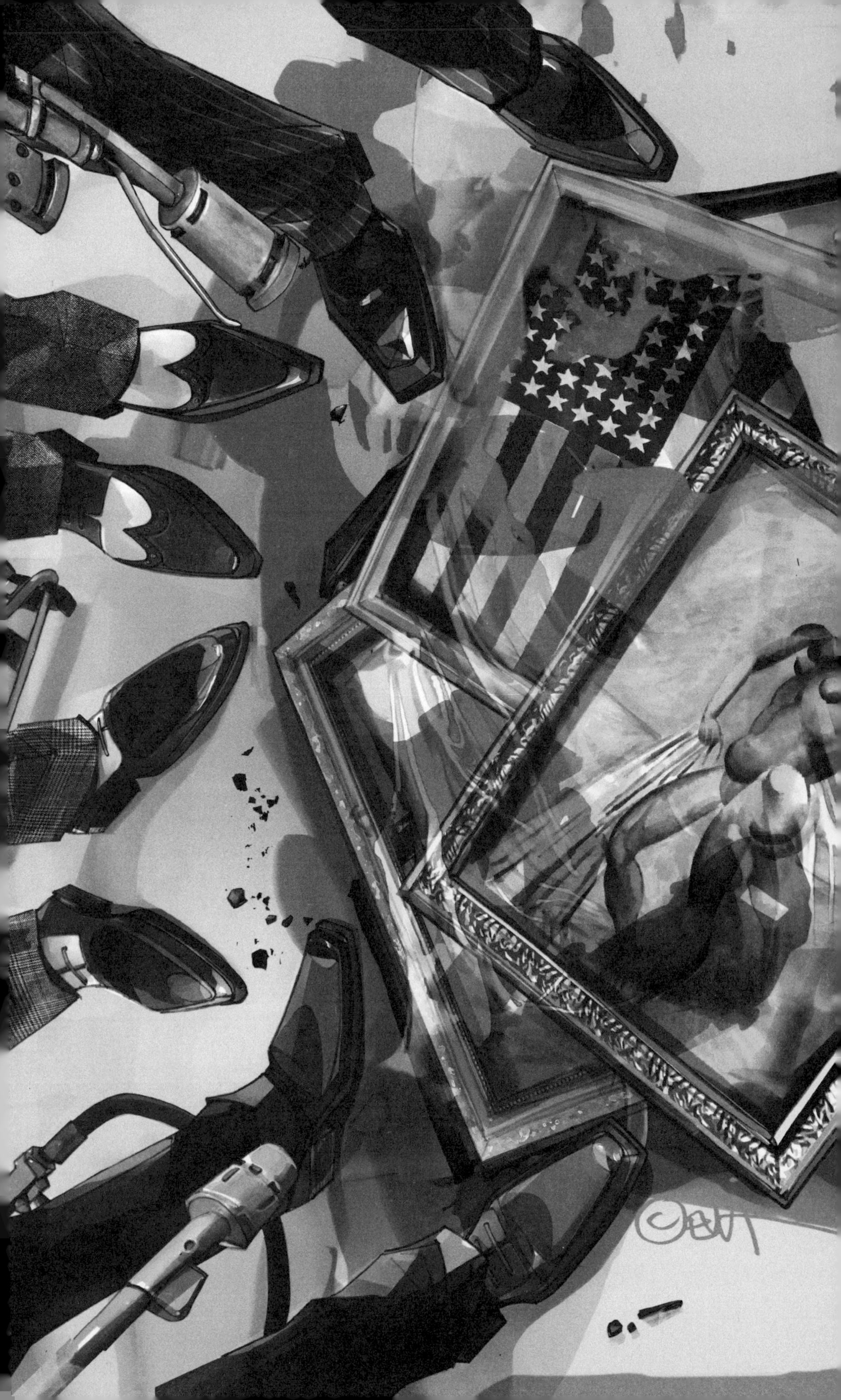

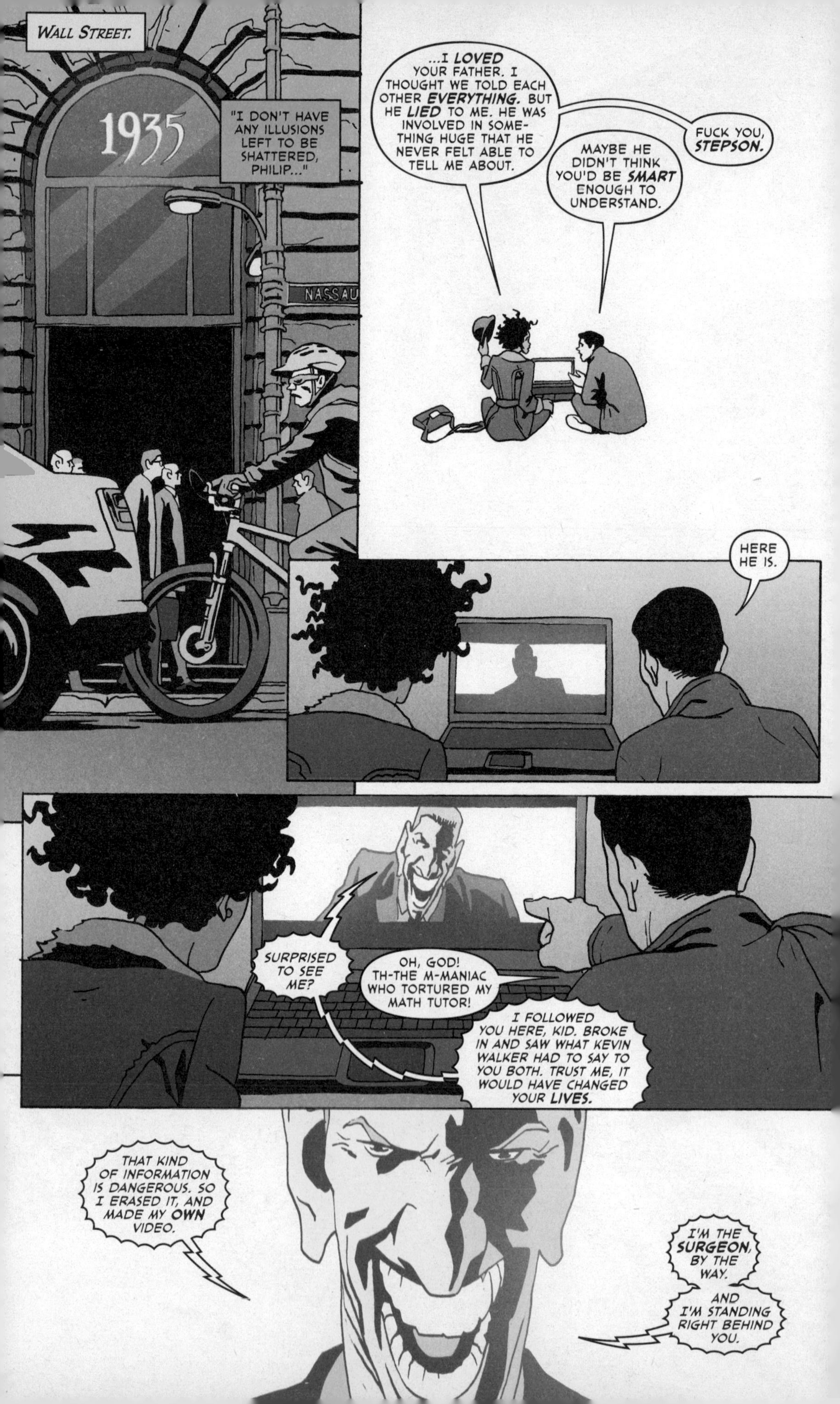
WALL STREET.
1935
"I DON'T HAVE ANY ILLUSIONS LEFT TO BE SHATTERED, PHILIP..."
NASSAU
...I LOVED YOUR FATHER. I THOUGHT WE TOLD EACH OTHER EVERYTHING. BUT HE LIED TO ME. HE WAS INVOLVED IN SOMETHING HUGE THAT HE NEVER FELT ABLE TO TELL ME ABOUT.
MAYBE HE DIDN'T THINK YOU'D BE SMART ENOUGH TO UNDERSTAND.
FUCK YOU, STEPSON.
HERE HE IS.
SURPRISED TO SEE ME?
OH, GOD! TH-THE M-MANIAC WHO TORTURED MY MATH TUTOR!
I FOLLOWED YOU HERE, KID. BROKE IN AND SAW WHAT KEVIN WALKER HAD TO SAY TO YOU BOTH. TRUST ME, IT WOULD HAVE CHANGED YOUR LIVES.
THAT KIND OF INFORMATION IS DANGEROUS. SO I ERASED IT, AND MADE MY OWN VIDEO.
I'M THE SURGEON, BY THE WAY.
AND I'M STANDING RIGHT BEHIND YOU.

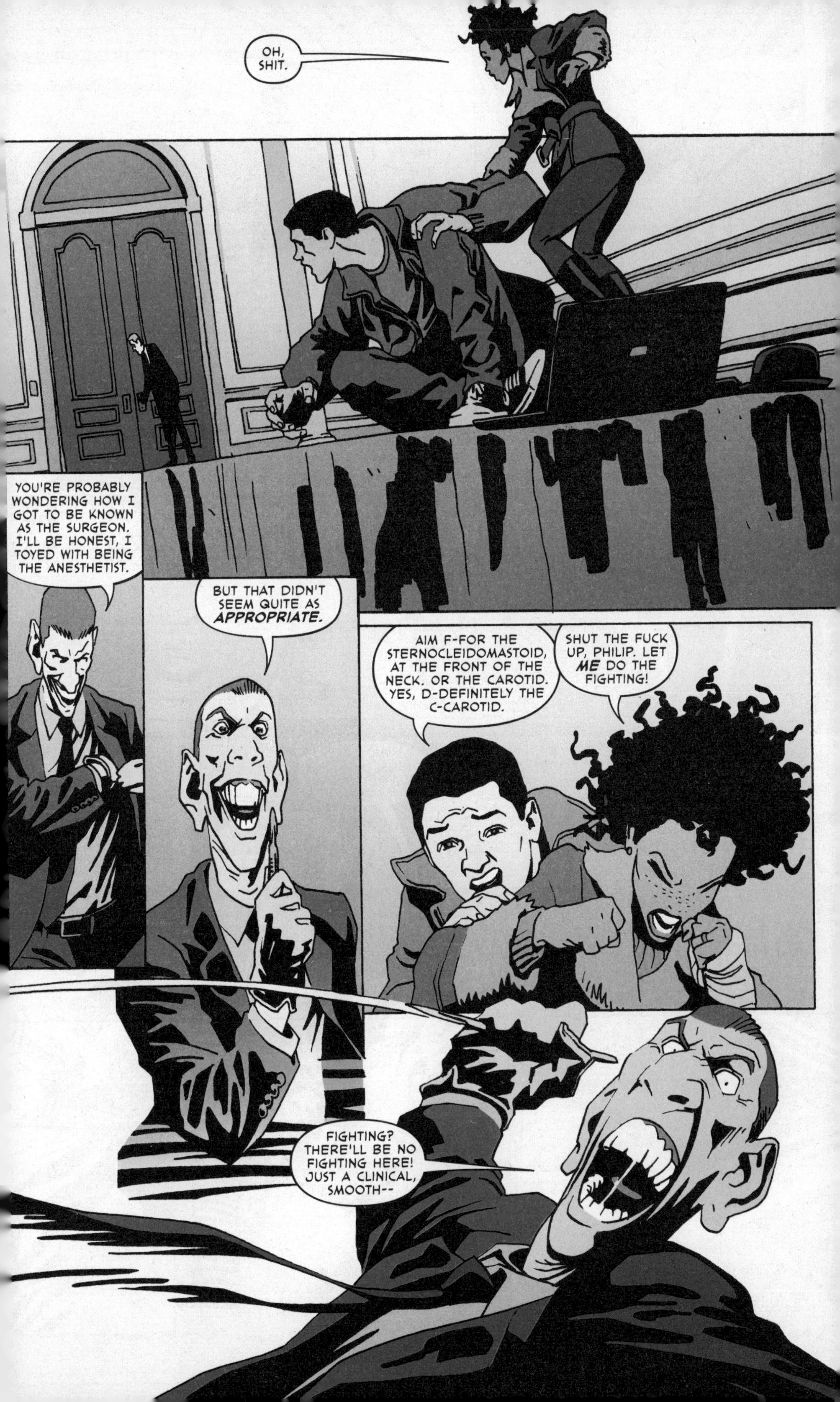
OH, SHIT.
YOU'RE PROBABLY WONDERING HOW I GOT TO BE KNOWN AS THE SURGEON. I'LL BE HONEST, I TOYED WITH BEING THE ANESTHETIST.
BUT THAT DIDN'T SEEM QUITE AS *APPROPRIATE.*
AIM F-FOR THE STERNOCLEIDOMASTOID, AT THE FRONT OF THE NECK. OR THE CAROTID. YES, D-DEFINITELY THE C-CAROTID.
SHUT THE FUCK UP, PHILIP. LET *ME* DO THE FIGHTING!
FIGHTING? THERE'LL BE NO FIGHTING HERE! JUST A CLINICAL, SMOOTH--

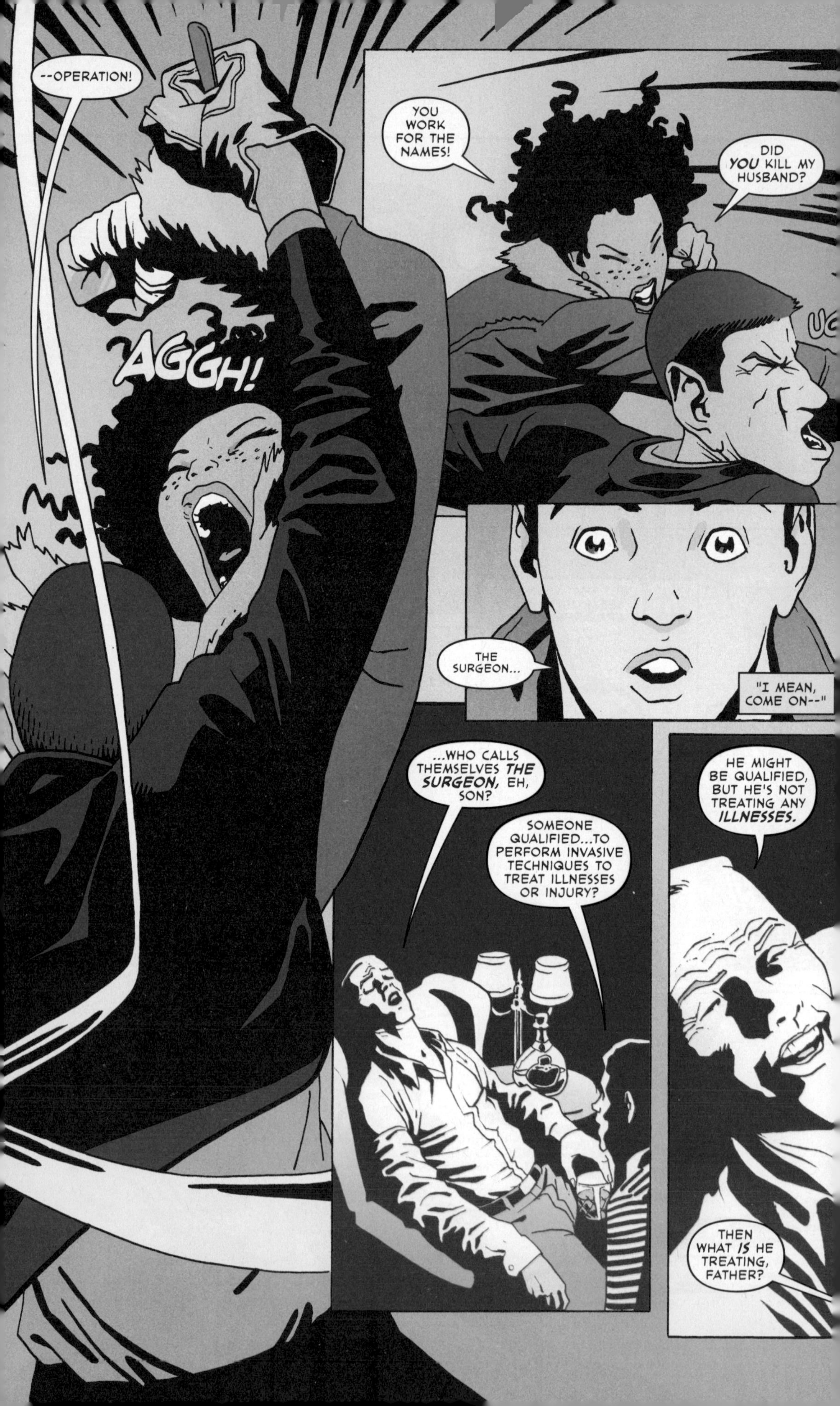
--OPERATION!
AGGH!
YOU WORK FOR THE NAMES!
DID YOU KILL MY HUSBAND?
UG
THE SURGEON...
"I MEAN, COME ON--"
...WHO CALLS THEMSELVES THE SURGEON, EH, SON?
SOMEONE QUALIFIED...TO PERFORM INVASIVE TECHNIQUES TO TREAT ILLNESSES OR INJURY?
HE MIGHT BE QUALIFIED, BUT HE'S NOT TREATING ANY ILLNESSES.
THEN WHAT IS HE TREATING, FATHER?

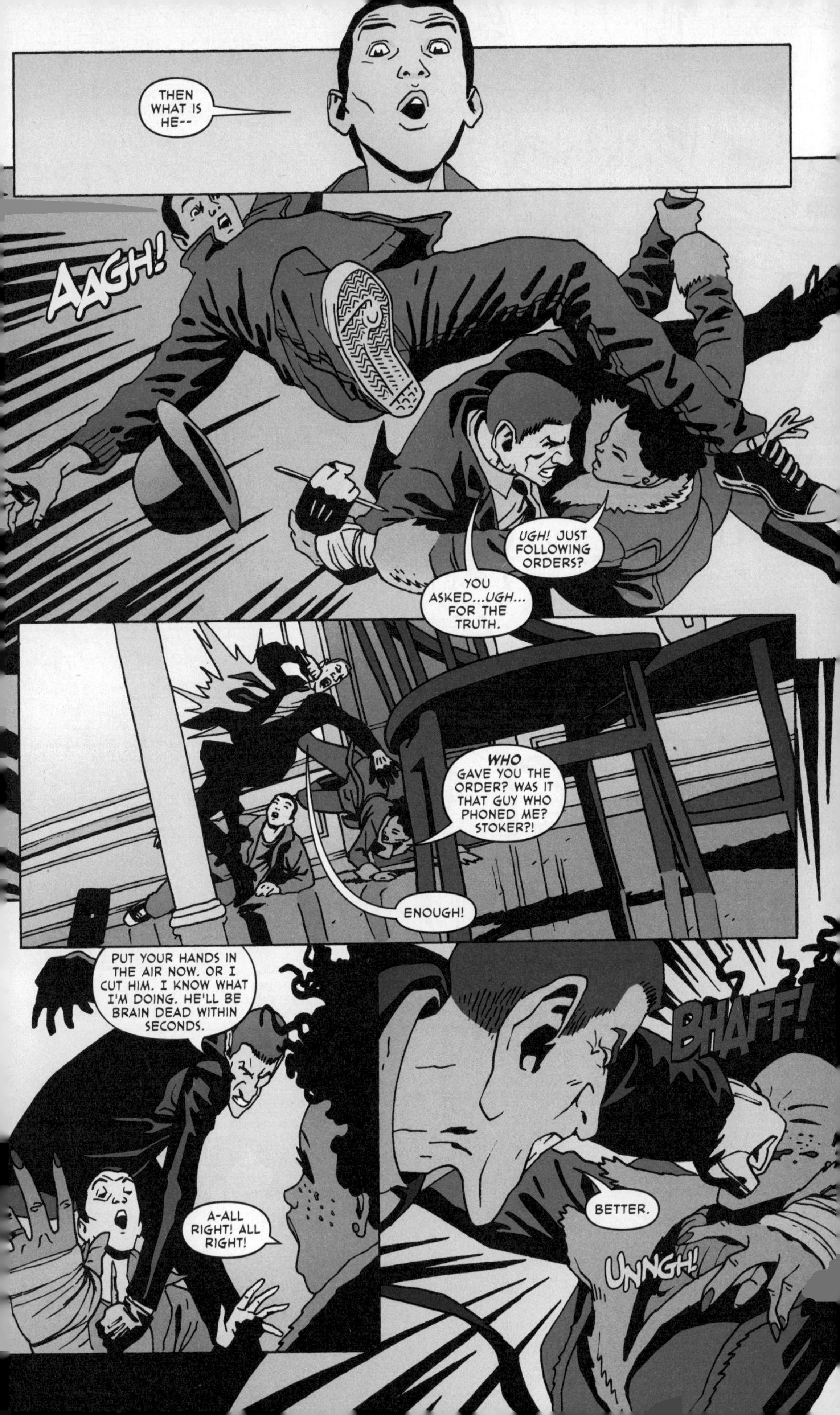

THEN WHAT IS HE--
AAGH!
UGH! JUST FOLLOWING ORDERS?
YOU ASKED...UGH... FOR THE TRUTH.
WHO GAVE YOU THE ORDER? WAS IT THAT GUY WHO PHONED ME? STOKER?!
ENOUGH!
PUT YOUR HANDS IN THE AIR NOW. OR I CUT HIM. I KNOW WHAT I'M DOING. HE'LL BE BRAIN DEAD WITHIN SECONDS.
A-ALL RIGHT! ALL RIGHT!
BHAFF!
BETTER.
UNNGH!

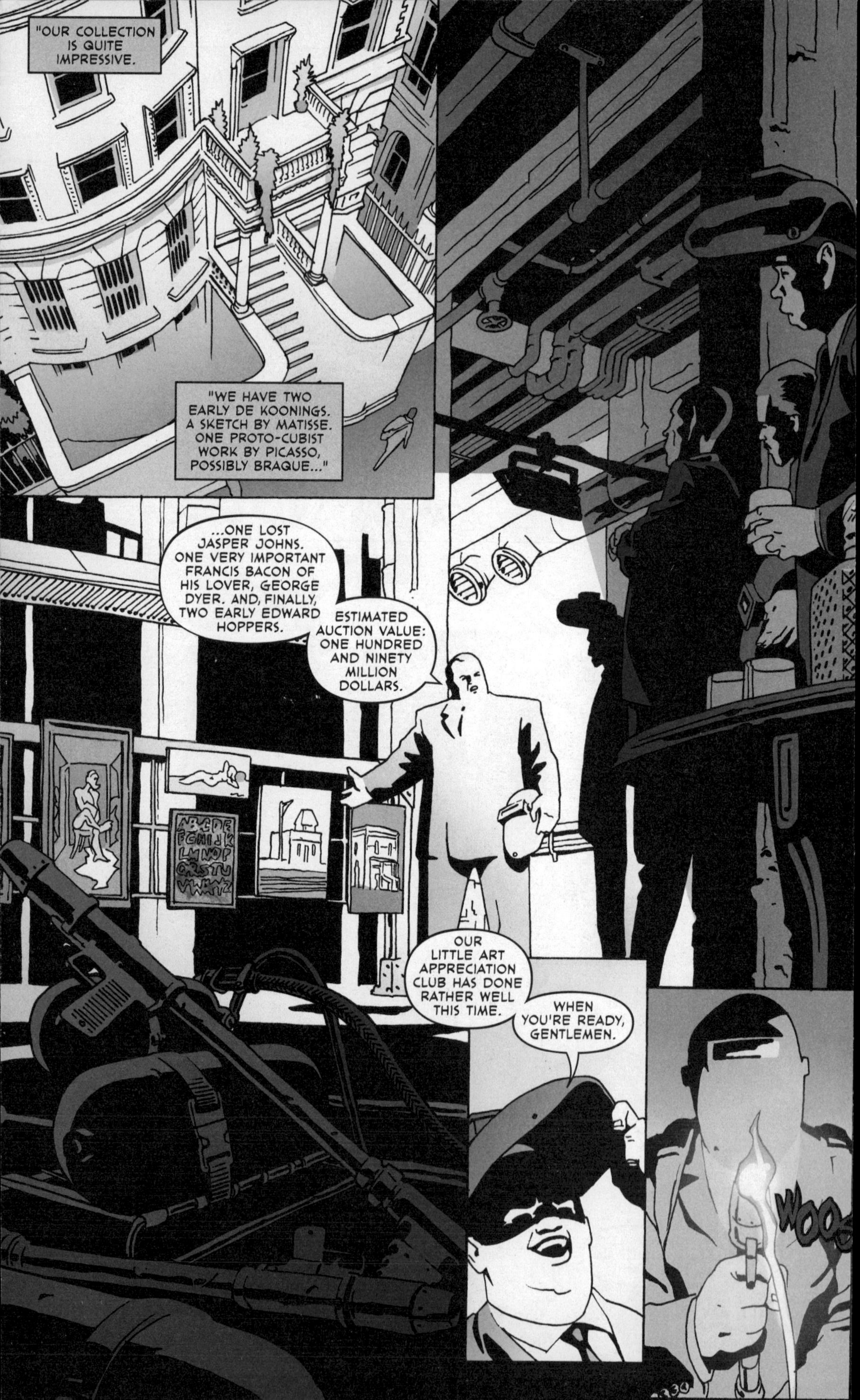
"OUR COLLECTION IS QUITE IMPRESSIVE.
"WE HAVE TWO EARLY DE KOONINGS. A SKETCH BY MATISSE. ONE PROTO-CUBIST WORK BY PICASSO, POSSIBLY BRAQUE..."
...ONE LOST JASPER JOHNS. ONE VERY IMPORTANT FRANCIS BACON OF HIS LOVER, GEORGE DYER. AND, FINALLY, TWO EARLY EDWARD HOPPERS.
ESTIMATED AUCTION VALUE: ONE HUNDRED AND NINETY MILLION DOLLARS.
OUR LITTLE ART APPRECIATION CLUB HAS DONE RATHER WELL THIS TIME.
WHEN YOU'RE READY, GENTLEMEN.
WOOS

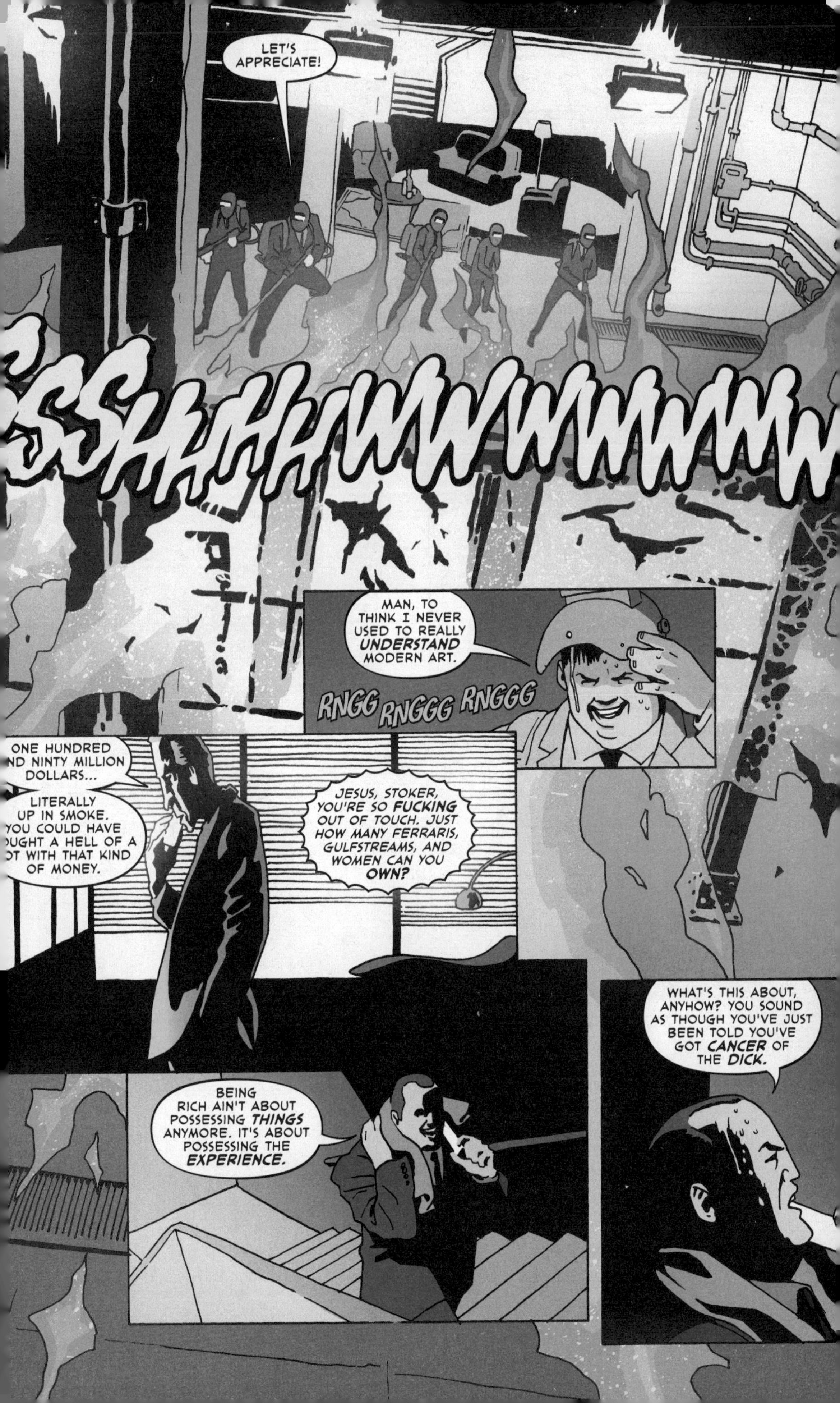
LET'S APPRECIATE!
SSHHHWWWWWWWWW
MAN, TO THINK I NEVER USED TO REALLY UNDERSTAND MODERN ART.
RNGG RNGGG RNGGG
ONE HUNDRED ND NINTY MILLION DOLLARS...
LITERALLY UP IN SMOKE. YOU COULD HAVE OUGHT A HELL OF A OT WITH THAT KIND OF MONEY.
JESUS, STOKER, YOU'RE SO FUCKING OUT OF TOUCH. JUST HOW MANY FERRARIS, GULFSTREAMS, AND WOMEN CAN YOU OWN?
BEING RICH AIN'T ABOUT POSSESSING THINGS ANYMORE. IT'S ABOUT POSSESSING THE EXPERIENCE.
WHAT'S THIS ABOUT, ANYHOW? YOU SOUND AS THOUGH YOU'VE JUST BEEN TOLD YOU'VE GOT CANCER OF THE DICK.

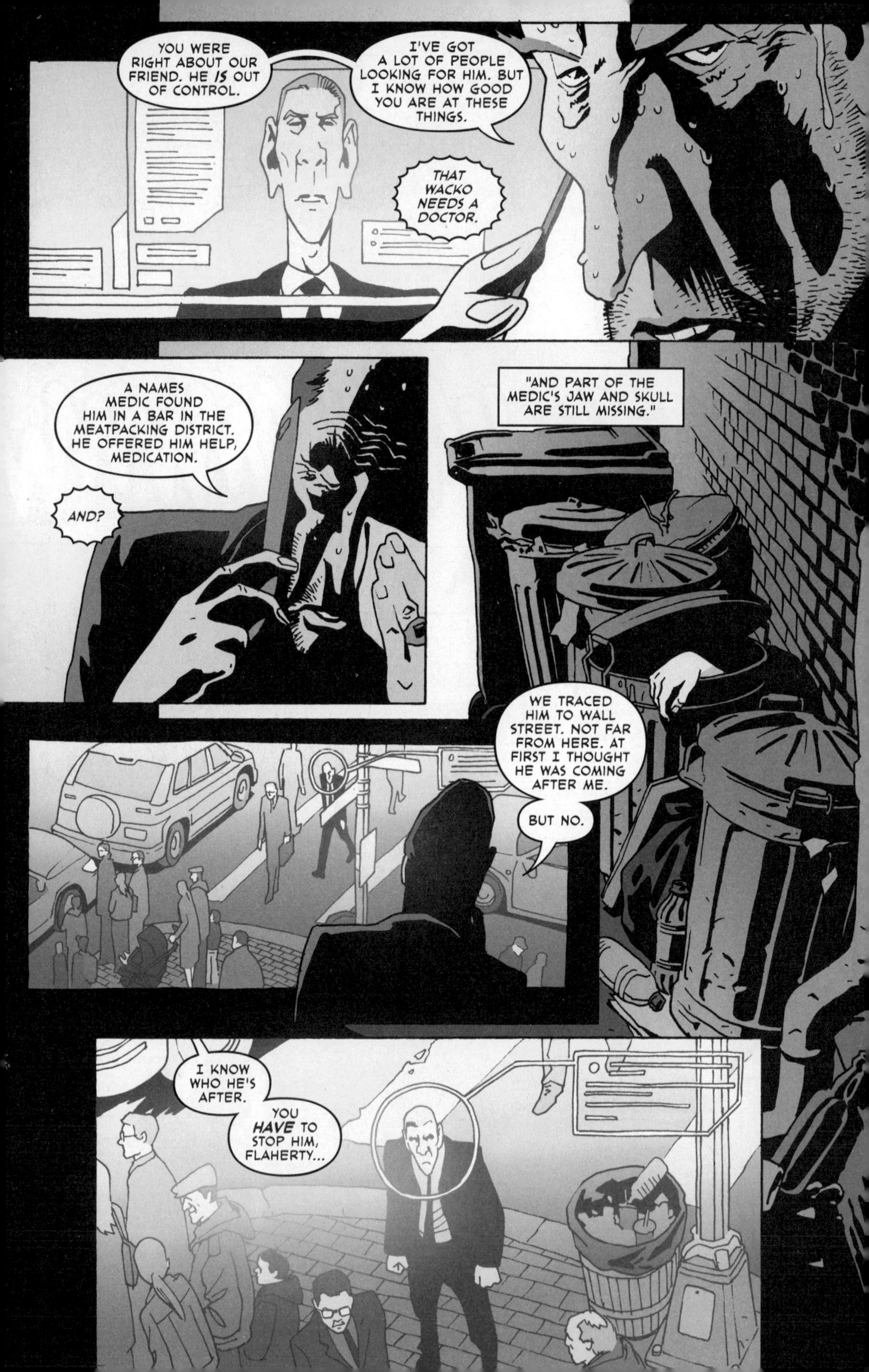
YOU WERE RIGHT ABOUT OUR FRIEND. HE IS OUT OF CONTROL.
I'VE GOT A LOT OF PEOPLE LOOKING FOR HIM. BUT I KNOW HOW GOOD YOU ARE AT THESE THINGS.
THAT WACKO NEEDS A DOCTOR.
A NAMES MEDIC FOUND HIM IN A BAR IN THE MEATPACKING DISTRICT. HE OFFERED HIM HELP, MEDICATION.
AND?
"AND PART OF THE MEDIC'S JAW AND SKULL ARE STILL MISSING."
WE TRACED HIM TO WALL STREET. NOT FAR FROM HERE. AT FIRST I THOUGHT HE WAS COMING AFTER ME.
BUT NO.
I KNOW WHO HE'S AFTER.
YOU HAVE TO STOP HIM, FLAHERTY...

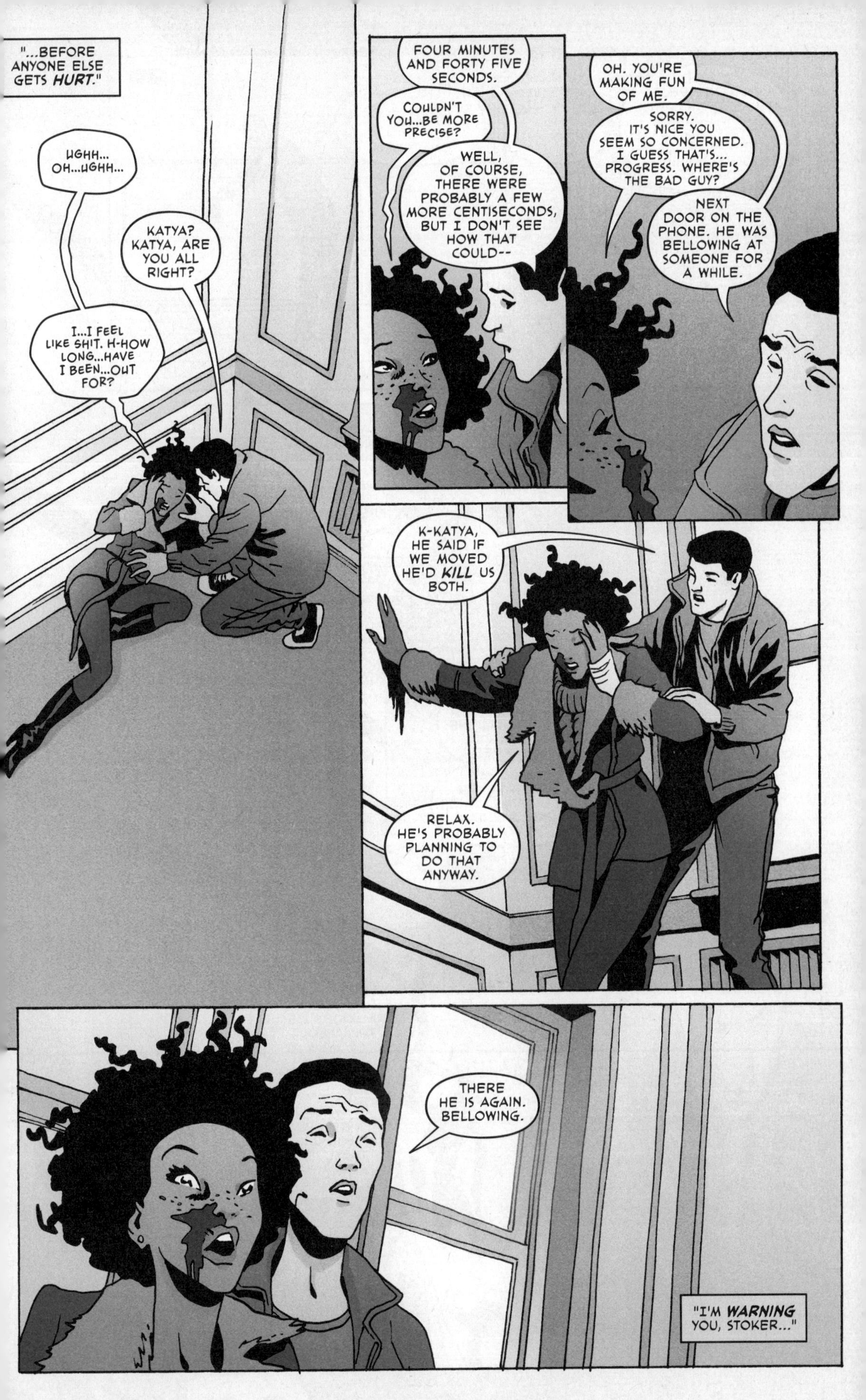
"...BEFORE ANYONE ELSE GETS *HURT*."
UGHH... OH...UGHH...
KATYA? KATYA, ARE YOU ALL RIGHT?
I...I FEEL LIKE SHIT. H-HOW LONG...HAVE I BEEN...OUT FOR?
FOUR MINUTES AND FORTY FIVE SECONDS.
COULDN'T YOU...BE MORE PRECISE?
WELL, OF COURSE, THERE WERE PROBABLY A FEW MORE CENTISECONDS, BUT I DON'T SEE HOW THAT COULD--
OH. YOU'RE MAKING FUN OF ME.
SORRY. IT'S NICE YOU SEEM SO CONCERNED. I GUESS THAT'S... PROGRESS. WHERE'S THE BAD GUY?
NEXT DOOR ON THE PHONE. HE WAS BELLOWING AT SOMEONE FOR A WHILE.
K-KATYA, HE SAID IF WE MOVED HE'D *KILL* US BOTH.
RELAX. HE'S PROBABLY PLANNING TO DO THAT ANYWAY.
THERE HE IS AGAIN. BELLOWING.
"I'M *WARNING* YOU, STOKER..."

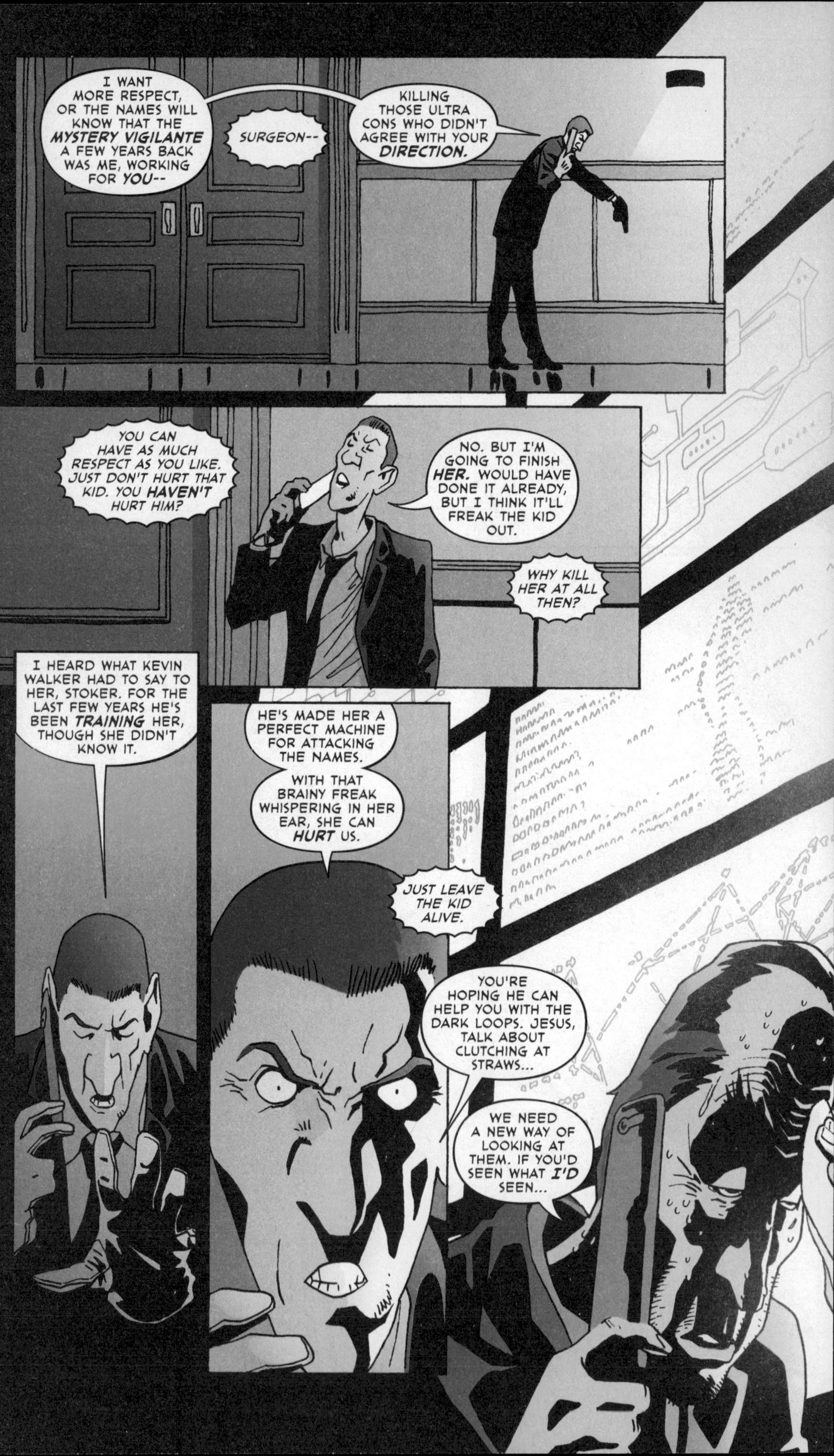
I WANT MORE RESPECT, OR THE NAMES WILL KNOW THAT THE MYSTERY VIGILANTE A FEW YEARS BACK WAS ME, WORKING FOR YOU--
SURGEON--
KILLING THOSE ULTRA CONS WHO DIDN'T AGREE WITH YOUR DIRECTION.
YOU CAN HAVE AS MUCH RESPECT AS YOU LIKE. JUST DON'T HURT THAT KID. YOU HAVEN'T HURT HIM?
NO. BUT I'M GOING TO FINISH HER. WOULD HAVE DONE IT ALREADY, BUT I THINK IT'LL FREAK THE KID OUT.
WHY KILL HER AT ALL THEN?
I HEARD WHAT KEVIN WALKER HAD TO SAY TO HER, STOKER. FOR THE LAST FEW YEARS HE'S BEEN TRAINING HER, THOUGH SHE DIDN'T KNOW IT.
HE'S MADE HER A PERFECT MACHINE FOR ATTACKING THE NAMES.
WITH THAT BRAINY FREAK WHISPERING IN HER EAR, SHE CAN HURT US.
JUST LEAVE THE KID ALIVE.
YOU'RE HOPING HE CAN HELP YOU WITH THE DARK LOOPS. JESUS, TALK ABOUT CLUTCHING AT STRAWS...
WE NEED A NEW WAY OF LOOKING AT THEM. IF YOU'D SEEN WHAT I'D SEEN...

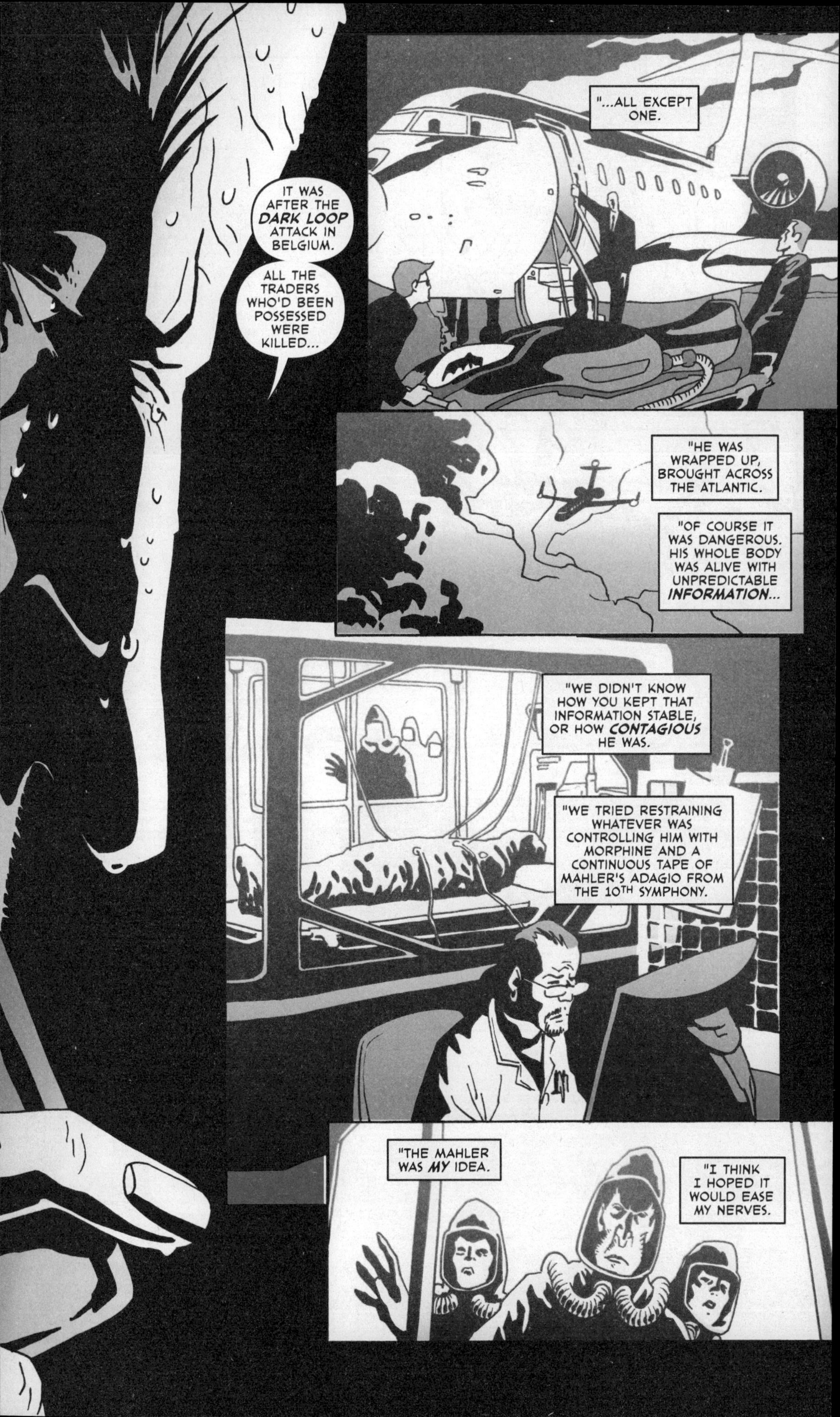
IT WAS AFTER THE DARK LOOP ATTACK IN BELGIUM.
ALL THE TRADERS WHO'D BEEN POSSESSED WERE KILLED...
"...ALL EXCEPT ONE.
"HE WAS WRAPPED UP, BROUGHT ACROSS THE ATLANTIC.
"OF COURSE IT WAS DANGEROUS. HIS WHOLE BODY WAS ALIVE WITH UNPREDICTABLE INFORMATION...
"WE DIDN'T KNOW HOW YOU KEPT THAT INFORMATION STABLE, OR HOW CONTAGIOUS HE WAS.
"WE TRIED RESTRAINING WHATEVER WAS CONTROLLING HIM WITH MORPHINE AND A CONTINUOUS TAPE OF MAHLER'S ADAGIO FROM THE 10TH SYMPHONY.
"THE MAHLER WAS MY IDEA.
"I THINK I HOPED IT WOULD EASE MY NERVES.

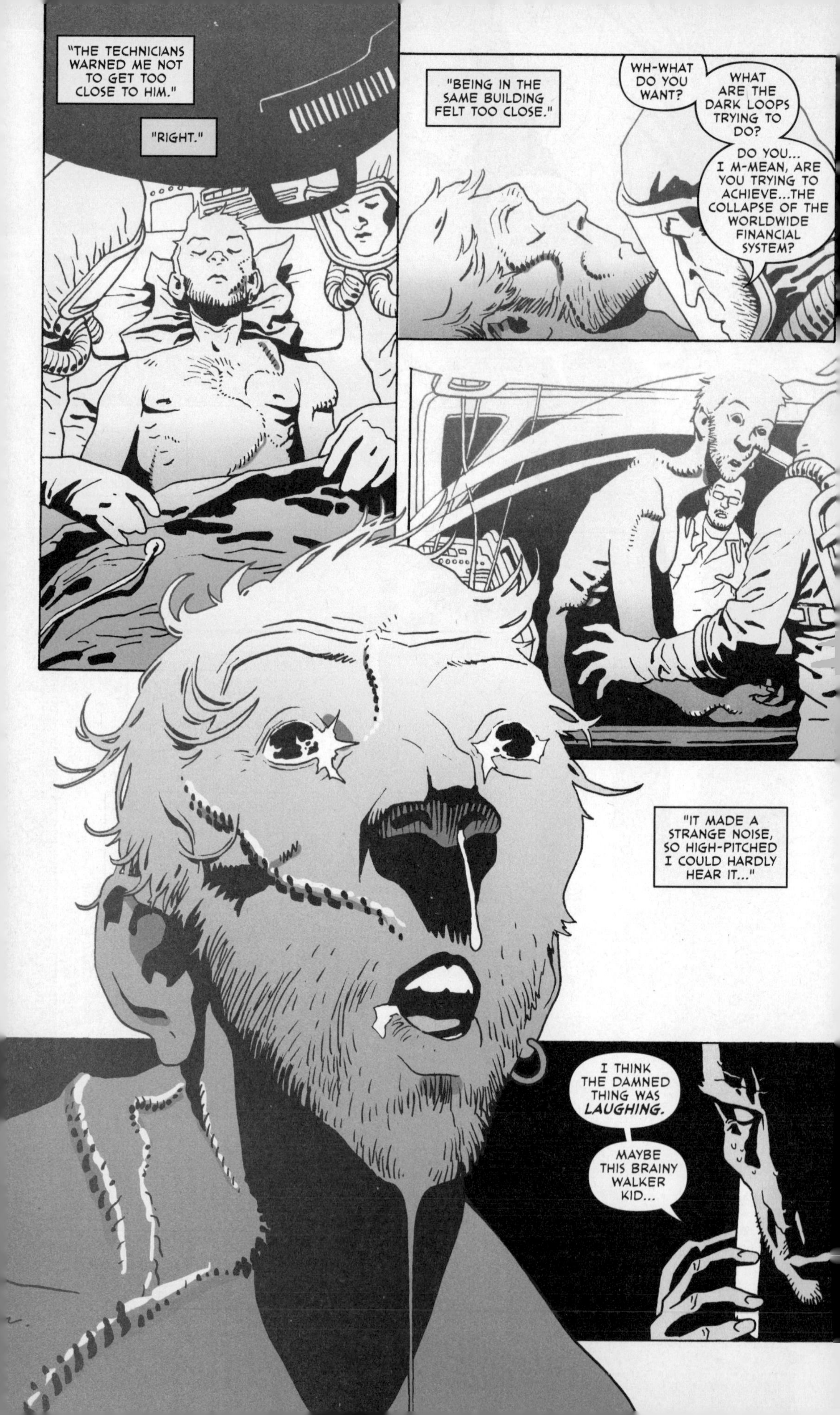
"THE TECHNICIANS WARNED ME NOT TO GET TOO CLOSE TO HIM."
"RIGHT."
"BEING IN THE SAME BUILDING FELT TOO CLOSE."
WH-WHAT DO YOU WANT?
WHAT ARE THE DARK LOOPS TRYING TO DO?
DO YOU... I M-MEAN, ARE YOU TRYING TO ACHIEVE...THE COLLAPSE OF THE WORLDWIDE FINANCIAL SYSTEM?
"IT MADE A STRANGE NOISE, SO HIGH-PITCHED I COULD HARDLY HEAR IT..."
I THINK THE DAMNED THING WAS *LAUGHING.*
MAYBE THIS BRAINY WALKER KID...

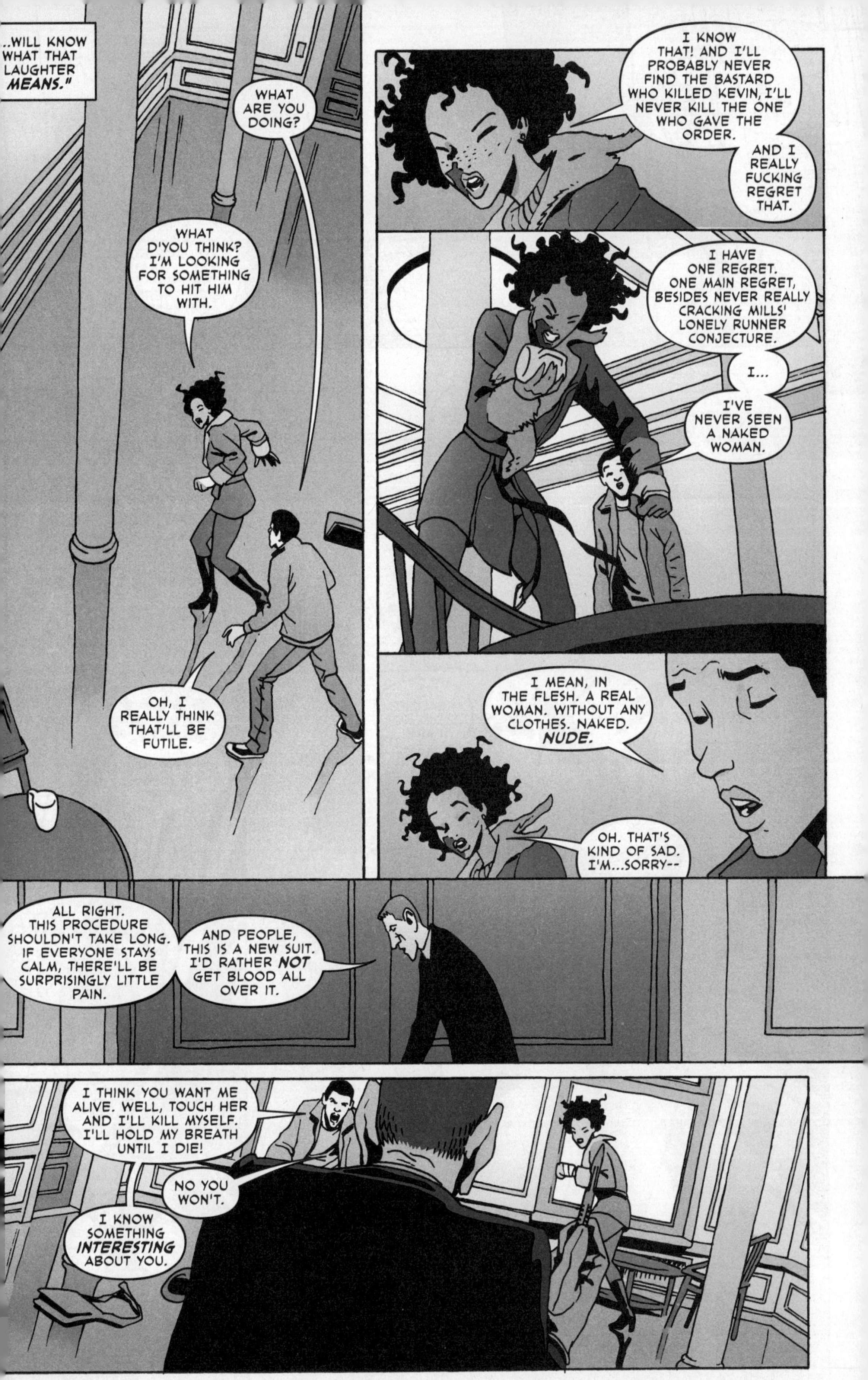
..WILL KNOW WHAT THAT LAUGHTER *MEANS."*
WHAT ARE YOU DOING?
WHAT D'YOU THINK? I'M LOOKING FOR SOMETHING TO HIT HIM WITH.
OH, I REALLY THINK THAT'LL BE FUTILE.
I KNOW THAT! AND I'LL PROBABLY NEVER FIND THE BASTARD WHO KILLED KEVIN, I'LL NEVER KILL THE ONE WHO GAVE THE ORDER.
AND I REALLY FUCKING REGRET THAT.
I HAVE ONE REGRET. ONE MAIN REGRET, BESIDES NEVER REALLY CRACKING MILLS' LONELY RUNNER CONJECTURE.
I...
I'VE NEVER SEEN A NAKED WOMAN.
I MEAN, IN THE FLESH. A REAL WOMAN. WITHOUT ANY CLOTHES. NAKED. ***NUDE.***
OH. THAT'S KIND OF SAD. I'M...SORRY--
ALL RIGHT. THIS PROCEDURE SHOULDN'T TAKE LONG. IF EVERYONE STAYS CALM, THERE'LL BE SURPRISINGLY LITTLE PAIN.
AND PEOPLE, THIS IS A NEW SUIT. I'D RATHER ***NOT*** GET BLOOD ALL OVER IT.
I THINK YOU WANT ME ALIVE. WELL, TOUCH HER AND I'LL KILL MYSELF. I'LL HOLD MY BREATH UNTIL I DIE!
NO YOU WON'T.
I KNOW SOMETHING ***INTERESTING*** ABOUT YOU.

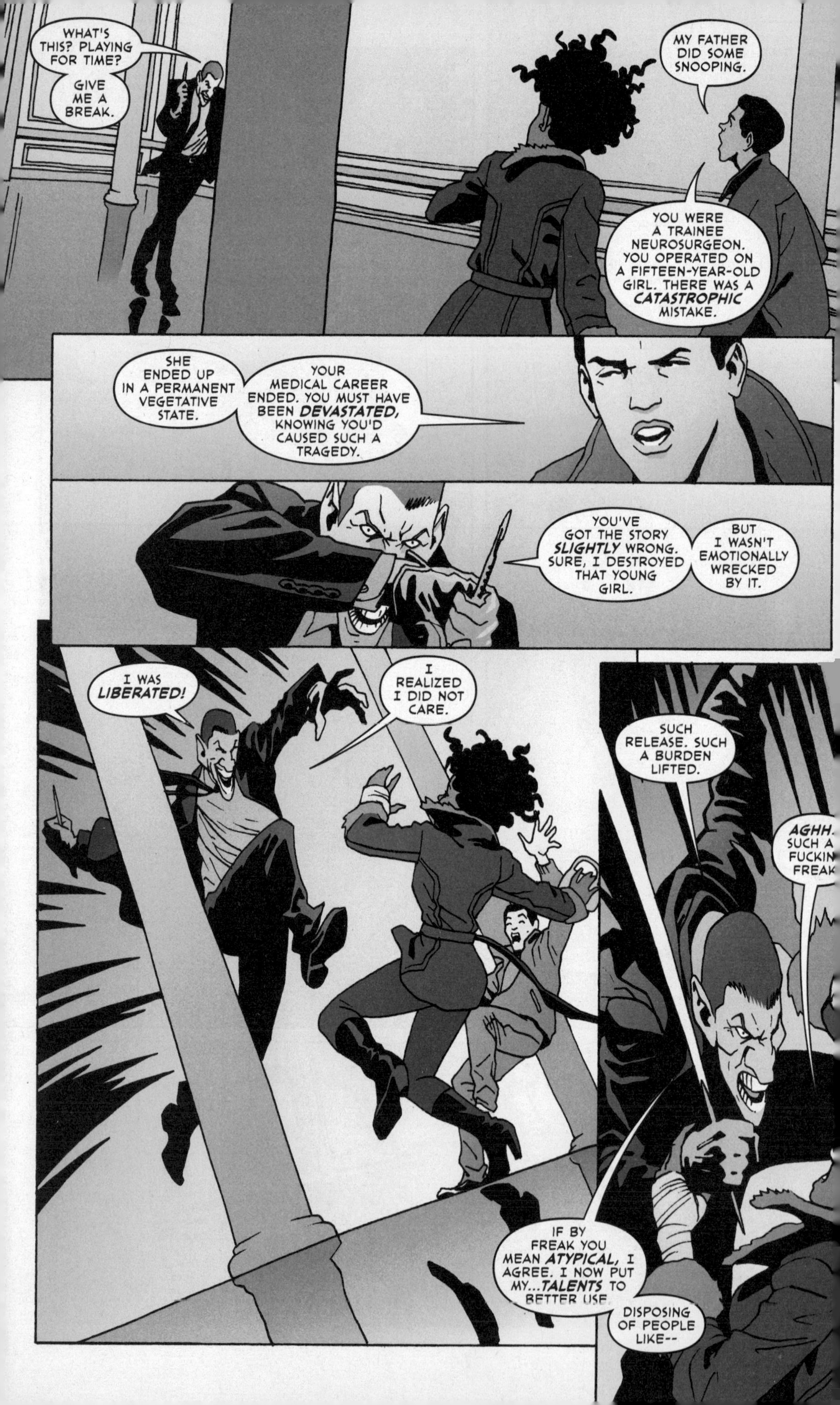
WHAT'S THIS? PLAYING FOR TIME?
GIVE ME A BREAK.
MY FATHER DID SOME SNOOPING.
YOU WERE A TRAINEE NEUROSURGEON. YOU OPERATED ON A FIFTEEN-YEAR-OLD GIRL. THERE WAS A CATASTROPHIC MISTAKE.
SHE ENDED UP IN A PERMANENT VEGETATIVE STATE.
YOUR MEDICAL CAREER ENDED. YOU MUST HAVE BEEN DEVASTATED, KNOWING YOU'D CAUSED SUCH A TRAGEDY.
YOU'VE GOT THE STORY SLIGHTLY WRONG. SURE, I DESTROYED THAT YOUNG GIRL.
BUT I WASN'T EMOTIONALLY WRECKED BY IT.
I WAS LIBERATED!
I REALIZED I DID NOT CARE.
SUCH RELEASE. SUCH A BURDEN LIFTED.
AGHH. SUCH A FUCKIN FREAK
IF BY FREAK YOU MEAN ATYPICAL, I AGREE. I NOW PUT MY...TALENTS TO BETTER USE.
DISPOSING OF PEOPLE LIKE--

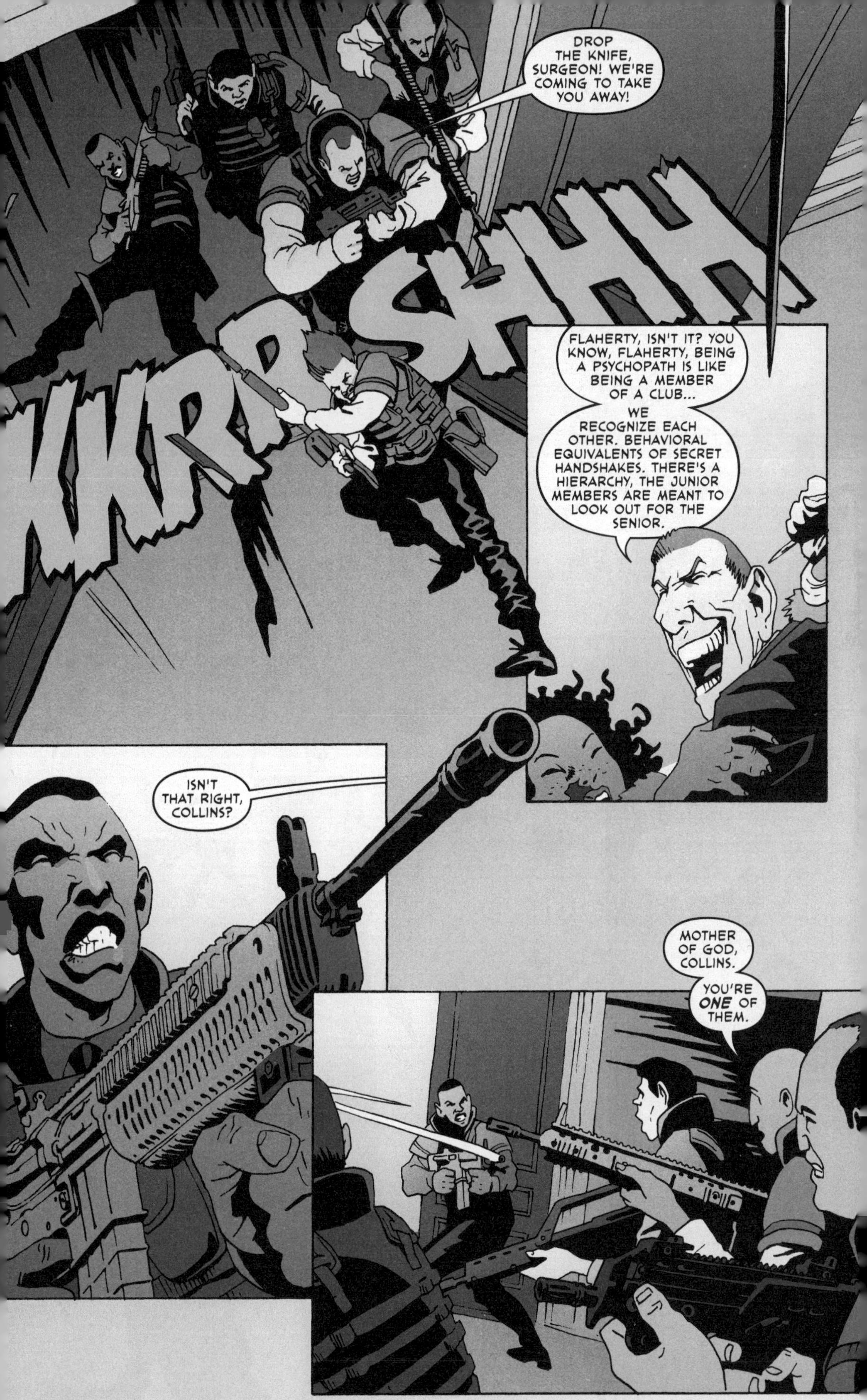
DROP THE KNIFE, SURGEON! WE'RE COMING TO TAKE YOU AWAY!
KKRRSHHH
FLAHERTY, ISN'T IT? YOU KNOW, FLAHERTY, BEING A PSYCHOPATH IS LIKE BEING A MEMBER OF A CLUB...
WE RECOGNIZE EACH OTHER. BEHAVIORAL EQUIVALENTS OF SECRET HANDSHAKES. THERE'S A HIERARCHY, THE JUNIOR MEMBERS ARE MEANT TO LOOK OUT FOR THE SENIOR.
ISN'T THAT RIGHT, COLLINS?
MOTHER OF GOD, COLLINS.
YOU'RE *ONE* OF THEM.

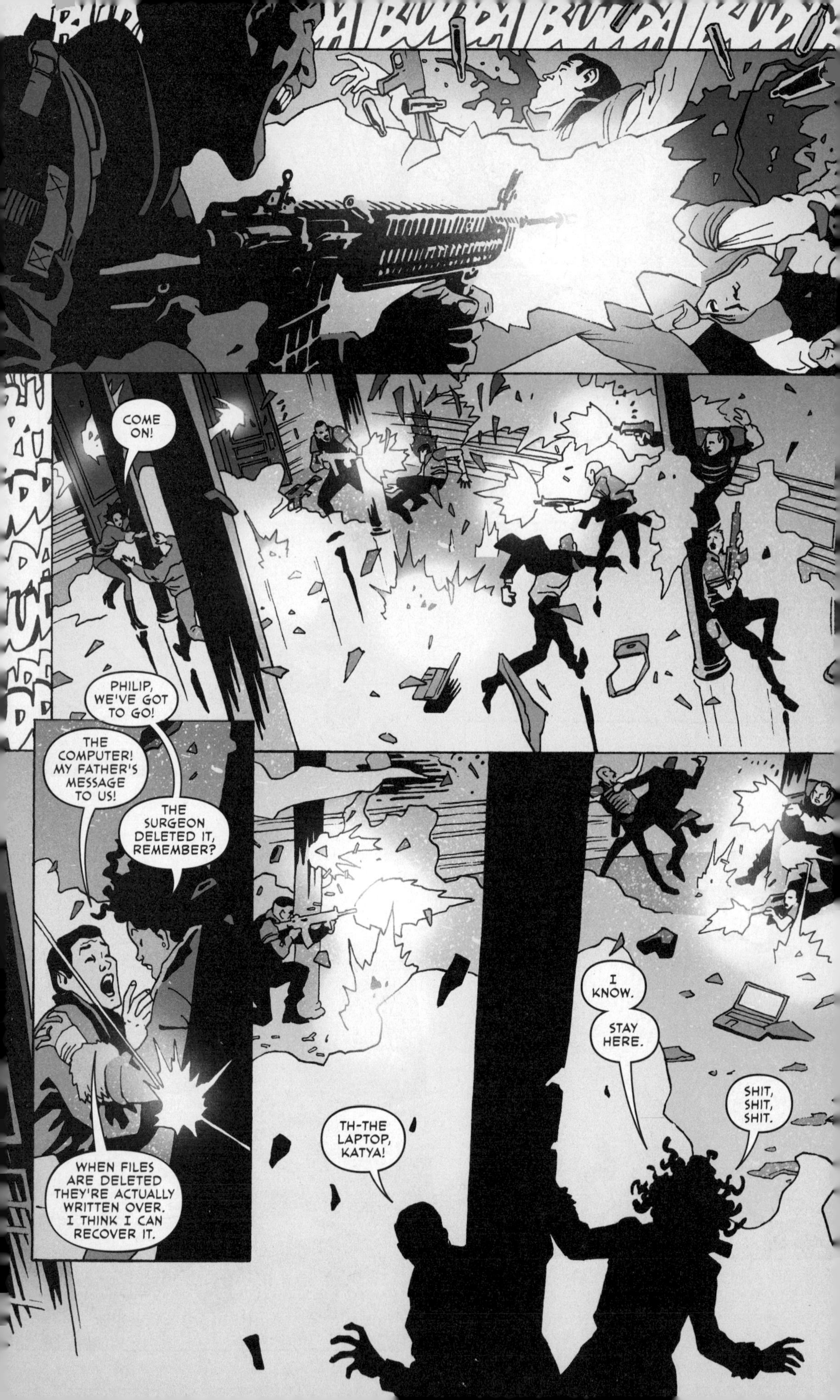
BUDDA BUDDA BUDDA BUDDA
COME ON!
PHILIP, WE'VE GOT TO GO!
THE COMPUTER! MY FATHER'S MESSAGE TO US!
THE SURGEON DELETED IT, REMEMBER?
WHEN FILES ARE DELETED THEY'RE ACTUALLY WRITTEN OVER. I THINK I CAN RECOVER IT.
TH-THE LAPTOP, KATYA!
I KNOW.
STAY HERE.
SHIT, SHIT, SHIT.

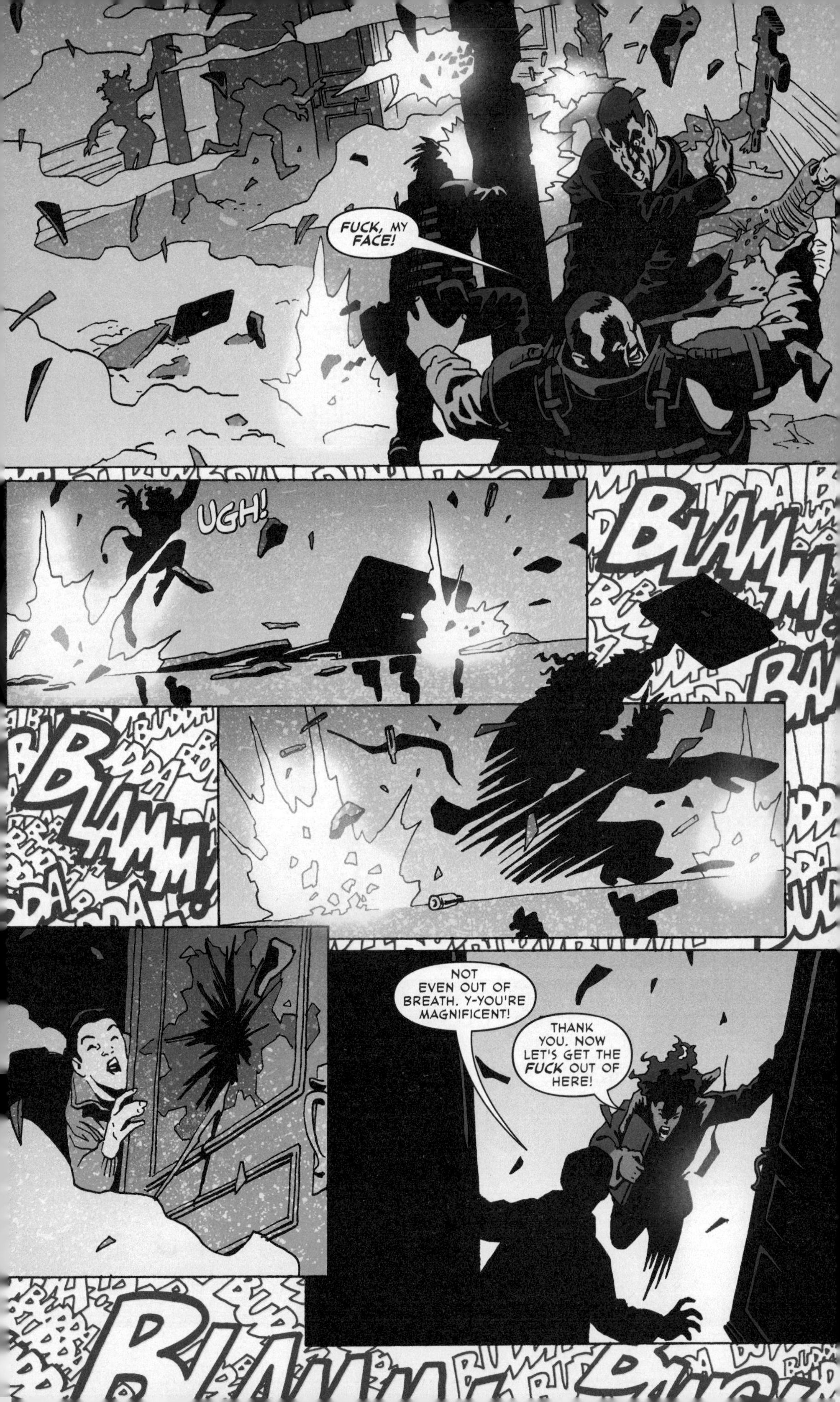
FUCK, MY FACE!
UGH!
BLAMM
BLAMM
NOT EVEN OUT OF BREATH. Y-YOU'RE MAGNIFICENT!
THANK YOU. NOW LET'S GET THE *FUCK* OUT OF HERE!

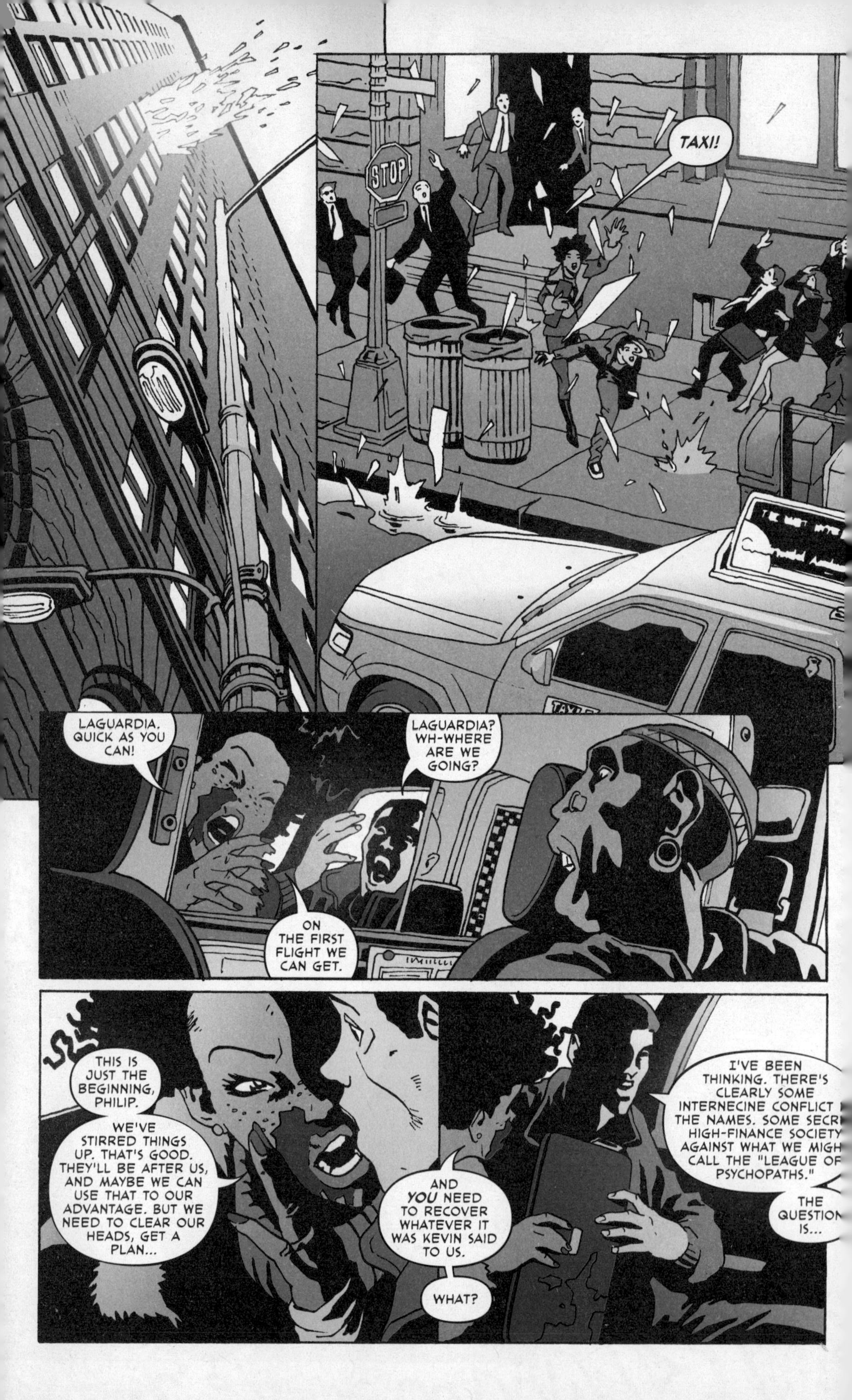

TAXI!
LAGUARDIA. QUICK AS YOU CAN!
LAGUARDIA? WH-WHERE ARE WE GOING?
ON THE FIRST FLIGHT WE CAN GET.
THIS IS JUST THE BEGINNING, PHILIP.
WE'VE STIRRED THINGS UP. THAT'S GOOD. THEY'LL BE AFTER US, AND MAYBE WE CAN USE THAT TO OUR ADVANTAGE. BUT WE NEED TO CLEAR OUR HEADS, GET A PLAN...
AND *YOU* NEED TO RECOVER WHATEVER IT WAS KEVIN SAID TO US.
WHAT?
I'VE BEEN THINKING. THERE'S CLEARLY SOME INTERNECINE CONFLICT THE NAMES. SOME SECR HIGH-FINANCE SOCIETY AGAINST WHAT WE MIGH CALL THE "LEAGUE OF PSYCHOPATHS."
THE QUESTION IS...

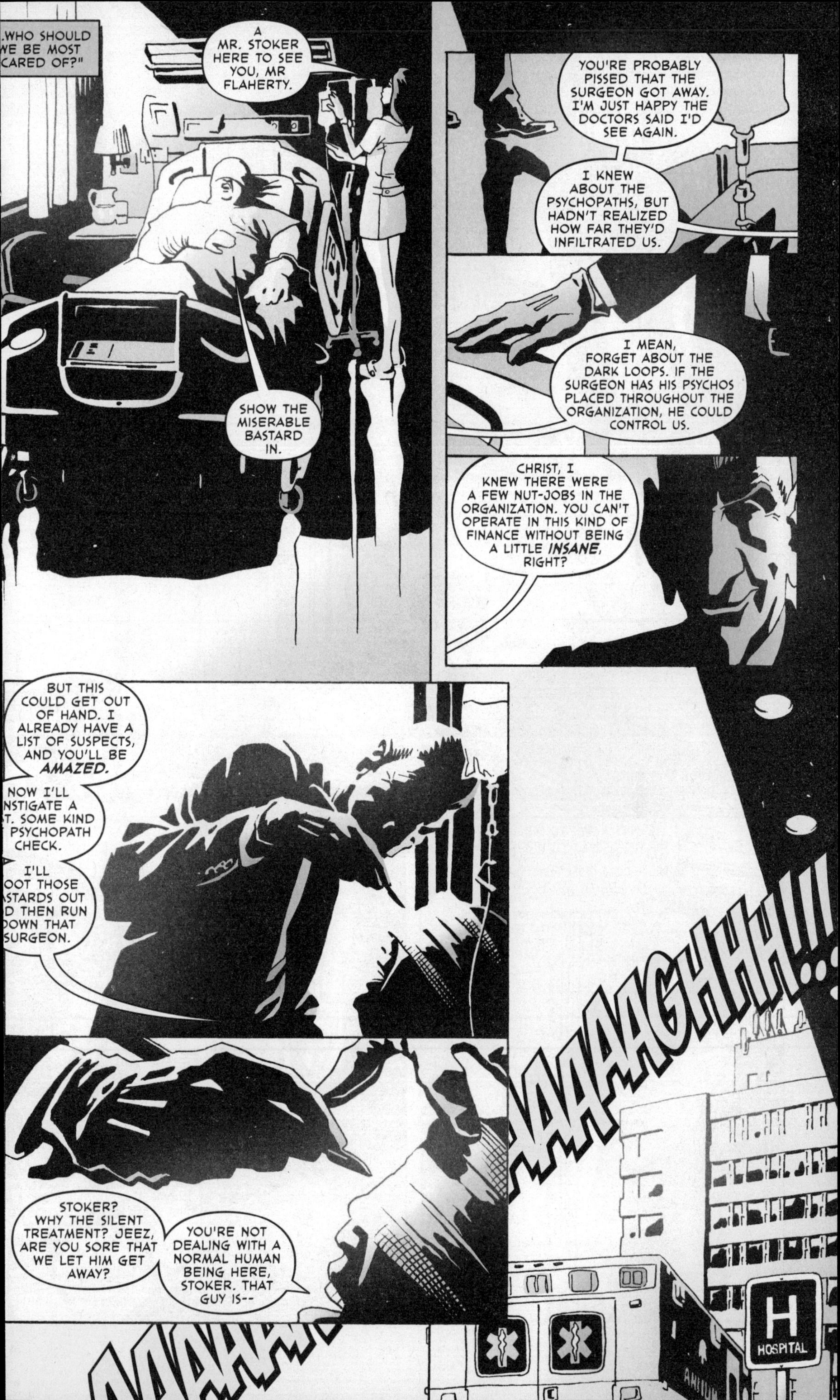
.WHO SHOULD WE BE MOST CARED OF?"
A MR. STOKER HERE TO SEE YOU, MR FLAHERTY.
SHOW THE MISERABLE BASTARD IN.
YOU'RE PROBABLY PISSED THAT THE SURGEON GOT AWAY. I'M JUST HAPPY THE DOCTORS SAID I'D SEE AGAIN.
I KNEW ABOUT THE PSYCHOPATHS, BUT HADN'T REALIZED HOW FAR THEY'D INFILTRATED US.
I MEAN, FORGET ABOUT THE DARK LOOPS. IF THE SURGEON HAS HIS PSYCHOS PLACED THROUGHOUT THE ORGANIZATION, HE COULD CONTROL US.
CHRIST, I KNEW THERE WERE A FEW NUT-JOBS IN THE ORGANIZATION. YOU CAN'T OPERATE IN THIS KIND OF FINANCE WITHOUT BEING A LITTLE *INSANE*, RIGHT?
BUT THIS COULD GET OUT OF HAND. I ALREADY HAVE A LIST OF SUSPECTS, AND YOU'LL BE ***AMAZED.***
NOW I'LL NSTIGATE A T. SOME KIND PSYCHOPATH CHECK.
I'LL OOT THOSE ASTARDS OUT D THEN RUN DOWN THAT SURGEON.
STOKER? WHY THE SILENT TREATMENT? JEEZ, ARE YOU SORE THAT WE LET HIM GET AWAY?
YOU'RE NOT DEALING WITH A NORMAL HUMAN BEING HERE, STOKER. THAT GUY IS--
AAAAAGHHH!!!
H
HOSPITAL

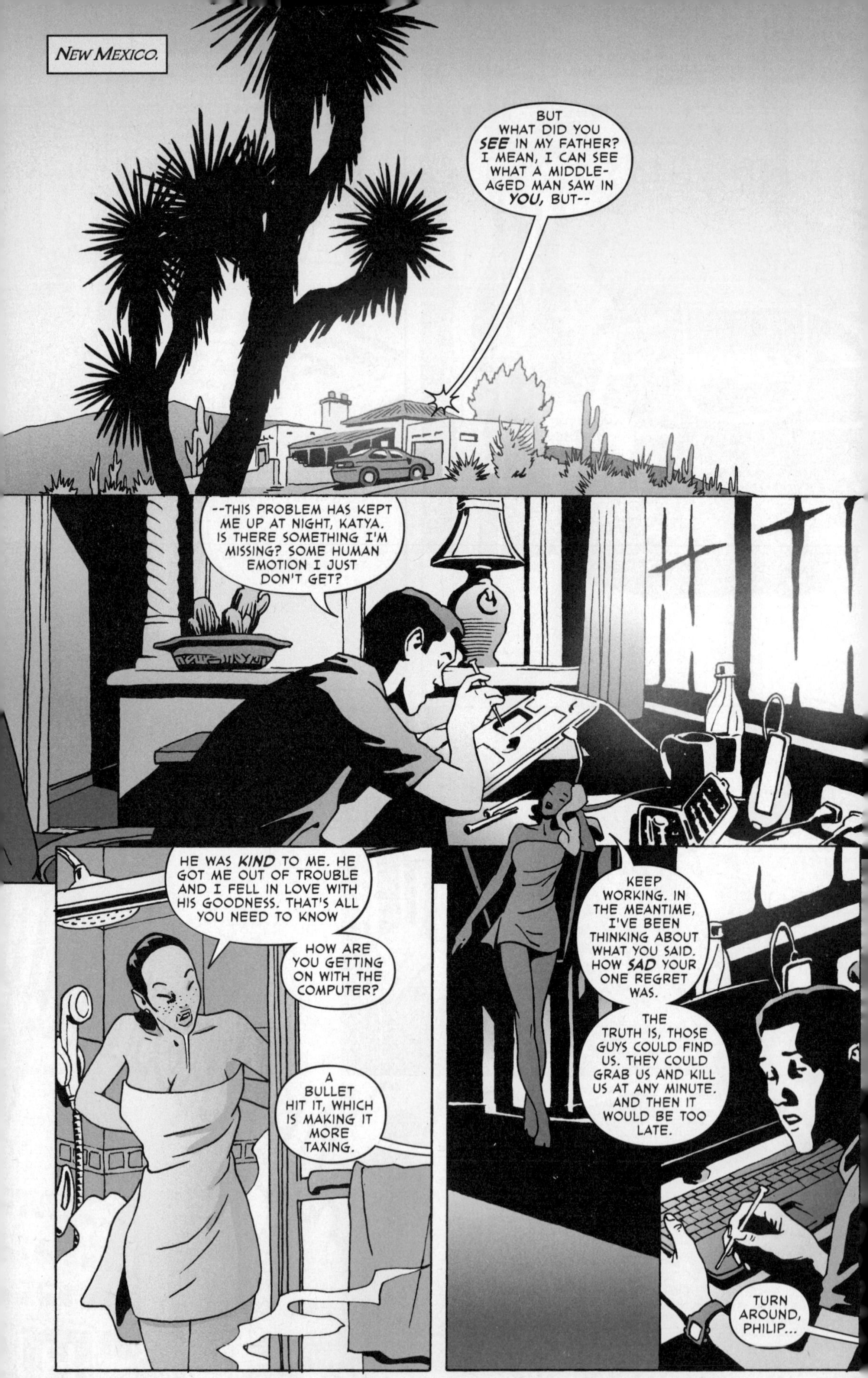
NEW MEXICO.
BUT WHAT DID YOU SEE IN MY FATHER? I MEAN, I CAN SEE WHAT A MIDDLE-AGED MAN SAW IN YOU, BUT--
--THIS PROBLEM HAS KEPT ME UP AT NIGHT, KATYA. IS THERE SOMETHING I'M MISSING? SOME HUMAN EMOTION I JUST DON'T GET?
HE WAS KIND TO ME. HE GOT ME OUT OF TROUBLE AND I FELL IN LOVE WITH HIS GOODNESS. THAT'S ALL YOU NEED TO KNOW
HOW ARE YOU GETTING ON WITH THE COMPUTER?
A BULLET HIT IT, WHICH IS MAKING IT MORE TAXING.
KEEP WORKING. IN THE MEANTIME, I'VE BEEN THINKING ABOUT WHAT YOU SAID. HOW SAD YOUR ONE REGRET WAS.
THE TRUTH IS, THOSE GUYS COULD FIND US. THEY COULD GRAB US AND KILL US AT ANY MINUTE. AND THEN IT WOULD BE TOO LATE.
TURN AROUND, PHILIP...

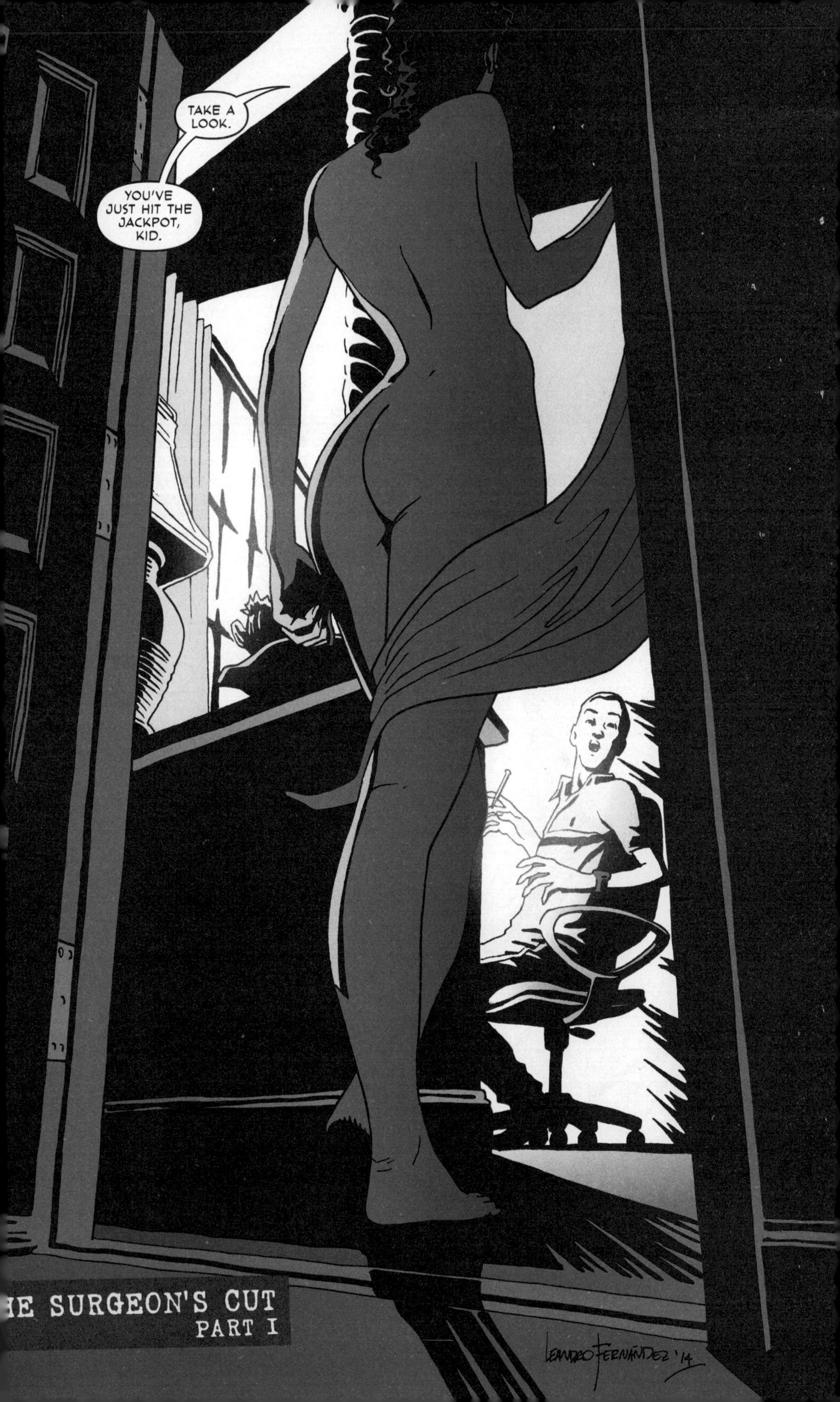
TAKE A LOOK.
YOU'VE JUST HIT THE JACKPOT, KID.
E SURGEON'S CUT
PART I
LEANDRO FERNÁNDEZ '14

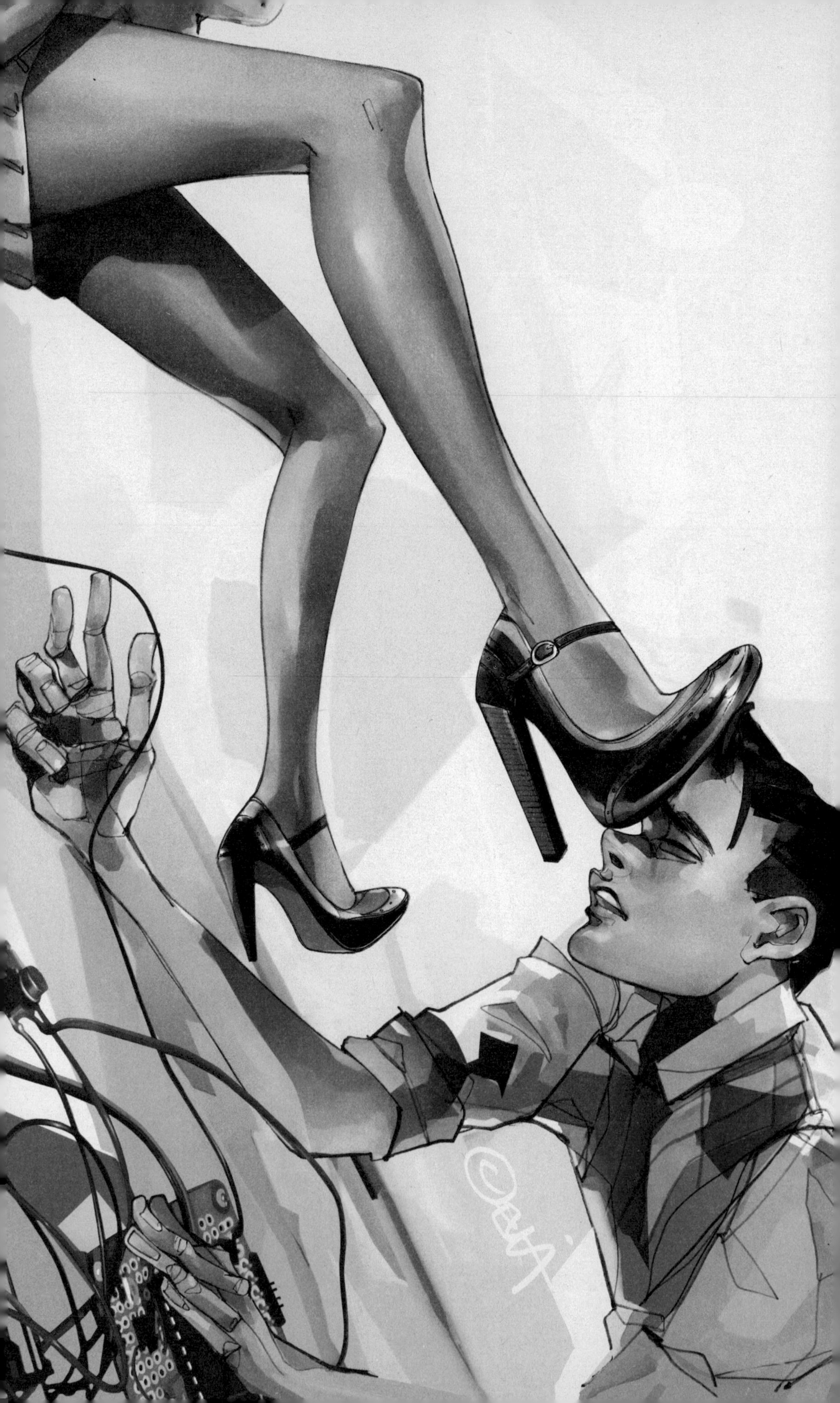

"THE SURGEON ONLY HAD A FEW SECONDS TO WORK IN. BUT THAT WAS ALL HE NEEDED.

"THE BLADE TRAVELLED THROUGH THE EYE AND ENTERED FLAHERTY'S BRAIN, ALL THE WAY IN TO THE TEMPORAL LOBE...

"...WHICH, I'M RELIABLY INFORMED, IS A *FUCKING* LONG WAY."

THE SURGEON'S CUT
PART II

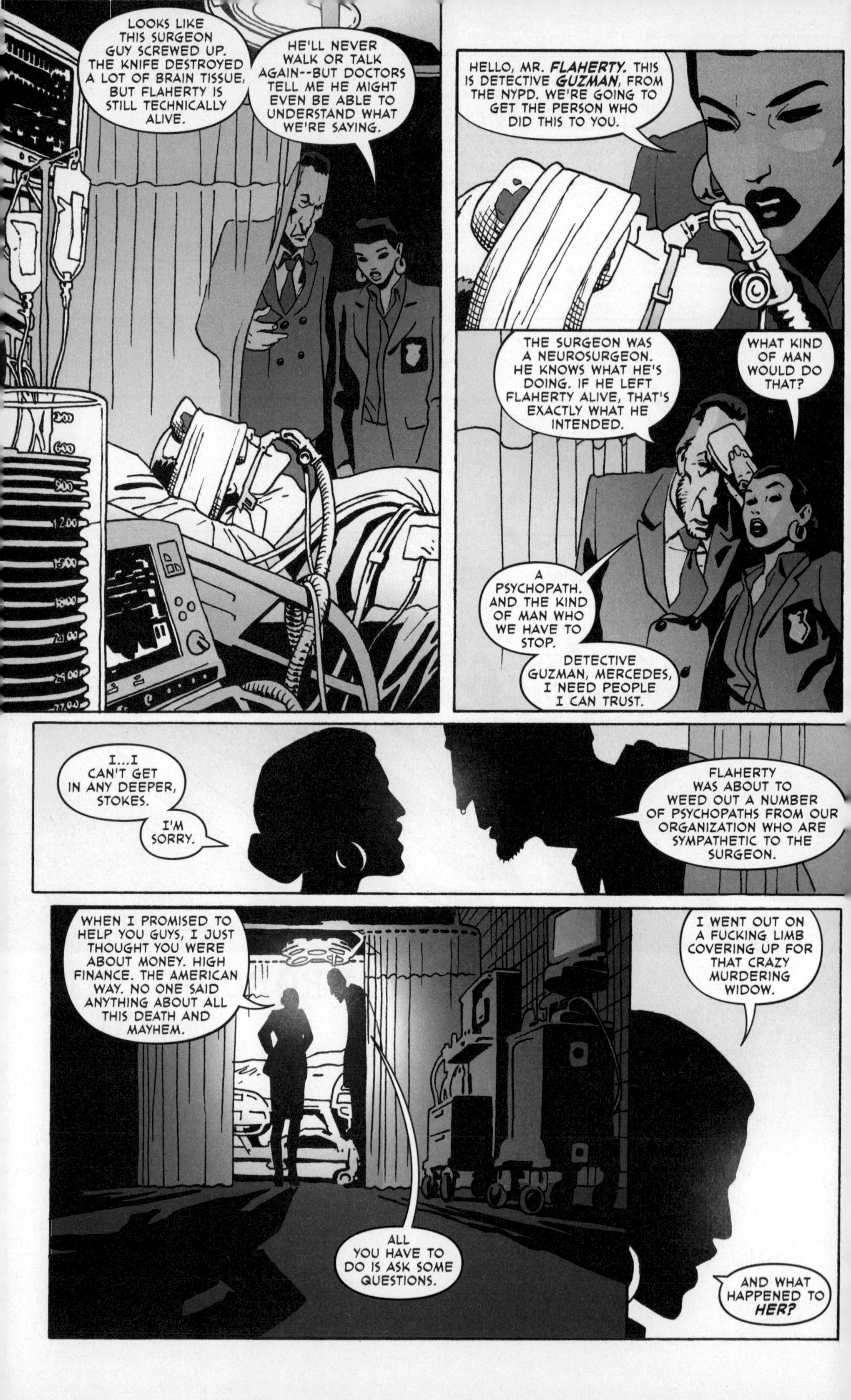
LOOKS LIKE THIS SURGEON GUY SCREWED UP. THE KNIFE DESTROYED A LOT OF BRAIN TISSUE, BUT FLAHERTY IS STILL TECHNICALLY ALIVE.
HE'LL NEVER WALK OR TALK AGAIN--BUT DOCTORS TELL ME HE MIGHT EVEN BE ABLE TO UNDERSTAND WHAT WE'RE SAYING.
HELLO, MR. *FLAHERTY.* THIS IS DETECTIVE *GUZMAN*, FROM THE NYPD. WE'RE GOING TO GET THE PERSON WHO DID THIS TO YOU.
THE SURGEON WAS A NEUROSURGEON. HE KNOWS WHAT HE'S DOING. IF HE LEFT FLAHERTY ALIVE, THAT'S EXACTLY WHAT HE INTENDED.
WHAT KIND OF MAN WOULD DO THAT?
A PSYCHOPATH. AND THE KIND OF MAN WHO WE HAVE TO STOP.
DETECTIVE GUZMAN, MERCEDES, I NEED PEOPLE I CAN TRUST.
I...I CAN'T GET IN ANY DEEPER, STOKES.
I'M SORRY.
FLAHERTY WAS ABOUT TO WEED OUT A NUMBER OF PSYCHOPATHS FROM OUR ORGANIZATION WHO ARE SYMPATHETIC TO THE SURGEON.
WHEN I PROMISED TO HELP YOU GUYS, I JUST THOUGHT YOU WERE ABOUT MONEY. HIGH FINANCE. THE AMERICAN WAY. NO ONE SAID ANYTHING ABOUT ALL THIS DEATH AND MAYHEM.
ALL YOU HAVE TO DO IS ASK SOME QUESTIONS.
I WENT OUT ON A FUCKING LIMB COVERING UP FOR THAT CRAZY MURDERING WIDOW.
AND WHAT HAPPENED TO *HER?*

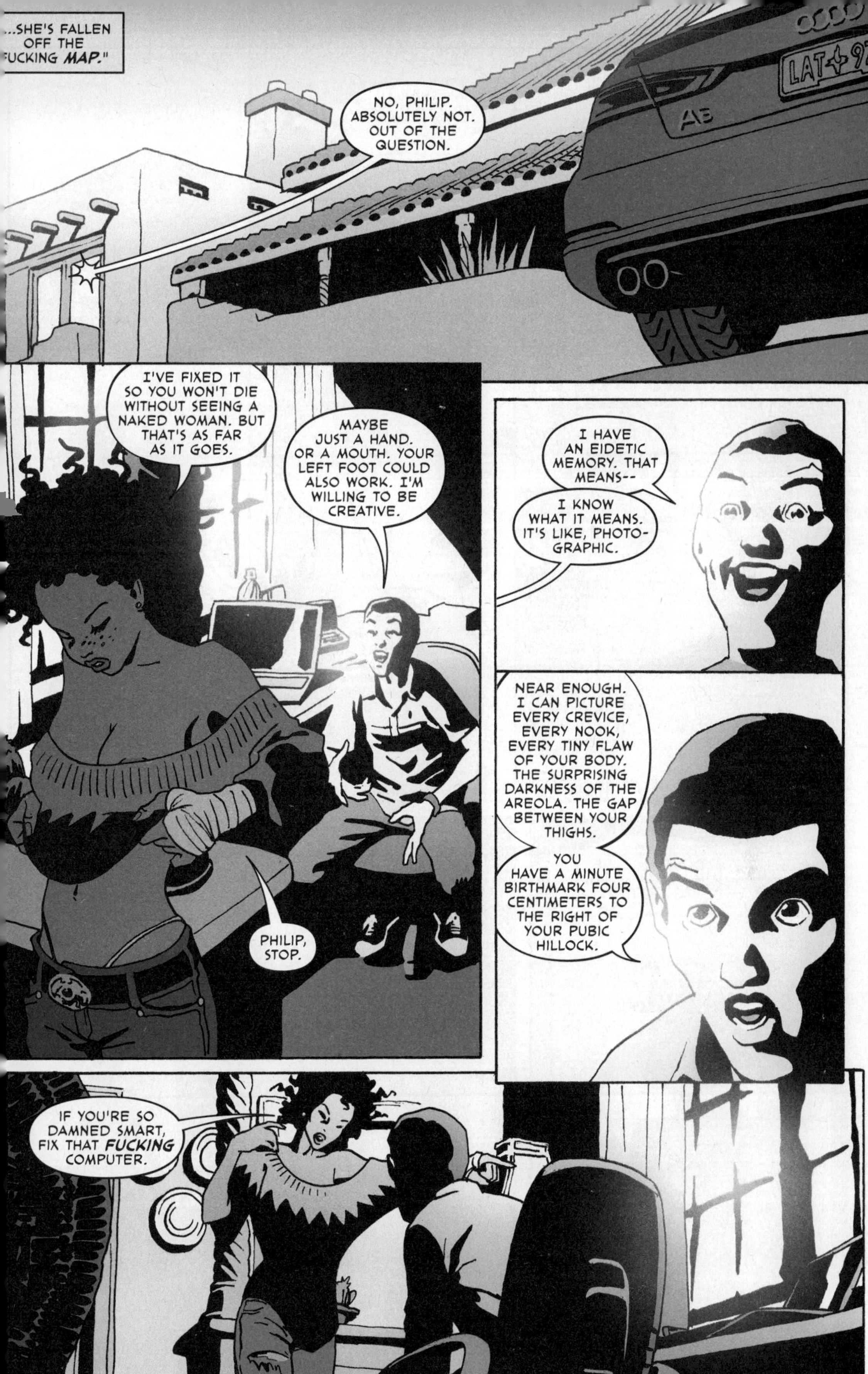

...SHE'S FALLEN OFF THE FUCKING *MAP.*"
LAT-974
A3
NO, PHILIP. ABSOLUTELY NOT. OUT OF THE QUESTION.
I'VE FIXED IT SO YOU WON'T DIE WITHOUT SEEING A NAKED WOMAN. BUT THAT'S AS FAR AS IT GOES.
MAYBE JUST A HAND. OR A MOUTH. YOUR LEFT FOOT COULD ALSO WORK. I'M WILLING TO BE CREATIVE.
PHILIP, STOP.
I HAVE AN EIDETIC MEMORY. THAT MEANS--
I KNOW WHAT IT MEANS. IT'S LIKE, PHOTO-GRAPHIC.
NEAR ENOUGH. I CAN PICTURE EVERY CREVICE, EVERY NOOK, EVERY TINY FLAW OF YOUR BODY. THE SURPRISING DARKNESS OF THE AREOLA. THE GAP BETWEEN YOUR THIGHS.
YOU HAVE A MINUTE BIRTHMARK FOUR CENTIMETERS TO THE RIGHT OF YOUR PUBIC HILLOCK.
IF YOU'RE SO DAMNED SMART, FIX THAT *FUCKING* COMPUTER.

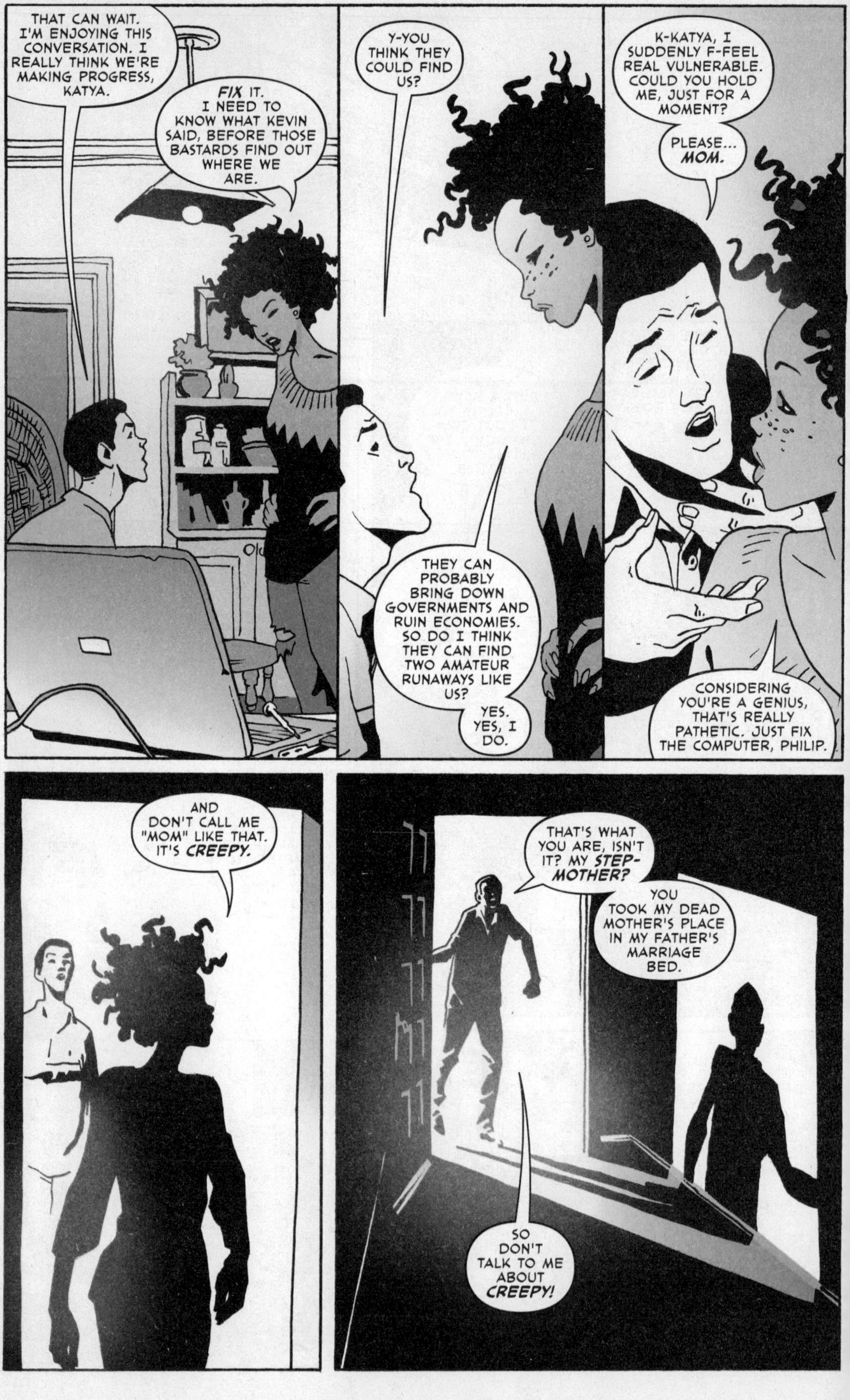
THAT CAN WAIT. I'M ENJOYING THIS CONVERSATION. I REALLY THINK WE'RE MAKING PROGRESS, KATYA.
FIX IT. I NEED TO KNOW WHAT KEVIN SAID, BEFORE THOSE BASTARDS FIND OUT WHERE WE ARE.
Y-YOU THINK THEY COULD FIND US?
THEY CAN PROBABLY BRING DOWN GOVERNMENTS AND RUIN ECONOMIES. SO DO I THINK THEY CAN FIND TWO AMATEUR RUNAWAYS LIKE US?
YES. YES, I DO.
K-KATYA, I SUDDENLY F-FEEL REAL VULNERABLE. COULD YOU HOLD ME, JUST FOR A MOMENT?
PLEASE... MOM.
CONSIDERING YOU'RE A GENIUS, THAT'S REALLY PATHETIC. JUST FIX THE COMPUTER, PHILIP.
AND DON'T CALL ME "MOM" LIKE THAT. IT'S CREEPY.
THAT'S WHAT YOU ARE, ISN'T IT? MY STEP-MOTHER?
YOU TOOK MY DEAD MOTHER'S PLACE IN MY FATHER'S MARRIAGE BED.
SO DON'T TALK TO ME ABOUT CREEPY!

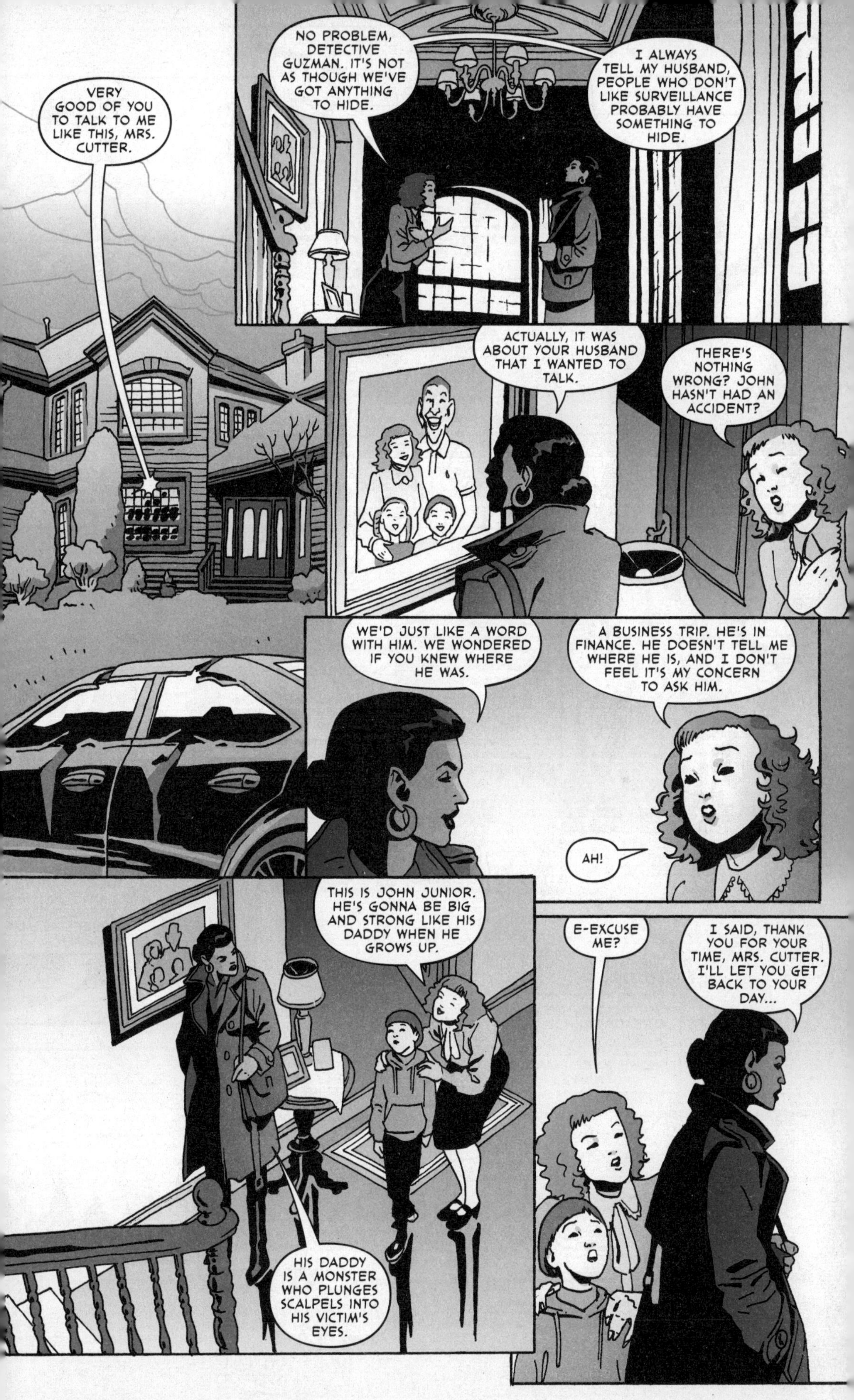
VERY GOOD OF YOU TO TALK TO ME LIKE THIS, MRS. CUTTER.
NO PROBLEM, DETECTIVE GUZMAN. IT'S NOT AS THOUGH WE'VE GOT ANYTHING TO HIDE.
I ALWAYS TELL MY HUSBAND, PEOPLE WHO DON'T LIKE SURVEILLANCE PROBABLY HAVE SOMETHING TO HIDE.
ACTUALLY, IT WAS ABOUT YOUR HUSBAND THAT I WANTED TO TALK.
THERE'S NOTHING WRONG? JOHN HASN'T HAD AN ACCIDENT?
WE'D JUST LIKE A WORD WITH HIM. WE WONDERED IF YOU KNEW WHERE HE WAS.
A BUSINESS TRIP. HE'S IN FINANCE. HE DOESN'T TELL ME WHERE HE IS, AND I DON'T FEEL IT'S MY CONCERN TO ASK HIM.
AH!
THIS IS JOHN JUNIOR. HE'S GONNA BE BIG AND STRONG LIKE HIS DADDY WHEN HE GROWS UP.
HIS DADDY IS A MONSTER WHO PLUNGES SCALPELS INTO HIS VICTIM'S EYES.
E-EXCUSE ME?
I SAID, THANK YOU FOR YOUR TIME, MRS. CUTTER. I'LL LET YOU GET BACK TO YOUR DAY...

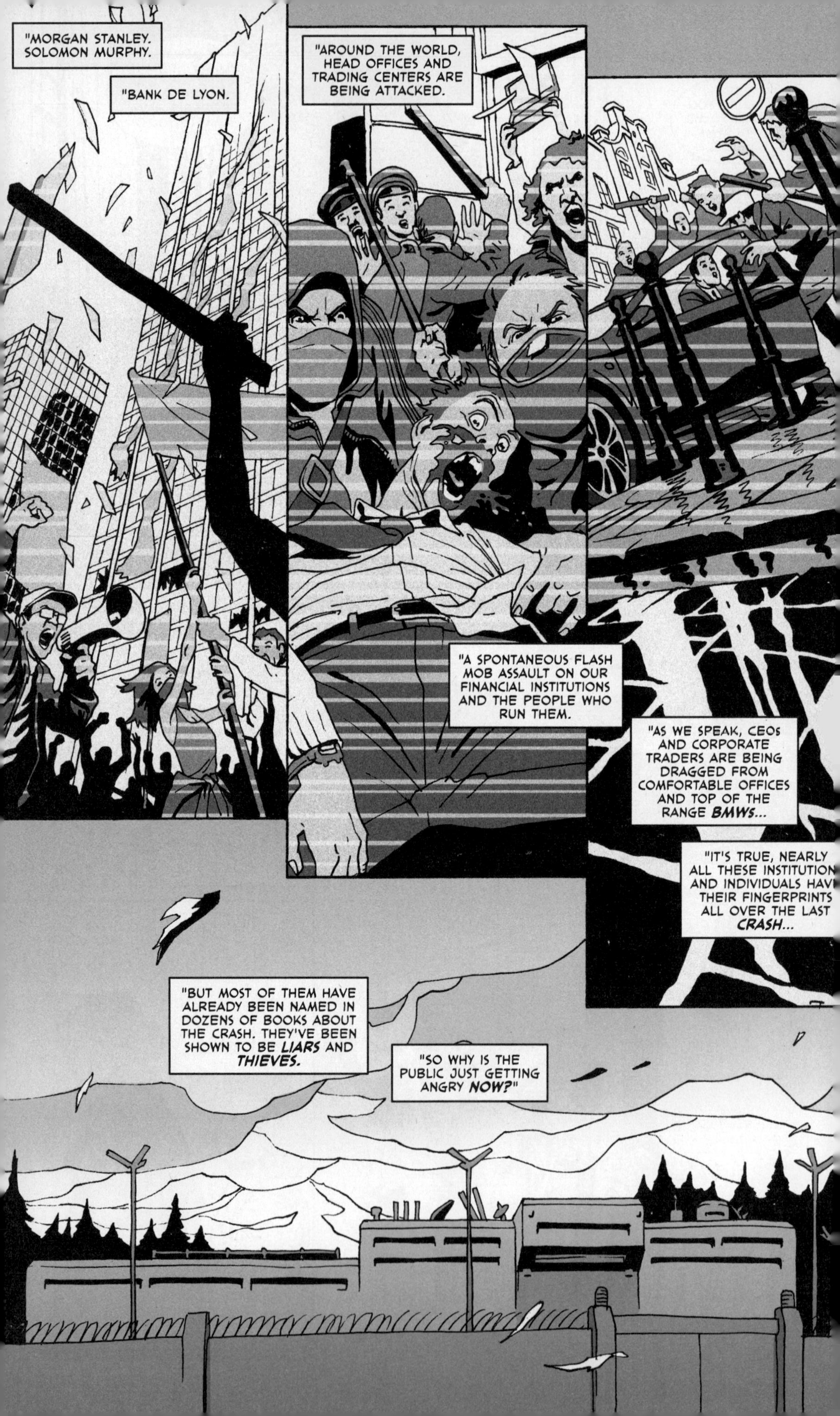
"MORGAN STANLEY. SOLOMON MURPHY.
"BANK DE LYON.
"AROUND THE WORLD, HEAD OFFICES AND TRADING CENTERS ARE BEING ATTACKED.
"A SPONTANEOUS FLASH MOB ASSAULT ON OUR FINANCIAL INSTITUTIONS AND THE PEOPLE WHO RUN THEM.
"AS WE SPEAK, CEOs AND CORPORATE TRADERS ARE BEING DRAGGED FROM COMFORTABLE OFFICES AND TOP OF THE RANGE BMWs...
"IT'S TRUE, NEARLY ALL THESE INSTITUTION AND INDIVIDUALS HAV THEIR FINGERPRINTS ALL OVER THE LAST CRASH...
"BUT MOST OF THEM HAVE ALREADY BEEN NAMED IN DOZENS OF BOOKS ABOUT THE CRASH. THEY'VE BEEN SHOWN TO BE LIARS AND THIEVES.
"SO WHY IS THE PUBLIC JUST GETTING ANGRY NOW?"

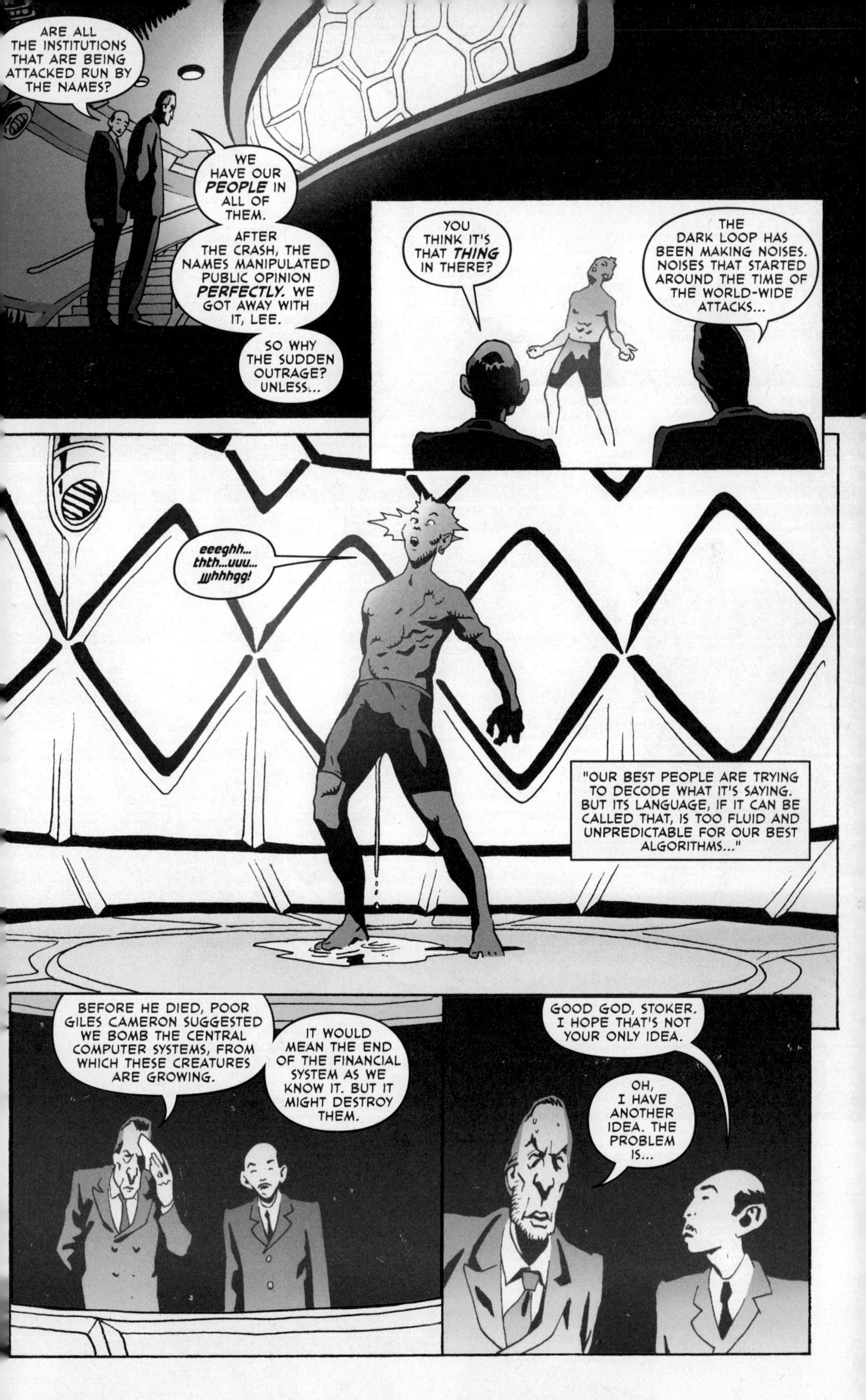
ARE ALL THE INSTITUTIONS THAT ARE BEING ATTACKED RUN BY THE NAMES?
WE HAVE OUR PEOPLE IN ALL OF THEM.
AFTER THE CRASH, THE NAMES MANIPULATED PUBLIC OPINION PERFECTLY. WE GOT AWAY WITH IT, LEE.
SO WHY THE SUDDEN OUTRAGE? UNLESS...
YOU THINK IT'S THAT THING IN THERE?
THE DARK LOOP HAS BEEN MAKING NOISES. NOISES THAT STARTED AROUND THE TIME OF THE WORLD-WIDE ATTACKS...
eeeghh... thth...uuu... jjjhhhgg!
"OUR BEST PEOPLE ARE TRYING TO DECODE WHAT IT'S SAYING. BUT ITS LANGUAGE, IF IT CAN BE CALLED THAT, IS TOO FLUID AND UNPREDICTABLE FOR OUR BEST ALGORITHMS..."
BEFORE HE DIED, POOR GILES CAMERON SUGGESTED WE BOMB THE CENTRAL COMPUTER SYSTEMS, FROM WHICH THESE CREATURES ARE GROWING.
IT WOULD MEAN THE END OF THE FINANCIAL SYSTEM AS WE KNOW IT. BUT IT MIGHT DESTROY THEM.
GOOD GOD, STOKER. I HOPE THAT'S NOT YOUR ONLY IDEA.
OH, I HAVE ANOTHER IDEA. THE PROBLEM IS...

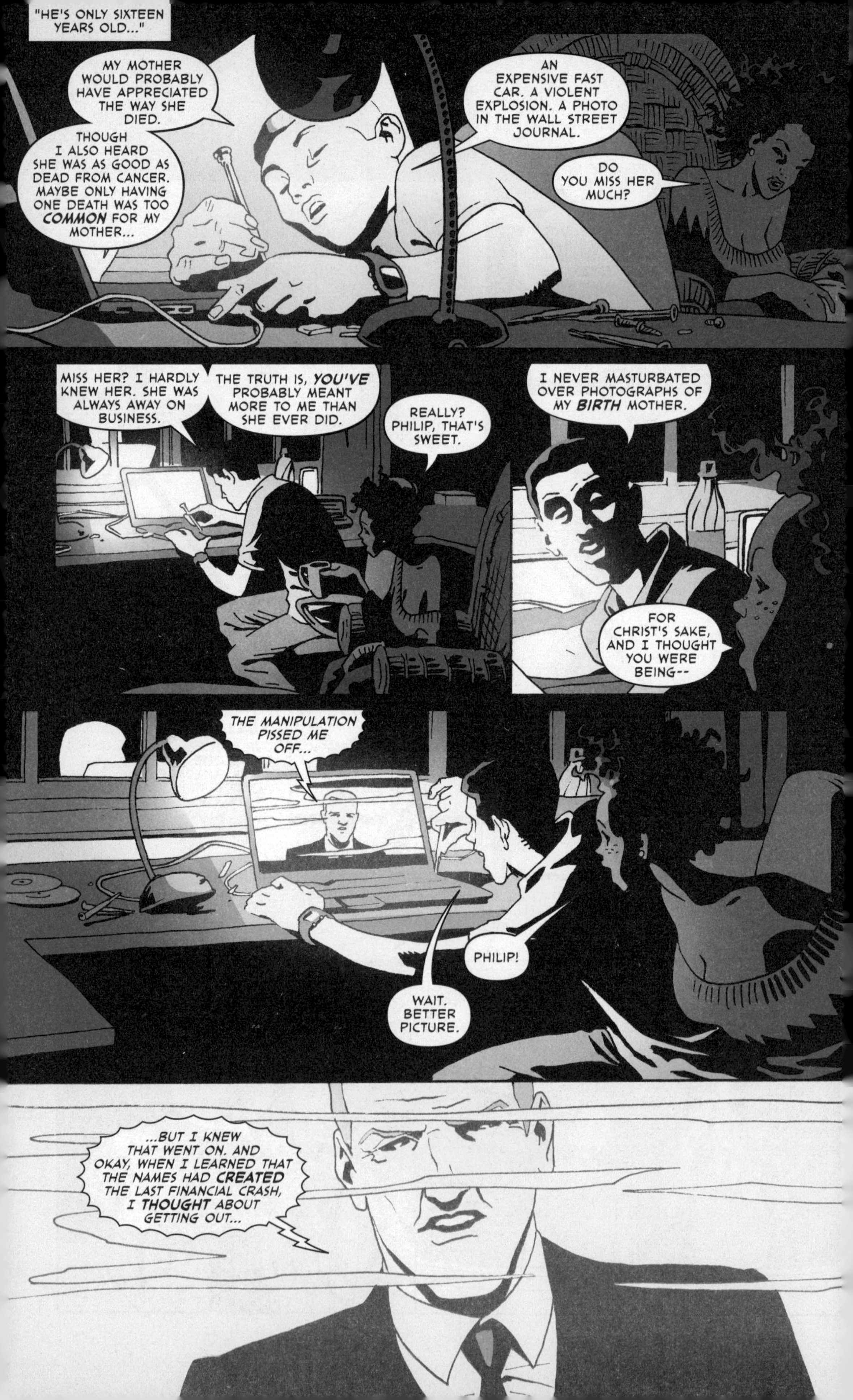
"HE'S ONLY SIXTEEN YEARS OLD..."
MY MOTHER WOULD PROBABLY HAVE APPRECIATED THE WAY SHE DIED.
THOUGH I ALSO HEARD SHE WAS AS GOOD AS DEAD FROM CANCER. MAYBE ONLY HAVING ONE DEATH WAS TOO COMMON FOR MY MOTHER...
AN EXPENSIVE FAST CAR. A VIOLENT EXPLOSION. A PHOTO IN THE WALL STREET JOURNAL.
DO YOU MISS HER MUCH?
MISS HER? I HARDLY KNEW HER. SHE WAS ALWAYS AWAY ON BUSINESS.
THE TRUTH IS, YOU'VE PROBABLY MEANT MORE TO ME THAN SHE EVER DID.
REALLY? PHILIP, THAT'S SWEET.
I NEVER MASTURBATED OVER PHOTOGRAPHS OF MY BIRTH MOTHER.
FOR CHRIST'S SAKE, AND I THOUGHT YOU WERE BEING--
THE MANIPULATION PISSED ME OFF...
PHILIP!
WAIT. BETTER PICTURE.
...BUT I KNEW THAT WENT ON. AND OKAY, WHEN I LEARNED THAT THE NAMES HAD CREATED THE LAST FINANCIAL CRASH, I THOUGHT ABOUT GETTING OUT...

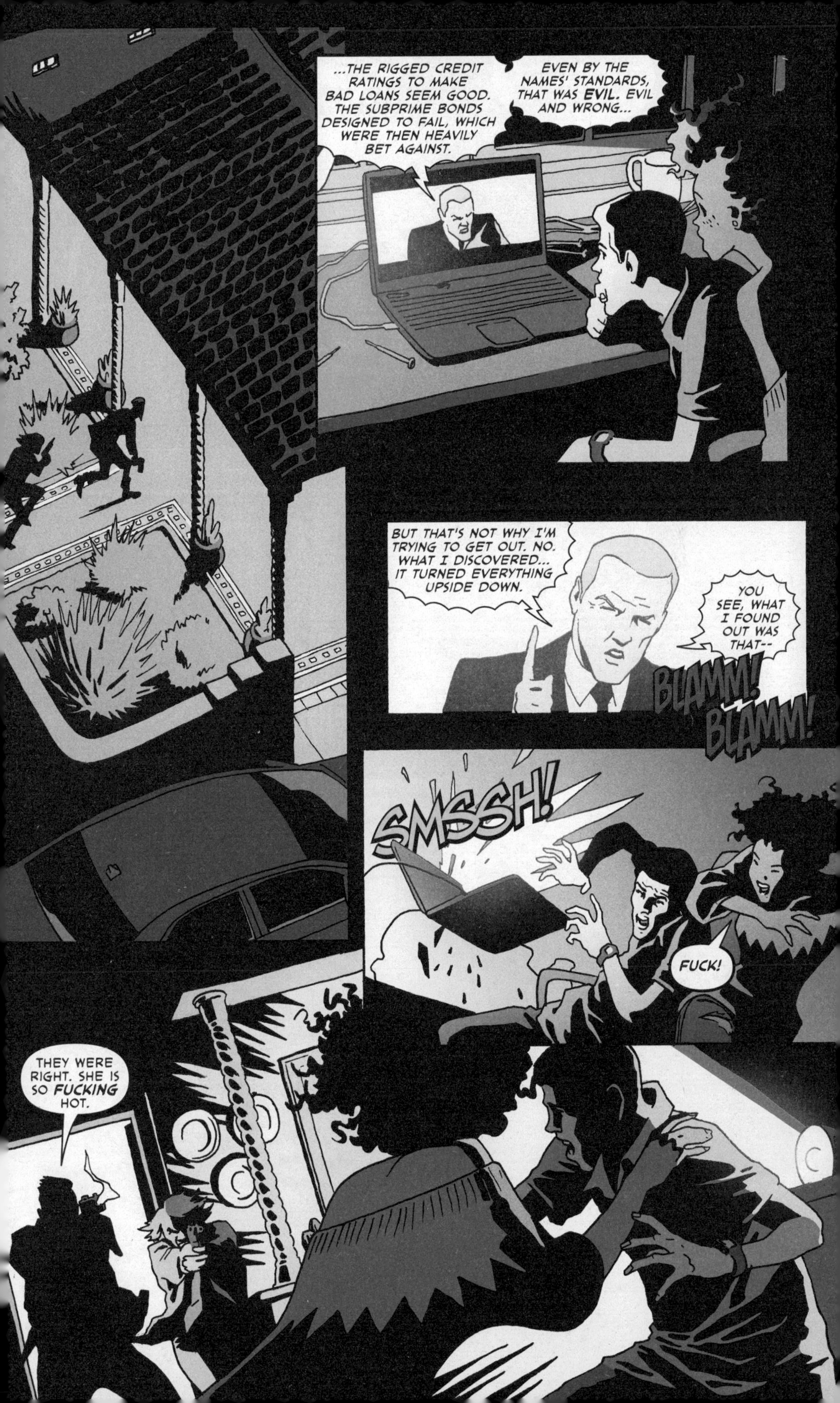
...THE RIGGED CREDIT RATINGS TO MAKE BAD LOANS SEEM GOOD. THE SUBPRIME BONDS DESIGNED TO FAIL, WHICH WERE THEN HEAVILY BET AGAINST.
EVEN BY THE NAMES' STANDARDS, THAT WAS EVIL. EVIL AND WRONG...
BUT THAT'S NOT WHY I'M TRYING TO GET OUT. NO. WHAT I DISCOVERED... IT TURNED EVERYTHING UPSIDE DOWN.
YOU SEE, WHAT I FOUND OUT WAS THAT--
BLAMM! BLAMM!
SMSSH!
FUCK!
THEY WERE RIGHT. SHE IS SO FUCKING HOT.

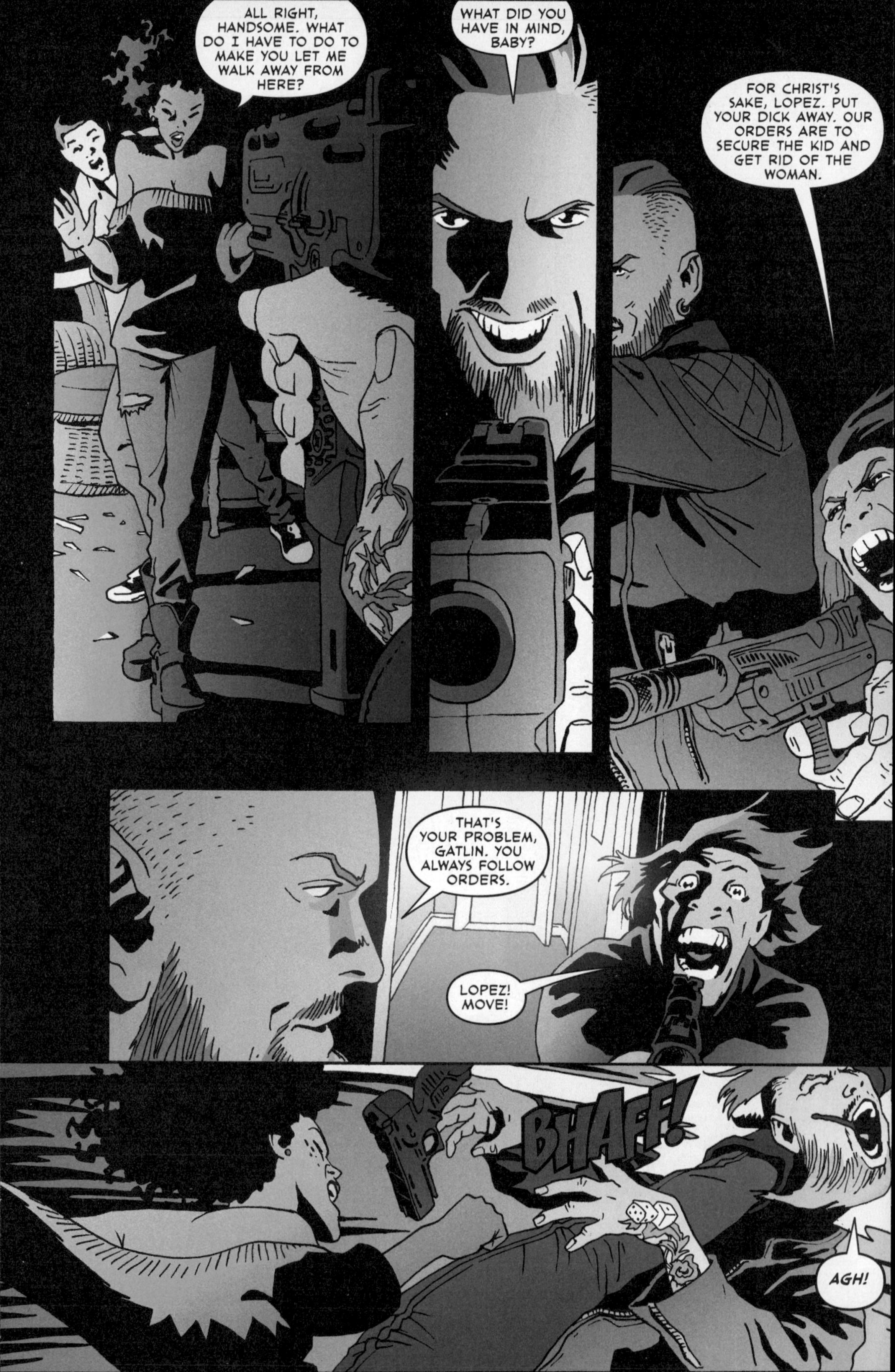
ALL RIGHT, HANDSOME. WHAT DO I HAVE TO DO TO MAKE YOU LET ME WALK AWAY FROM HERE?
WHAT DID YOU HAVE IN MIND, BABY?
FOR CHRIST'S SAKE, LOPEZ. PUT YOUR DICK AWAY. OUR ORDERS ARE TO SECURE THE KID AND GET RID OF THE WOMAN.
THAT'S YOUR PROBLEM, GATLIN. YOU ALWAYS FOLLOW ORDERS.
LOPEZ! MOVE!
BHAFF!
AGH!

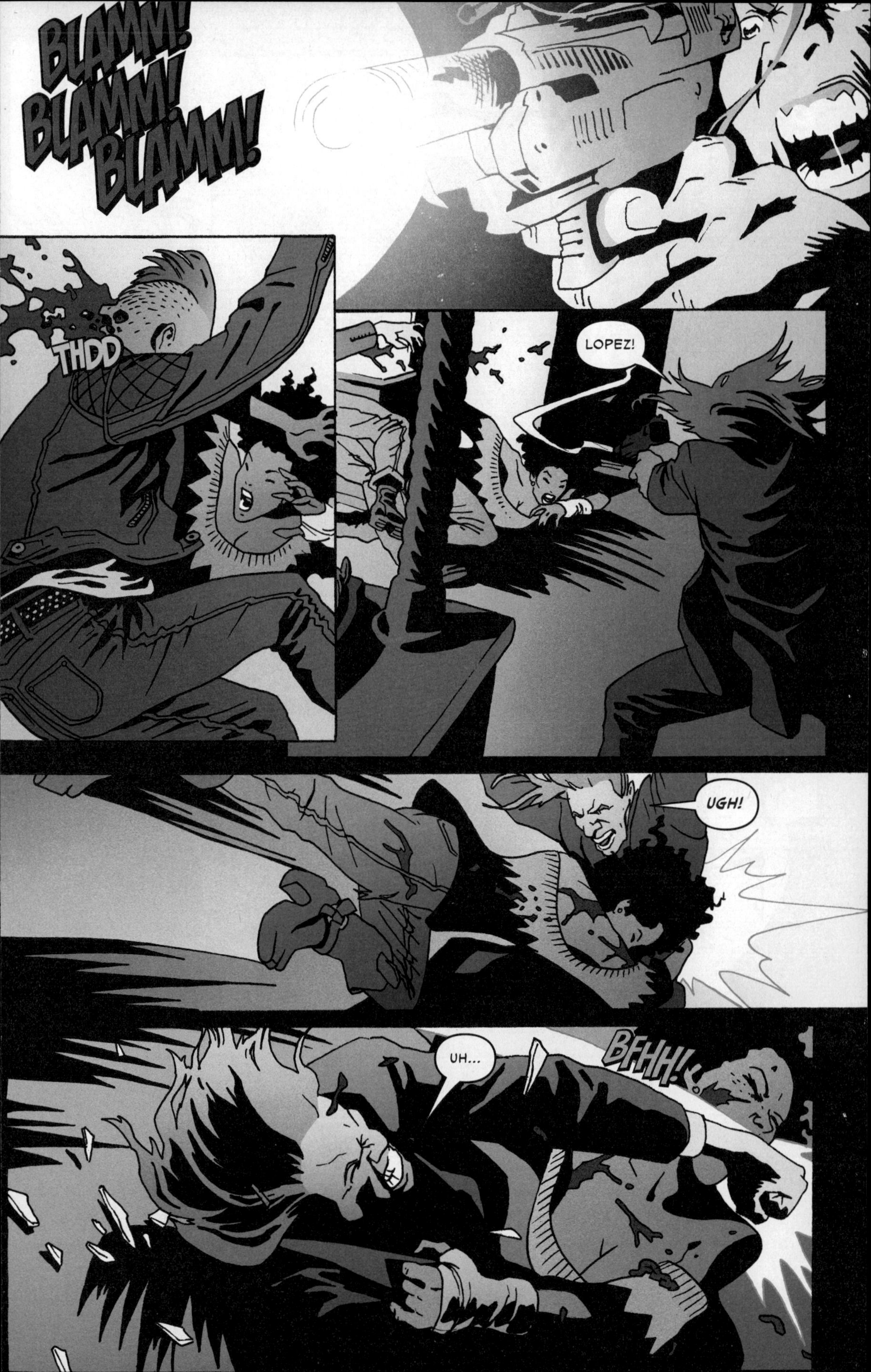
BLAMM! BLAMM! BLAMM!
THDD
LOPEZ!
UGH!
UH...
BFHH!

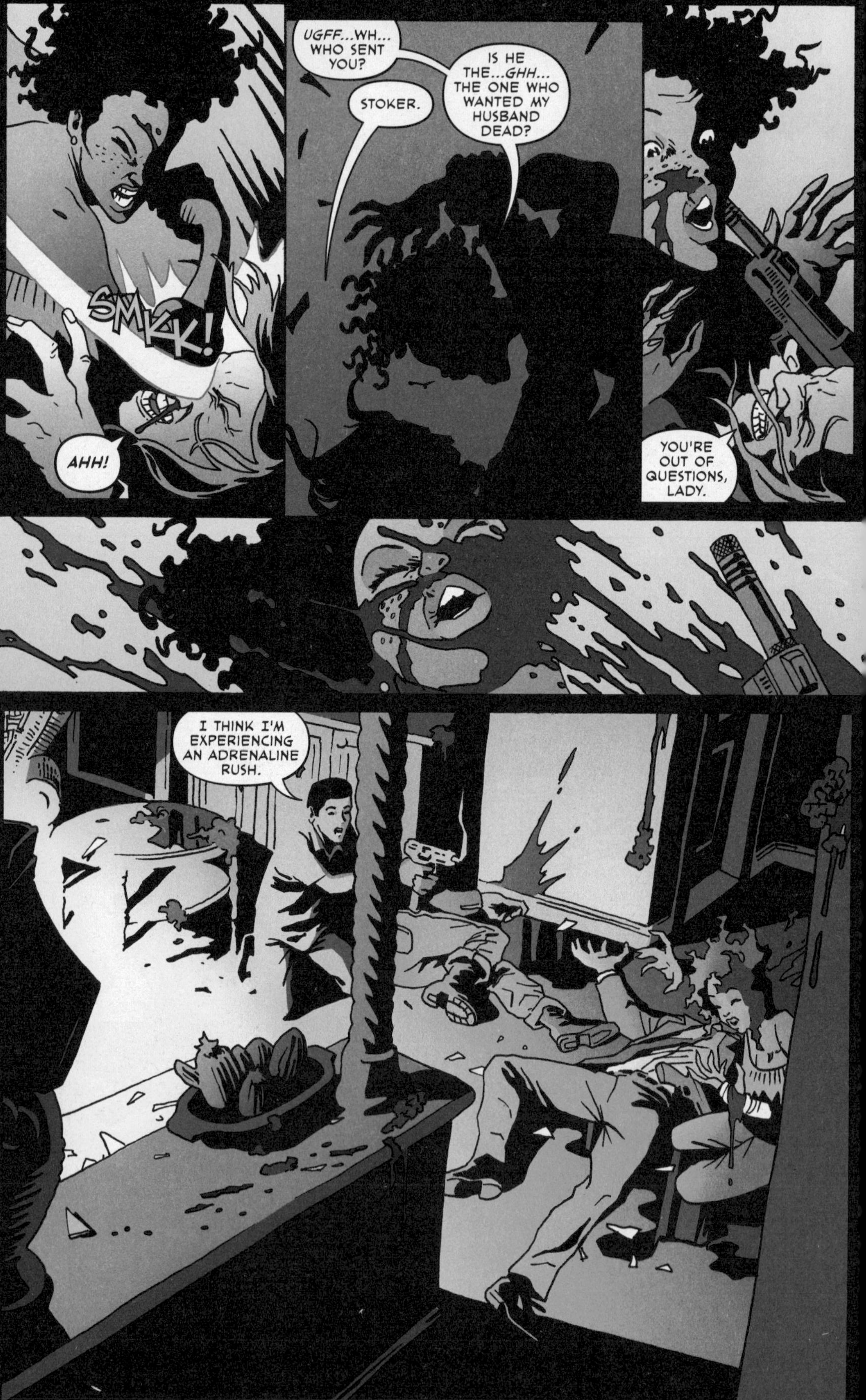
SMKAK!
AHH!
UGFF...WH... WHO SENT YOU?
STOKER.
IS HE THE...GHH... THE ONE WHO WANTED MY HUSBAND DEAD?
YOU'RE OUT OF QUESTIONS, LADY.
I THINK I'M EXPERIENCING AN ADRENALINE RUSH.

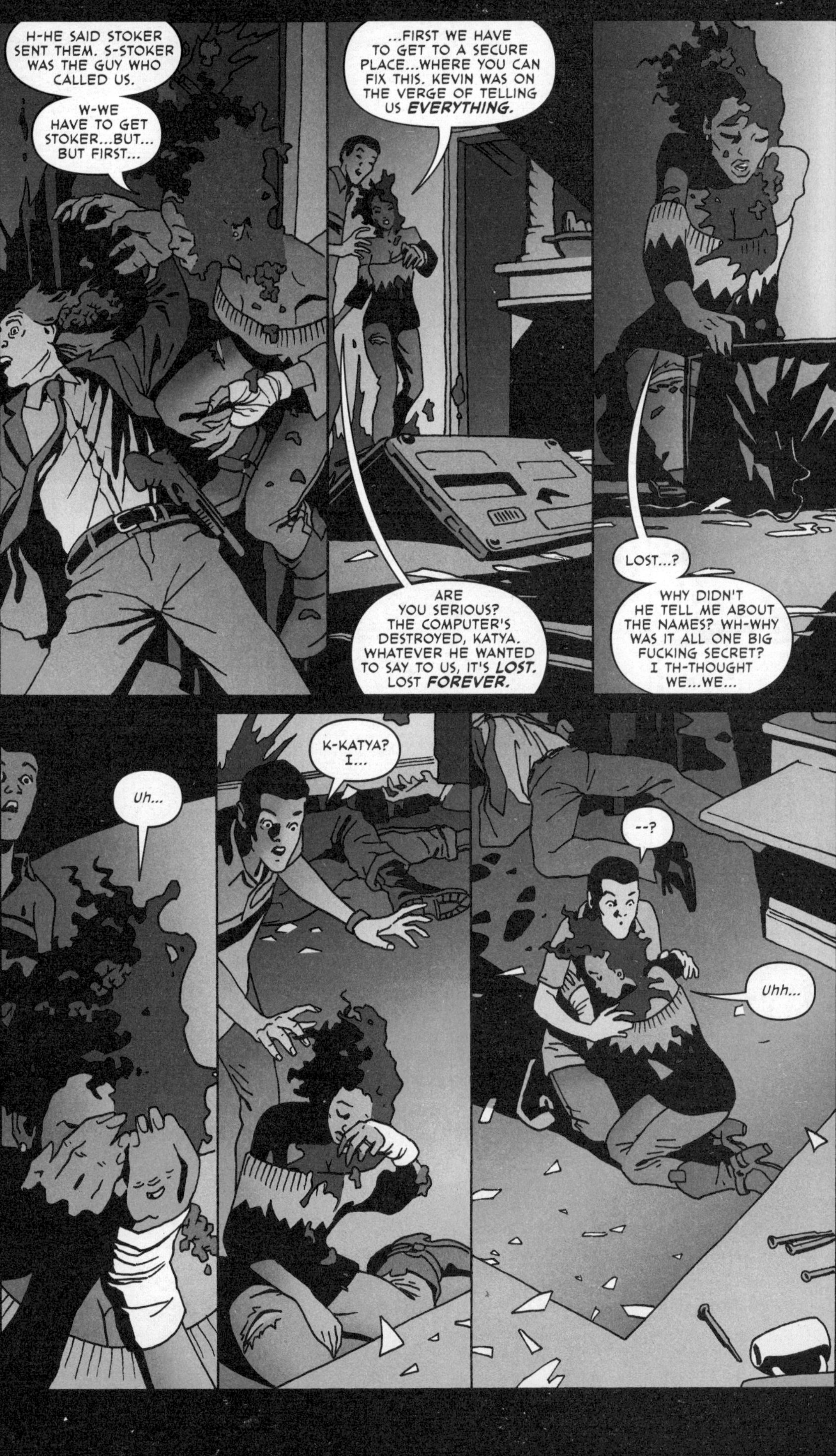
H-HE SAID STOKER SENT THEM. S-STOKER WAS THE GUY WHO CALLED US.
W-WE HAVE TO GET STOKER...BUT... BUT FIRST...
...FIRST WE HAVE TO GET TO A SECURE PLACE...WHERE YOU CAN FIX THIS. KEVIN WAS ON THE VERGE OF TELLING US *EVERYTHING.*
ARE YOU SERIOUS? THE COMPUTER'S DESTROYED, KATYA. WHATEVER HE WANTED TO SAY TO US, IT'S *LOST.* LOST *FOREVER.*
LOST...?
WHY DIDN'T HE TELL ME ABOUT THE NAMES? WH-WHY WAS IT ALL ONE BIG FUCKING SECRET? I TH-THOUGHT WE...WE...
Uh...
K-KATYA? I...
--?
Uhh...

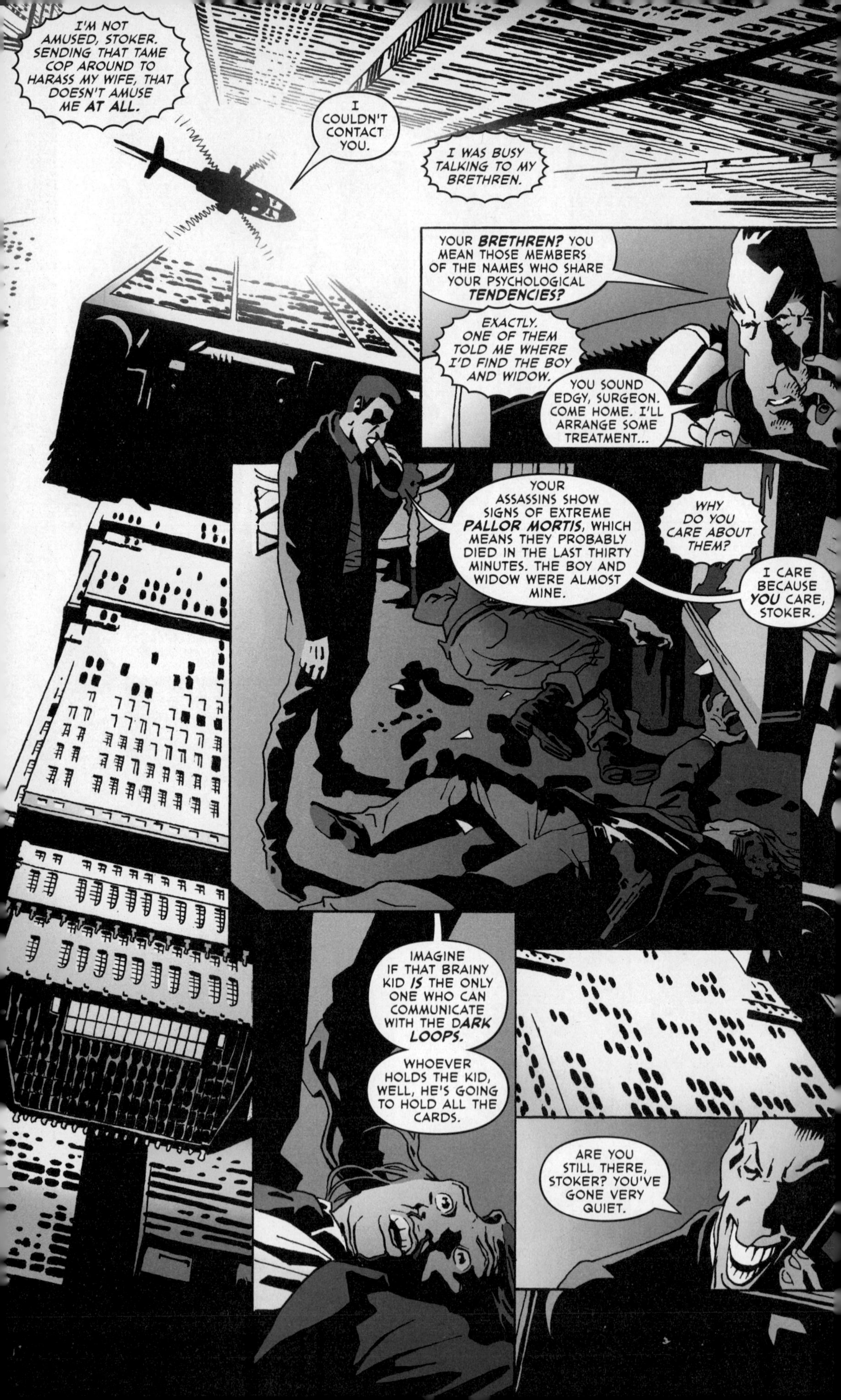
I'M NOT AMUSED, STOKER. SENDING THAT TAME COP AROUND TO HARASS MY WIFE, THAT DOESN'T AMUSE ME AT ALL.
I COULDN'T CONTACT YOU.
I WAS BUSY TALKING TO MY BRETHREN.
YOUR BRETHREN? YOU MEAN THOSE MEMBERS OF THE NAMES WHO SHARE YOUR PSYCHOLOGICAL TENDENCIES?
EXACTLY. ONE OF THEM TOLD ME WHERE I'D FIND THE BOY AND WIDOW.
YOU SOUND EDGY, SURGEON. COME HOME. I'LL ARRANGE SOME TREATMENT...
YOUR ASSASSINS SHOW SIGNS OF EXTREME PALLOR MORTIS, WHICH MEANS THEY PROBABLY DIED IN THE LAST THIRTY MINUTES. THE BOY AND WIDOW WERE ALMOST MINE.
WHY DO YOU CARE ABOUT THEM?
I CARE BECAUSE YOU CARE, STOKER.
IMAGINE IF THAT BRAINY KID IS THE ONLY ONE WHO CAN COMMUNICATE WITH THE DARK LOOPS.
WHOEVER HOLDS THE KID, WELL, HE'S GOING TO HOLD ALL THE CARDS.
ARE YOU STILL THERE, STOKER? YOU'VE GONE VERY QUIET.

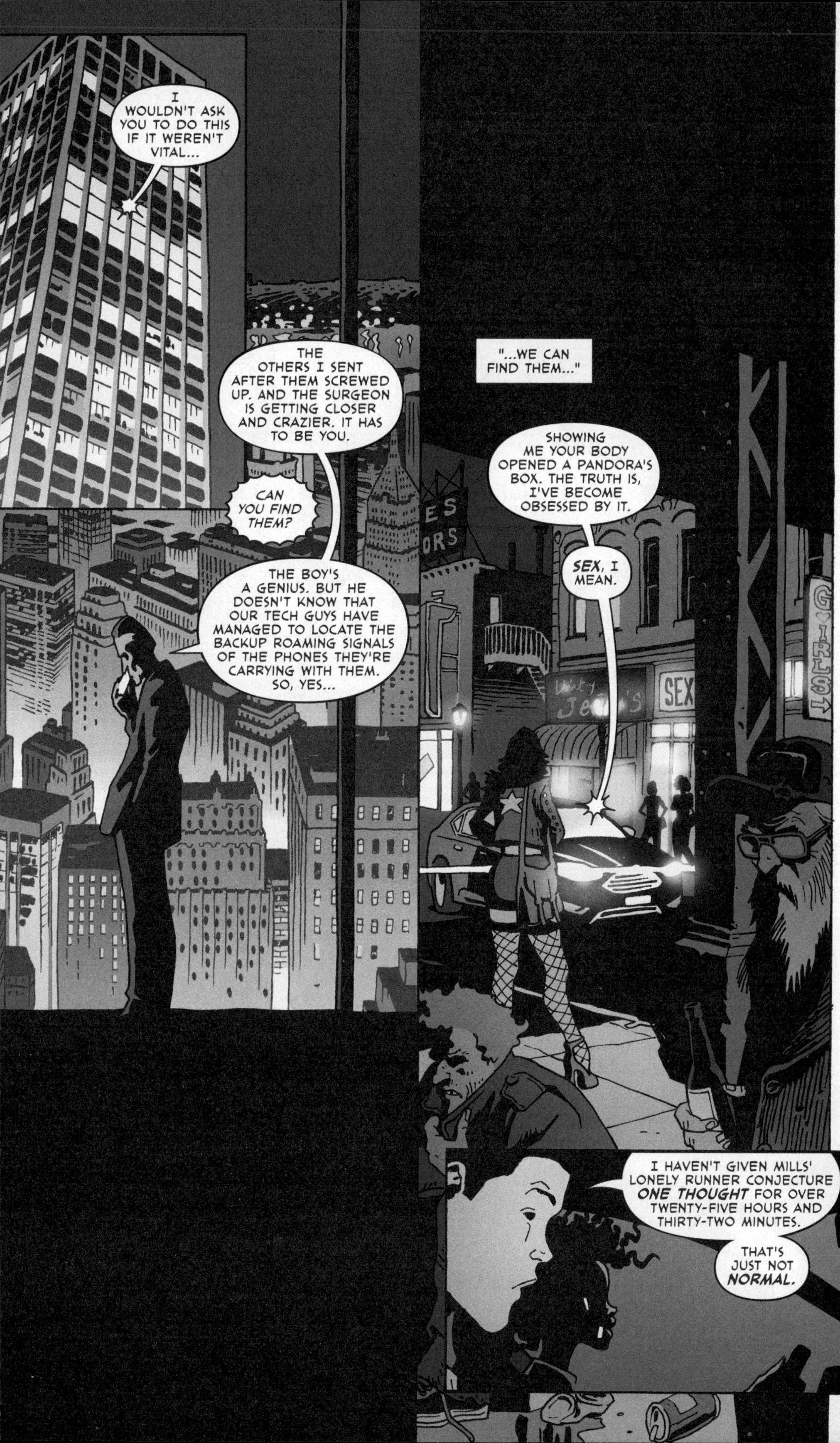
I WOULDN'T ASK YOU TO DO THIS IF IT WEREN'T VITAL...
THE OTHERS I SENT AFTER THEM SCREWED UP. AND THE SURGEON IS GETTING CLOSER AND CRAZIER. IT HAS TO BE YOU.
CAN YOU FIND THEM?
THE BOY'S A GENIUS. BUT HE DOESN'T KNOW THAT OUR TECH GUYS HAVE MANAGED TO LOCATE THE BACKUP ROAMING SIGNALS OF THE PHONES THEY'RE CARRYING WITH THEM. SO, YES...
"...WE CAN FIND THEM..."
SHOWING ME YOUR BODY OPENED A PANDORA'S BOX. THE TRUTH IS, I'VE BECOME OBSESSED BY IT.
SEX, I MEAN.
SEX
GIRLS
I HAVEN'T GIVEN MILLS' LONELY RUNNER CONJECTURE *ONE THOUGHT* FOR OVER TWENTY-FIVE HOURS AND THIRTY-TWO MINUTES.
THAT'S JUST NOT *NORMAL.*

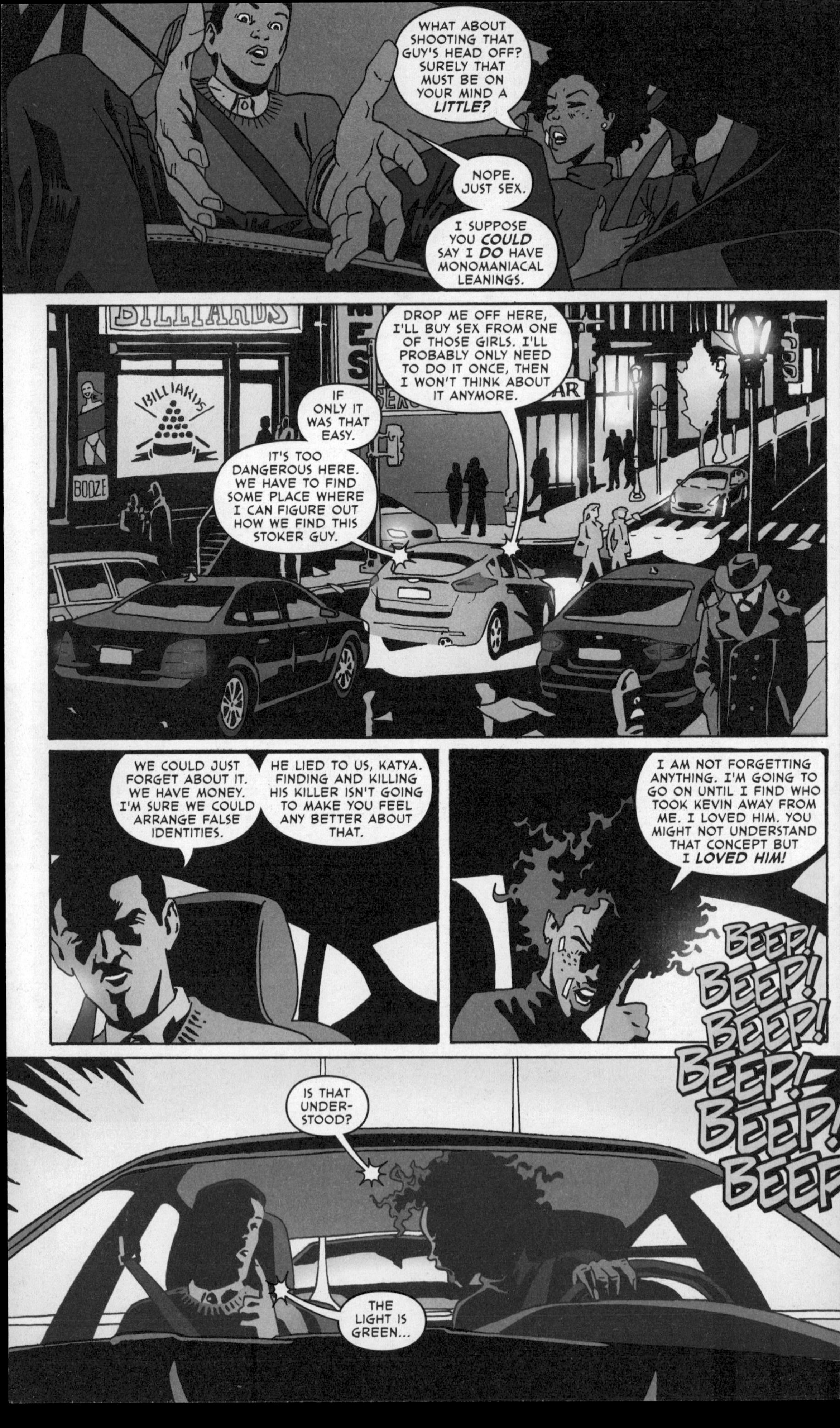
WHAT ABOUT SHOOTING THAT GUY'S HEAD OFF? SURELY THAT MUST BE ON YOUR MIND A *LITTLE?*
NOPE. JUST SEX.
I SUPPOSE YOU *COULD* SAY I *DO* HAVE MONOMANIACAL LEANINGS.
BILLIARDS
BILLIARDS
BOOZE
DROP ME OFF HERE, I'LL BUY SEX FROM ONE OF THOSE GIRLS. I'LL PROBABLY ONLY NEED TO DO IT ONCE, THEN I WON'T THINK ABOUT IT ANYMORE.
IF ONLY IT WAS THAT EASY.
IT'S TOO DANGEROUS HERE. WE HAVE TO FIND SOME PLACE WHERE I CAN FIGURE OUT HOW WE FIND THIS STOKER GUY.
WE COULD JUST FORGET ABOUT IT. WE HAVE MONEY. I'M SURE WE COULD ARRANGE FALSE IDENTITIES.
HE LIED TO US, KATYA. FINDING AND KILLING HIS KILLER ISN'T GOING TO MAKE YOU FEEL ANY BETTER ABOUT THAT.
I AM NOT FORGETTING ANYTHING. I'M GOING TO GO ON UNTIL I FIND WHO TOOK KEVIN AWAY FROM ME. I LOVED HIM. YOU MIGHT NOT UNDERSTAND THAT CONCEPT BUT I *LOVED HIM!*
BEEP! BEEP! BEEP! BEEP! BEEP! BEEP
IS THAT UNDER-STOOD?
THE LIGHT IS GREEN...

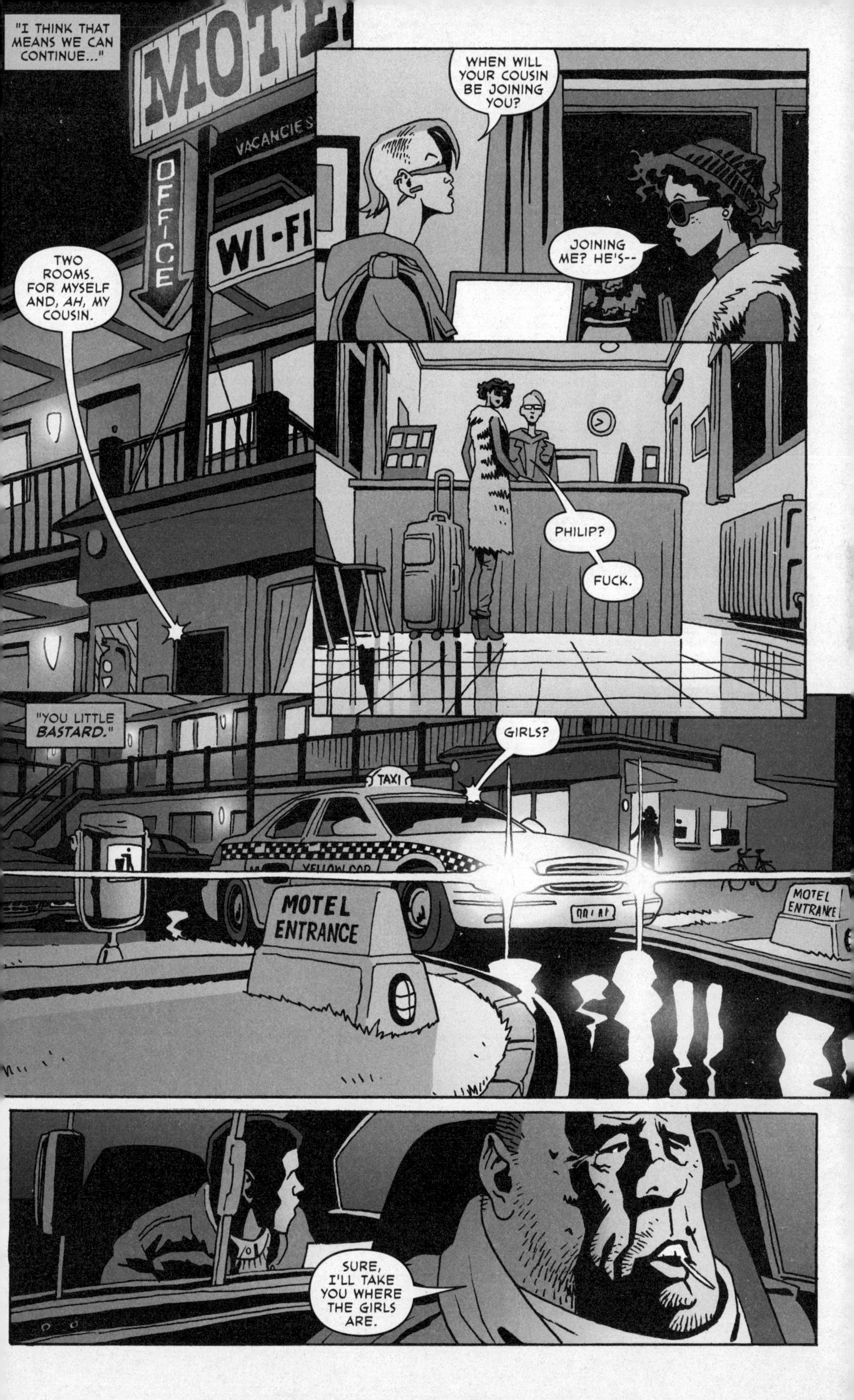
"I THINK THAT MEANS WE CAN CONTINUE..."
MOTE
VACANCIES
OFFICE
WI-FI
TWO ROOMS. FOR MYSELF AND, *AH,* MY COUSIN.
WHEN WILL YOUR COUSIN BE JOINING YOU?
JOINING ME? HE'S--
PHILIP?
FUCK.
"YOU LITTLE *BASTARD.*"
GIRLS?
TAXI
MOTEL ENTRANCE
MOTEL ENTRANCE
SURE, I'LL TAKE YOU WHERE THE GIRLS ARE.

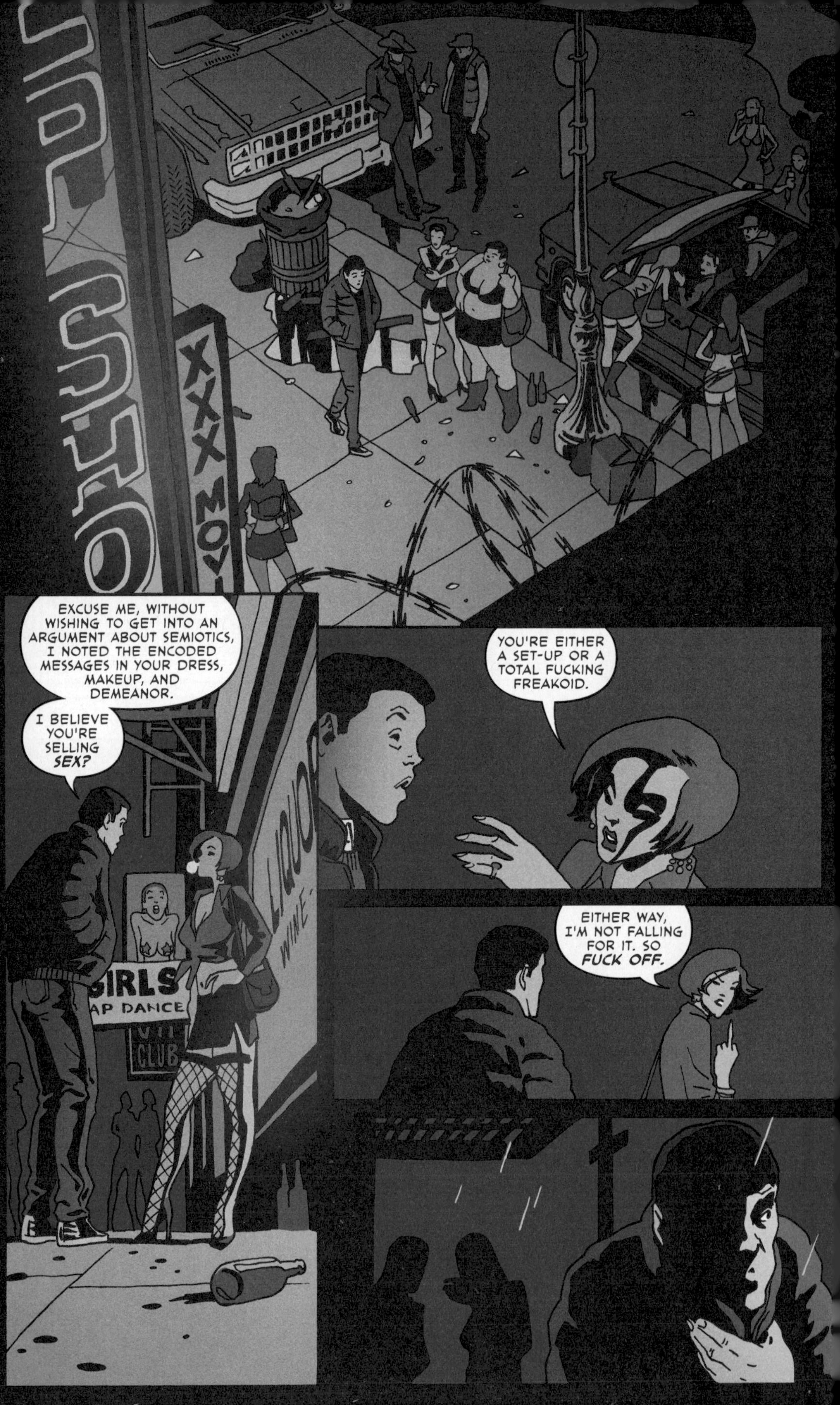
XXX MOV
EXCUSE ME, WITHOUT WISHING TO GET INTO AN ARGUMENT ABOUT SEMIOTICS, I NOTED THE ENCODED MESSAGES IN YOUR DRESS, MAKEUP, AND DEMEANOR.
I BELIEVE YOU'RE SELLING *SEX?*
GIRLS
AP DANCE
CLUB
LIQUO
WINE
YOU'RE EITHER A SET-UP OR A TOTAL FUCKING FREAKOID.
EITHER WAY, I'M NOT FALLING FOR IT. SO *FUCK OFF.*

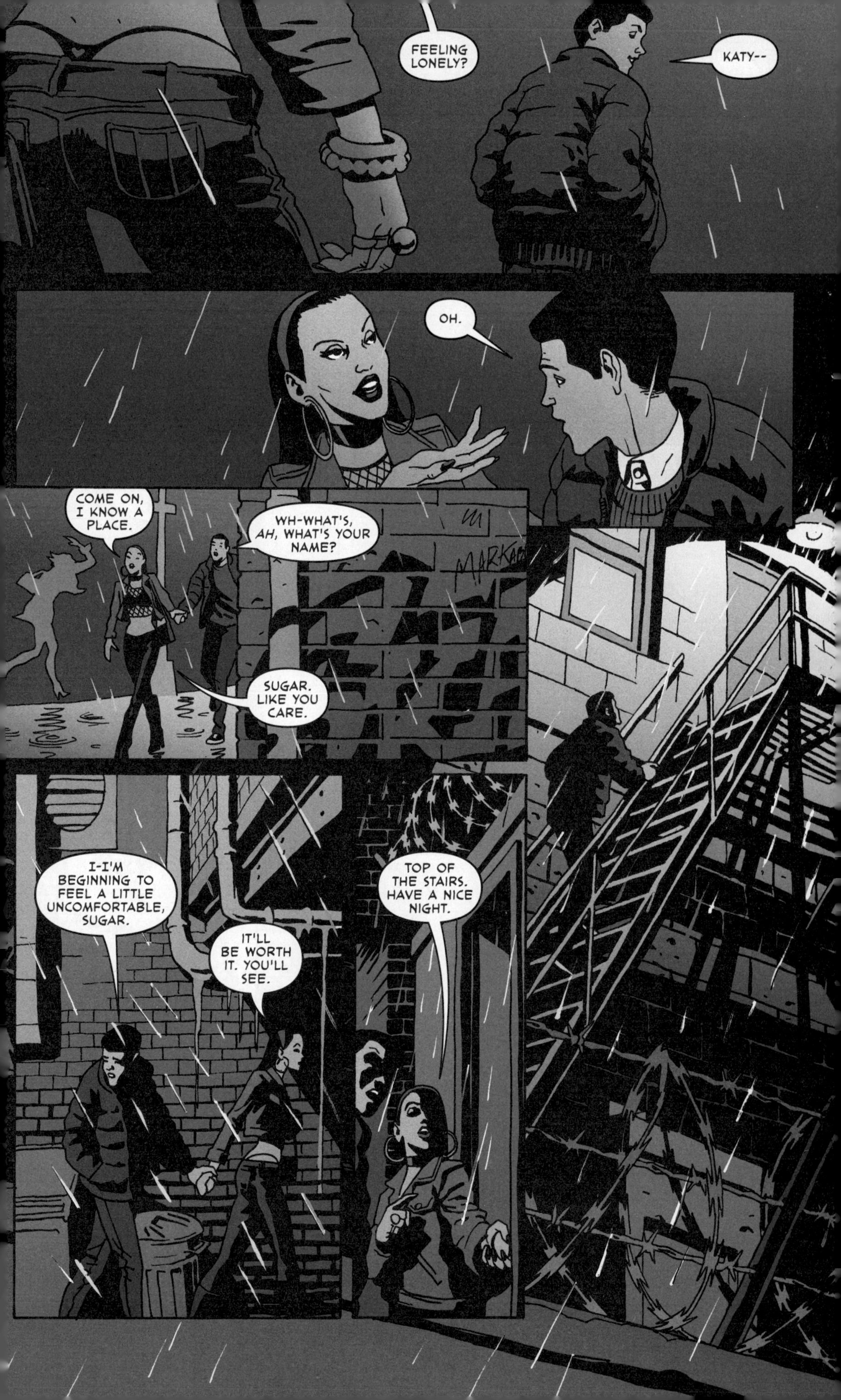
FEELING LONELY?
KATY--
OH.
COME ON, I KNOW A PLACE.
WH-WHAT'S, *AH*, WHAT'S YOUR NAME?
SUGAR. LIKE YOU CARE.
I-I'M BEGINNING TO FEEL A LITTLE UNCOMFORTABLE, SUGAR.
IT'LL BE WORTH IT. YOU'LL SEE.
TOP OF THE STAIRS. HAVE A NICE NIGHT.

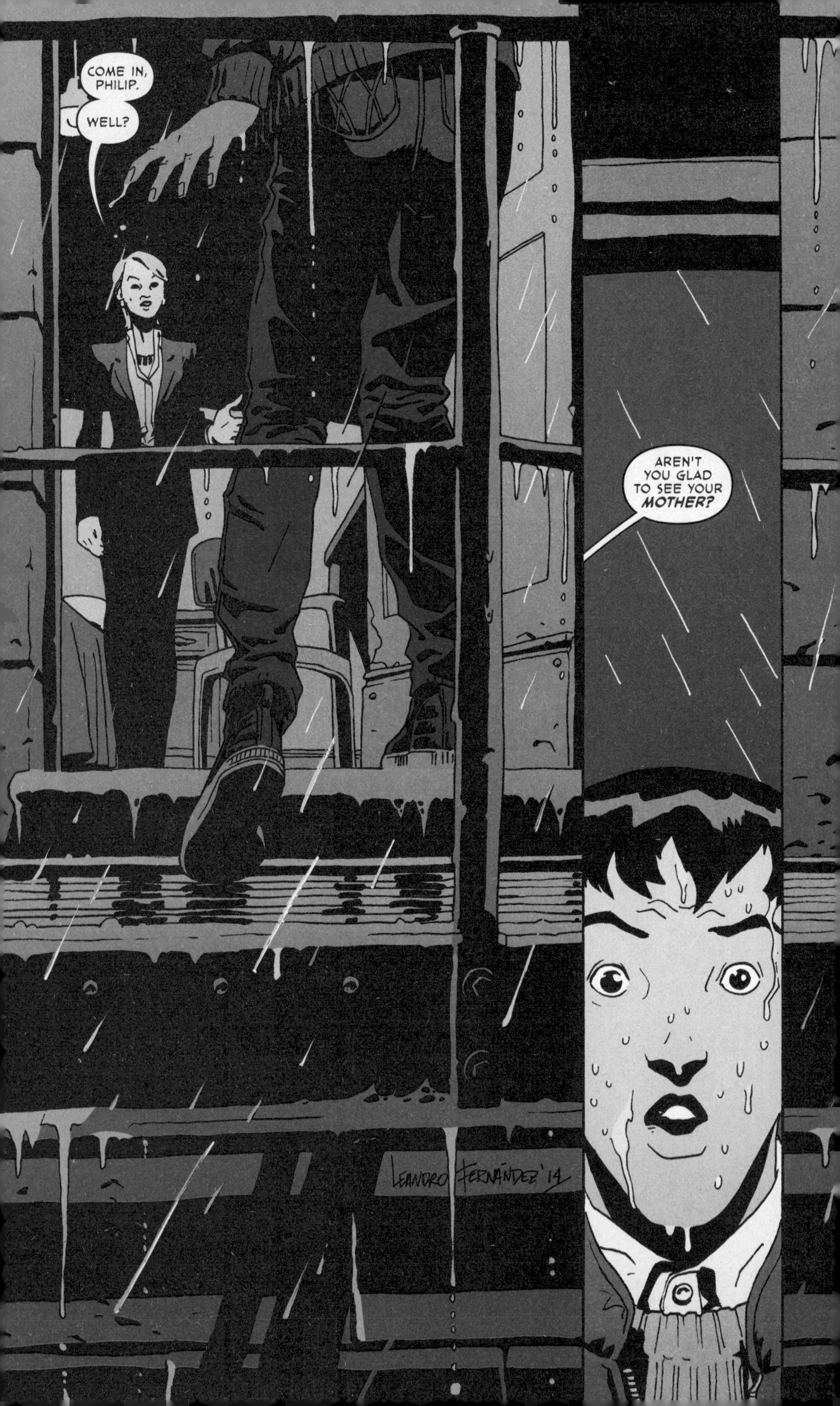
COME IN, PHILIP.
WELL?
AREN'T YOU GLAD TO SEE YOUR *MOTHER?*
LEANDRO FERNÁNDEZ '14

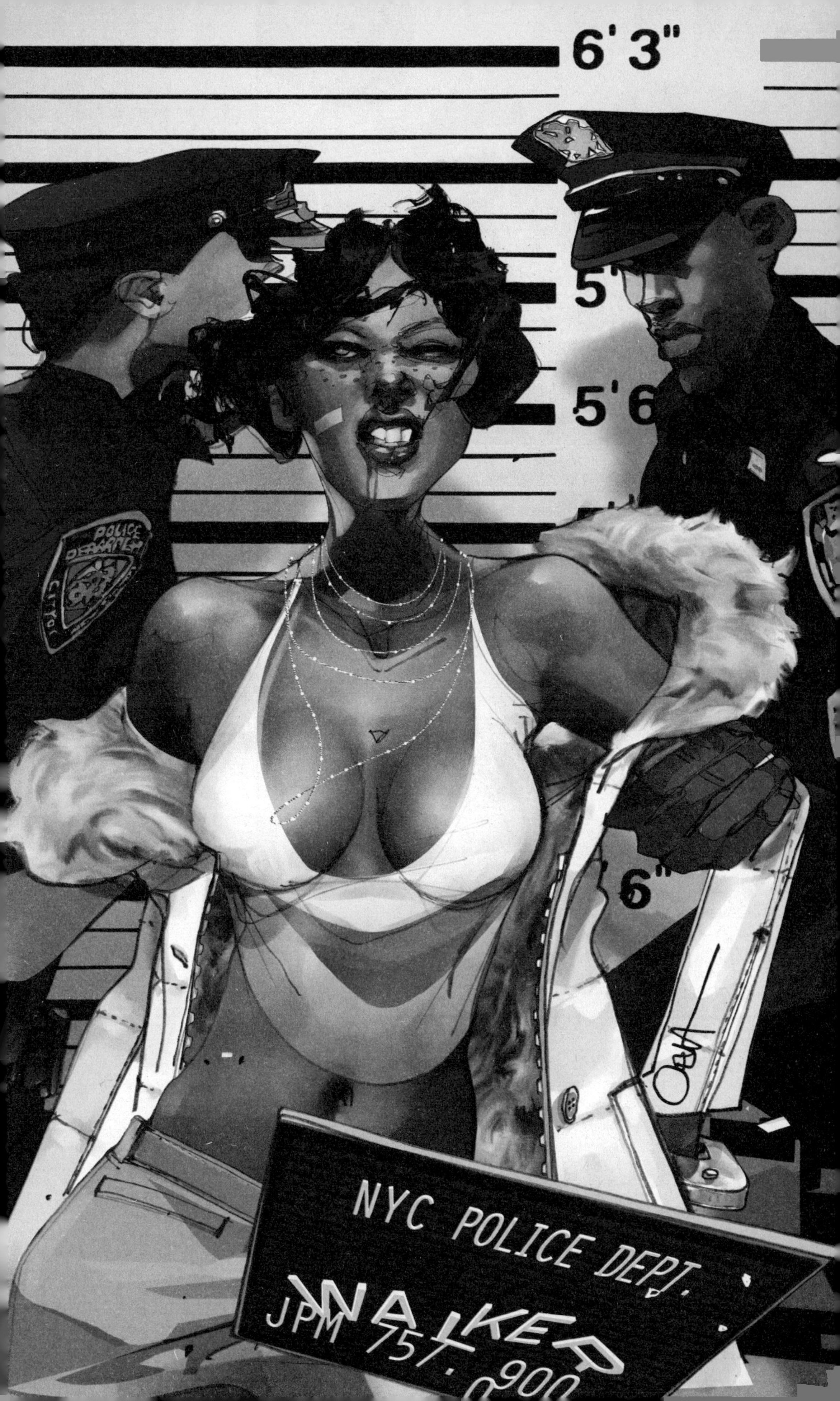
6'3"
5'
5'6
6"
POLICE
NYC POLICE DEPT.

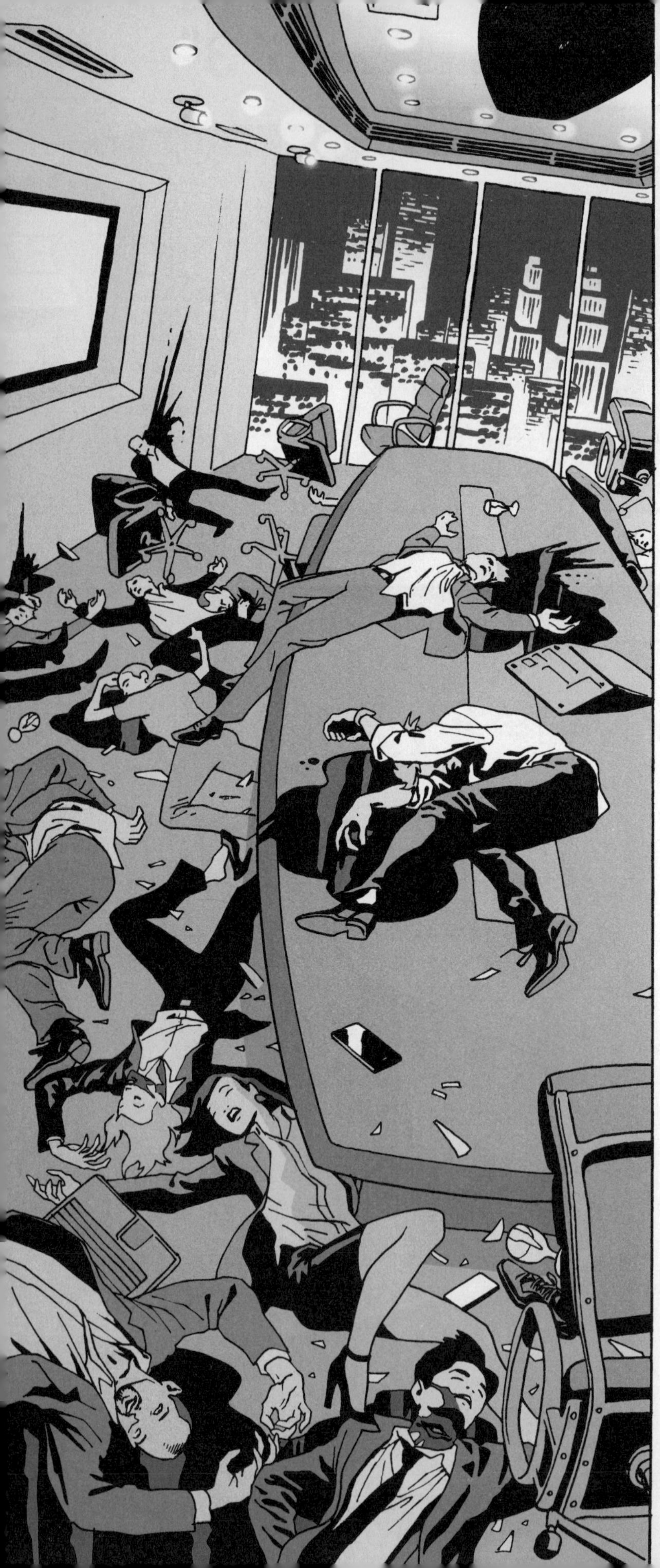
"LAST NIGHT IN LA JOLLA WAS BRUTAL, ONLY WORD FOR IT.
"*SOMETHING* GATE-CRASHED A SECRET MEETING OF SOME OF AMERICA'S MOST HIGHLY-PAID HEDGE FUND MANAGERS, ELECTRONIC TRADERS, QUANTITATIVE ANALYSTS, AND STOCHASTIC CALCULUS GURUS.
"THIRTY MINUTES LATER, ALL OF THE ABOVE WERE *DEAD.*
"THEY'D KILLED EACH OTHER.
"CORRECTION..."

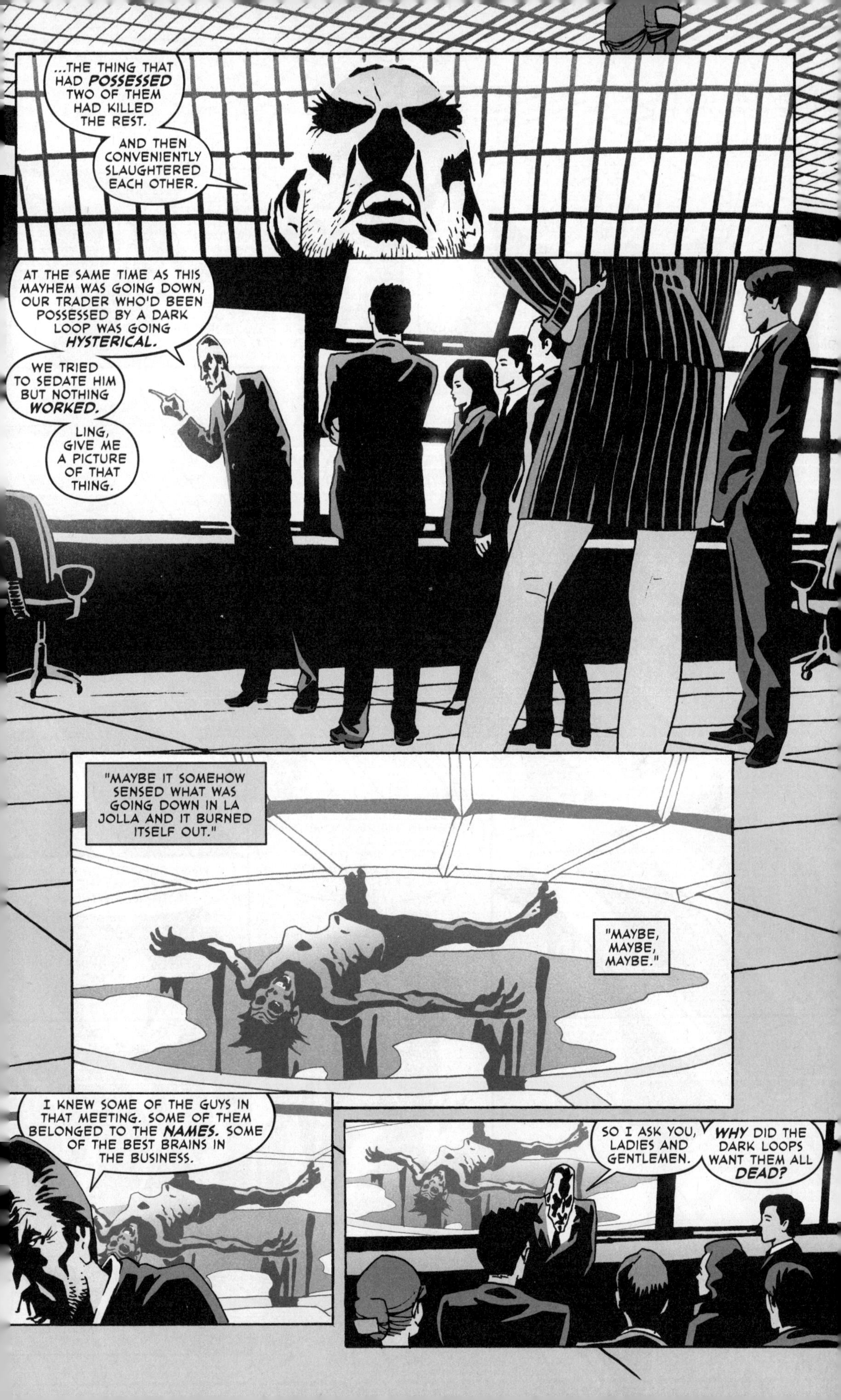
...THE THING THAT HAD POSSESSED TWO OF THEM HAD KILLED THE REST.
AND THEN CONVENIENTLY SLAUGHTERED EACH OTHER.
AT THE SAME TIME AS THIS MAYHEM WAS GOING DOWN, OUR TRADER WHO'D BEEN POSSESSED BY A DARK LOOP WAS GOING HYSTERICAL.
WE TRIED TO SEDATE HIM BUT NOTHING WORKED.
LING, GIVE ME A PICTURE OF THAT THING.
"MAYBE IT SOMEHOW SENSED WHAT WAS GOING DOWN IN LA JOLLA AND IT BURNED ITSELF OUT."
"MAYBE, MAYBE, MAYBE."
I KNEW SOME OF THE GUYS IN THAT MEETING. SOME OF THEM BELONGED TO THE NAMES. SOME OF THE BEST BRAINS IN THE BUSINESS.
SO I ASK YOU, LADIES AND GENTLEMEN.
WHY DID THE DARK LOOPS WANT THEM ALL DEAD?

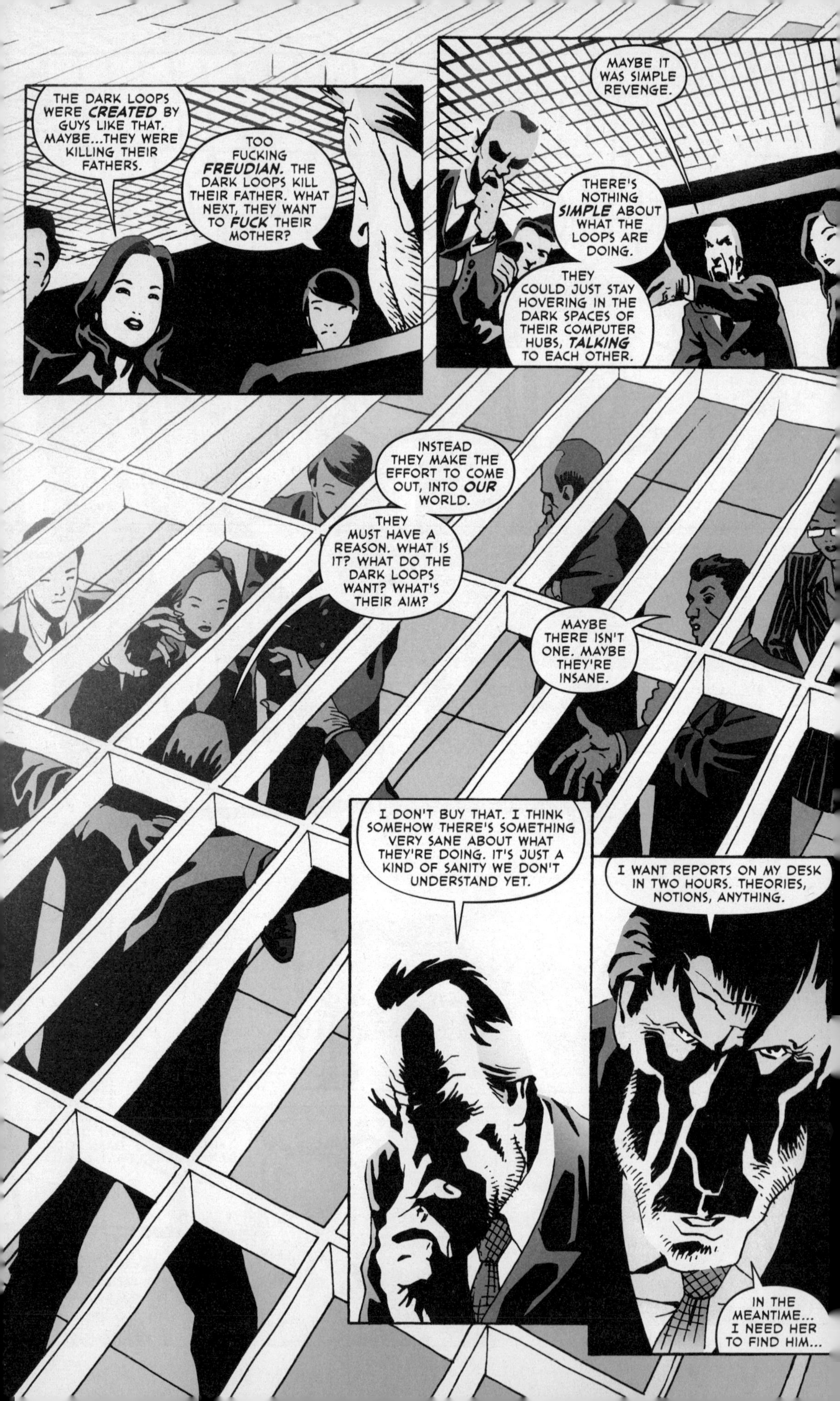
THE DARK LOOPS WERE CREATED BY GUYS LIKE THAT. MAYBE...THEY WERE KILLING THEIR FATHERS.
TOO FUCKING FREUDIAN. THE DARK LOOPS KILL THEIR FATHER. WHAT NEXT, THEY WANT TO FUCK THEIR MOTHER?
MAYBE IT WAS SIMPLE REVENGE.
THERE'S NOTHING SIMPLE ABOUT WHAT THE LOOPS ARE DOING.
THEY COULD JUST STAY HOVERING IN THE DARK SPACES OF THEIR COMPUTER HUBS, TALKING TO EACH OTHER.
INSTEAD THEY MAKE THE EFFORT TO COME OUT, INTO OUR WORLD.
THEY MUST HAVE A REASON. WHAT IS IT? WHAT DO THE DARK LOOPS WANT? WHAT'S THEIR AIM?
MAYBE THERE ISN'T ONE. MAYBE THEY'RE INSANE.
I DON'T BUY THAT. I THINK SOMEHOW THERE'S SOMETHING VERY SANE ABOUT WHAT THEY'RE DOING. IT'S JUST A KIND OF SANITY WE DON'T UNDERSTAND YET.
I WANT REPORTS ON MY DESK IN TWO HOURS. THEORIES, NOTIONS, ANYTHING.
IN THE MEANTIME... I NEED HER TO FIND HIM...

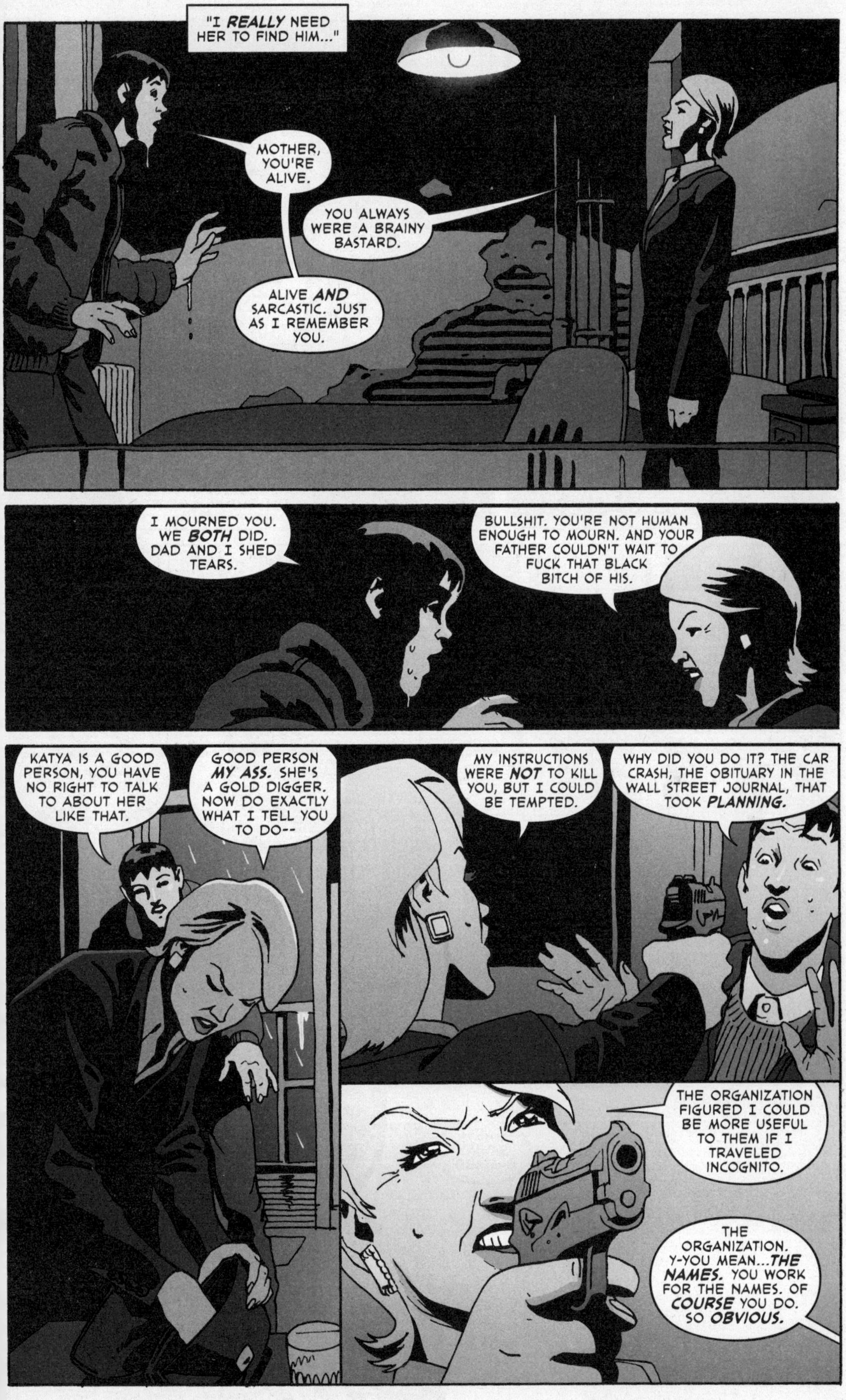
"I REALLY NEED HER TO FIND HIM..."
MOTHER, YOU'RE ALIVE.
YOU ALWAYS WERE A BRAINY BASTARD.
ALIVE AND SARCASTIC. JUST AS I REMEMBER YOU.
I MOURNED YOU. WE BOTH DID. DAD AND I SHED TEARS.
BULLSHIT. YOU'RE NOT HUMAN ENOUGH TO MOURN. AND YOUR FATHER COULDN'T WAIT TO FUCK THAT BLACK BITCH OF HIS.
KATYA IS A GOOD PERSON, YOU HAVE NO RIGHT TO TALK TO ABOUT HER LIKE THAT.
GOOD PERSON MY ASS. SHE'S A GOLD DIGGER. NOW DO EXACTLY WHAT I TELL YOU TO DO--
MY INSTRUCTIONS WERE NOT TO KILL YOU, BUT I COULD BE TEMPTED.
WHY DID YOU DO IT? THE CAR CRASH, THE OBITUARY IN THE WALL STREET JOURNAL, THAT TOOK PLANNING.
THE ORGANIZATION FIGURED I COULD BE MORE USEFUL TO THEM IF I TRAVELED INCOGNITO.
THE ORGANIZATION. Y-YOU MEAN...THE NAMES. YOU WORK FOR THE NAMES. OF COURSE YOU DO. SO OBVIOUS.

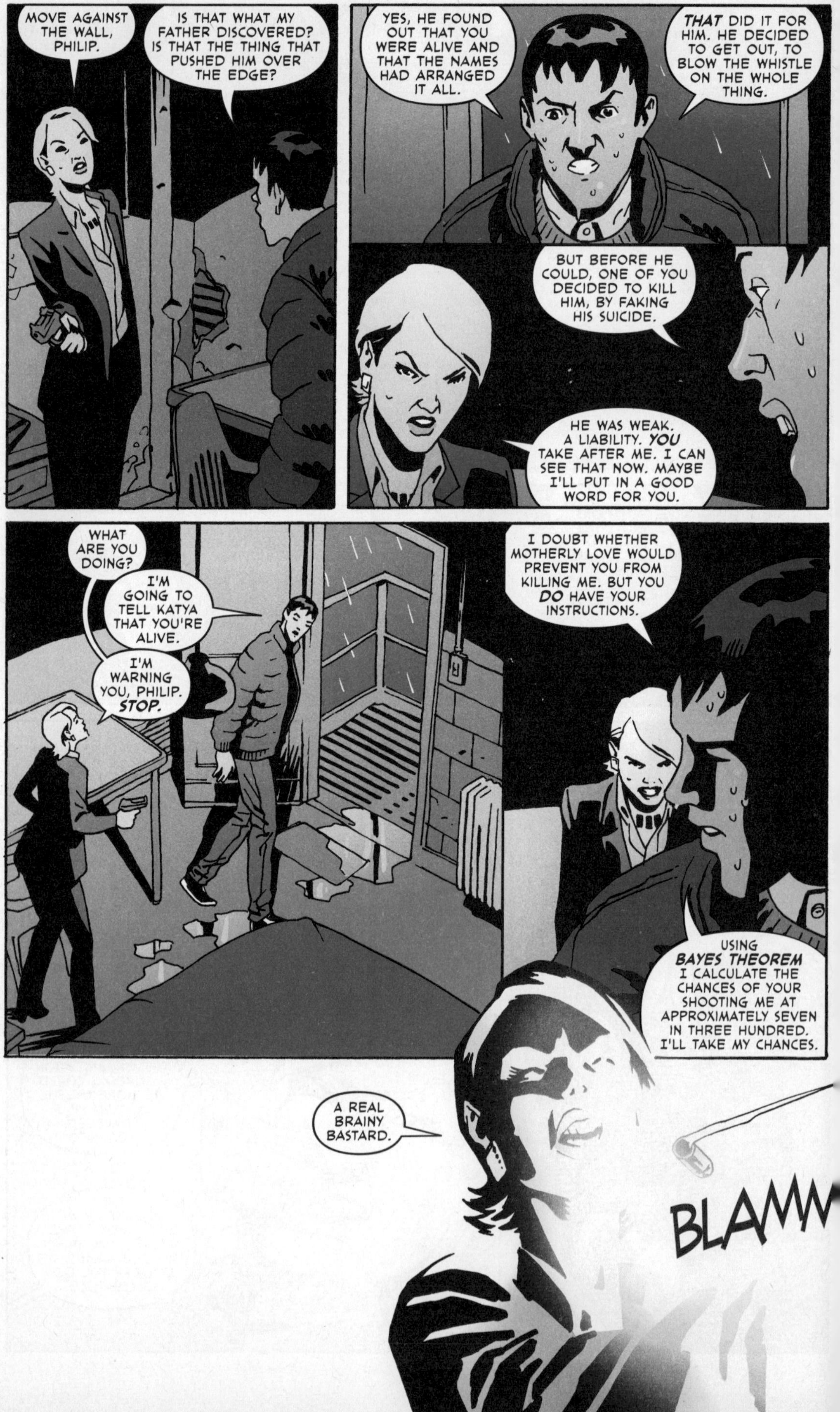

MOVE AGAINST THE WALL, PHILIP.
IS THAT WHAT MY FATHER DISCOVERED? IS THAT THE THING THAT PUSHED HIM OVER THE EDGE?
YES, HE FOUND OUT THAT YOU WERE ALIVE AND THAT THE NAMES HAD ARRANGED IT ALL.
THAT DID IT FOR HIM. HE DECIDED TO GET OUT, TO BLOW THE WHISTLE ON THE WHOLE THING.
BUT BEFORE HE COULD, ONE OF YOU DECIDED TO KILL HIM, BY FAKING HIS SUICIDE.
HE WAS WEAK. A LIABILITY. YOU TAKE AFTER ME. I CAN SEE THAT NOW. MAYBE I'LL PUT IN A GOOD WORD FOR YOU.
WHAT ARE YOU DOING?
I'M GOING TO TELL KATYA THAT YOU'RE ALIVE.
I'M WARNING YOU, PHILIP. STOP.
I DOUBT WHETHER MOTHERLY LOVE WOULD PREVENT YOU FROM KILLING ME. BUT YOU DO HAVE YOUR INSTRUCTIONS.
USING BAYES THEOREM I CALCULATE THE CHANCES OF YOUR SHOOTING ME AT APPROXIMATELY SEVEN IN THREE HUNDRED. I'LL TAKE MY CHANCES.
A REAL BRAINY BASTARD.
BLAMM

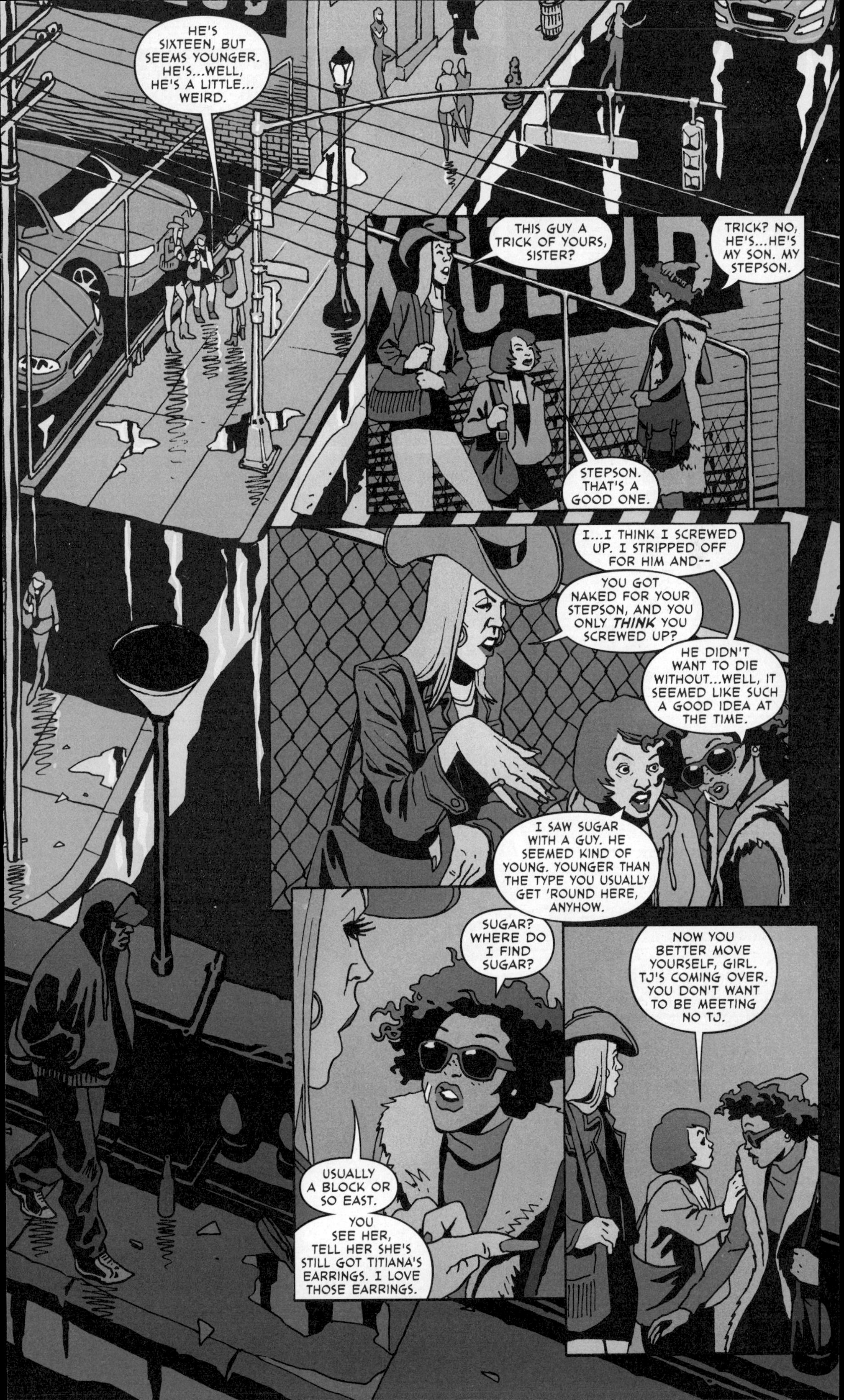

HE'S SIXTEEN, BUT SEEMS YOUNGER. HE'S...WELL, HE'S A LITTLE... WEIRD.
THIS GUY A TRICK OF YOURS, SISTER?
TRICK? NO, HE'S...HE'S MY SON. MY STEPSON.
STEPSON. THAT'S A GOOD ONE.
I...I THINK I SCREWED UP. I STRIPPED OFF FOR HIM AND--
YOU GOT NAKED FOR YOUR STEPSON, AND YOU ONLY *THINK* YOU SCREWED UP?
HE DIDN'T WANT TO DIE WITHOUT...WELL, IT SEEMED LIKE SUCH A GOOD IDEA AT THE TIME.
I SAW SUGAR WITH A GUY. HE SEEMED KIND OF YOUNG. YOUNGER THAN THE TYPE YOU USUALLY GET 'ROUND HERE, ANYHOW.
SUGAR? WHERE DO I FIND SUGAR?
USUALLY A BLOCK OR SO EAST.
YOU SEE HER, TELL HER SHE'S STILL GOT TITIANA'S EARRINGS. I LOVE THOSE EARRINGS.
NOW YOU BETTER MOVE YOURSELF, GIRL. TJ'S COMING OVER. YOU DON'T WANT TO BE MEETING NO TJ.

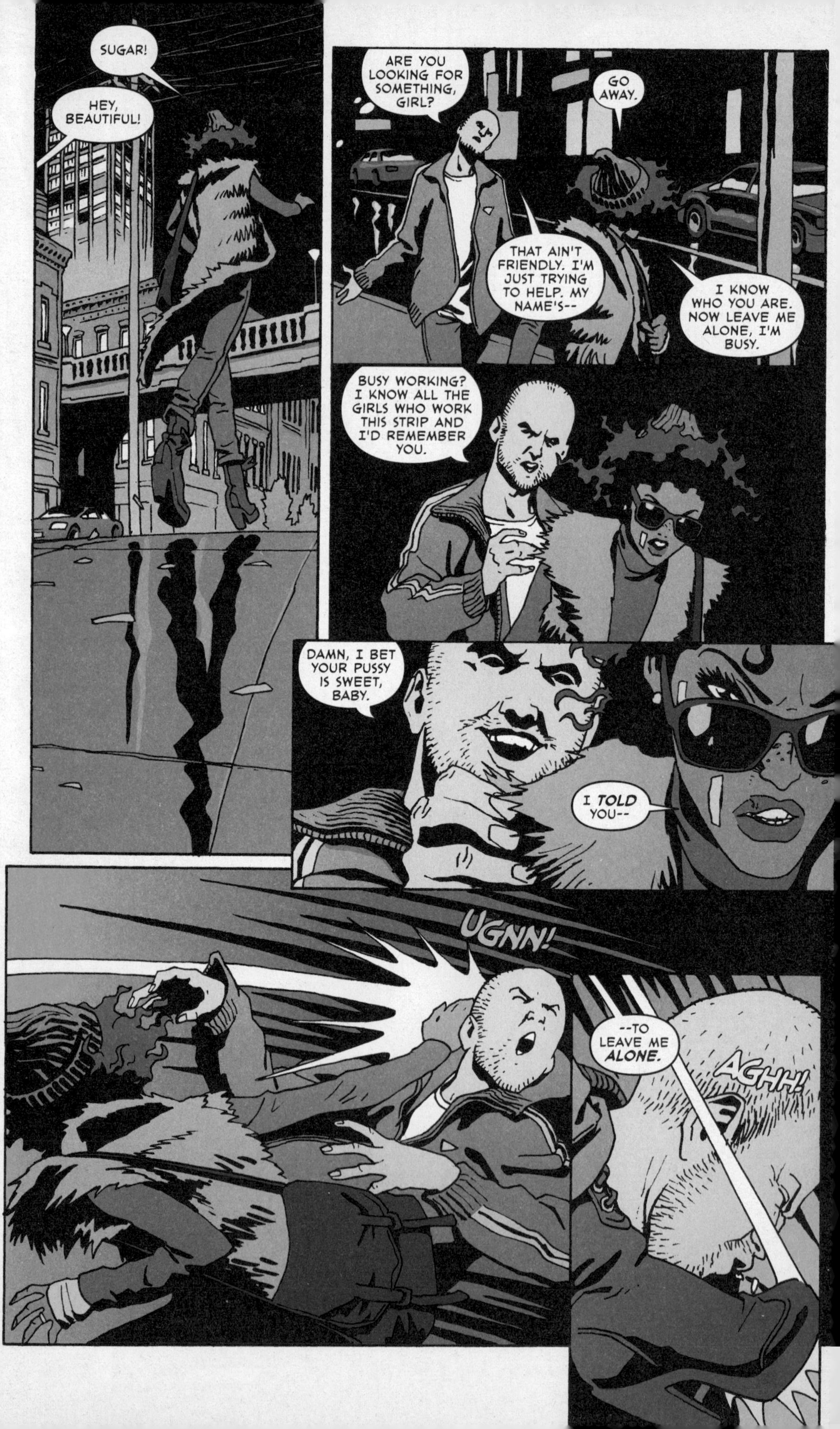
SUGAR!
HEY, BEAUTIFUL!
ARE YOU LOOKING FOR SOMETHING, GIRL?
GO AWAY.
THAT AIN'T FRIENDLY. I'M JUST TRYING TO HELP. MY NAME'S--
I KNOW WHO YOU ARE. NOW LEAVE ME ALONE, I'M BUSY.
BUSY WORKING? I KNOW ALL THE GIRLS WHO WORK THIS STRIP AND I'D REMEMBER YOU.
DAMN, I BET YOUR PUSSY IS SWEET, BABY.
I *TOLD* YOU--
UGNN!
--TO LEAVE ME *ALONE.*
AGHH!

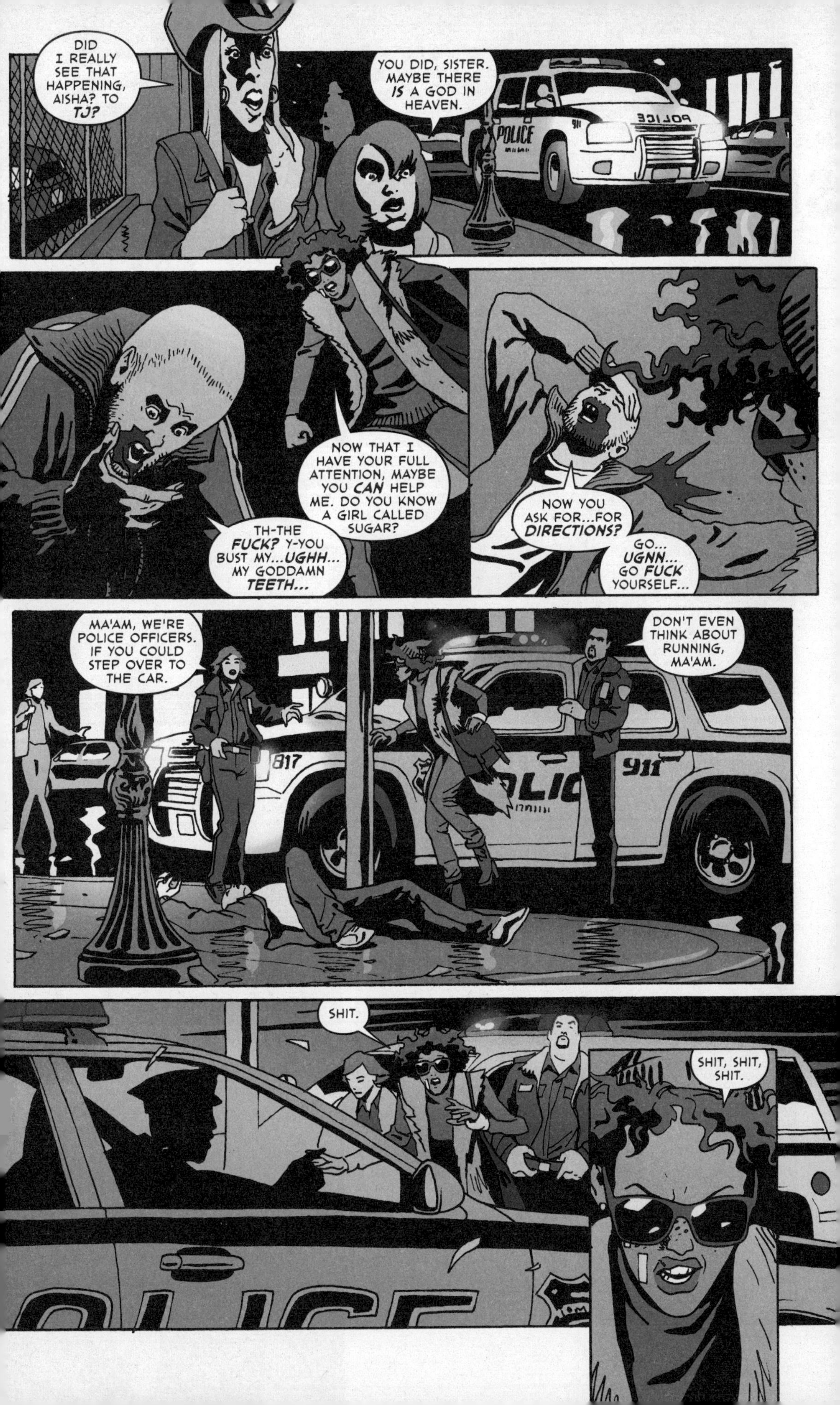
DID I REALLY SEE THAT HAPPENING, AISHA? TO TJ?
YOU DID, SISTER. MAYBE THERE IS A GOD IN HEAVEN.
POLICE
NOW THAT I HAVE YOUR FULL ATTENTION, MAYBE YOU CAN HELP ME. DO YOU KNOW A GIRL CALLED SUGAR?
TH-THE FUCK? Y-YOU BUST MY...UGHH... MY GODDAMN TEETH...
NOW YOU ASK FOR...FOR DIRECTIONS?
GO... UGNN... GO FUCK YOURSELF...
MA'AM, WE'RE POLICE OFFICERS. IF YOU COULD STEP OVER TO THE CAR.
DON'T EVEN THINK ABOUT RUNNING, MA'AM.
817
911
SHIT.
SHIT, SHIT, SHIT.

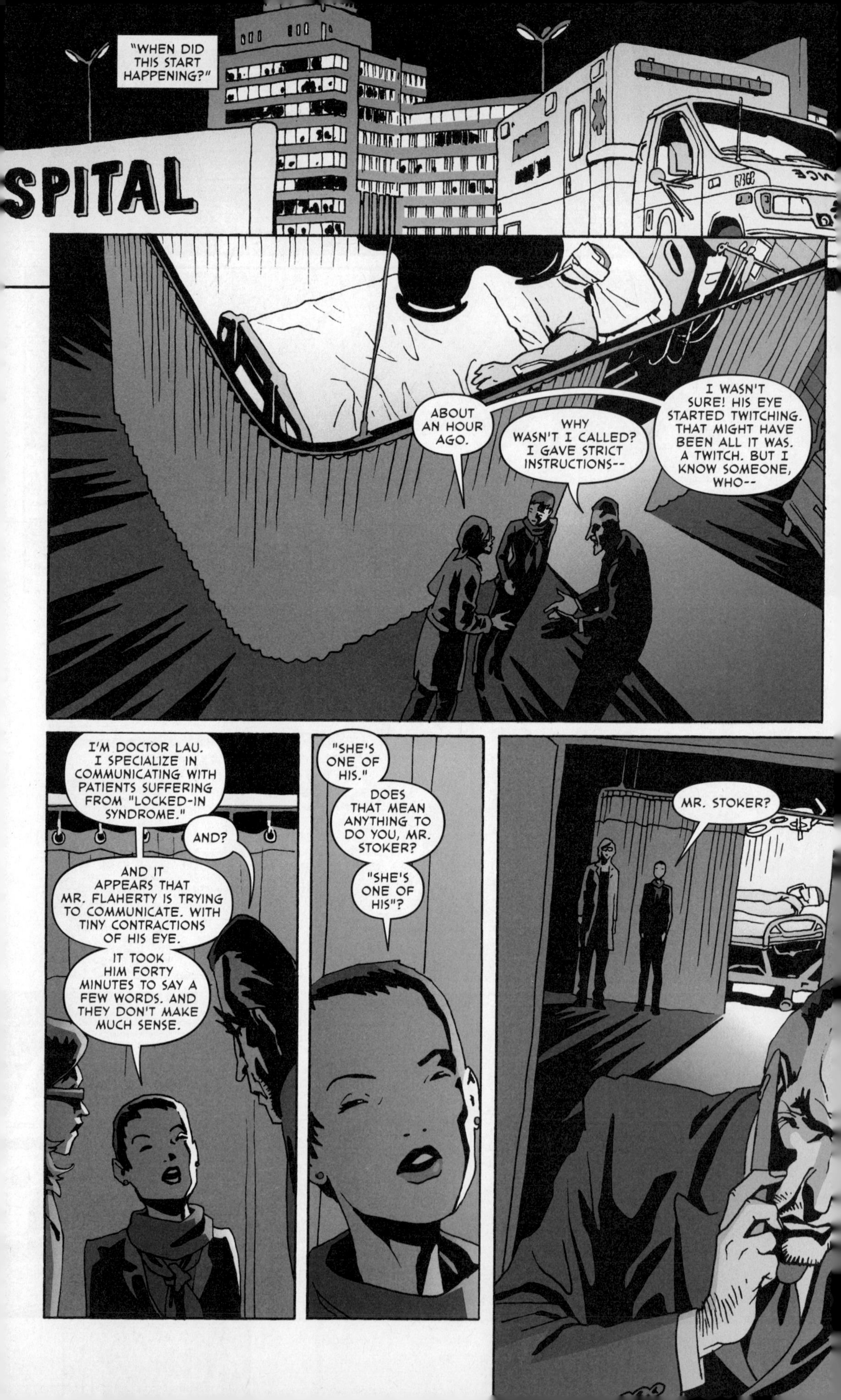
"WHEN DID THIS START HAPPENING?"
SPITAL
ABOUT AN HOUR AGO.
WHY WASN'T I CALLED? I GAVE STRICT INSTRUCTIONS--
I WASN'T SURE! HIS EYE STARTED TWITCHING. THAT MIGHT HAVE BEEN ALL IT WAS. A TWITCH. BUT I KNOW SOMEONE, WHO--
I'M DOCTOR LAU. I SPECIALIZE IN COMMUNICATING WITH PATIENTS SUFFERING FROM "LOCKED-IN SYNDROME."
AND?
AND IT APPEARS THAT MR. FLAHERTY IS TRYING TO COMMUNICATE. WITH TINY CONTRACTIONS OF HIS EYE.
IT TOOK HIM FORTY MINUTES TO SAY A FEW WORDS. AND THEY DON'T MAKE MUCH SENSE.
"SHE'S ONE OF HIS."
DOES THAT MEAN ANYTHING TO DO YOU, MR. STOKER?
"SHE'S ONE OF HIS"?
MR. STOKER?

UGHH... UGHH...

I'VE PUT A TOURNIQUET ON YOUR LEG AND GIVEN YOU A SHOT OF SOMETHING. YOU'LL LIVE.

MY...MY CALCULATIONS. BAYES THEOREM. H-HOW COULD I HAVE BEEN... SO WRONG? UNLESS...

UNLESS I DIDN'T FACTOR IN...

MAYBE YOU JUST AIN'T AS CLEVER AS YOU THINK YOU ARE, SONNY BOY.

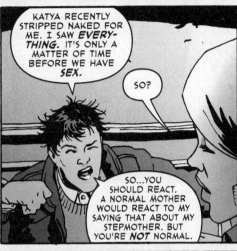

KATYA RECENTLY STRIPPED NAKED FOR ME. I SAW *EVERYTHING.* IT'S ONLY A MATTER OF TIME BEFORE WE HAVE *SEX.*

SO?

SO...YOU SHOULD REACT. A NORMAL MOTHER WOULD REACT TO MY SAYING THAT ABOUT MY STEPMOTHER. BUT YOU'RE *NOT* NORMAL.

"...YOU'RE ONE OF THEM..."

IT'S ME. HOW'S IT LOOKING?

"...THE LEAGUE OF PSYCHOPATHS..."

KEEP THE PRIZE ALIVE. I'LL BE THERE IN UNDER TWO HOURS.

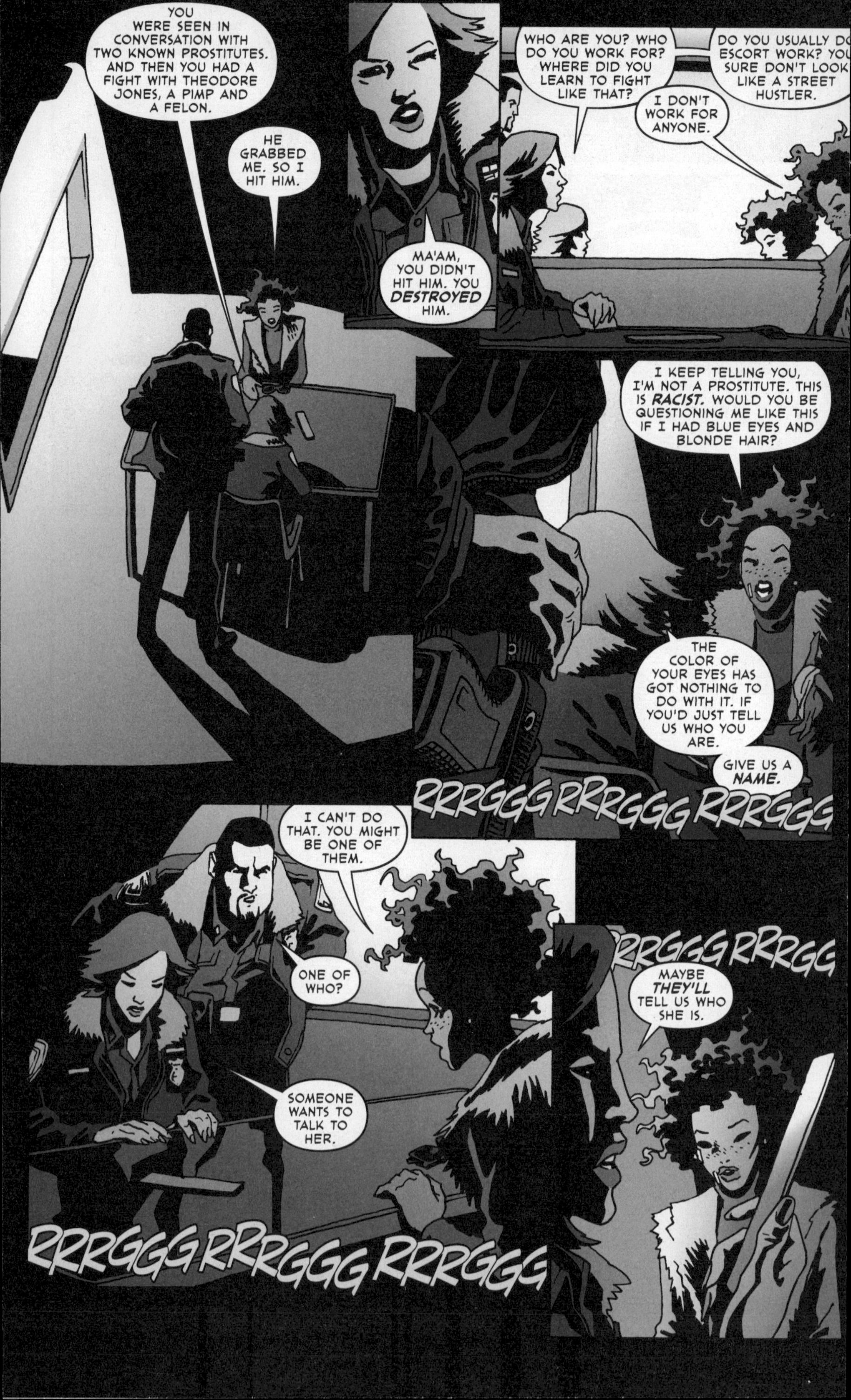

YOU WERE SEEN IN CONVERSATION WITH TWO KNOWN PROSTITUTES. AND THEN YOU HAD A FIGHT WITH THEODORE JONES, A PIMP AND A FELON.
HE GRABBED ME. SO I HIT HIM.
MA'AM, YOU DIDN'T HIT HIM. YOU DESTROYED HIM.
WHO ARE YOU? WHO DO YOU WORK FOR? WHERE DID YOU LEARN TO FIGHT LIKE THAT?
DO YOU USUALLY DO ESCORT WORK? YOU SURE DON'T LOOK LIKE A STREET HUSTLER.
I DON'T WORK FOR ANYONE.
I KEEP TELLING YOU, I'M NOT A PROSTITUTE. THIS IS RACIST. WOULD YOU BE QUESTIONING ME LIKE THIS IF I HAD BLUE EYES AND BLONDE HAIR?
THE COLOR OF YOUR EYES HAS GOT NOTHING TO DO WITH IT. IF YOU'D JUST TELL US WHO YOU ARE.
GIVE US A NAME.
RRRGGG RRRGGG RRRGGG
I CAN'T DO THAT. YOU MIGHT BE ONE OF THEM.
ONE OF WHO?
SOMEONE WANTS TO TALK TO HER.
RRRGGG RRRGGG RRRGGG
RRRGGG RRRGG
MAYBE THEY'LL TELL US WHO SHE IS.

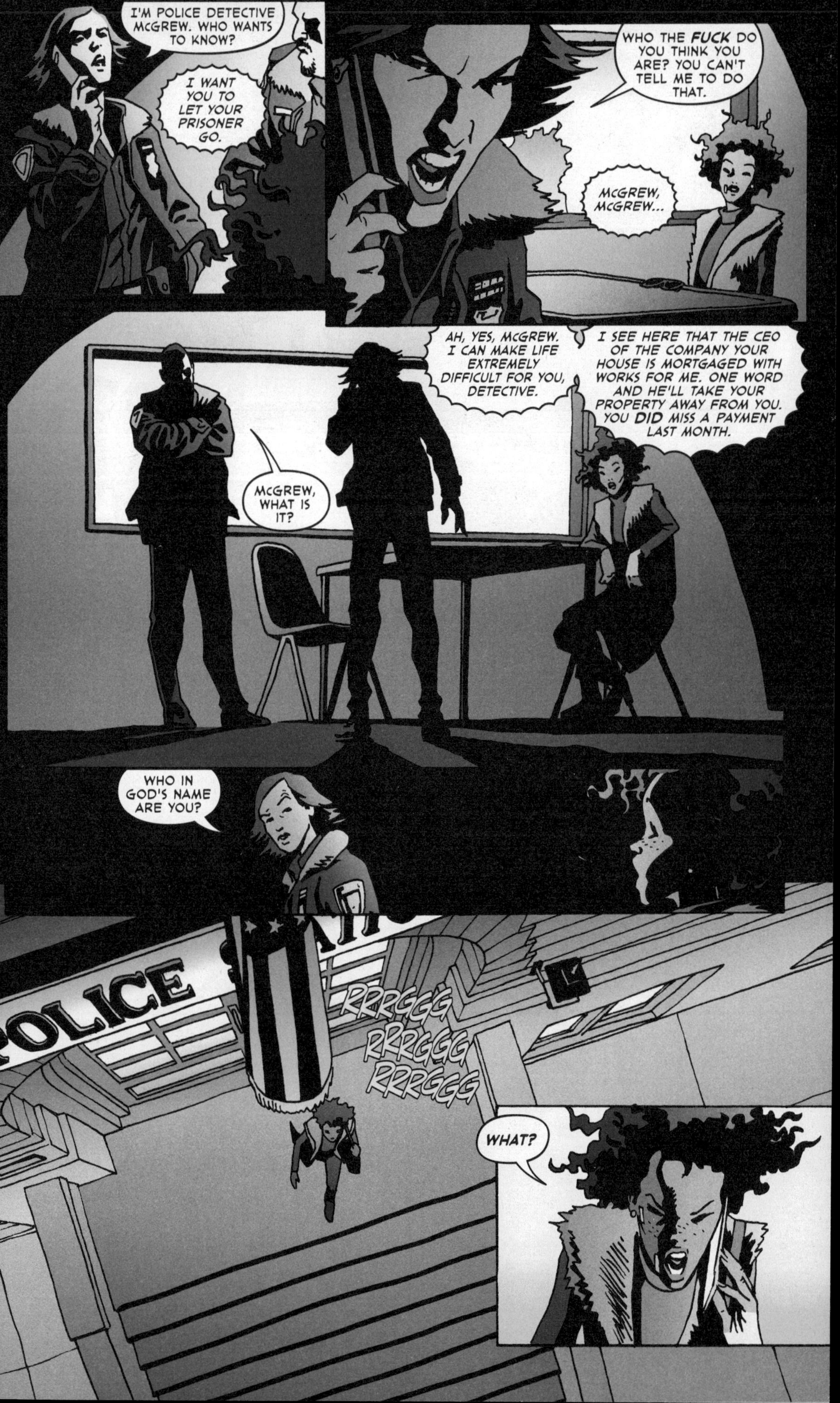
I'M POLICE DETECTIVE McGREW. WHO WANTS TO KNOW?
I WANT YOU TO LET YOUR PRISONER GO.
WHO THE FUCK DO YOU THINK YOU ARE? YOU CAN'T TELL ME TO DO THAT.
McGREW, McGREW...
AH, YES, McGREW. I CAN MAKE LIFE EXTREMELY DIFFICULT FOR YOU, DETECTIVE.
I SEE HERE THAT THE CEO OF THE COMPANY YOUR HOUSE IS MORTGAGED WITH WORKS FOR ME. ONE WORD AND HE'LL TAKE YOUR PROPERTY AWAY FROM YOU. YOU DID MISS A PAYMENT LAST MONTH.
McGREW, WHAT IS IT?
WHO IN GOD'S NAME ARE YOU?
POLICE
RRRGGG
RRRGGG
RRRGGG
WHAT?

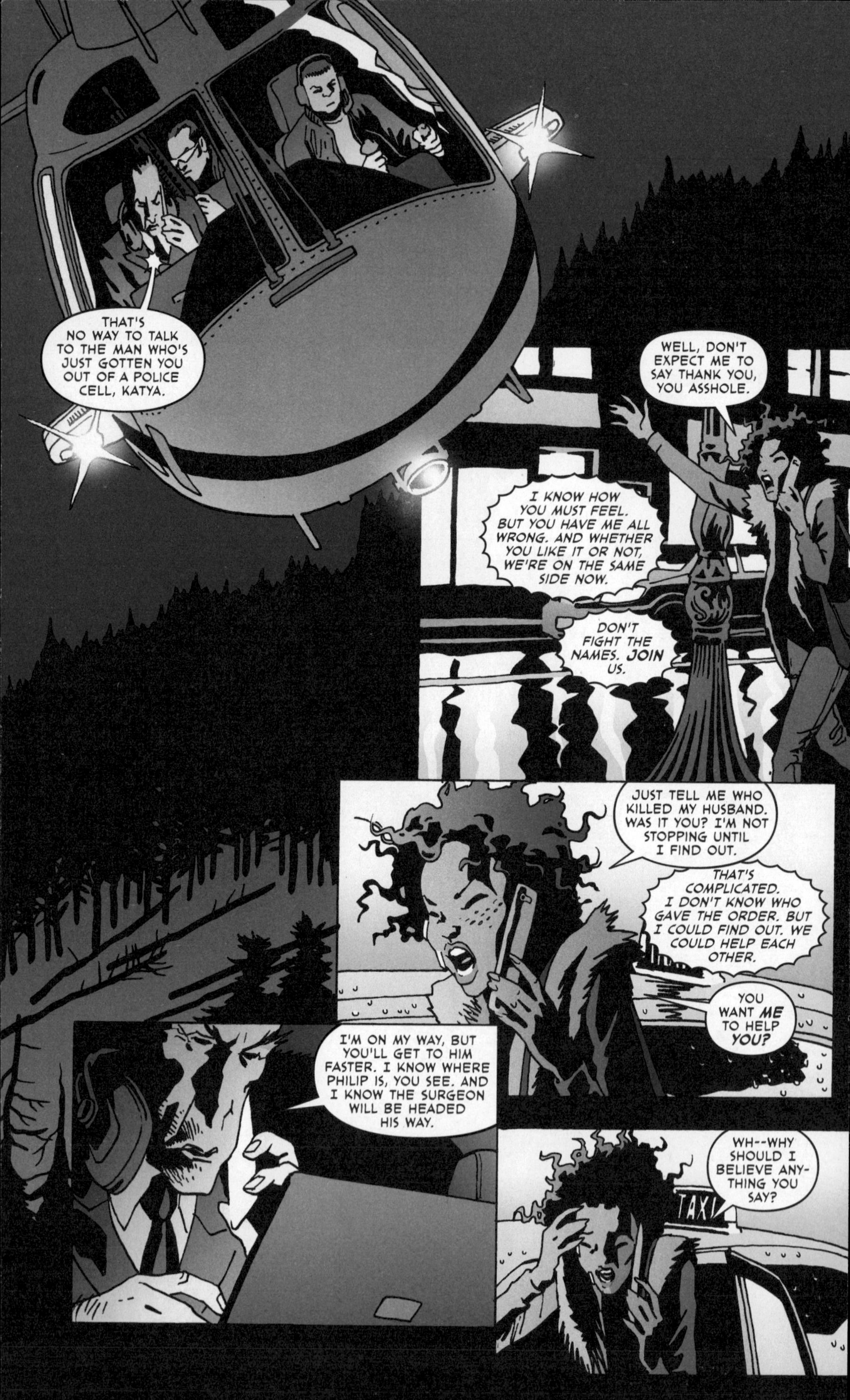
THAT'S NO WAY TO TALK TO THE MAN WHO'S JUST GOTTEN YOU OUT OF A POLICE CELL, KATYA.
WELL, DON'T EXPECT ME TO SAY THANK YOU, YOU ASSHOLE.
I KNOW HOW YOU MUST FEEL. BUT YOU HAVE ME ALL WRONG. AND WHETHER YOU LIKE IT OR NOT, WE'RE ON THE SAME SIDE NOW.
DON'T FIGHT THE NAMES. JOIN US.
JUST TELL ME WHO KILLED MY HUSBAND. WAS IT YOU? I'M NOT STOPPING UNTIL I FIND OUT.
THAT'S COMPLICATED. I DON'T KNOW WHO GAVE THE ORDER. BUT I COULD FIND OUT. WE COULD HELP EACH OTHER.
YOU WANT ME TO HELP YOU?
I'M ON MY WAY, BUT YOU'LL GET TO HIM FASTER. I KNOW WHERE PHILIP IS, YOU SEE. AND I KNOW THE SURGEON WILL BE HEADED HIS WAY.
WH--WHY SHOULD I BELIEVE ANYTHING YOU SAY?
TAXI

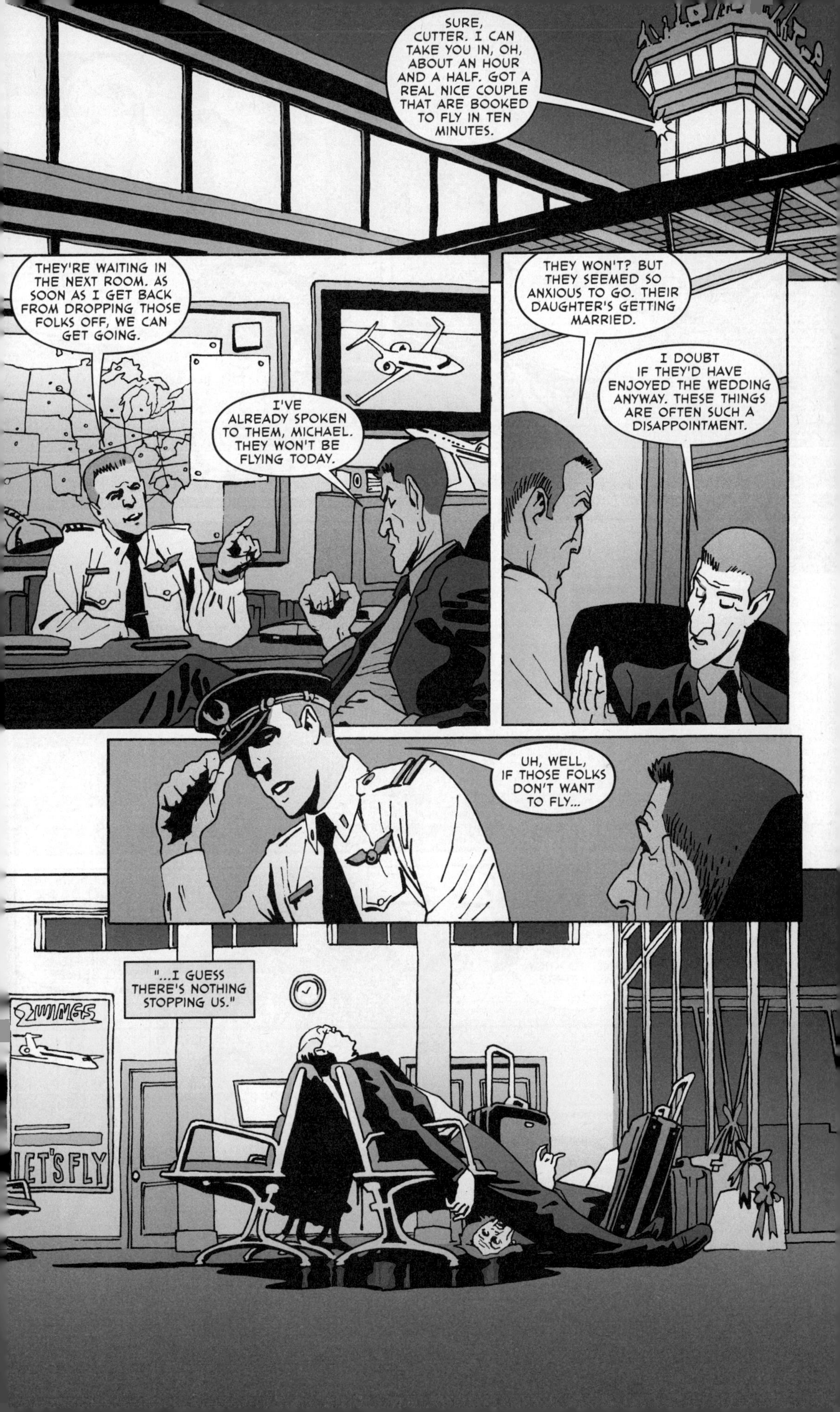
SURE, CUTTER. I CAN TAKE YOU IN, OH, ABOUT AN HOUR AND A HALF. GOT A REAL NICE COUPLE THAT ARE BOOKED TO FLY IN TEN MINUTES.
THEY'RE WAITING IN THE NEXT ROOM. AS SOON AS I GET BACK FROM DROPPING THOSE FOLKS OFF, WE CAN GET GOING.
I'VE ALREADY SPOKEN TO THEM, MICHAEL. THEY WON'T BE FLYING TODAY.
THEY WON'T? BUT THEY SEEMED SO ANXIOUS TO GO. THEIR DAUGHTER'S GETTING MARRIED.
I DOUBT IF THEY'D HAVE ENJOYED THE WEDDING ANYWAY. THESE THINGS ARE OFTEN SUCH A DISAPPOINTMENT.
UH, WELL, IF THOSE FOLKS DON'T WANT TO FLY...
"...I GUESS THERE'S NOTHING STOPPING US."
2WINGS
LET'S FLY

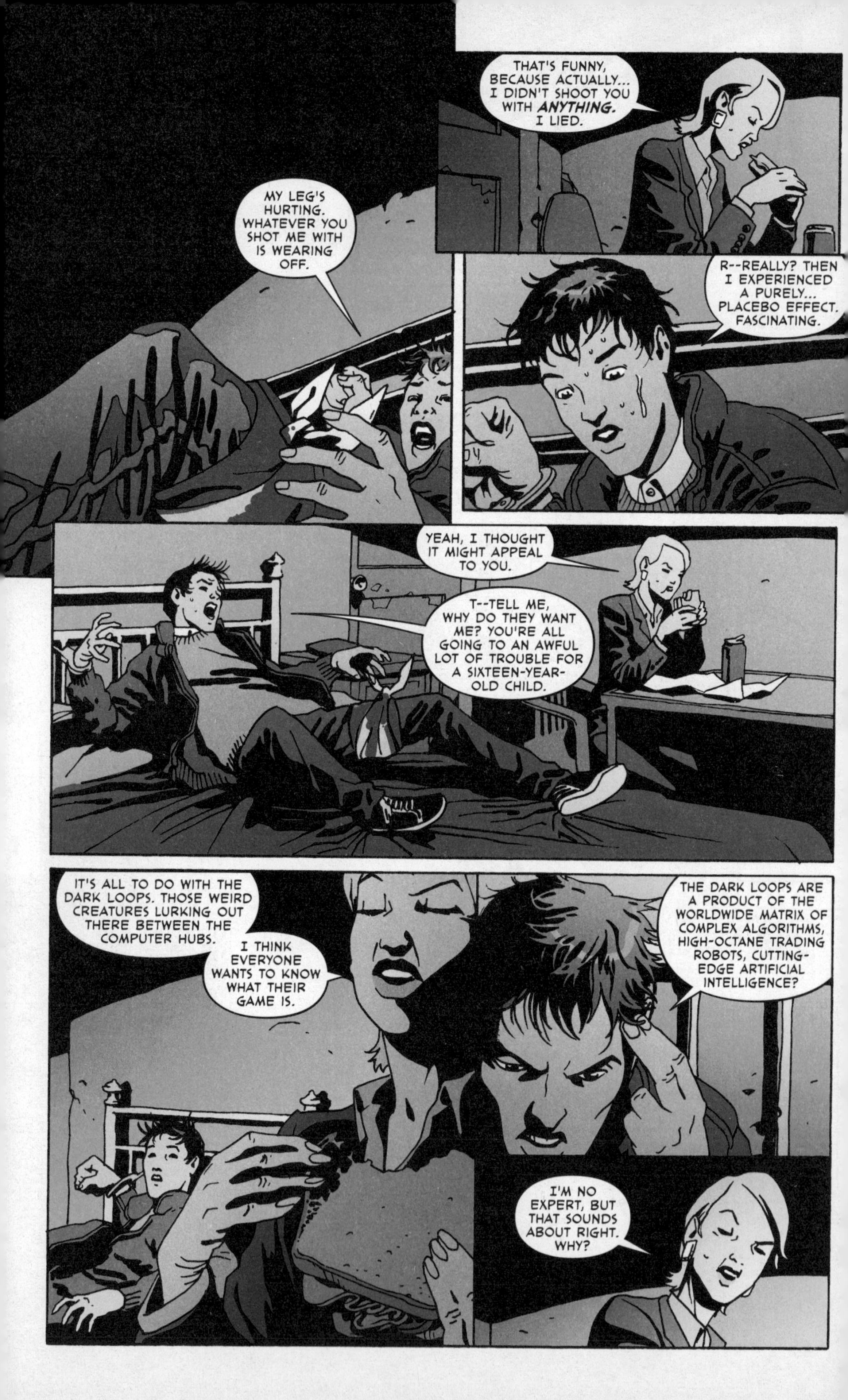
MY LEG'S HURTING. WHATEVER YOU SHOT ME WITH IS WEARING OFF.
THAT'S FUNNY, BECAUSE ACTUALLY... I DIDN'T SHOOT YOU WITH ANYTHING. I LIED.
R--REALLY? THEN I EXPERIENCED A PURELY... PLACEBO EFFECT. FASCINATING.
YEAH, I THOUGHT IT MIGHT APPEAL TO YOU.
T--TELL ME, WHY DO THEY WANT ME? YOU'RE ALL GOING TO AN AWFUL LOT OF TROUBLE FOR A SIXTEEN-YEAR-OLD CHILD.
IT'S ALL TO DO WITH THE DARK LOOPS. THOSE WEIRD CREATURES LURKING OUT THERE BETWEEN THE COMPUTER HUBS.
I THINK EVERYONE WANTS TO KNOW WHAT THEIR GAME IS.
THE DARK LOOPS ARE A PRODUCT OF THE WORLDWIDE MATRIX OF COMPLEX ALGORITHMS, HIGH-OCTANE TRADING ROBOTS, CUTTING-EDGE ARTIFICIAL INTELLIGENCE?
I'M NO EXPERT, BUT THAT SOUNDS ABOUT RIGHT. WHY?

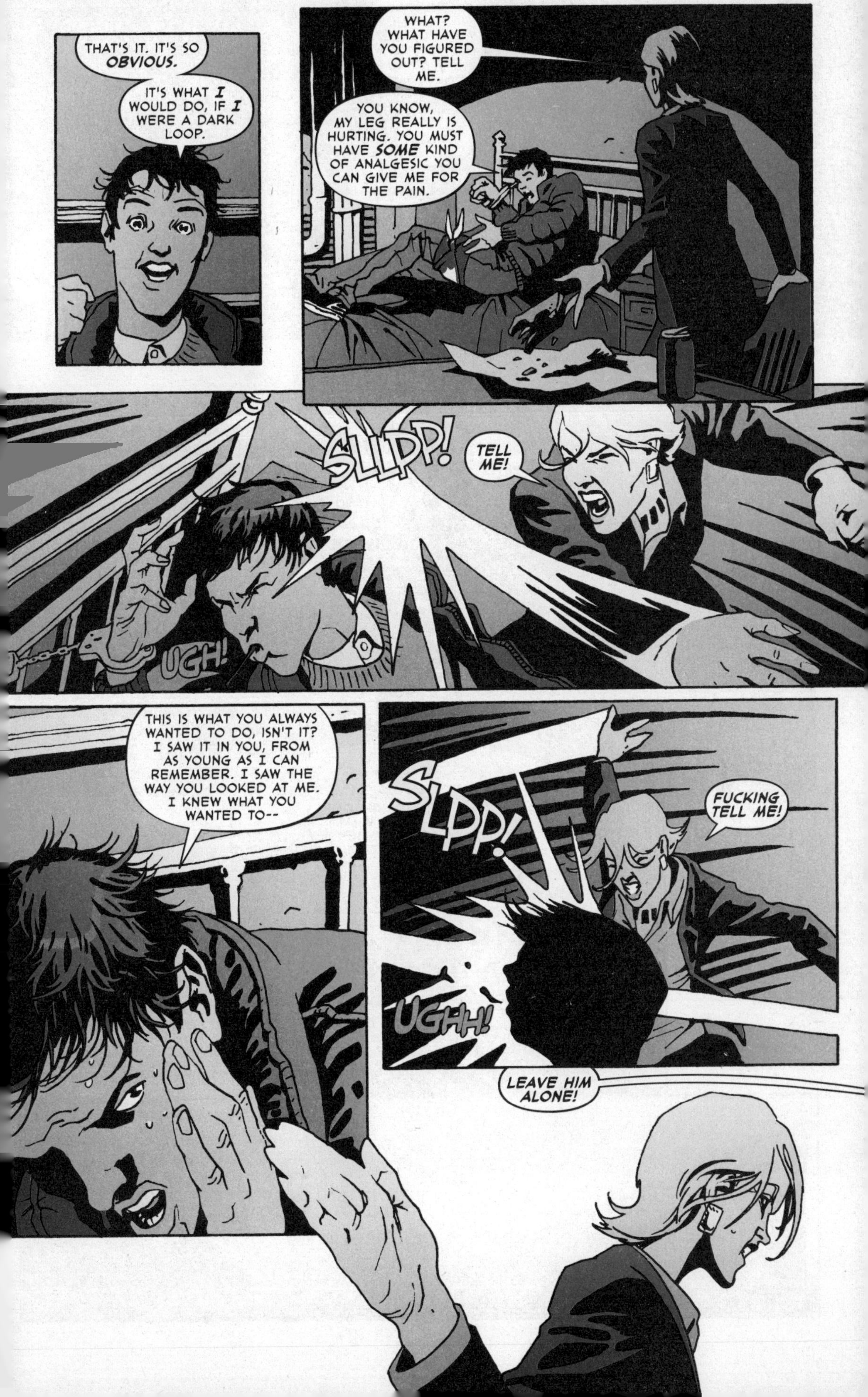
THAT'S IT. IT'S SO *OBVIOUS.*
IT'S WHAT *I* WOULD DO, IF *I* WERE A DARK LOOP.
WHAT? WHAT HAVE YOU FIGURED OUT? TELL ME.
YOU KNOW, MY LEG REALLY IS HURTING. YOU MUST HAVE *SOME* KIND OF ANALGESIC YOU CAN GIVE ME FOR THE PAIN.
SLLPP!
TELL ME!
UGH!
THIS IS WHAT YOU ALWAYS WANTED TO DO, ISN'T IT? I SAW IT IN YOU, FROM AS YOUNG AS I CAN REMEMBER. I SAW THE WAY YOU LOOKED AT ME. I KNEW WHAT YOU WANTED TO--
SLPP!
FUCKING TELL ME!
UGHH!
LEAVE HIM ALONE!

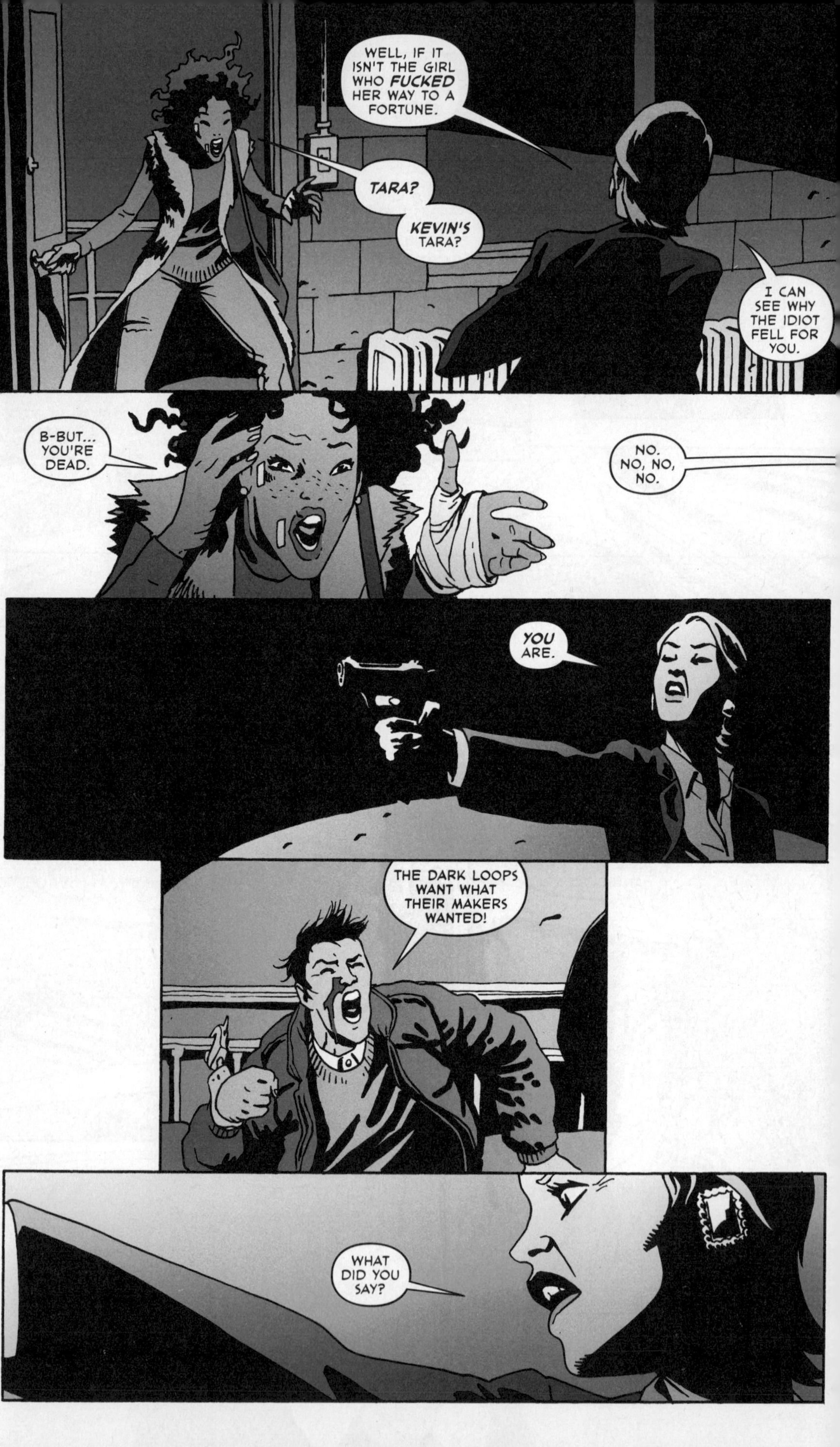
WELL, IF IT ISN'T THE GIRL WHO FUCKED HER WAY TO A FORTUNE.
TARA?
KEVIN'S TARA?
I CAN SEE WHY THE IDIOT FELL FOR YOU.
B-BUT... YOU'RE DEAD.
NO. NO, NO, NO.
YOU ARE.
THE DARK LOOPS WANT WHAT THEIR MAKERS WANTED!
WHAT DID YOU SAY?

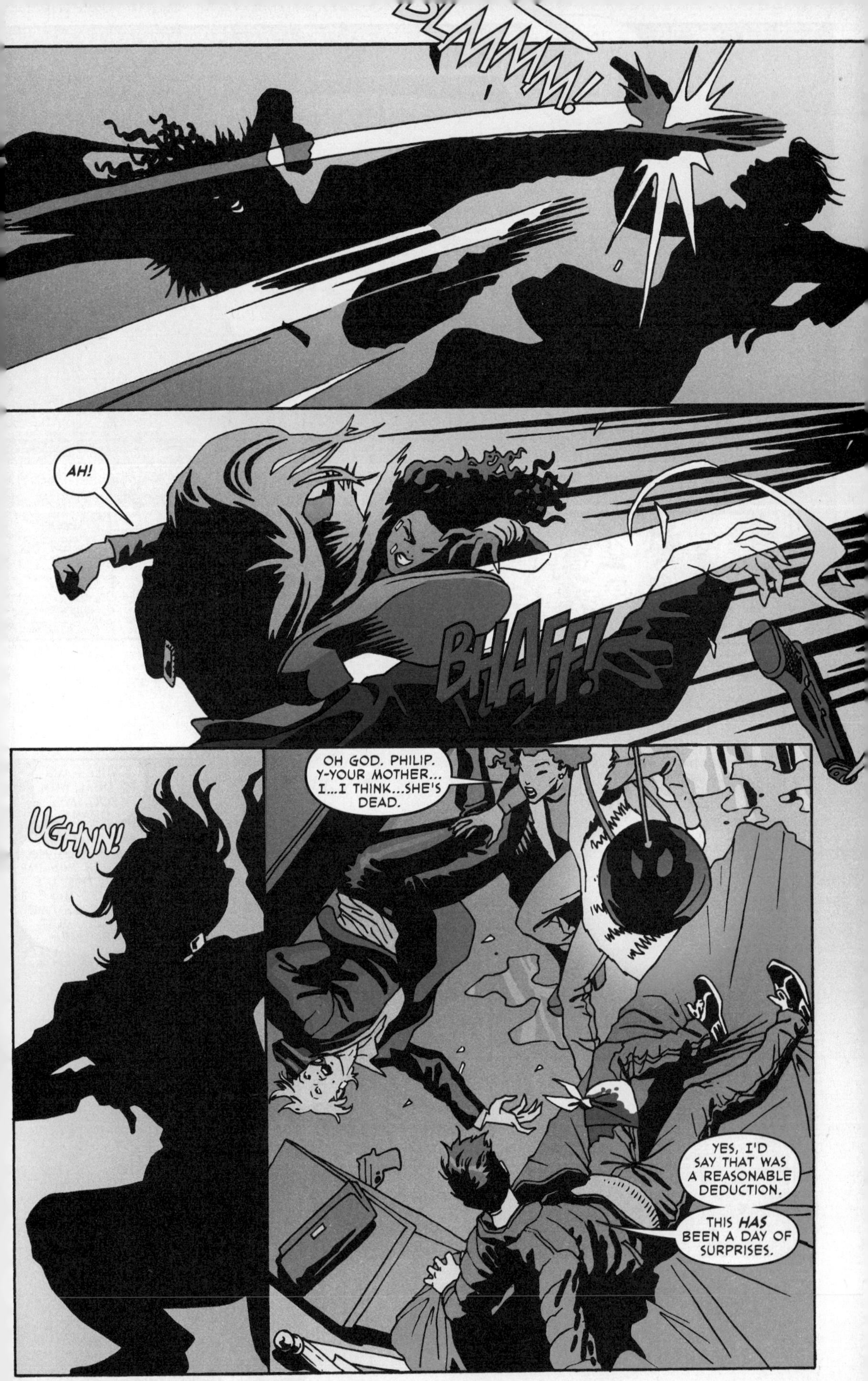
BLAMMM!
AH!
BHAFF!
UGHNN!
OH GOD. PHILIP. Y-YOUR MOTHER... I...I THINK...SHE'S DEAD.
YES, I'D SAY THAT WAS A REASONABLE DEDUCTION.
THIS HAS BEEN A DAY OF SURPRISES.

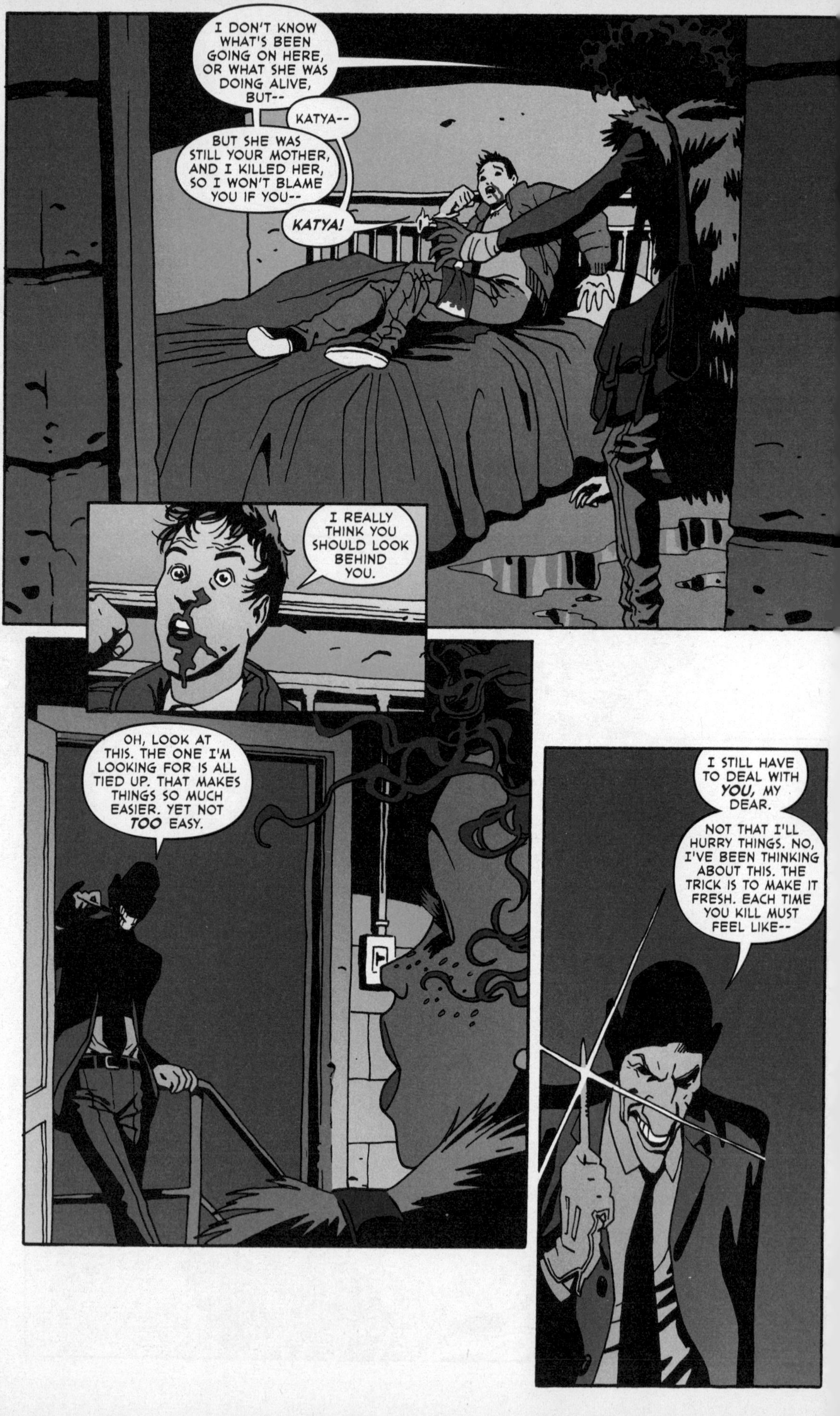
I DON'T KNOW WHAT'S BEEN GOING ON HERE, OR WHAT SHE WAS DOING ALIVE, BUT--
KATYA--
BUT SHE WAS STILL YOUR MOTHER, AND I KILLED HER, SO I WON'T BLAME YOU IF YOU--
KATYA!
I REALLY THINK YOU SHOULD LOOK BEHIND YOU.
OH, LOOK AT THIS. THE ONE I'M LOOKING FOR IS ALL TIED UP. THAT MAKES THINGS SO MUCH EASIER. YET NOT TOO EASY.
I STILL HAVE TO DEAL WITH YOU, MY DEAR.
NOT THAT I'LL HURRY THINGS. NO, I'VE BEEN THINKING ABOUT THIS. THE TRICK IS TO MAKE IT FRESH. EACH TIME YOU KILL MUST FEEL LIKE--

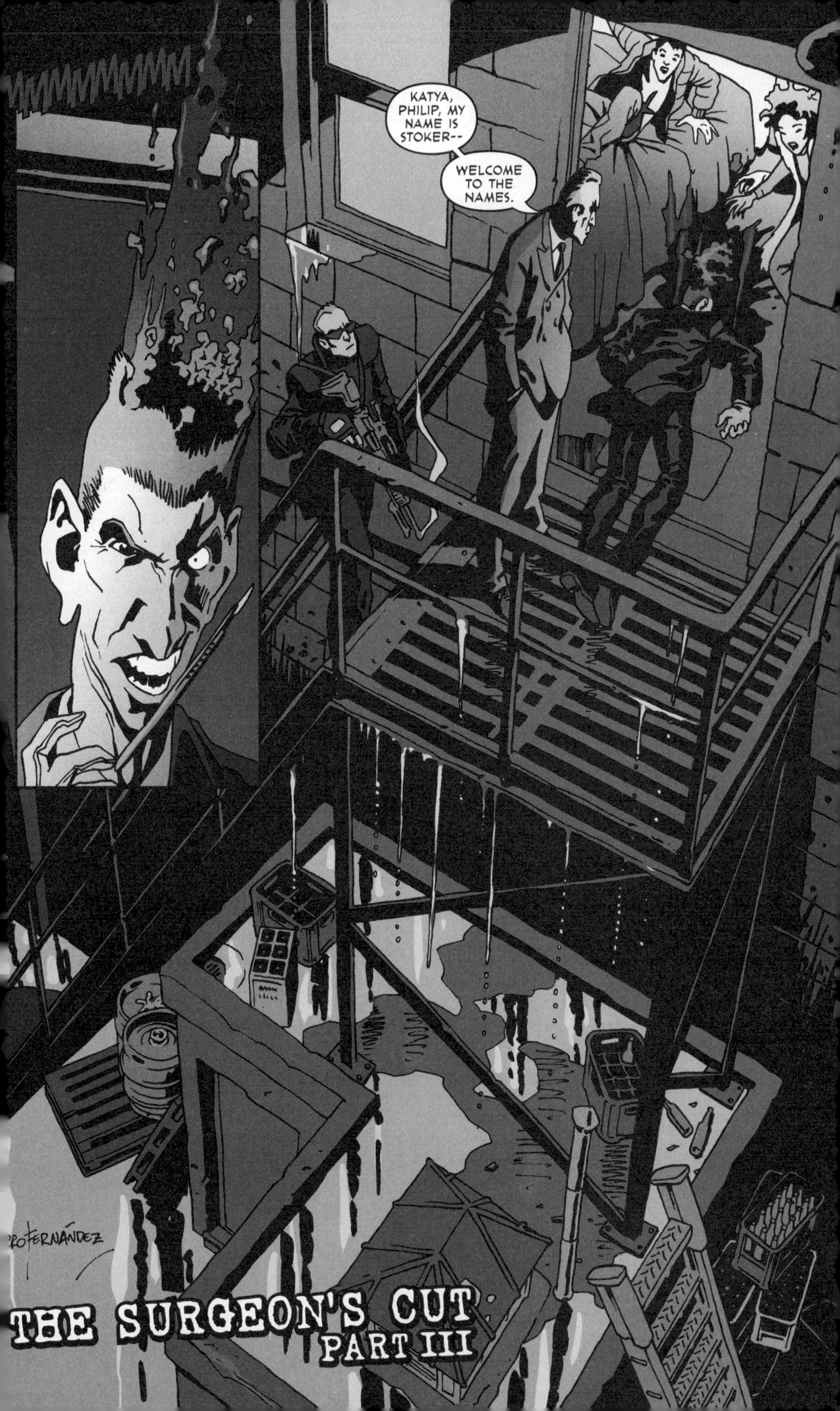
KATYA, PHILIP, MY NAME IS STOKER--
WELCOME TO THE NAMES.
FERNÁNDEZ
THE SURGEON'S CUT
PART III

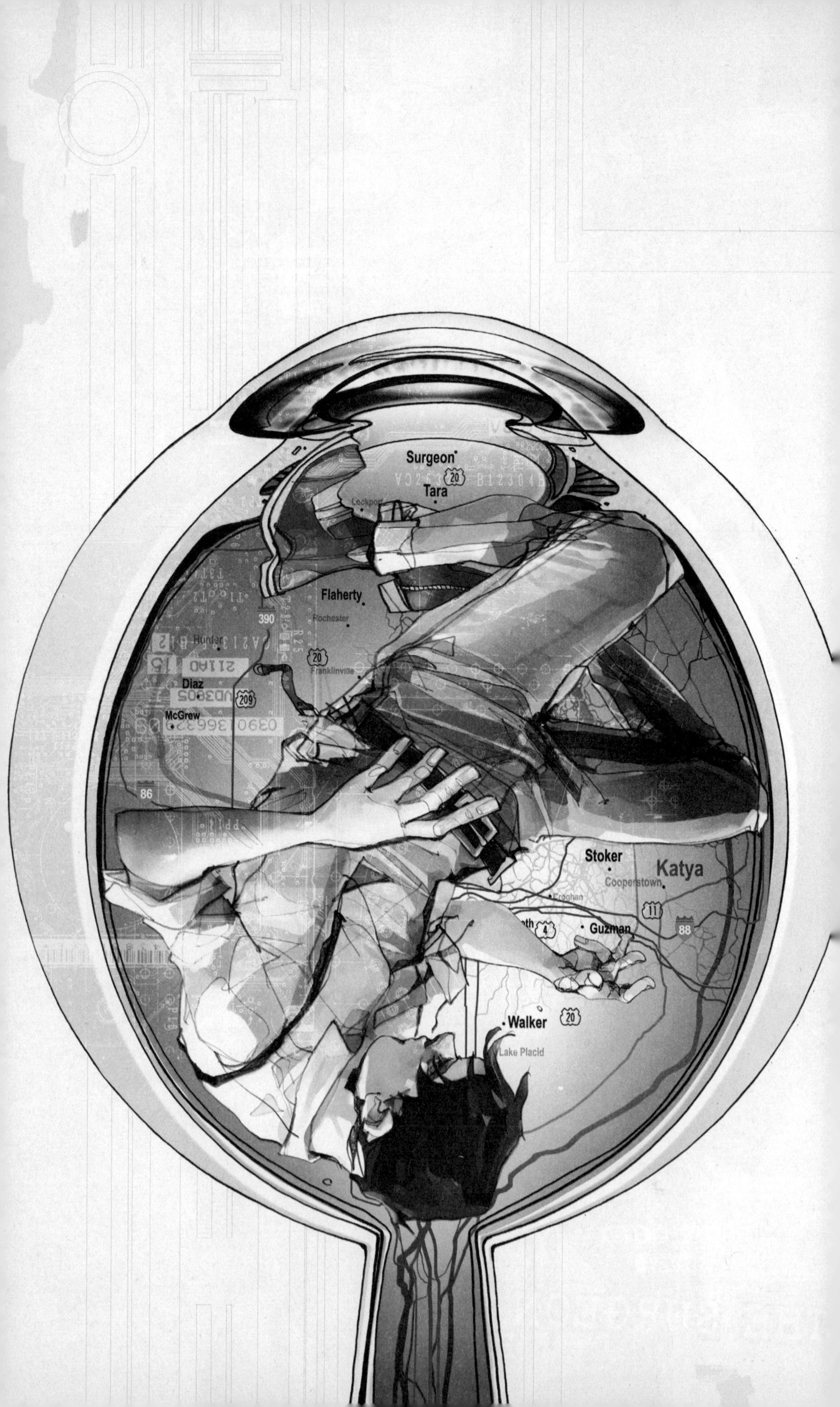
Surgeon
20
Tara
Lockport
Flaherty
390
Rochester
Hunter
20
Franklinville
Diaz
209
McGrew
86
Stoker
Katya
Cooperstown
11
4
Guzman
88
Walker
20
Lake Placid

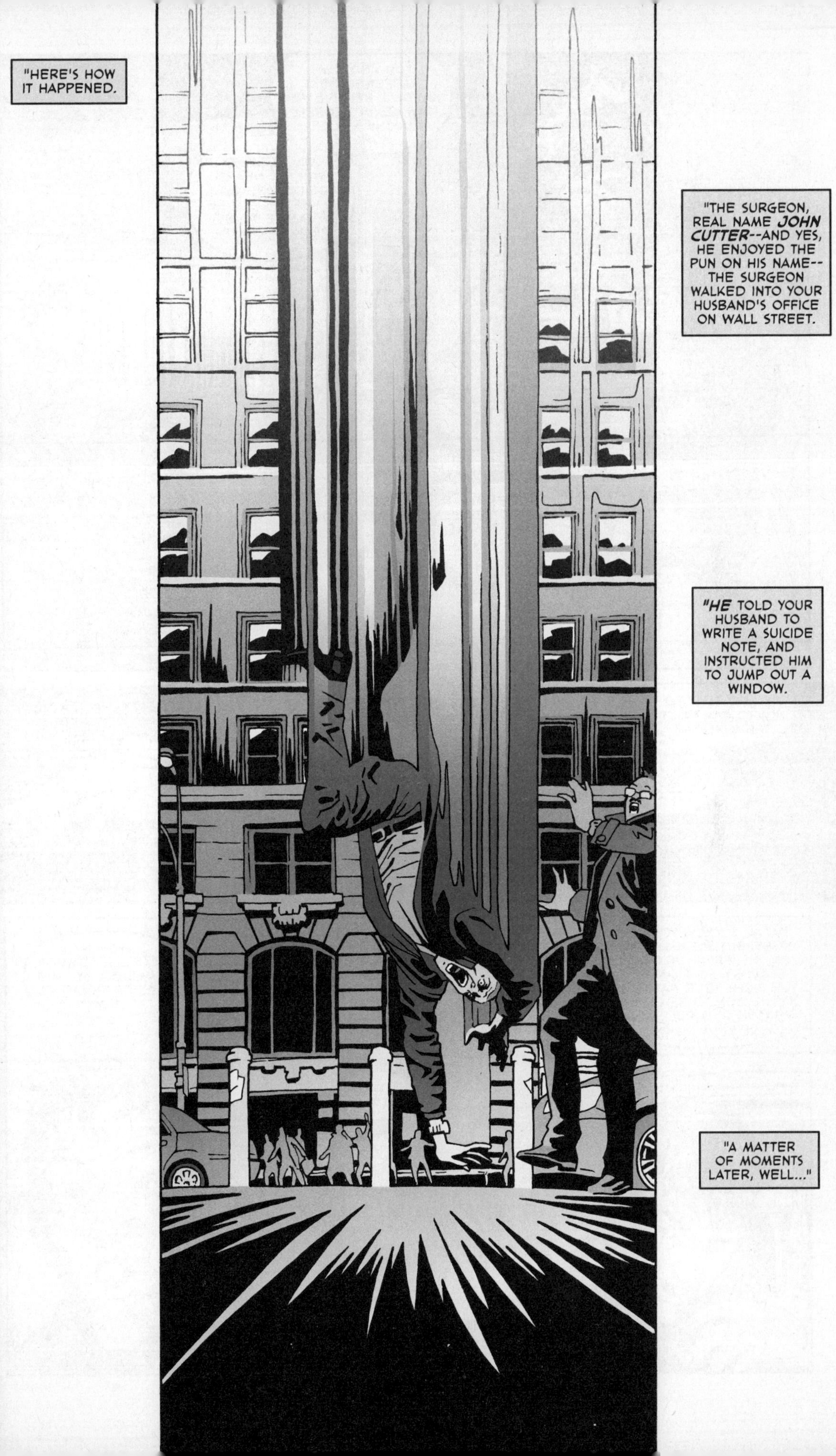
"HERE'S HOW IT HAPPENED.
"THE SURGEON, REAL NAME *JOHN CUTTER*--AND YES, HE ENJOYED THE PUN ON HIS NAME-- THE SURGEON WALKED INTO YOUR HUSBAND'S OFFICE ON WALL STREET.
"*HE* TOLD YOUR HUSBAND TO WRITE A SUICIDE NOTE, AND INSTRUCTED HIM TO JUMP OUT A WINDOW.
"A MATTER OF MOMENTS LATER, WELL..."

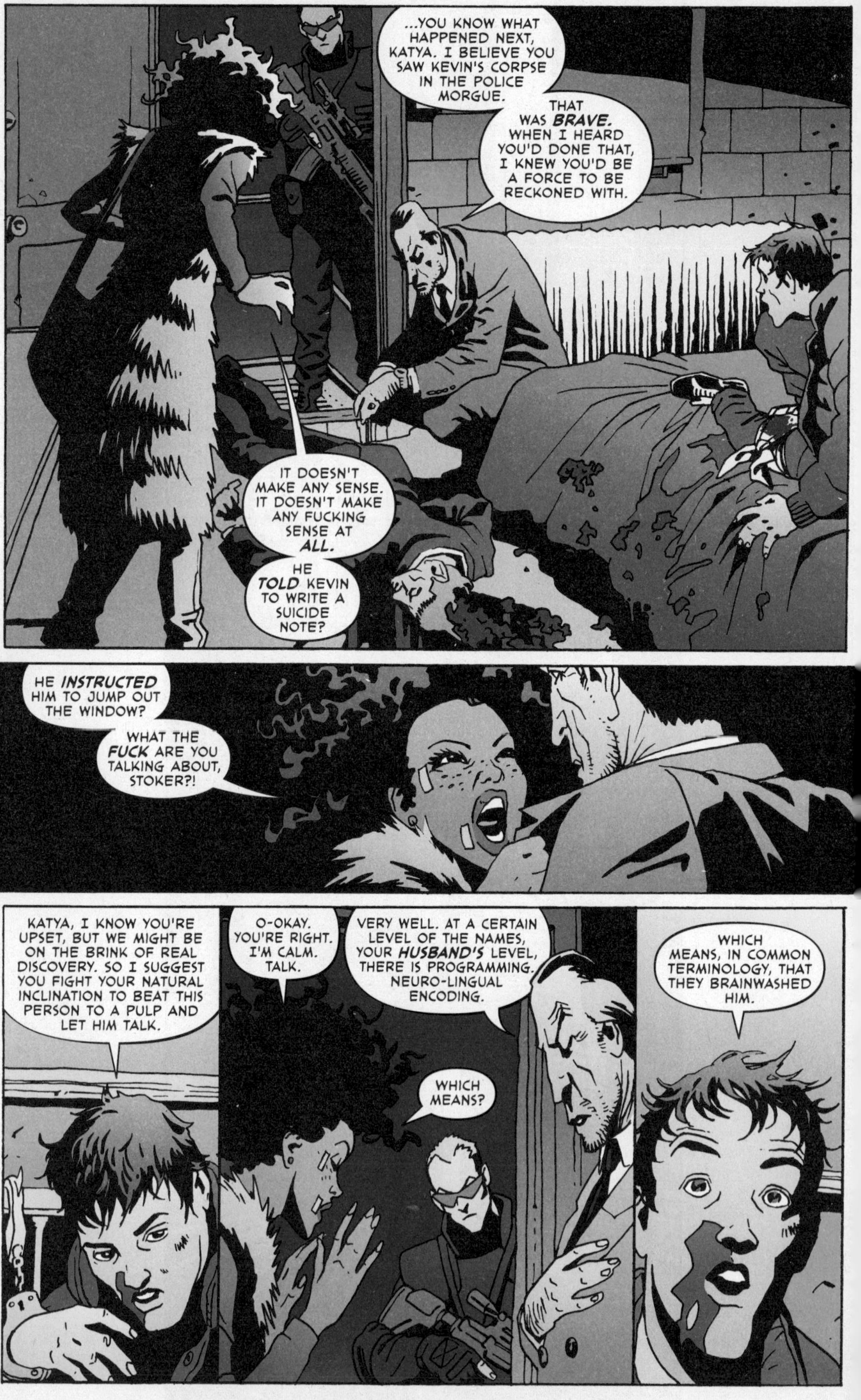
...YOU KNOW WHAT HAPPENED NEXT, KATYA. I BELIEVE YOU SAW KEVIN'S CORPSE IN THE POLICE MORGUE.
THAT WAS BRAVE. WHEN I HEARD YOU'D DONE THAT, I KNEW YOU'D BE A FORCE TO BE RECKONED WITH.
IT DOESN'T MAKE ANY SENSE. IT DOESN'T MAKE ANY FUCKING SENSE AT ALL.
HE TOLD KEVIN TO WRITE A SUICIDE NOTE?
HE INSTRUCTED HIM TO JUMP OUT THE WINDOW?
WHAT THE FUCK ARE YOU TALKING ABOUT, STOKER?!
KATYA, I KNOW YOU'RE UPSET, BUT WE MIGHT BE ON THE BRINK OF REAL DISCOVERY. SO I SUGGEST YOU FIGHT YOUR NATURAL INCLINATION TO BEAT THIS PERSON TO A PULP AND LET HIM TALK.
O-OKAY. YOU'RE RIGHT. I'M CALM. TALK.
VERY WELL. AT A CERTAIN LEVEL OF THE NAMES, YOUR HUSBAND'S LEVEL, THERE IS PROGRAMMING. NEURO-LINGUAL ENCODING.
WHICH MEANS?
WHICH MEANS, IN COMMON TERMINOLOGY, THAT THEY BRAINWASHED HIM.

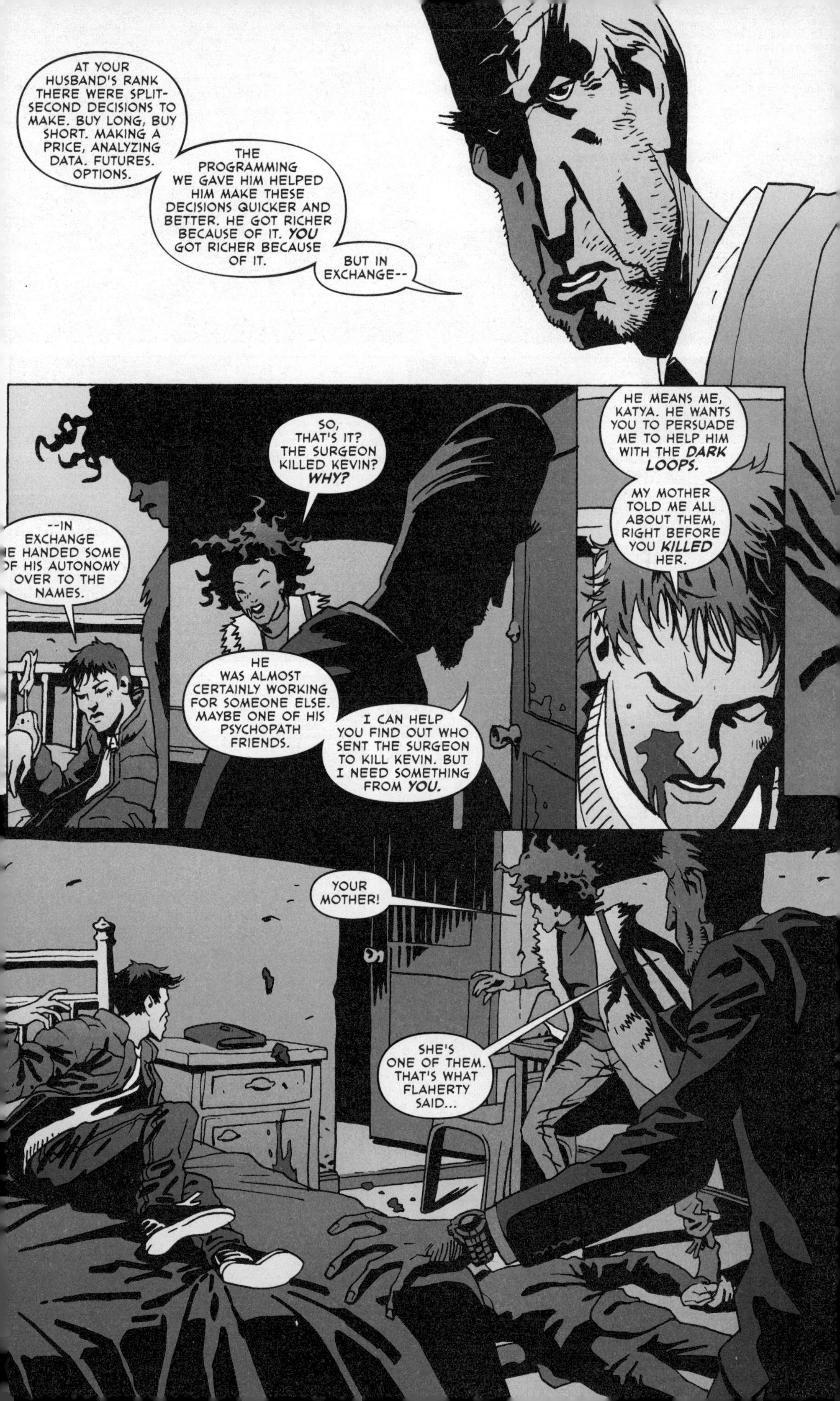
AT YOUR HUSBAND'S RANK THERE WERE SPLIT-SECOND DECISIONS TO MAKE. BUY LONG, BUY SHORT. MAKING A PRICE, ANALYZING DATA. FUTURES. OPTIONS.
THE PROGRAMMING WE GAVE HIM HELPED HIM MAKE THESE DECISIONS QUICKER AND BETTER. HE GOT RICHER BECAUSE OF IT. YOU GOT RICHER BECAUSE OF IT.
BUT IN EXCHANGE--
--IN EXCHANGE HE HANDED SOME OF HIS AUTONOMY OVER TO THE NAMES.
SO, THAT'S IT? THE SURGEON KILLED KEVIN? WHY?
HE WAS ALMOST CERTAINLY WORKING FOR SOMEONE ELSE. MAYBE ONE OF HIS PSYCHOPATH FRIENDS.
I CAN HELP YOU FIND OUT WHO SENT THE SURGEON TO KILL KEVIN. BUT I NEED SOMETHING FROM YOU.
HE MEANS ME, KATYA. HE WANTS YOU TO PERSUADE ME TO HELP HIM WITH THE DARK LOOPS.
MY MOTHER TOLD ME ALL ABOUT THEM, RIGHT BEFORE YOU KILLED HER.
YOUR MOTHER!
SHE'S ONE OF THEM. THAT'S WHAT FLAHERTY SAID...

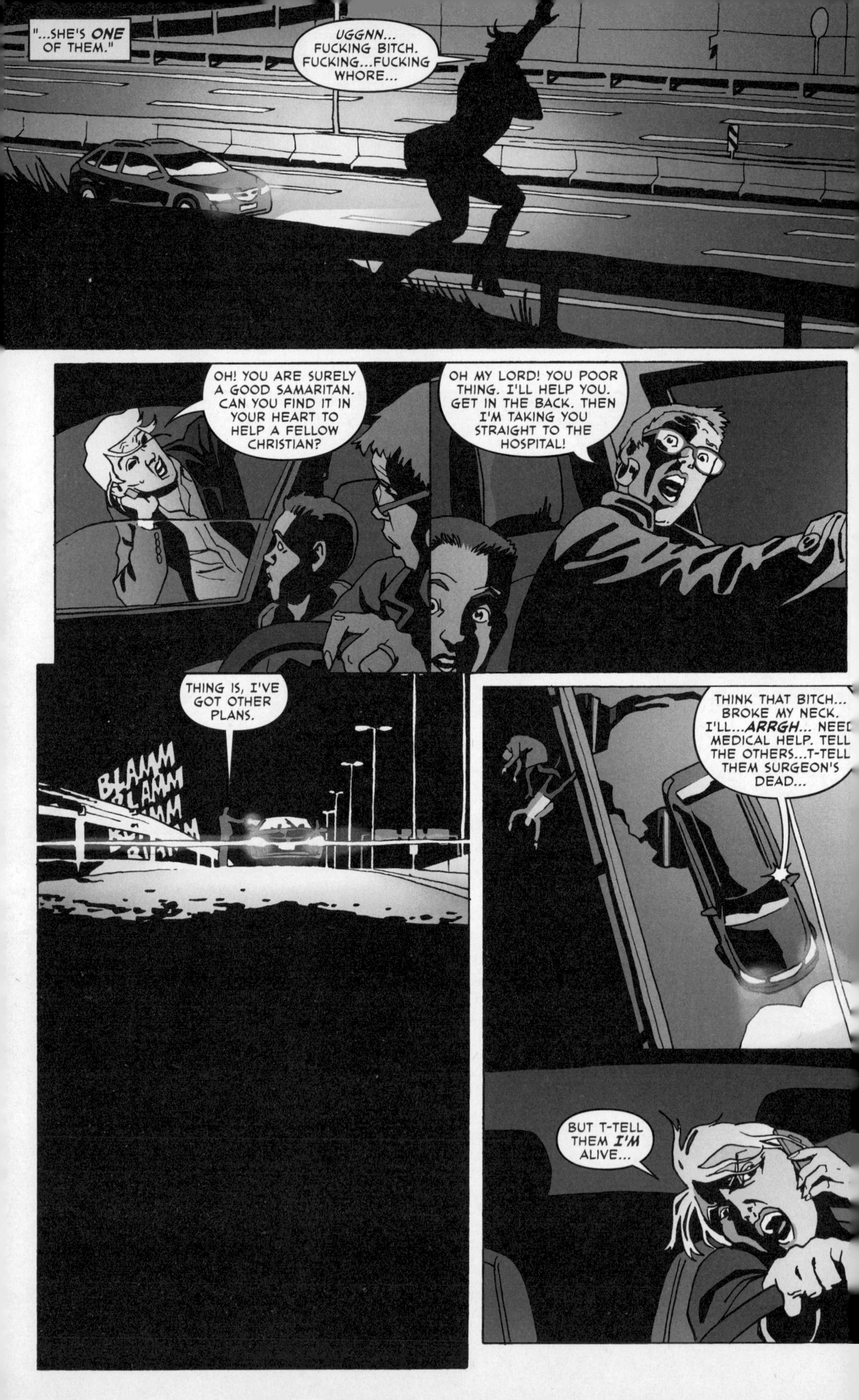
"...SHE'S ONE OF THEM."
UGGNN... FUCKING BITCH. FUCKING...FUCKING WHORE...
OH! YOU ARE SURELY A GOOD SAMARITAN. CAN YOU FIND IT IN YOUR HEART TO HELP A FELLOW CHRISTIAN?
OH MY LORD! YOU POOR THING. I'LL HELP YOU. GET IN THE BACK. THEN I'M TAKING YOU STRAIGHT TO THE HOSPITAL!
THING IS, I'VE GOT OTHER PLANS.
BLAMM
BLAMM
THINK THAT BITCH... BROKE MY NECK. I'LL...ARRGH... NEED MEDICAL HELP. TELL THE OTHERS...T-TELL THEM SURGEON'S DEAD...
BUT T-TELL THEM I'M ALIVE...

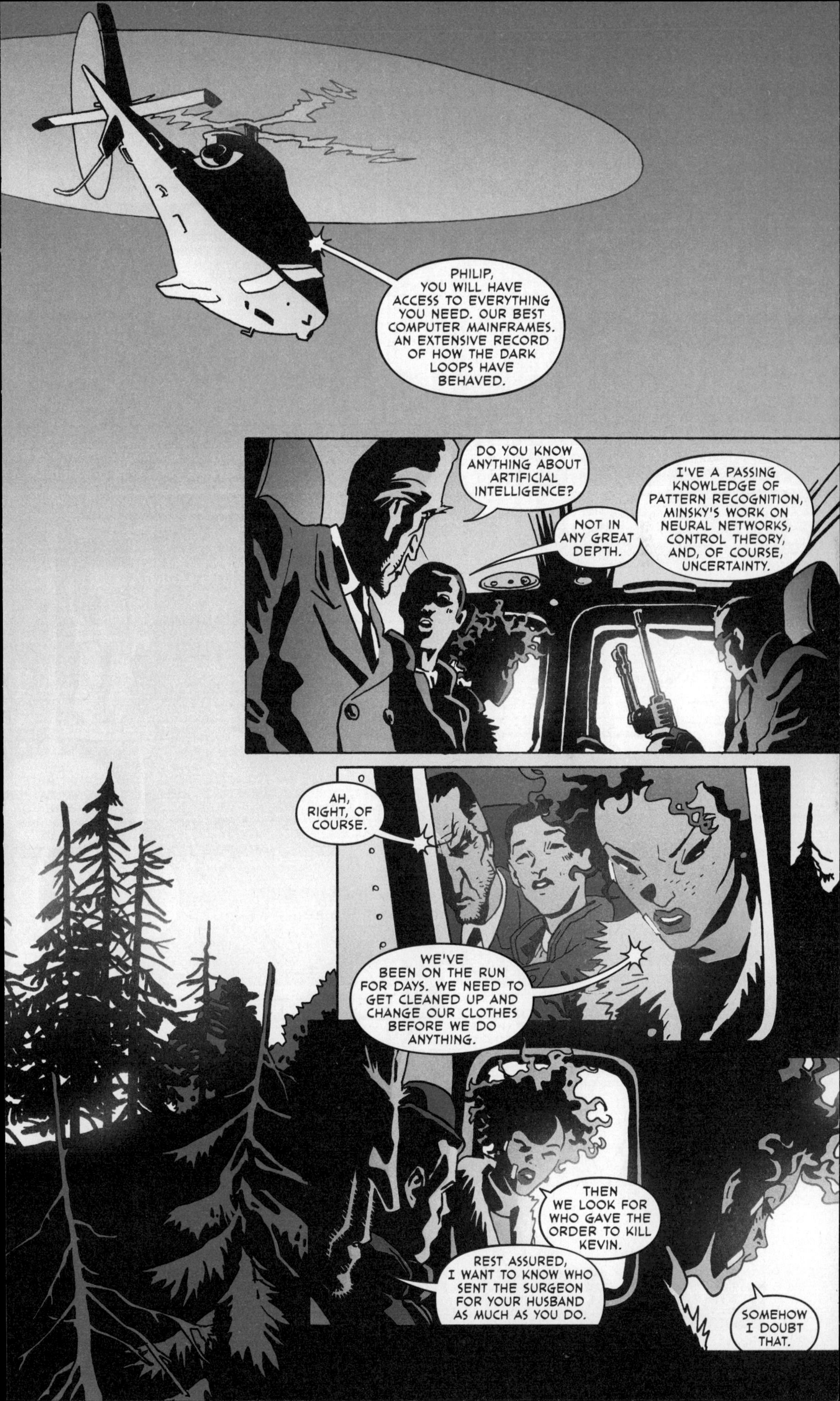
PHILIP, YOU WILL HAVE ACCESS TO EVERYTHING YOU NEED. OUR BEST COMPUTER MAINFRAMES. AN EXTENSIVE RECORD OF HOW THE DARK LOOPS HAVE BEHAVED.
DO YOU KNOW ANYTHING ABOUT ARTIFICIAL INTELLIGENCE?
NOT IN ANY GREAT DEPTH.
I'VE A PASSING KNOWLEDGE OF PATTERN RECOGNITION, MINSKY'S WORK ON NEURAL NETWORKS, CONTROL THEORY, AND, OF COURSE, UNCERTAINTY.
AH, RIGHT, OF COURSE.
WE'VE BEEN ON THE RUN FOR DAYS. WE NEED TO GET CLEANED UP AND CHANGE OUR CLOTHES BEFORE WE DO ANYTHING.
THEN WE LOOK FOR WHO GAVE THE ORDER TO KILL KEVIN.
REST ASSURED, I WANT TO KNOW WHO SENT THE SURGEON FOR YOUR HUSBAND AS MUCH AS YOU DO.
SOMEHOW I DOUBT THAT.

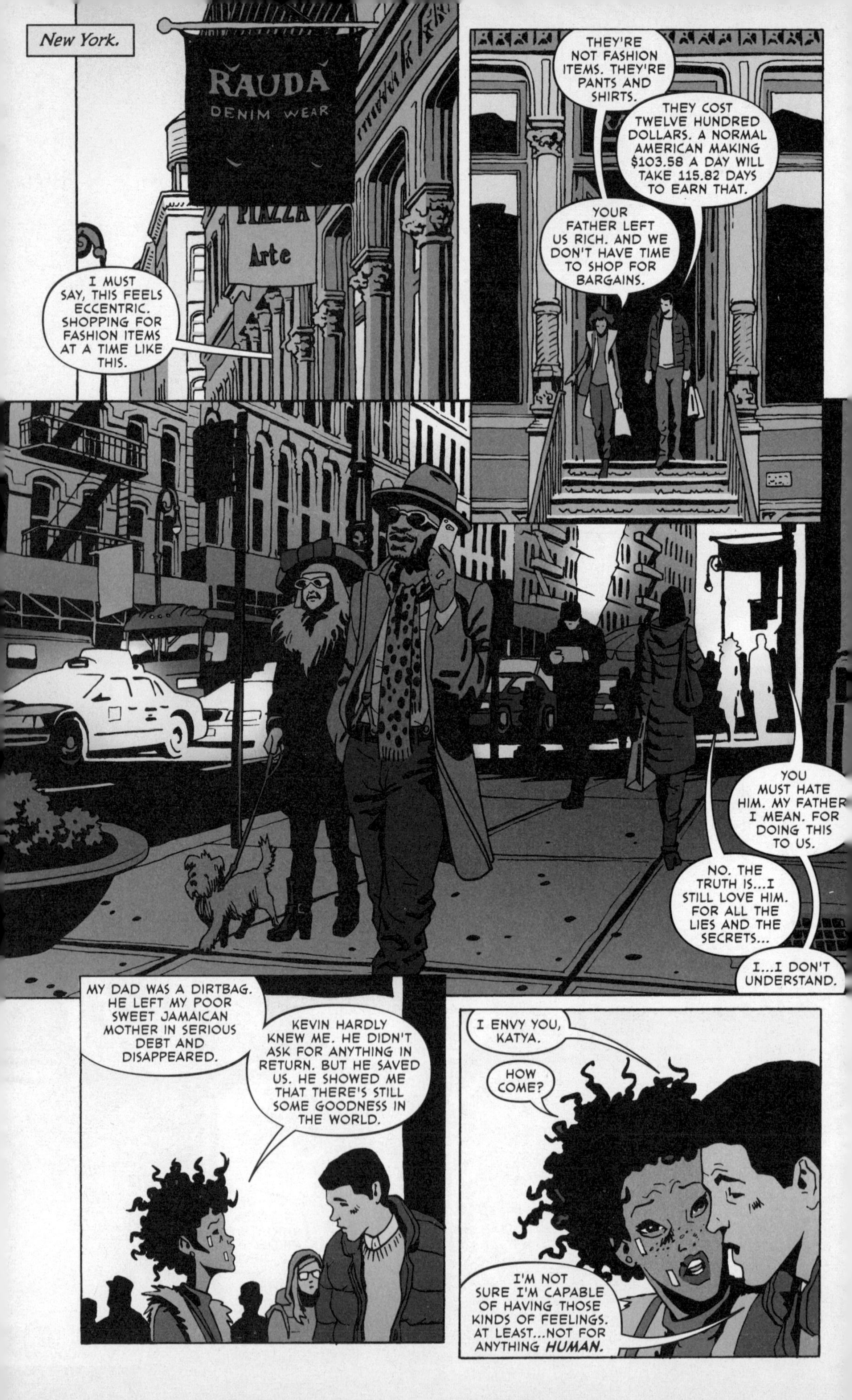

New York.
RAUDA DENIM WEAR
PIZZA Arte
I MUST SAY, THIS FEELS ECCENTRIC. SHOPPING FOR FASHION ITEMS AT A TIME LIKE THIS.
THEY'RE NOT FASHION ITEMS. THEY'RE PANTS AND SHIRTS.
THEY COST TWELVE HUNDRED DOLLARS. A NORMAL AMERICAN MAKING $103.58 A DAY WILL TAKE 115.82 DAYS TO EARN THAT.
YOUR FATHER LEFT US RICH. AND WE DON'T HAVE TIME TO SHOP FOR BARGAINS.
YOU MUST HATE HIM. MY FATHER I MEAN. FOR DOING THIS TO US.
NO. THE TRUTH IS...I STILL LOVE HIM. FOR ALL THE LIES AND THE SECRETS...
I...I DON'T UNDERSTAND.
MY DAD WAS A DIRTBAG. HE LEFT MY POOR SWEET JAMAICAN MOTHER IN SERIOUS DEBT AND DISAPPEARED.
KEVIN HARDLY KNEW ME. HE DIDN'T ASK FOR ANYTHING IN RETURN. BUT HE SAVED US. HE SHOWED ME THAT THERE'S STILL SOME GOODNESS IN THE WORLD.
I ENVY YOU, KATYA.
HOW COME?
I'M NOT SURE I'M CAPABLE OF HAVING THOSE KINDS OF FEELINGS. AT LEAST...NOT FOR ANYTHING *HUMAN.*

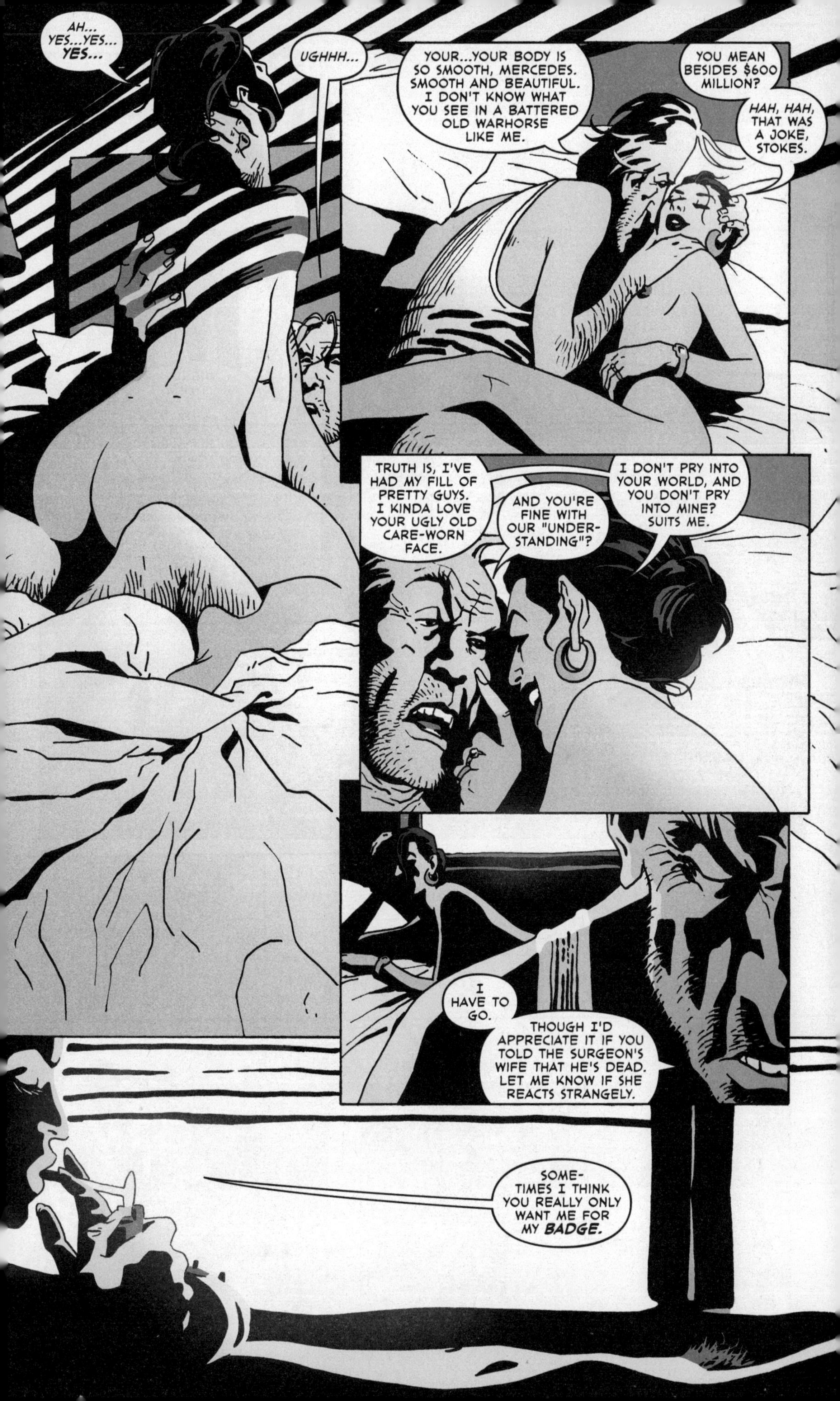

AH... YES...YES... *YES...*
UGHHH...
YOUR...YOUR BODY IS SO SMOOTH, MERCEDES. SMOOTH AND BEAUTIFUL. I DON'T KNOW WHAT YOU SEE IN A BATTERED OLD WARHORSE LIKE ME.
YOU MEAN BESIDES $600 MILLION?
HAH, HAH, THAT WAS A JOKE, STOKES.
TRUTH IS, I'VE HAD MY FILL OF PRETTY GUYS. I KINDA LOVE YOUR UGLY OLD CARE-WORN FACE.
AND YOU'RE FINE WITH OUR "UNDER-STANDING"?
I DON'T PRY INTO YOUR WORLD, AND YOU DON'T PRY INTO MINE? SUITS ME.
I HAVE TO GO.
THOUGH I'D APPRECIATE IT IF YOU TOLD THE SURGEON'S WIFE THAT HE'S DEAD. LET ME KNOW IF SHE REACTS STRANGELY.
SOME-TIMES I THINK YOU REALLY ONLY WANT ME FOR MY *BADGE.*

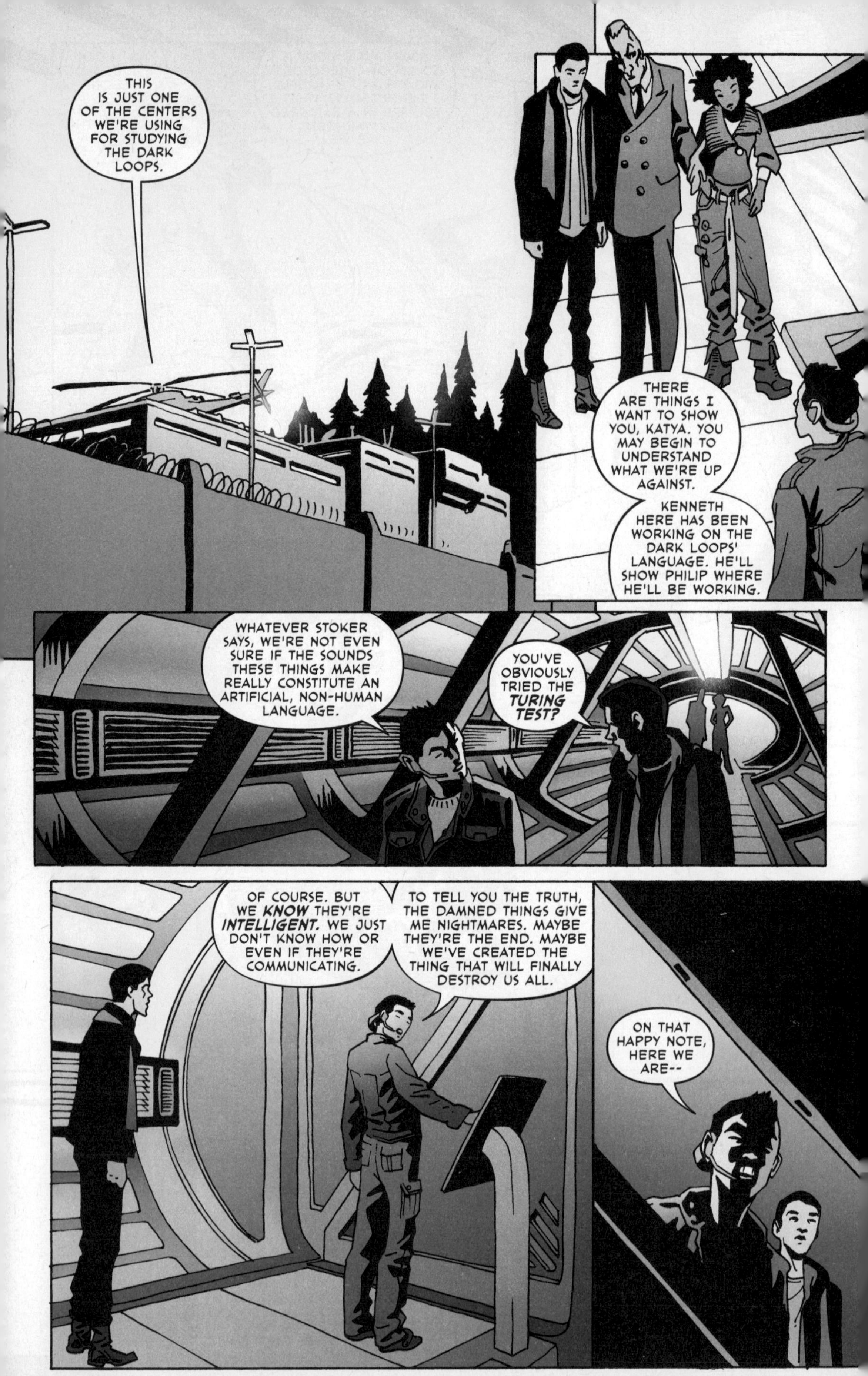
THIS IS JUST ONE OF THE CENTERS WE'RE USING FOR STUDYING THE DARK LOOPS.
THERE ARE THINGS I WANT TO SHOW YOU, KATYA. YOU MAY BEGIN TO UNDERSTAND WHAT WE'RE UP AGAINST.
KENNETH HERE HAS BEEN WORKING ON THE DARK LOOPS' LANGUAGE. HE'LL SHOW PHILIP WHERE HE'LL BE WORKING.
WHATEVER STOKER SAYS, WE'RE NOT EVEN SURE IF THE SOUNDS THESE THINGS MAKE REALLY CONSTITUTE AN ARTIFICIAL, NON-HUMAN LANGUAGE.
YOU'VE OBVIOUSLY TRIED THE *TURING TEST?*
OF COURSE. BUT WE ***KNOW*** THEY'RE ***INTELLIGENT.*** WE JUST DON'T KNOW HOW OR EVEN IF THEY'RE COMMUNICATING.
TO TELL YOU THE TRUTH, THE DAMNED THINGS GIVE ME NIGHTMARES. MAYBE THEY'RE THE END. MAYBE WE'VE CREATED THE THING THAT WILL FINALLY DESTROY US ALL.
ON THAT HAPPY NOTE, HERE WE ARE--

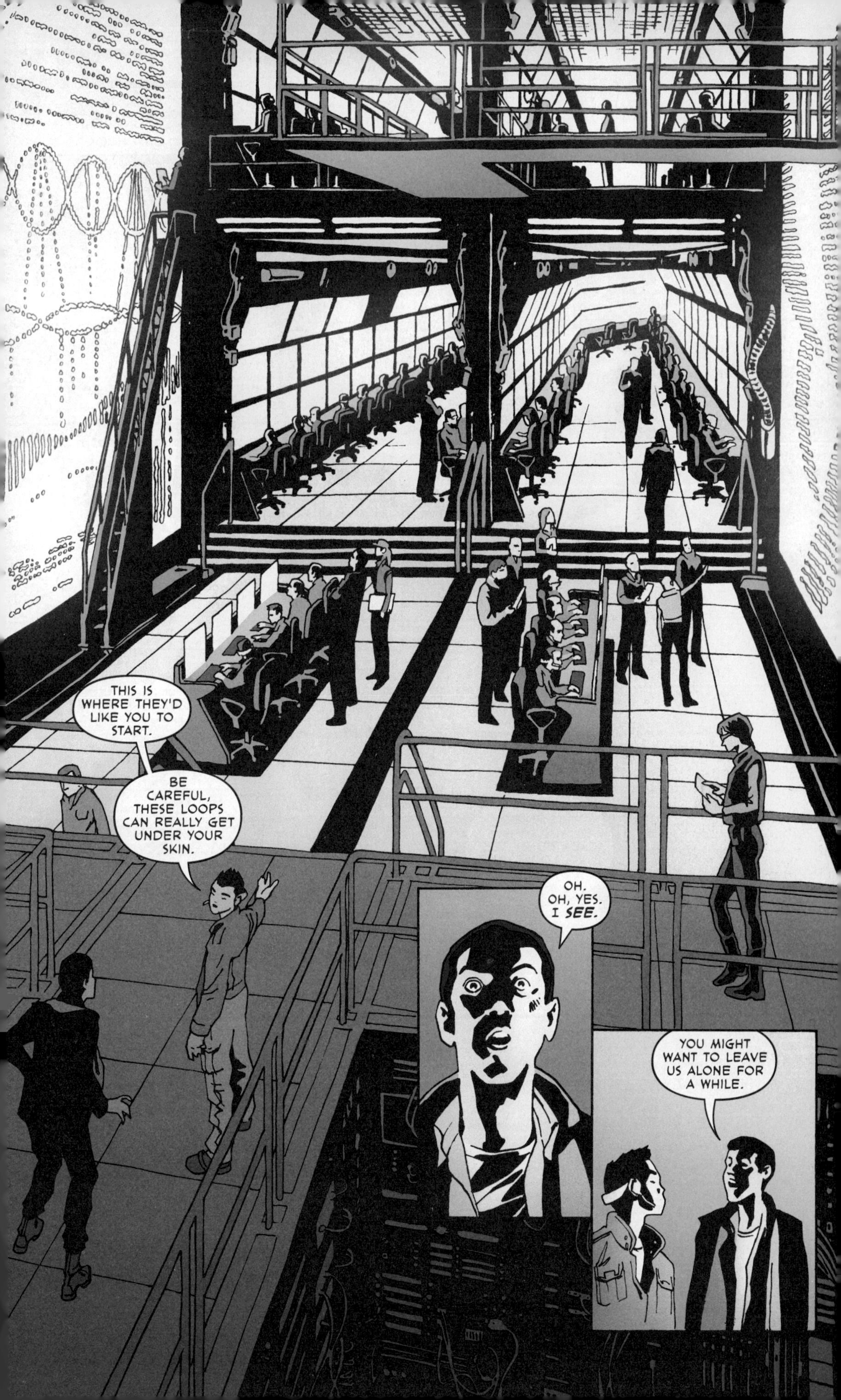
THIS IS WHERE THEY'D LIKE YOU TO START.
BE CAREFUL, THESE LOOPS CAN REALLY GET UNDER YOUR SKIN.
OH. OH, YES. I *SEE.*
YOU MIGHT WANT TO LEAVE US ALONE FOR A WHILE.

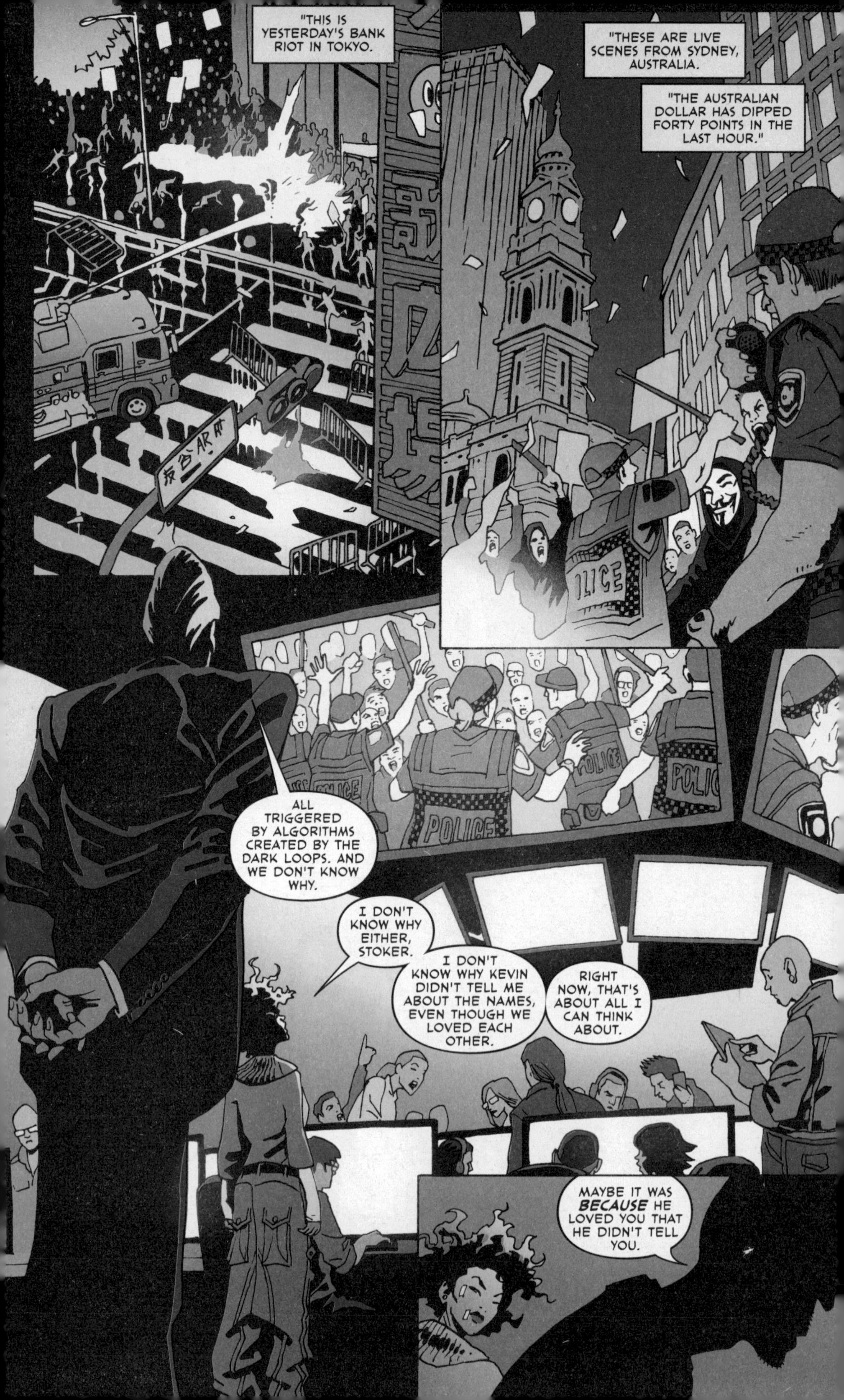
"THIS IS YESTERDAY'S BANK RIOT IN TOKYO.
"THESE ARE LIVE SCENES FROM SYDNEY, AUSTRALIA.
"THE AUSTRALIAN DOLLAR HAS DIPPED FORTY POINTS IN THE LAST HOUR."
POLICE
ALL TRIGGERED BY ALGORITHMS CREATED BY THE DARK LOOPS. AND WE DON'T KNOW WHY.
I DON'T KNOW WHY EITHER, STOKER.
I DON'T KNOW WHY KEVIN DIDN'T TELL ME ABOUT THE NAMES, EVEN THOUGH WE LOVED EACH OTHER.
RIGHT NOW, THAT'S ABOUT ALL I CAN THINK ABOUT.
MAYBE IT WAS *BECAUSE* HE LOVED YOU THAT HE DIDN'T TELL YOU.

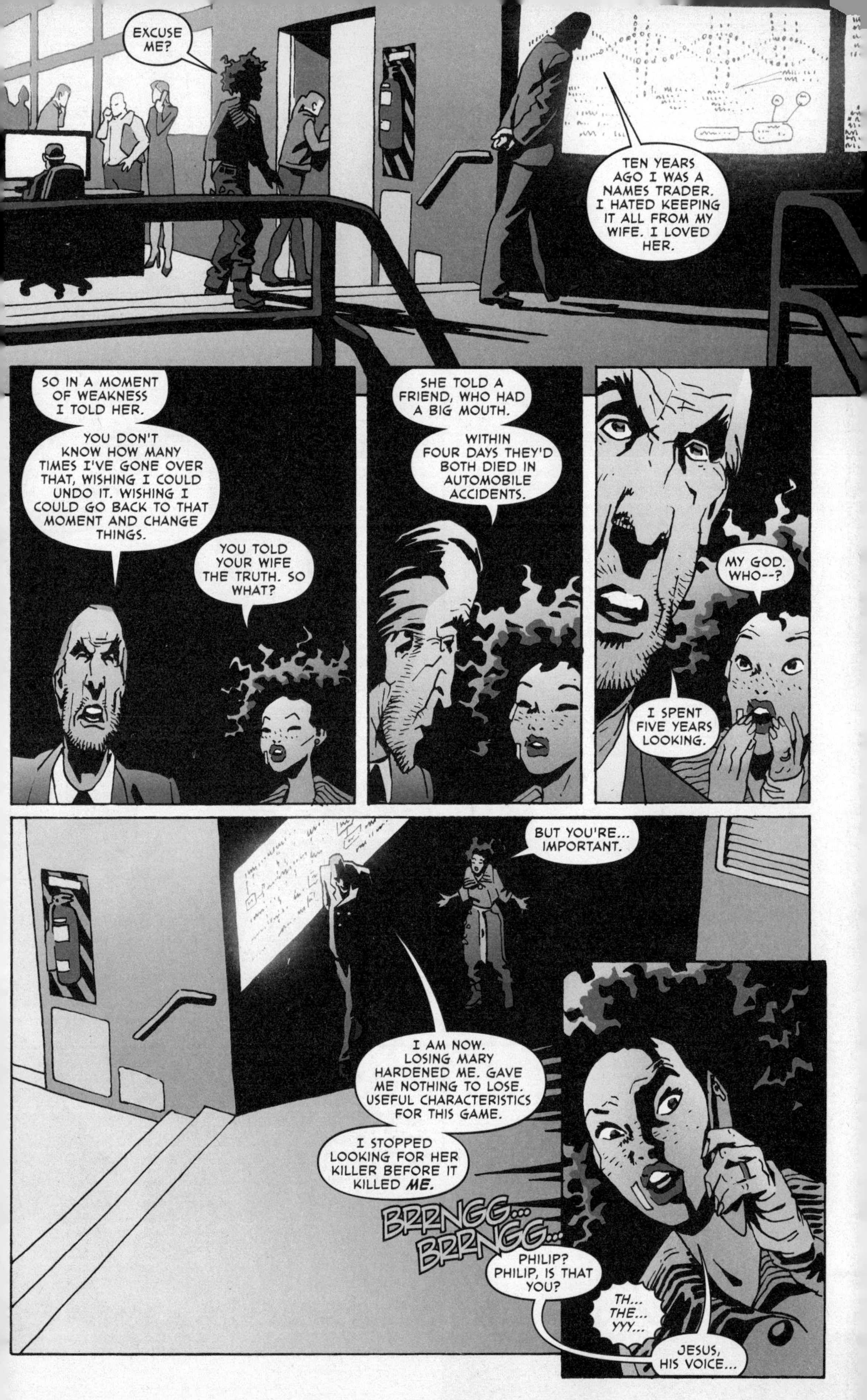
EXCUSE ME?
TEN YEARS AGO I WAS A NAMES TRADER. I HATED KEEPING IT ALL FROM MY WIFE. I LOVED HER.
SO IN A MOMENT OF WEAKNESS I TOLD HER.
YOU DON'T KNOW HOW MANY TIMES I'VE GONE OVER THAT, WISHING I COULD UNDO IT. WISHING I COULD GO BACK TO THAT MOMENT AND CHANGE THINGS.
YOU TOLD YOUR WIFE THE TRUTH. SO WHAT?
SHE TOLD A FRIEND, WHO HAD A BIG MOUTH.
WITHIN FOUR DAYS THEY'D BOTH DIED IN AUTOMOBILE ACCIDENTS.
MY GOD. WHO--?
I SPENT FIVE YEARS LOOKING.
BUT YOU'RE... IMPORTANT.
I AM NOW. LOSING MARY HARDENED ME. GAVE ME NOTHING TO LOSE. USEFUL CHARACTERISTICS FOR THIS GAME.
I STOPPED LOOKING FOR HER KILLER BEFORE IT KILLED ME.
BRRNGG... BRRNGG...
PHILIP? PHILIP, IS THAT YOU?
TH... THE... YYY...
JESUS, HIS VOICE...

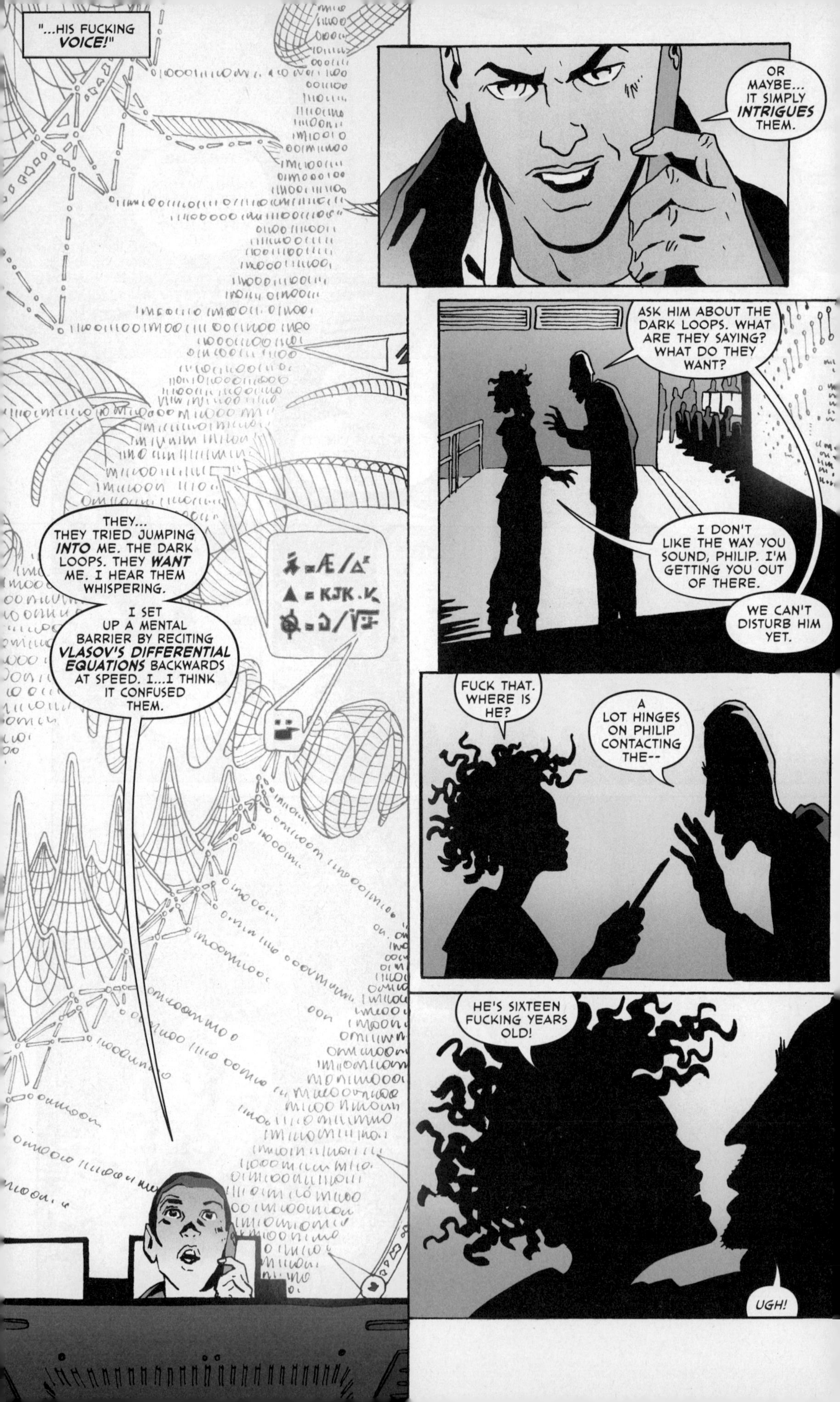

"...HIS FUCKING VOICE!"
THEY... THEY TRIED JUMPING INTO ME. THE DARK LOOPS. THEY WANT ME. I HEAR THEM WHISPERING.
I SET UP A MENTAL BARRIER BY RECITING VLASOV'S DIFFERENTIAL EQUATIONS BACKWARDS AT SPEED. I...I THINK IT CONFUSED THEM.
OR MAYBE... IT SIMPLY INTRIGUES THEM.
ASK HIM ABOUT THE DARK LOOPS. WHAT ARE THEY SAYING? WHAT DO THEY WANT?
I DON'T LIKE THE WAY YOU SOUND, PHILIP. I'M GETTING YOU OUT OF THERE.
WE CAN'T DISTURB HIM YET.
FUCK THAT. WHERE IS HE?
A LOT HINGES ON PHILIP CONTACTING THE--
HE'S SIXTEEN FUCKING YEARS OLD!
UGH!

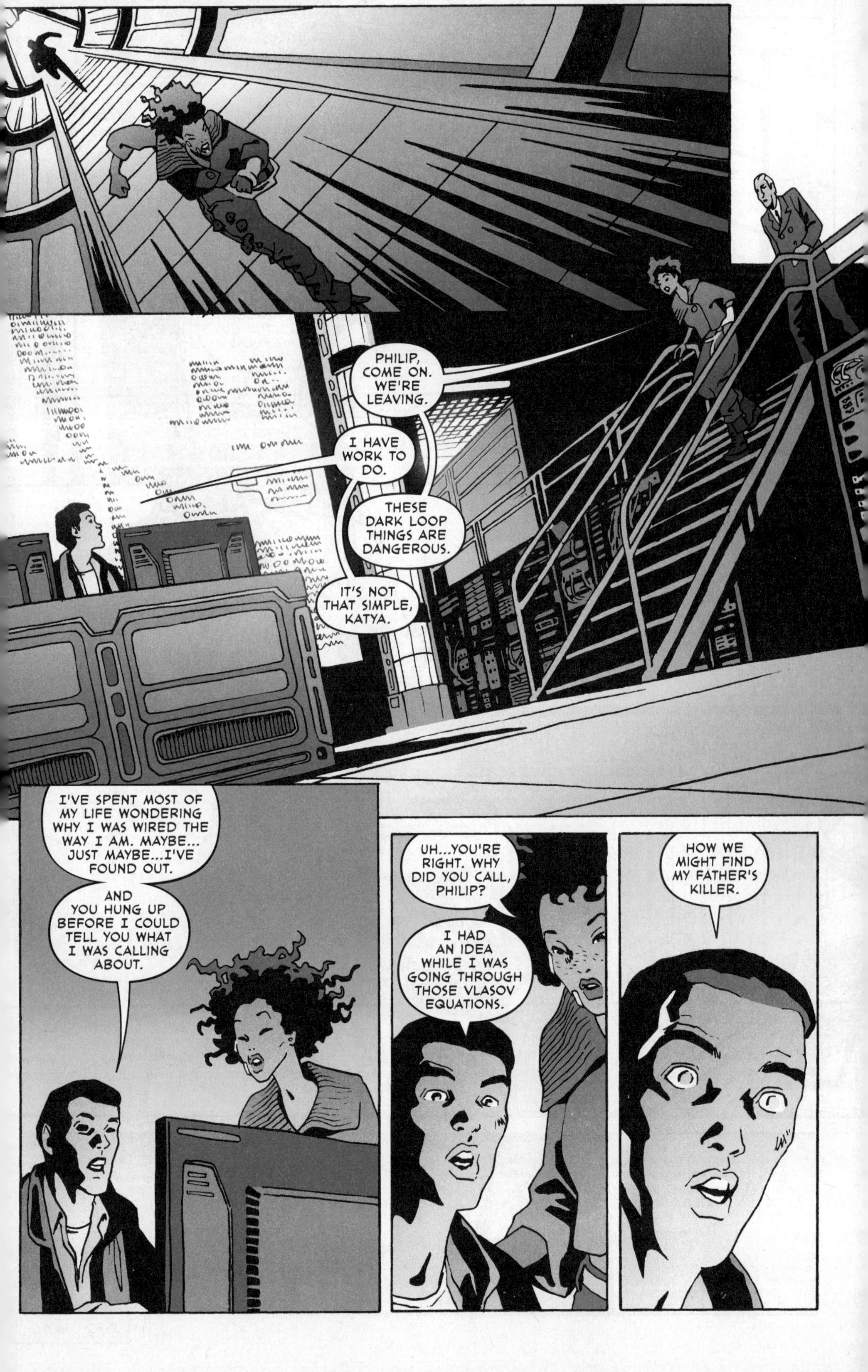
PHILIP, COME ON. WE'RE LEAVING.
I HAVE WORK TO DO.
THESE DARK LOOP THINGS ARE DANGEROUS.
IT'S NOT THAT SIMPLE, KATYA.
I'VE SPENT MOST OF MY LIFE WONDERING WHY I WAS WIRED THE WAY I AM. MAYBE... JUST MAYBE...I'VE FOUND OUT.
AND YOU HUNG UP BEFORE I COULD TELL YOU WHAT I WAS CALLING ABOUT.
UH...YOU'RE RIGHT. WHY DID YOU CALL, PHILIP?
I HAD AN IDEA WHILE I WAS GOING THROUGH THOSE VLASOV EQUATIONS.
HOW WE MIGHT FIND MY FATHER'S KILLER.

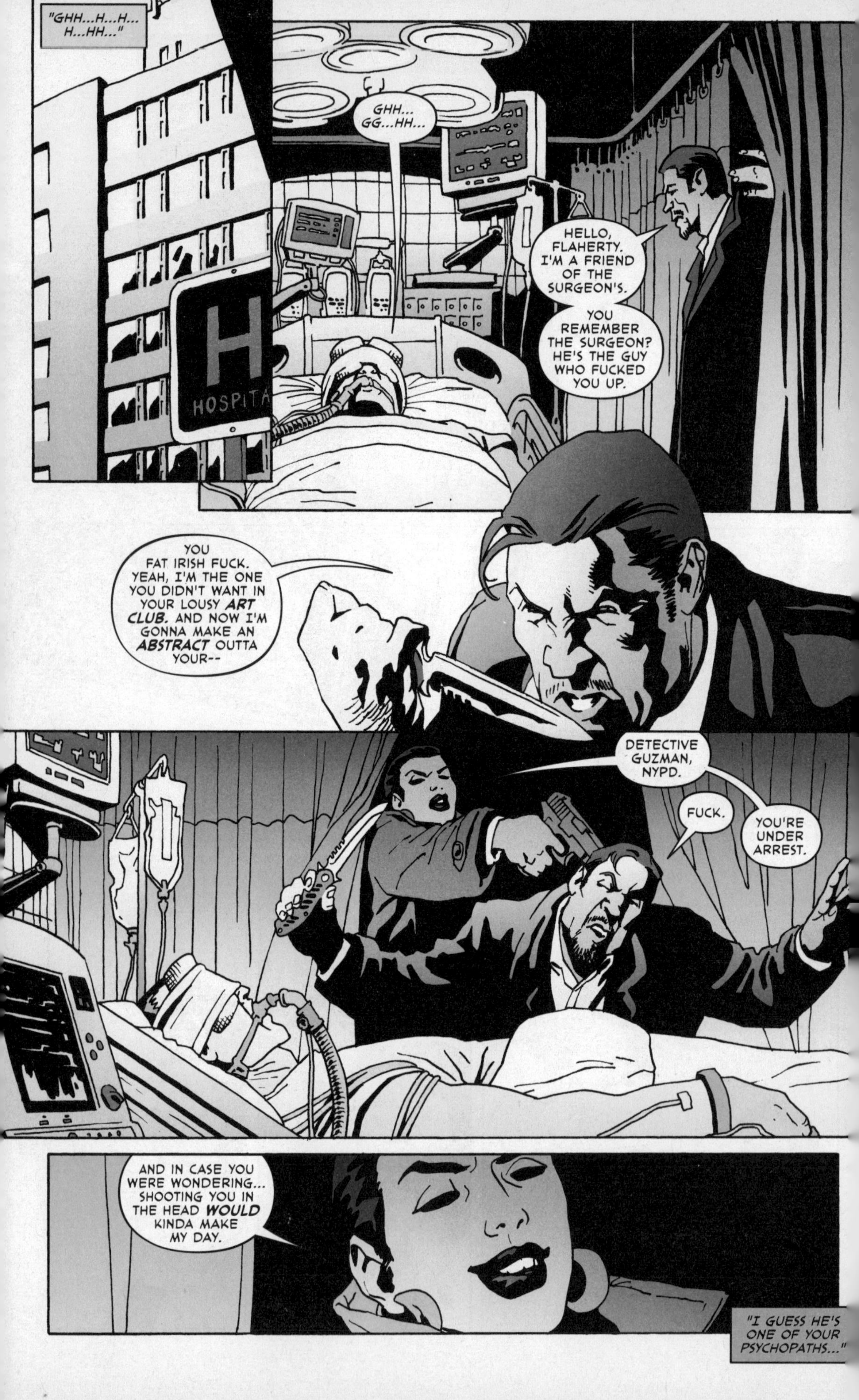
"GHH...H...H... H...HH..."
GHH... GG...HH...
HELLO, FLAHERTY. I'M A FRIEND OF THE SURGEON'S.
YOU REMEMBER THE SURGEON? HE'S THE GUY WHO FUCKED YOU UP.
HOSPITA
YOU FAT IRISH FUCK. YEAH, I'M THE ONE YOU DIDN'T WANT IN YOUR LOUSY ART CLUB. AND NOW I'M GONNA MAKE AN ABSTRACT OUTTA YOUR--
DETECTIVE GUZMAN, NYPD.
FUCK.
YOU'RE UNDER ARREST.
AND IN CASE YOU WERE WONDERING... SHOOTING YOU IN THE HEAD WOULD KINDA MAKE MY DAY.
"I GUESS HE'S ONE OF YOUR PSYCHOPATHS..."

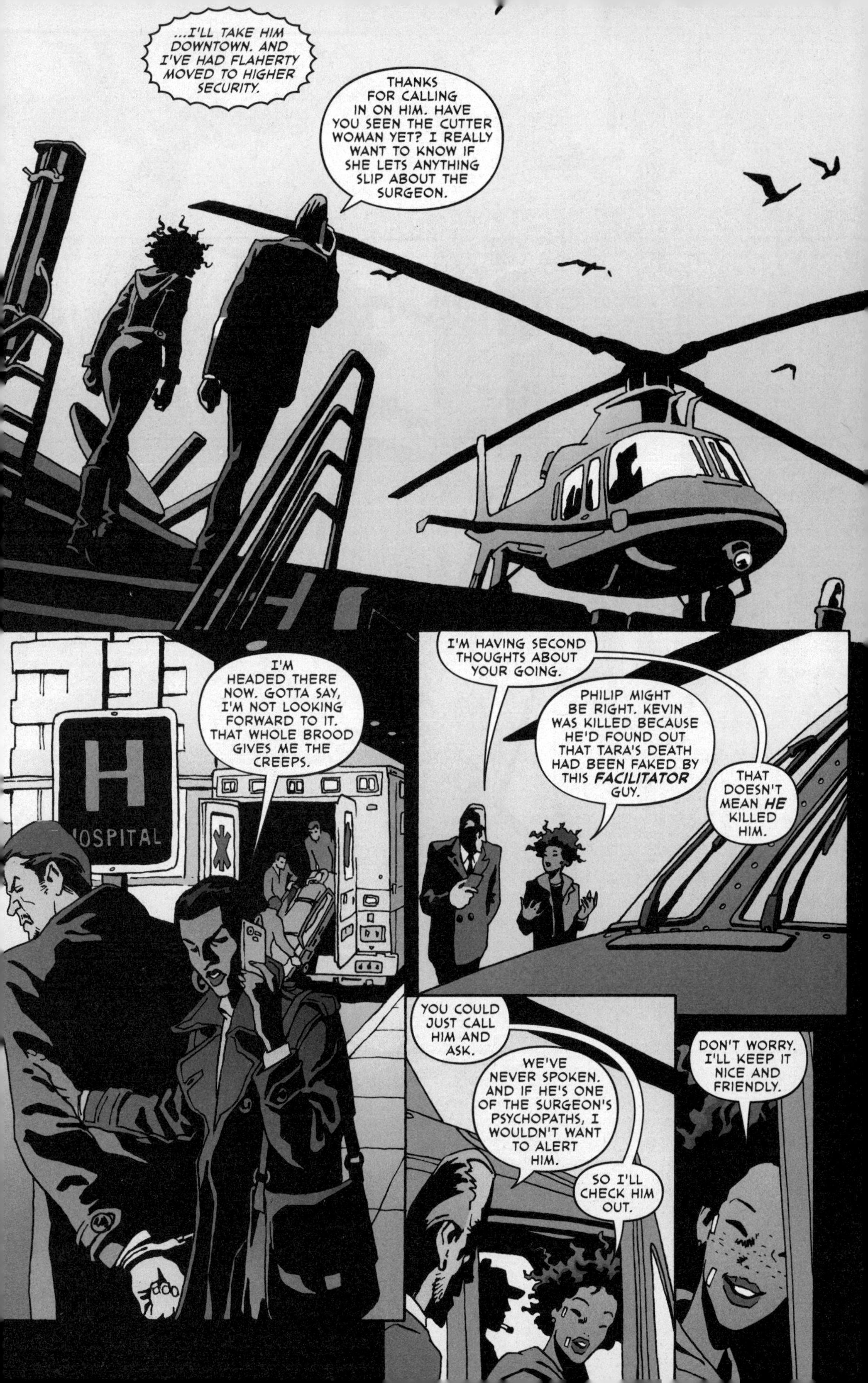
...I'LL TAKE HIM DOWNTOWN. AND I'VE HAD FLAHERTY MOVED TO HIGHER SECURITY.
THANKS FOR CALLING IN ON HIM. HAVE YOU SEEN THE CUTTER WOMAN YET? I REALLY WANT TO KNOW IF SHE LETS ANYTHING SLIP ABOUT THE SURGEON.
I'M HEADED THERE NOW. GOTTA SAY, I'M NOT LOOKING FORWARD TO IT. THAT WHOLE BROOD GIVES ME THE CREEPS.
H
HOSPITAL
I'M HAVING SECOND THOUGHTS ABOUT YOUR GOING.
PHILIP MIGHT BE RIGHT. KEVIN WAS KILLED BECAUSE HE'D FOUND OUT THAT TARA'S DEATH HAD BEEN FAKED BY THIS FACILITATOR GUY.
THAT DOESN'T MEAN HE KILLED HIM.
YOU COULD JUST CALL HIM AND ASK.
WE'VE NEVER SPOKEN. AND IF HE'S ONE OF THE SURGEON'S PSYCHOPATHS, I WOULDN'T WANT TO ALERT HIM.
SO I'LL CHECK HIM OUT.
DON'T WORRY. I'LL KEEP IT NICE AND FRIENDLY.

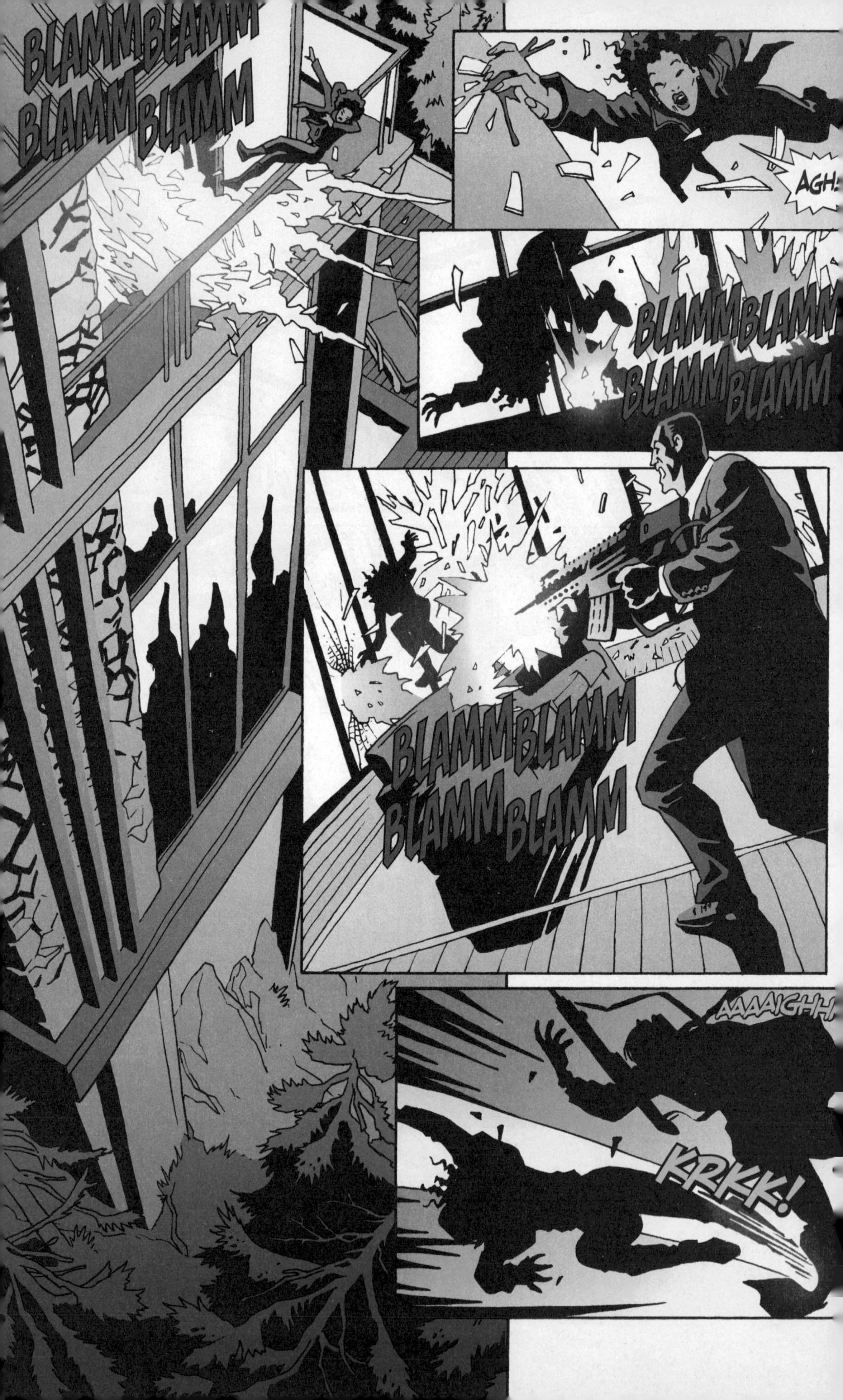
BLAMM BLAMM BLAMM BLAMM
AGH!
BLAMM BLAMM BLAMM BLAMM
BLAMM BLAMM BLAMM BLAMM
AAAAIGHH
KRKK!

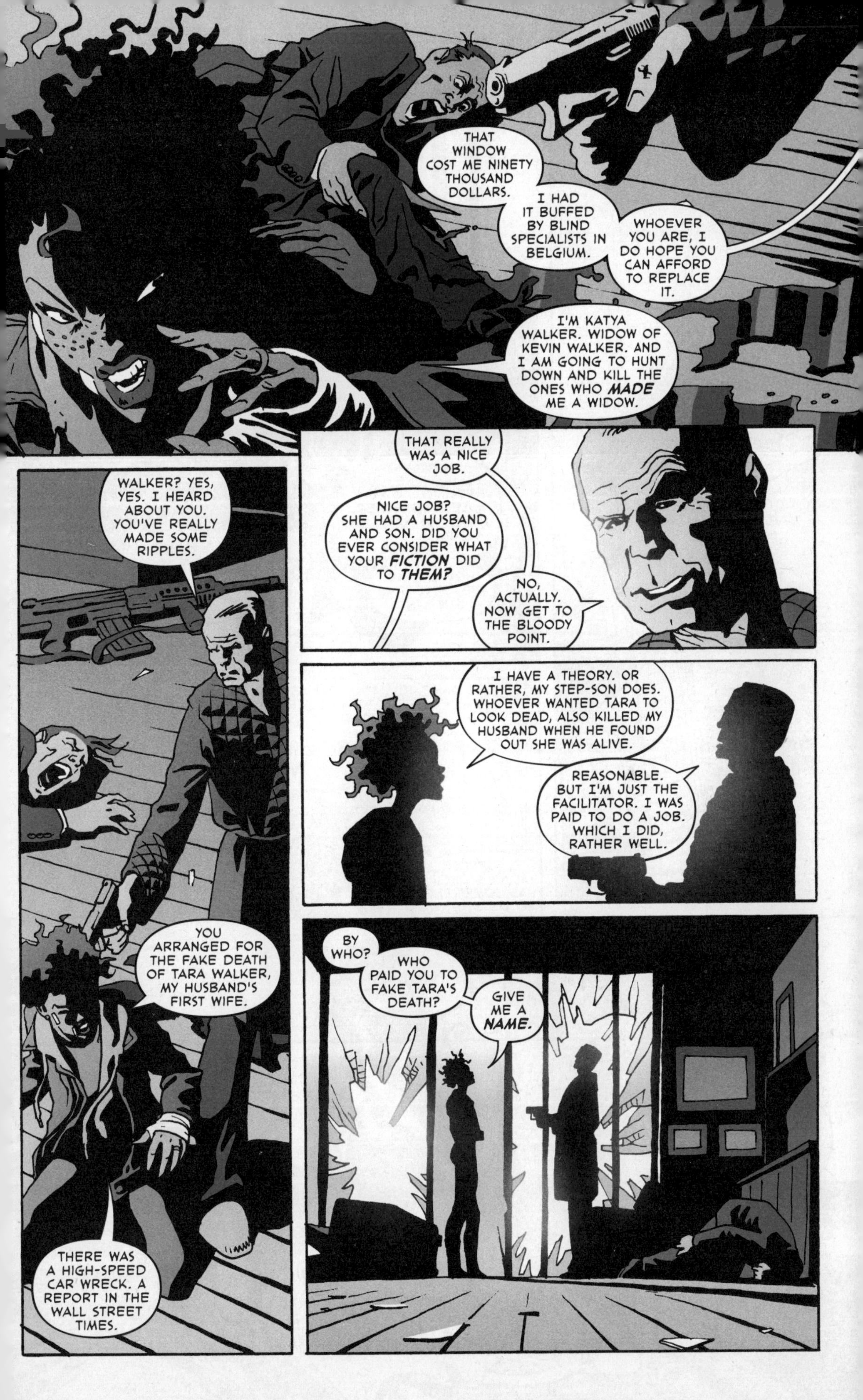
THAT WINDOW COST ME NINETY THOUSAND DOLLARS.
I HAD IT BUFFED BY BLIND SPECIALISTS IN BELGIUM.
WHOEVER YOU ARE, I DO HOPE YOU CAN AFFORD TO REPLACE IT.
I'M KATYA WALKER. WIDOW OF KEVIN WALKER. AND I AM GOING TO HUNT DOWN AND KILL THE ONES WHO MADE ME A WIDOW.
WALKER? YES, YES. I HEARD ABOUT YOU. YOU'VE REALLY MADE SOME RIPPLES.
YOU ARRANGED FOR THE FAKE DEATH OF TARA WALKER, MY HUSBAND'S FIRST WIFE.
THERE WAS A HIGH-SPEED CAR WRECK. A REPORT IN THE WALL STREET TIMES.
THAT REALLY WAS A NICE JOB.
NICE JOB? SHE HAD A HUSBAND AND SON. DID YOU EVER CONSIDER WHAT YOUR FICTION DID TO THEM?
NO, ACTUALLY. NOW GET TO THE BLOODY POINT.
I HAVE A THEORY. OR RATHER, MY STEP-SON DOES. WHOEVER WANTED TARA TO LOOK DEAD, ALSO KILLED MY HUSBAND WHEN HE FOUND OUT SHE WAS ALIVE.
REASONABLE. BUT I'M JUST THE FACILITATOR. I WAS PAID TO DO A JOB. WHICH I DID, RATHER WELL.
BY WHO?
WHO PAID YOU TO FAKE TARA'S DEATH?
GIVE ME A NAME.

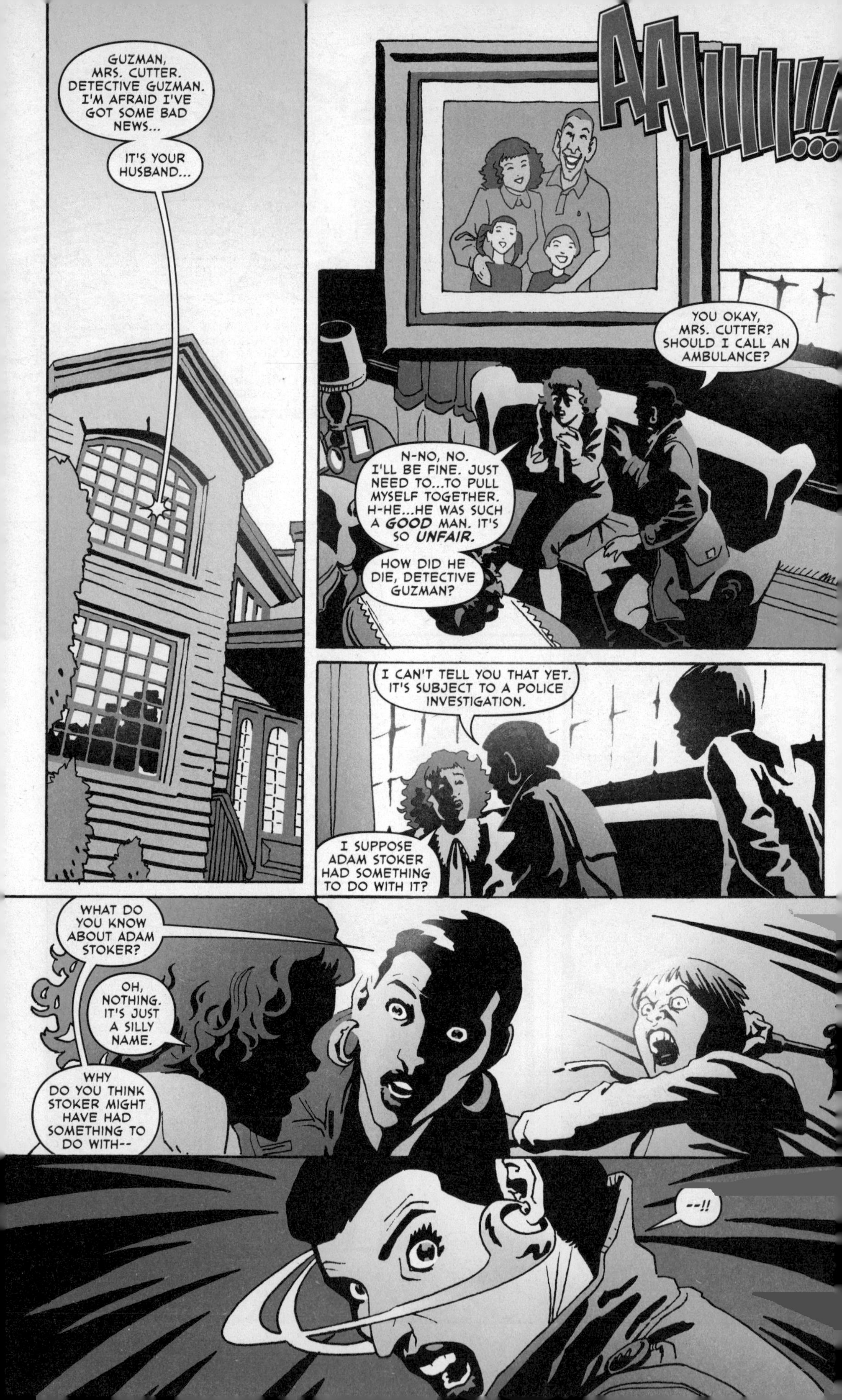
GUZMAN, MRS. CUTTER. DETECTIVE GUZMAN. I'M AFRAID I'VE GOT SOME BAD NEWS...
IT'S YOUR HUSBAND...
AAIIIIIII!!!...
YOU OKAY, MRS. CUTTER? SHOULD I CALL AN AMBULANCE?
N-NO, NO. I'LL BE FINE. JUST NEED TO...TO PULL MYSELF TOGETHER. H-HE...HE WAS SUCH A GOOD MAN. IT'S SO UNFAIR.
HOW DID HE DIE, DETECTIVE GUZMAN?
I CAN'T TELL YOU THAT YET. IT'S SUBJECT TO A POLICE INVESTIGATION.
I SUPPOSE ADAM STOKER HAD SOMETHING TO DO WITH IT?
WHAT DO YOU KNOW ABOUT ADAM STOKER?
OH, NOTHING. IT'S JUST A SILLY NAME.
WHY DO YOU THINK STOKER MIGHT HAVE HAD SOMETHING TO DO WITH--
--!!

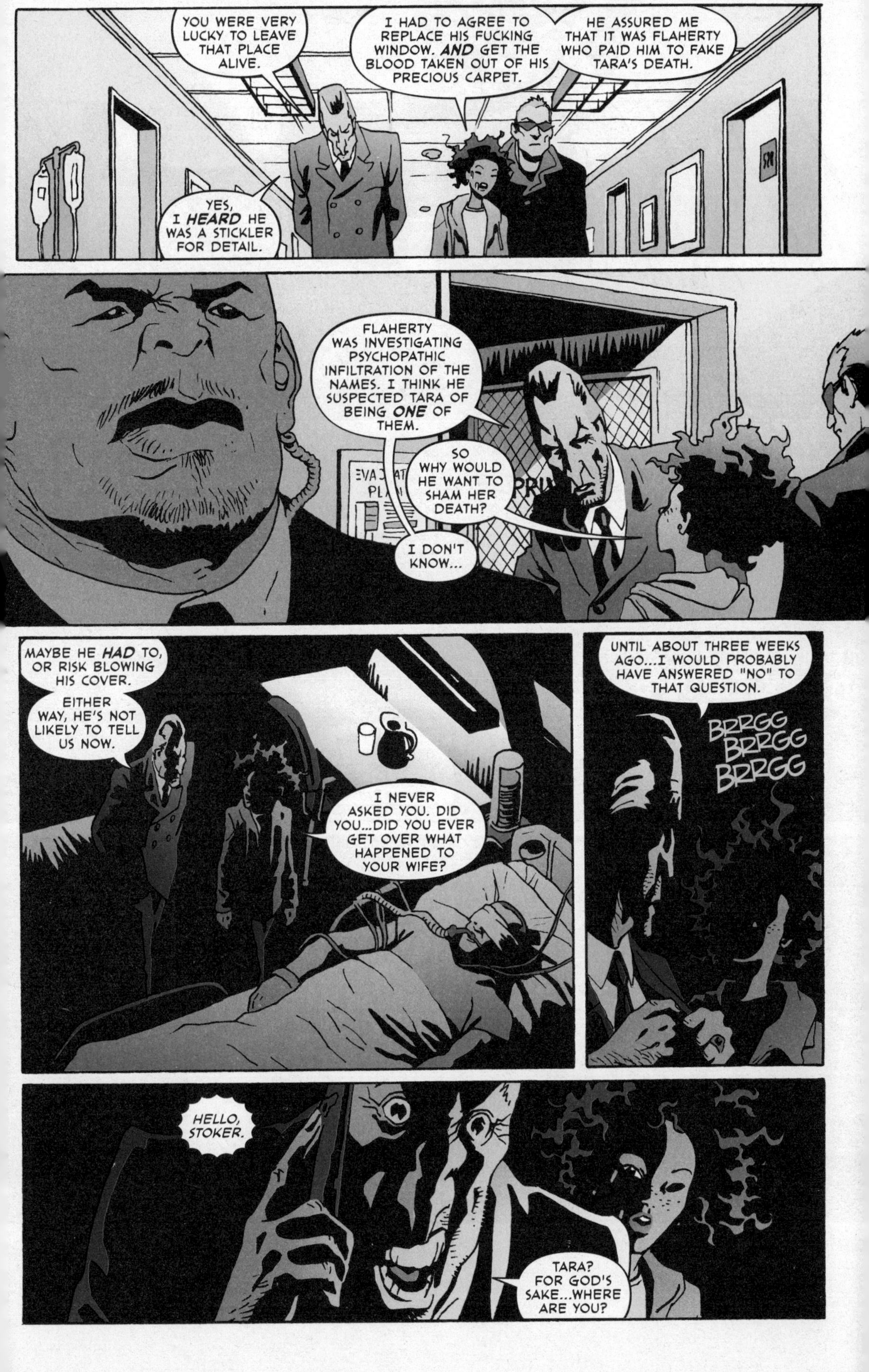
YOU WERE VERY LUCKY TO LEAVE THAT PLACE ALIVE.
YES, I HEARD HE WAS A STICKLER FOR DETAIL.
I HAD TO AGREE TO REPLACE HIS FUCKING WINDOW. AND GET THE BLOOD TAKEN OUT OF HIS PRECIOUS CARPET.
HE ASSURED ME THAT IT WAS FLAHERTY WHO PAID HIM TO FAKE TARA'S DEATH.
FLAHERTY WAS INVESTIGATING PSYCHOPATHIC INFILTRATION OF THE NAMES. I THINK HE SUSPECTED TARA OF BEING ONE OF THEM.
SO WHY WOULD HE WANT TO SHAM HER DEATH?
I DON'T KNOW...
MAYBE HE HAD TO, OR RISK BLOWING HIS COVER.
EITHER WAY, HE'S NOT LIKELY TO TELL US NOW.
I NEVER ASKED YOU. DID YOU...DID YOU EVER GET OVER WHAT HAPPENED TO YOUR WIFE?
UNTIL ABOUT THREE WEEKS AGO...I WOULD PROBABLY HAVE ANSWERED "NO" TO THAT QUESTION.
BRRGG BRRGG BRRGG
HELLO, STOKER.
TARA? FOR GOD'S SAKE...WHERE ARE YOU?

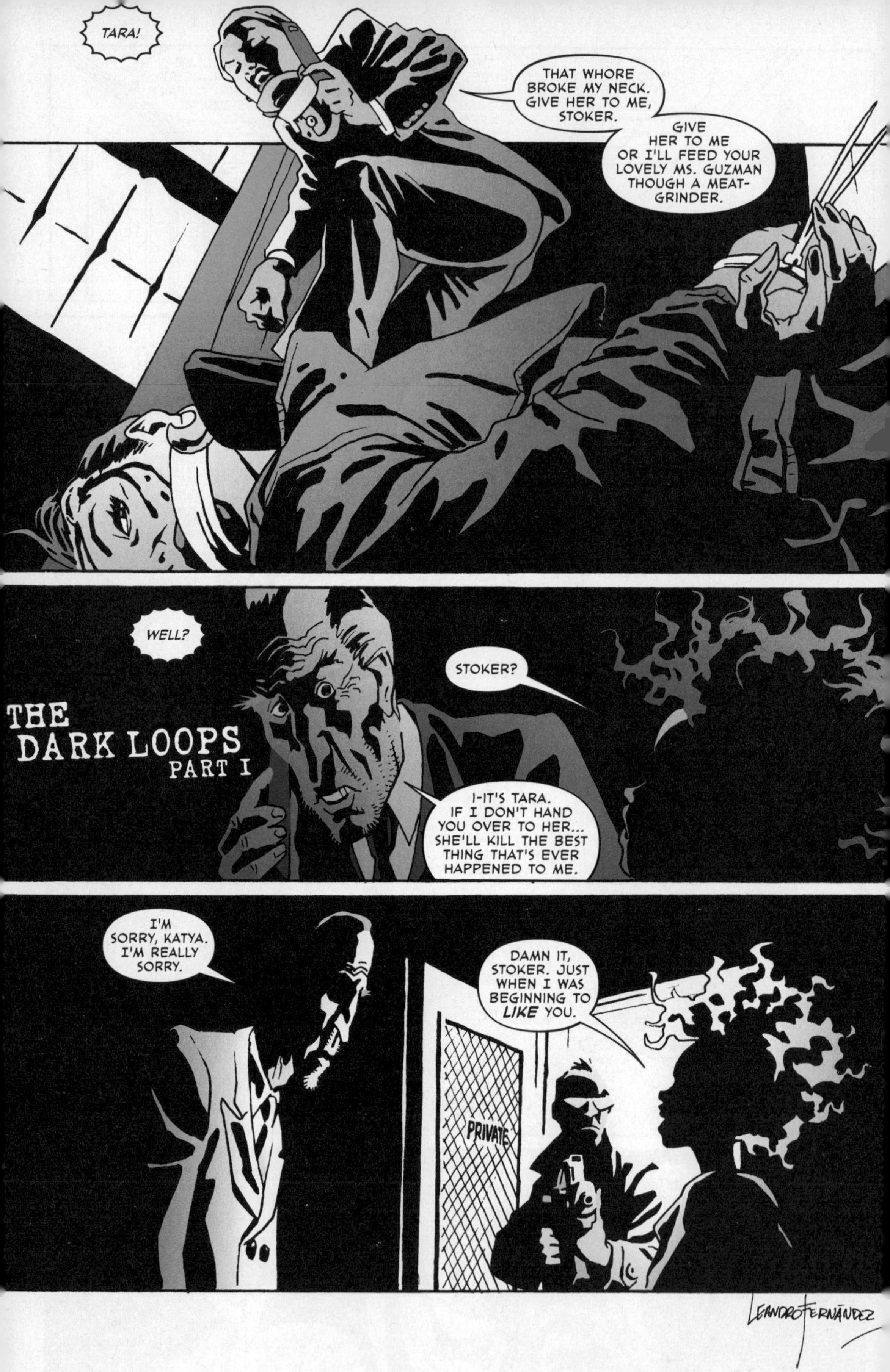
TARA!
THAT WHORE BROKE MY NECK. GIVE HER TO ME, STOKER.
GIVE HER TO ME OR I'LL FEED YOUR LOVELY MS. GUZMAN THOUGH A MEAT-GRINDER.
WELL?
STOKER?
THE DARK LOOPS PART I
I-IT'S TARA. IF I DON'T HAND YOU OVER TO HER... SHE'LL KILL THE BEST THING THAT'S EVER HAPPENED TO ME.
I'M SORRY, KATYA. I'M REALLY SORRY.
DAMN IT, STOKER. JUST WHEN I WAS BEGINNING TO LIKE YOU.
PRIVATE
LEANDRO FERNANDEZ

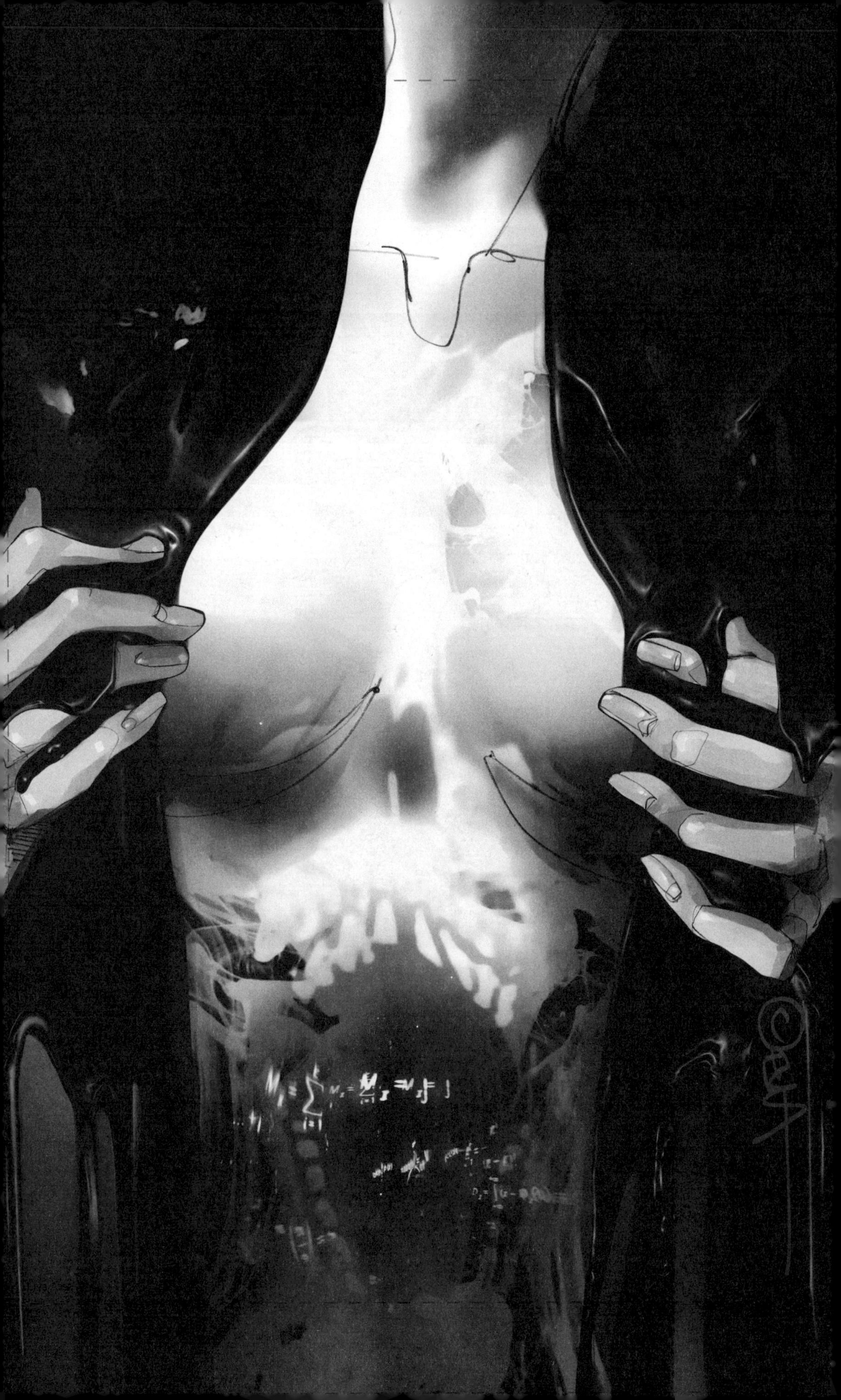

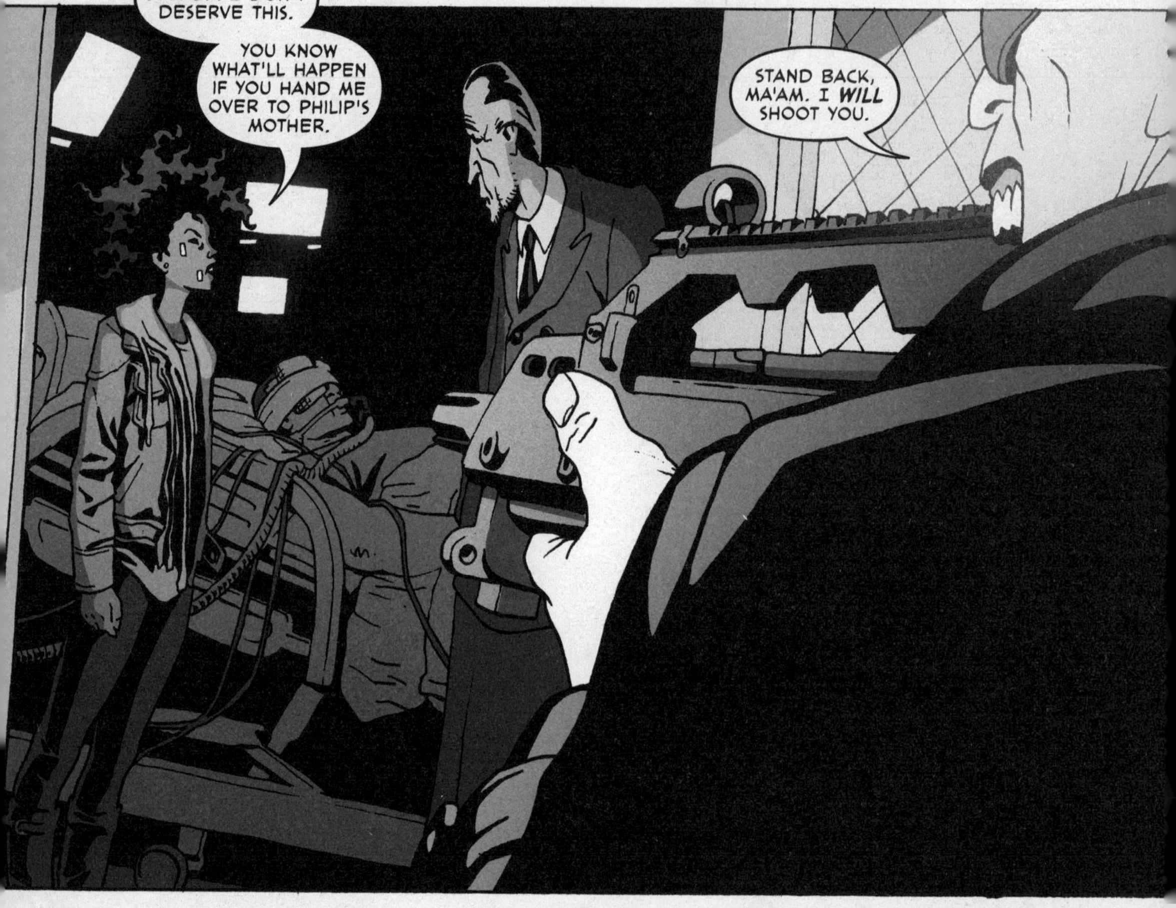
PLEASE, STOKER. I DON'T DESERVE THIS.
YOU KNOW WHAT'LL HAPPEN IF YOU HAND ME OVER TO PHILIP'S MOTHER.
STAND BACK, MA'AM. I *WILL* SHOOT YOU.

THE DARK LOOPS
PART II

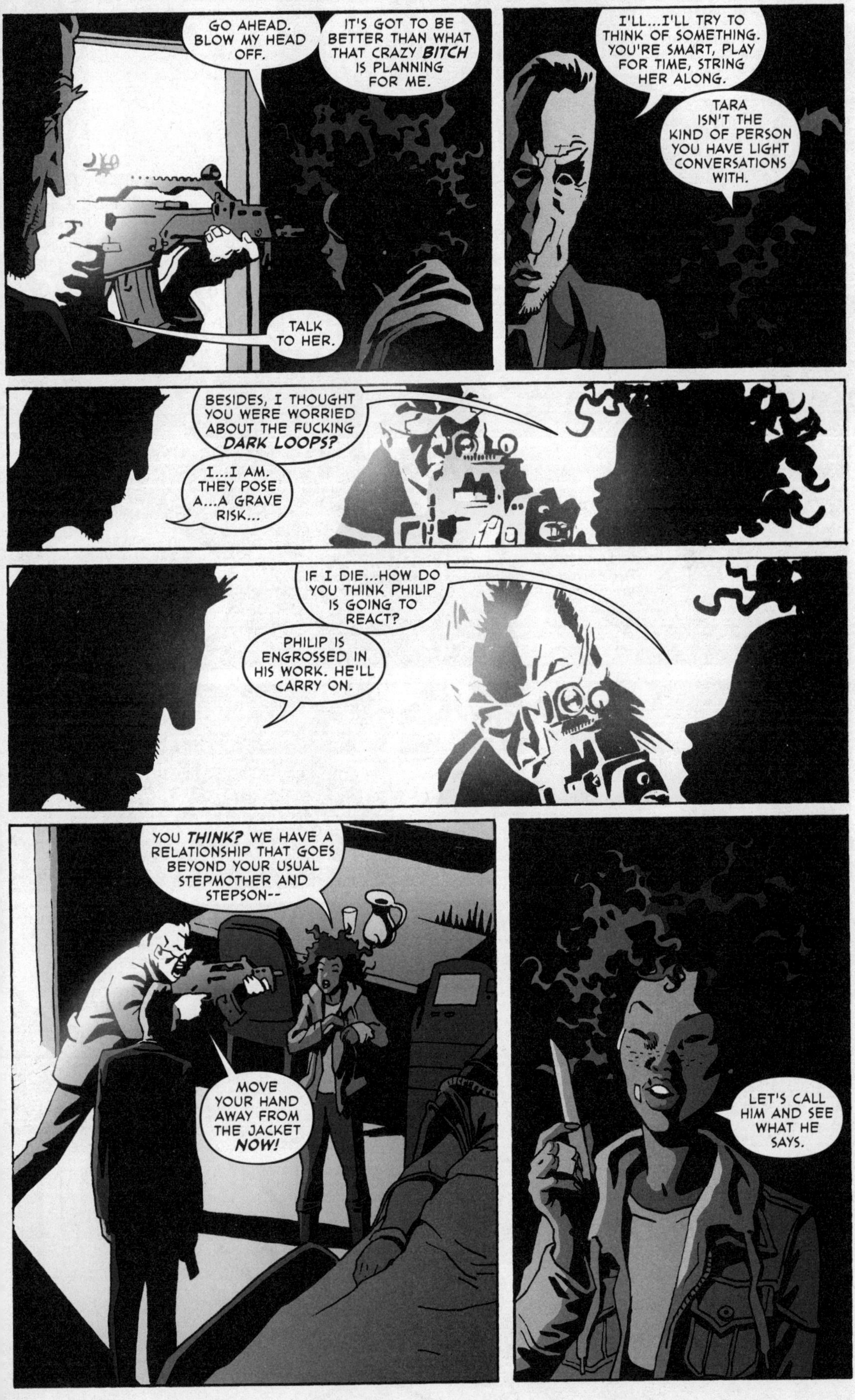
GO AHEAD. BLOW MY HEAD OFF.
IT'S GOT TO BE BETTER THAN WHAT THAT CRAZY BITCH IS PLANNING FOR ME.
TALK TO HER.
I'LL...I'LL TRY TO THINK OF SOMETHING. YOU'RE SMART, PLAY FOR TIME, STRING HER ALONG.
TARA ISN'T THE KIND OF PERSON YOU HAVE LIGHT CONVERSATIONS WITH.
BESIDES, I THOUGHT YOU WERE WORRIED ABOUT THE FUCKING DARK LOOPS?
I...I AM. THEY POSE A...A GRAVE RISK...
IF I DIE...HOW DO YOU THINK PHILIP IS GOING TO REACT?
PHILIP IS ENGROSSED IN HIS WORK. HE'LL CARRY ON.
YOU THINK? WE HAVE A RELATIONSHIP THAT GOES BEYOND YOUR USUAL STEPMOTHER AND STEPSON--
MOVE YOUR HAND AWAY FROM THE JACKET NOW!
LET'S CALL HIM AND SEE WHAT HE SAYS.

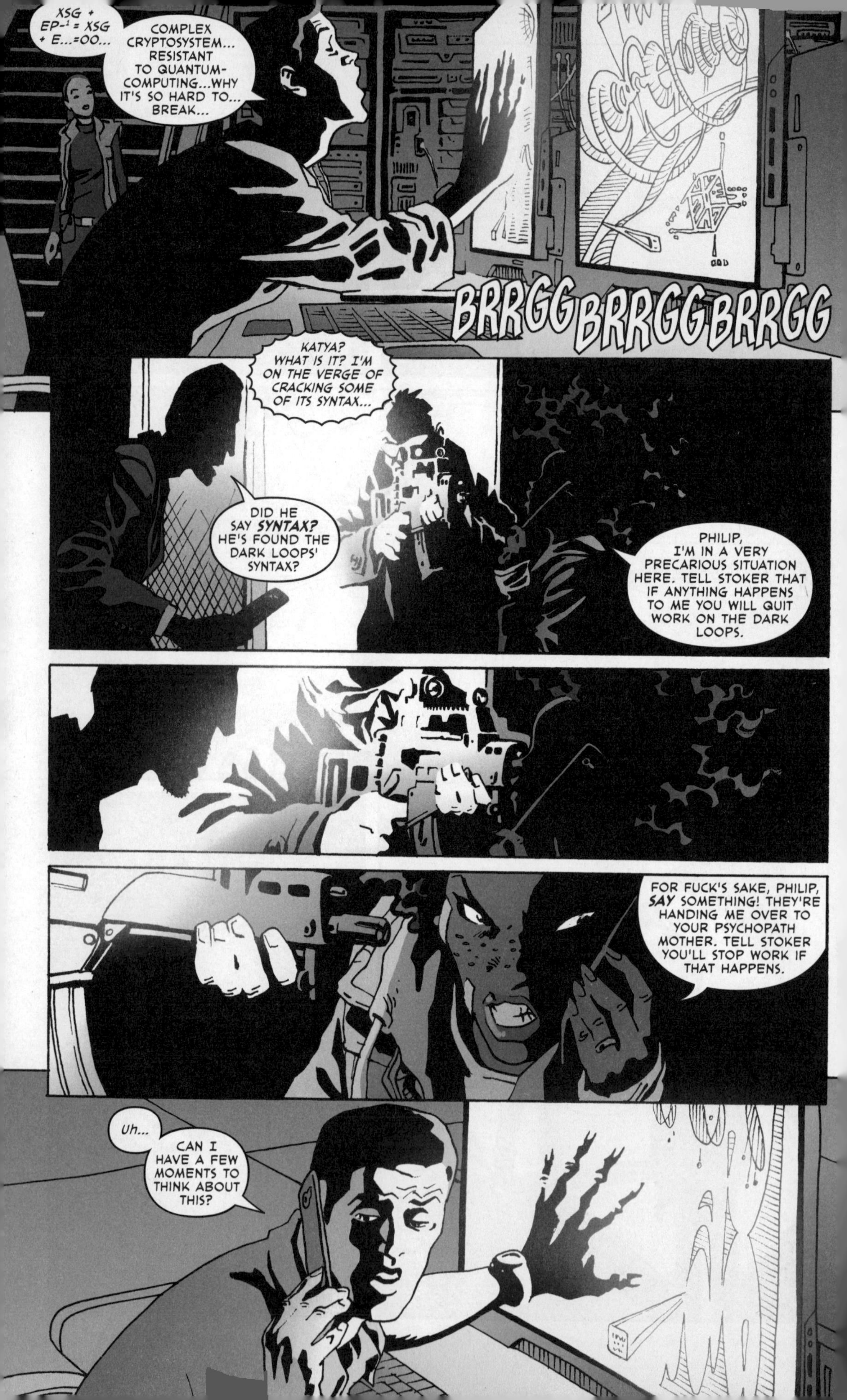
XSG + EP-1 = XSG + E...=OO...
COMPLEX CRYPTOSYSTEM... RESISTANT TO QUANTUM-COMPUTING...WHY IT'S SO HARD TO... BREAK...
BRRGG BRRGG BRRGG
KATYA? WHAT IS IT? I'M ON THE VERGE OF CRACKING SOME OF ITS SYNTAX...
DID HE SAY SYNTAX? HE'S FOUND THE DARK LOOPS' SYNTAX?
PHILIP, I'M IN A VERY PRECARIOUS SITUATION HERE. TELL STOKER THAT IF ANYTHING HAPPENS TO ME YOU WILL QUIT WORK ON THE DARK LOOPS.
FOR FUCK'S SAKE, PHILIP, SAY SOMETHING! THEY'RE HANDING ME OVER TO YOUR PSYCHOPATH MOTHER. TELL STOKER YOU'LL STOP WORK IF THAT HAPPENS.
Uh...
CAN I HAVE A FEW MOMENTS TO THINK ABOUT THIS?

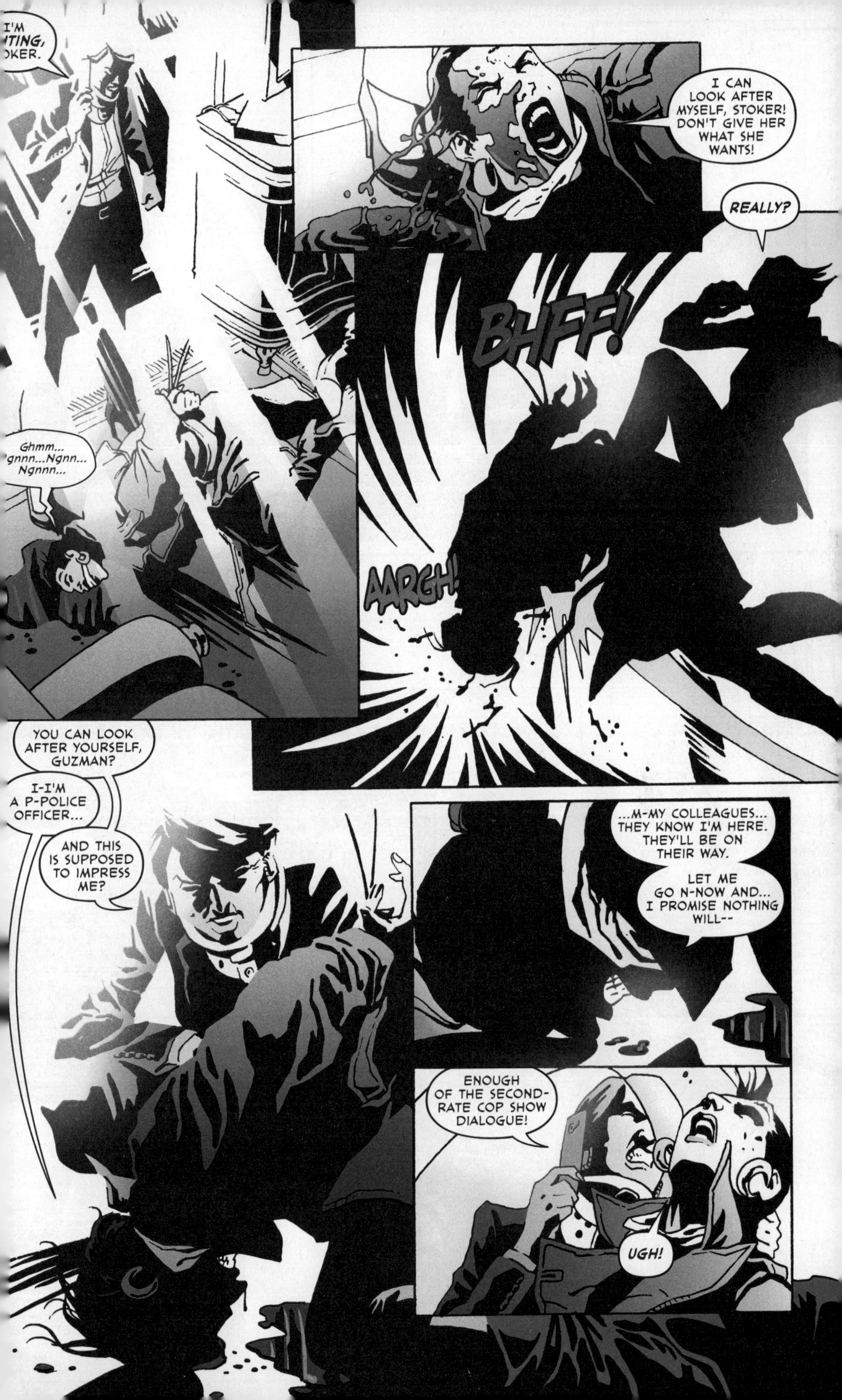
I'M
...TING,
...OKER.
I CAN LOOK AFTER MYSELF, STOKER! DON'T GIVE HER WHAT SHE WANTS!
REALLY?
Ghmm... ...gnnn...Ngnn... Ngnnn...
BHFF!
AARGH!
YOU CAN LOOK AFTER YOURSELF, GUZMAN?
I-I'M A P-POLICE OFFICER...
AND THIS IS SUPPOSED TO IMPRESS ME?
...M-MY COLLEAGUES... THEY KNOW I'M HERE. THEY'LL BE ON THEIR WAY.
LET ME GO N-NOW AND... I PROMISE NOTHING WILL--
ENOUGH OF THE SECOND-RATE COP SHOW DIALOGUE!
UGH!

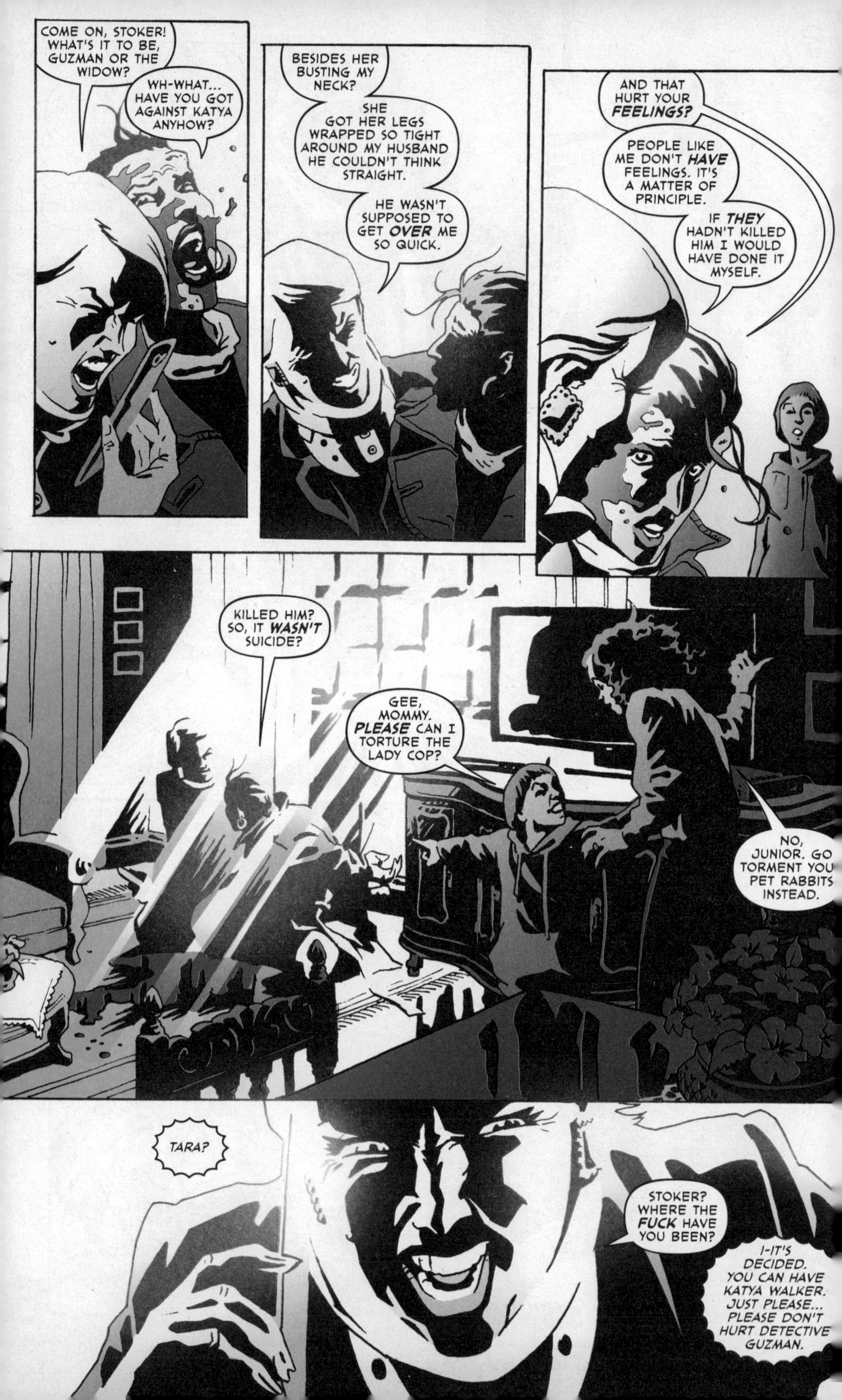
COME ON, STOKER! WHAT'S IT TO BE, GUZMAN OR THE WIDOW?
WH-WHAT... HAVE YOU GOT AGAINST KATYA ANYHOW?
BESIDES HER BUSTING MY NECK?
SHE GOT HER LEGS WRAPPED SO TIGHT AROUND MY HUSBAND HE COULDN'T THINK STRAIGHT.
HE WASN'T SUPPOSED TO GET OVER ME SO QUICK.
AND THAT HURT YOUR FEELINGS?
PEOPLE LIKE ME DON'T HAVE FEELINGS. IT'S A MATTER OF PRINCIPLE.
IF THEY HADN'T KILLED HIM I WOULD HAVE DONE IT MYSELF.
KILLED HIM? SO, IT WASN'T SUICIDE?
GEE, MOMMY. PLEASE CAN I TORTURE THE LADY COP?
NO, JUNIOR. GO TORMENT YOU PET RABBITS INSTEAD.
TARA?
STOKER? WHERE THE FUCK HAVE YOU BEEN?
I-IT'S DECIDED. YOU CAN HAVE KATYA WALKER. JUST PLEASE... PLEASE DON'T HURT DETECTIVE GUZMAN.

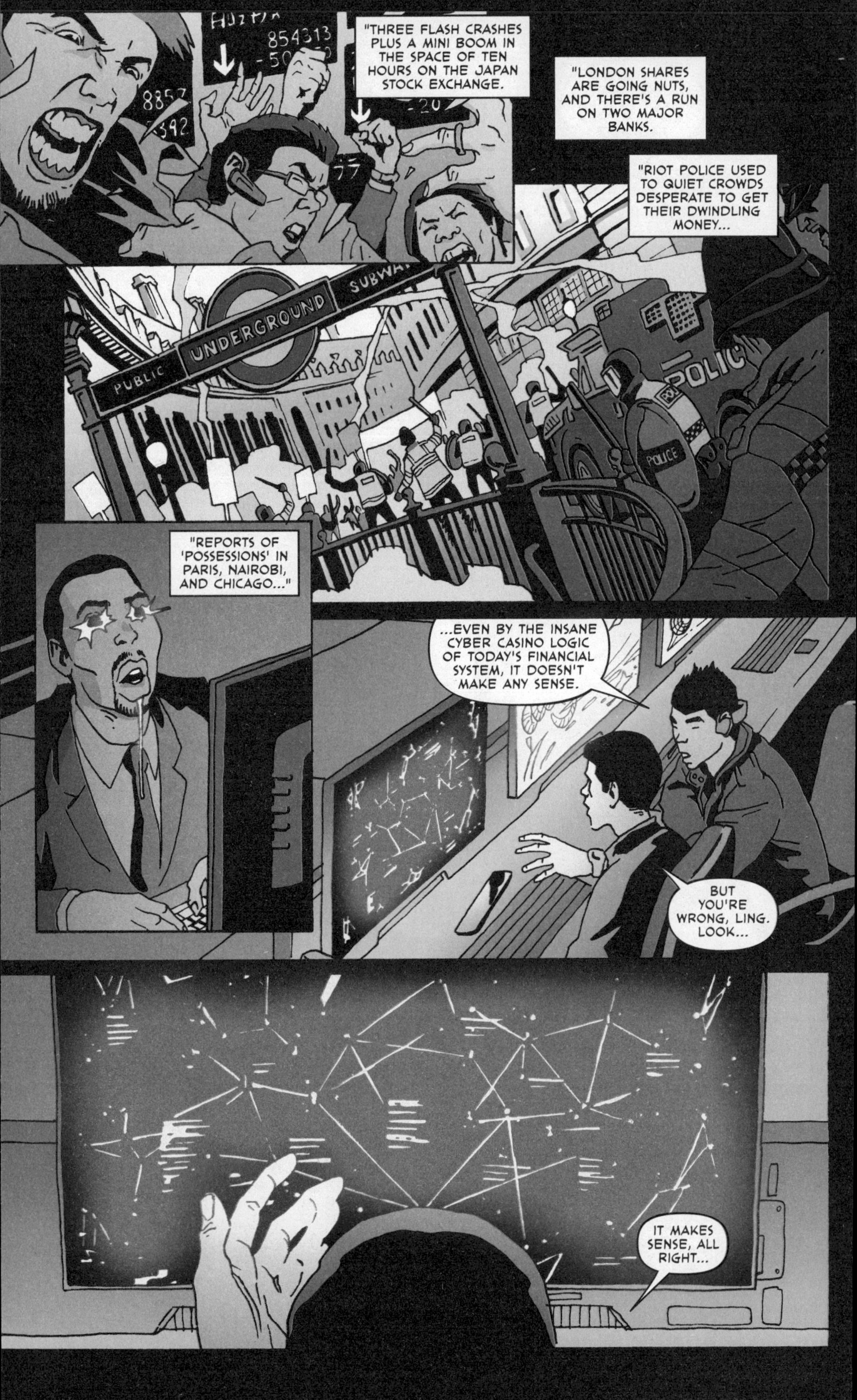
"THREE FLASH CRASHES PLUS A MINI BOOM IN THE SPACE OF TEN HOURS ON THE JAPAN STOCK EXCHANGE.
"LONDON SHARES ARE GOING NUTS, AND THERE'S A RUN ON TWO MAJOR BANKS.
"RIOT POLICE USED TO QUIET CROWDS DESPERATE TO GET THEIR DWINDLING MONEY...
UNDERGROUND
PUBLIC
SUBWAY
POLIC
POLICE
"REPORTS OF 'POSSESSIONS' IN PARIS, NAIROBI, AND CHICAGO..."
...EVEN BY THE INSANE CYBER CASINO LOGIC OF TODAY'S FINANCIAL SYSTEM, IT DOESN'T MAKE ANY SENSE.
BUT YOU'RE WRONG, LING. LOOK...
IT MAKES SENSE, ALL RIGHT...

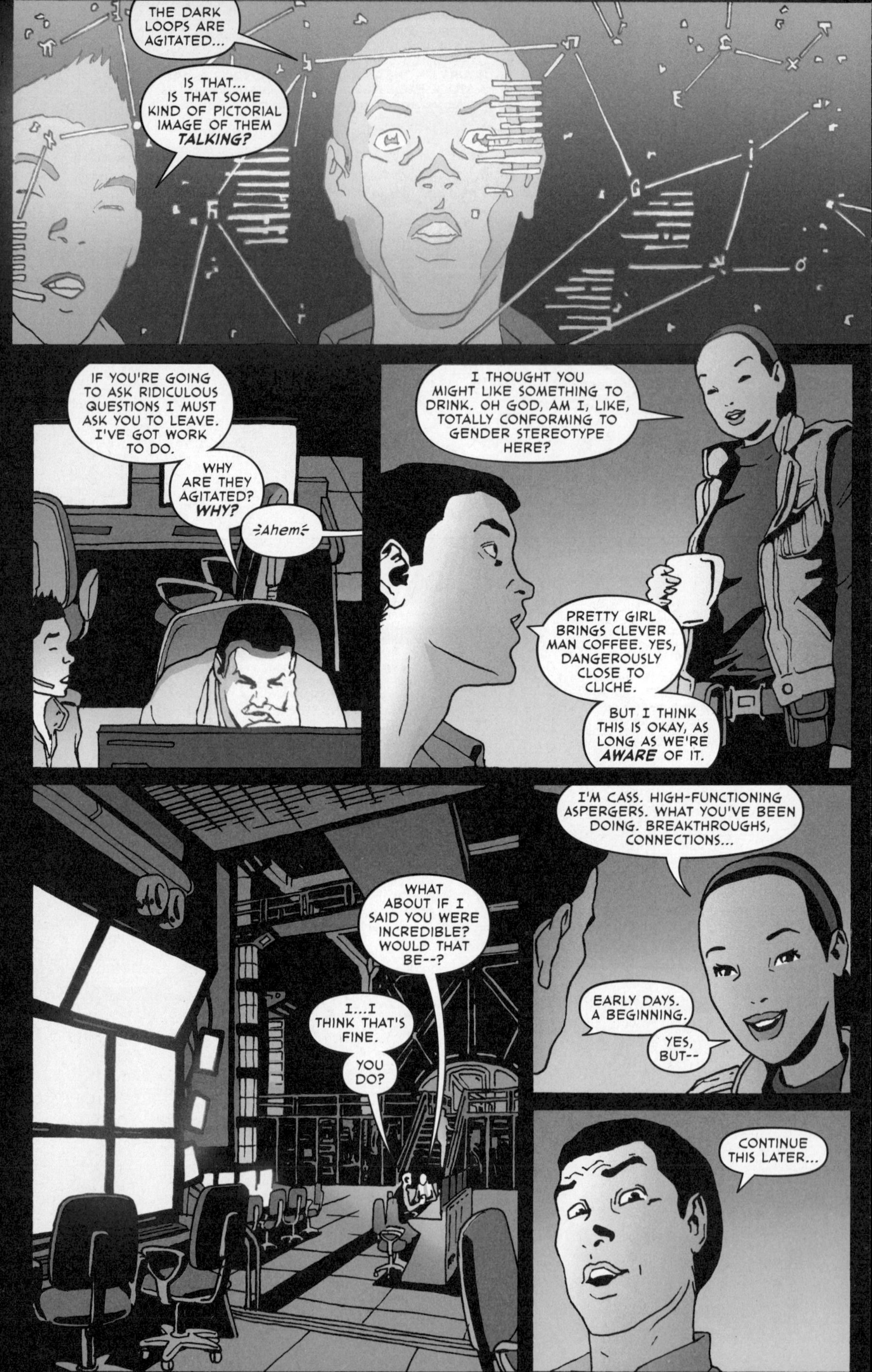
THE DARK LOOPS ARE AGITATED...
IS THAT... IS THAT SOME KIND OF PICTORIAL IMAGE OF THEM TALKING?
IF YOU'RE GOING TO ASK RIDICULOUS QUESTIONS I MUST ASK YOU TO LEAVE. I'VE GOT WORK TO DO.
WHY ARE THEY AGITATED? WHY?
Ahem
I THOUGHT YOU MIGHT LIKE SOMETHING TO DRINK. OH GOD, AM I, LIKE, TOTALLY CONFORMING TO GENDER STEREOTYPE HERE?
PRETTY GIRL BRINGS CLEVER MAN COFFEE. YES, DANGEROUSLY CLOSE TO CLICHÉ.
BUT I THINK THIS IS OKAY, AS LONG AS WE'RE AWARE OF IT.
WHAT ABOUT IF I SAID YOU WERE INCREDIBLE? WOULD THAT BE--?
I...I THINK THAT'S FINE.
YOU DO?
I'M CASS. HIGH-FUNCTIONING ASPERGERS. WHAT YOU'VE BEEN DOING. BREAKTHROUGHS, CONNECTIONS...
EARLY DAYS. A BEGINNING.
YES, BUT--
CONTINUE THIS LATER...

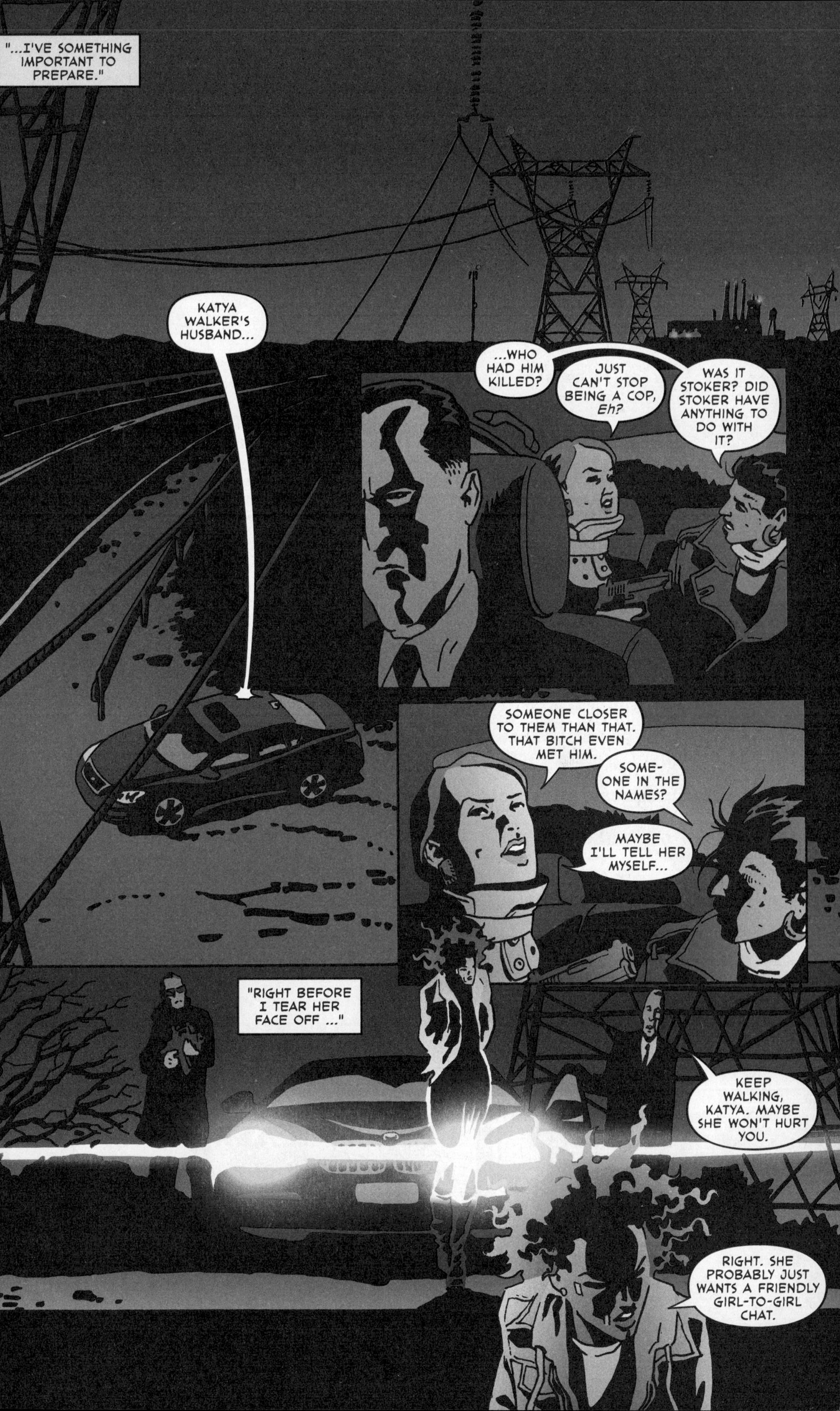
"...I'VE SOMETHING IMPORTANT TO PREPARE."
KATYA WALKER'S HUSBAND...
...WHO HAD HIM KILLED?
JUST CAN'T STOP BEING A COP, *Eh?*
WAS IT STOKER? DID STOKER HAVE ANYTHING TO DO WITH IT?
SOMEONE CLOSER TO THEM THAN THAT. THAT BITCH EVEN MET HIM.
SOME-ONE IN THE NAMES?
MAYBE I'LL TELL HER MYSELF...
"RIGHT BEFORE I TEAR HER FACE OFF ..."
KEEP WALKING, KATYA. MAYBE SHE WON'T HURT YOU.
RIGHT. SHE PROBABLY JUST WANTS A FRIENDLY GIRL-TO-GIRL CHAT.

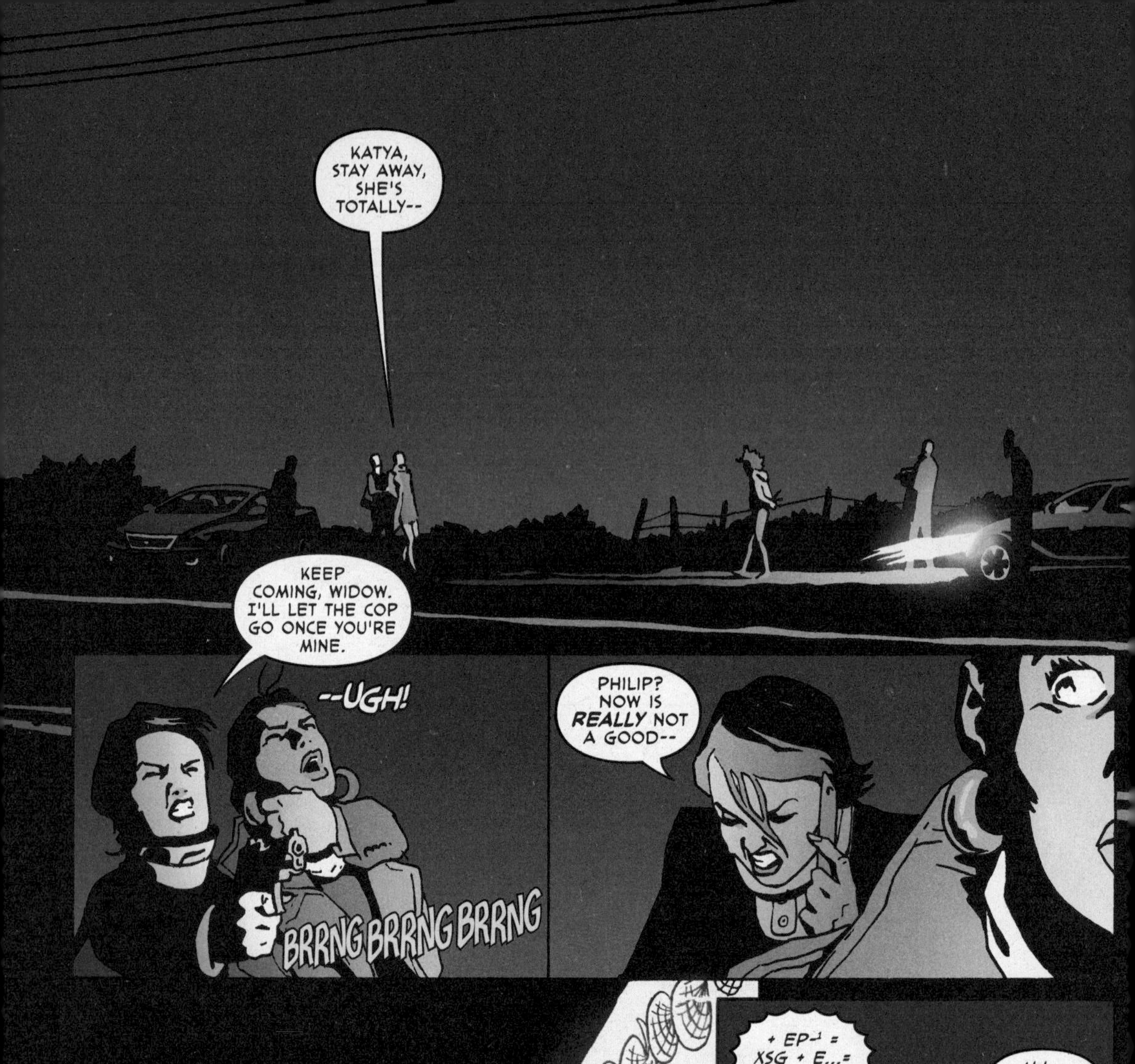

KATYA, STAY AWAY, SHE'S TOTALLY--
KEEP COMING, WIDOW. I'LL LET THE COP GO ONCE YOU'RE MINE.
--UGH!
BRRNG BRRNG BRRNG
PHILIP? NOW IS *REALLY* NOT A GOOD--
YP^{-1} = (XG' + E)P^{-1} = XSG + EP^{-1} = XSG + E... =OOO (FQ)ß^¥¥∏OO P^{-1} = XSG...
+ EP^{-1} = XSG + E...= OOOOO)ß...
Ahh... WH-WHAT... THE...
Ahh... Gngng... Ahah... Gngn...

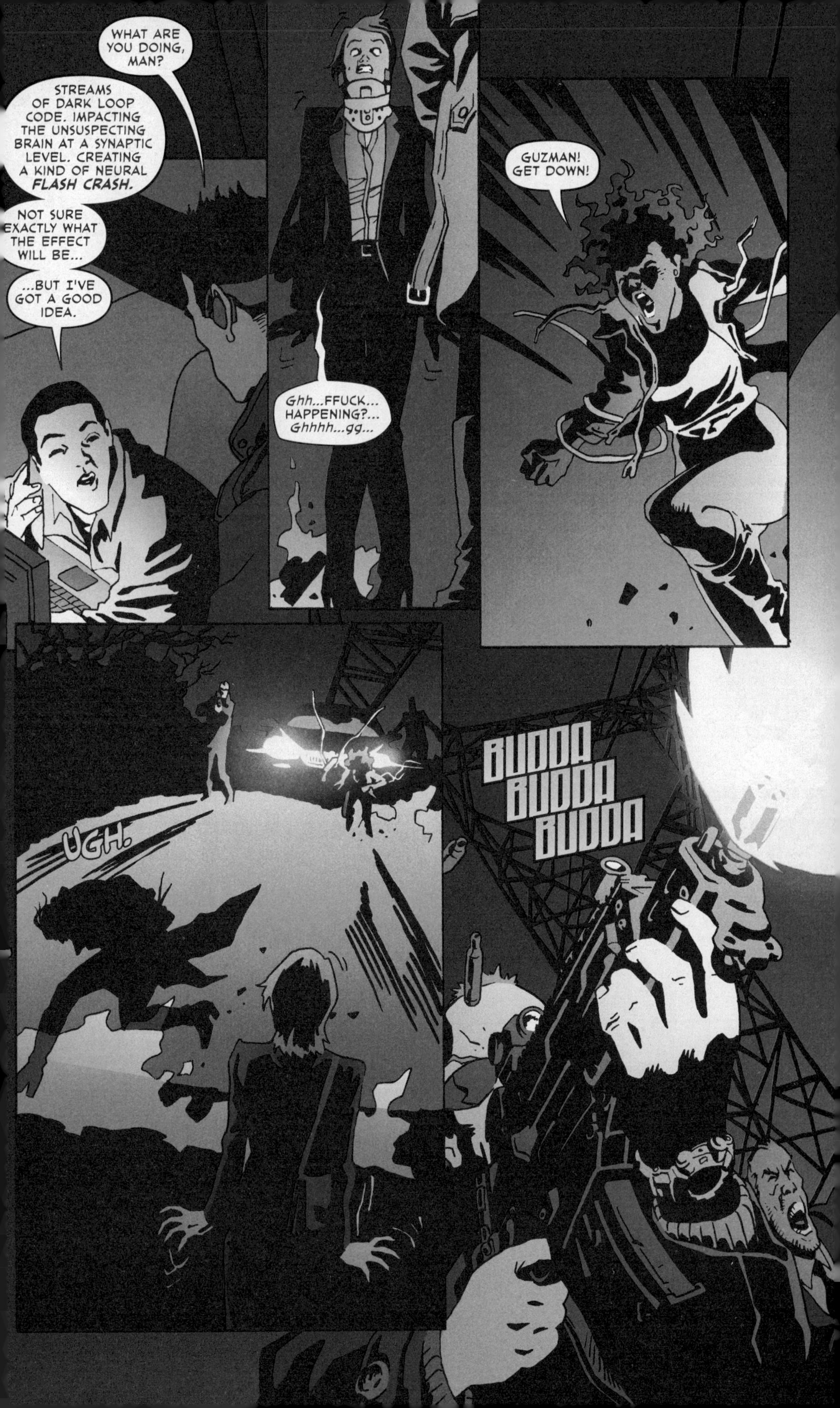
WHAT ARE YOU DOING, MAN?
STREAMS OF DARK LOOP CODE. IMPACTING THE UNSUSPECTING BRAIN AT A SYNAPTIC LEVEL. CREATING A KIND OF NEURAL FLASH CRASH.
NOT SURE EXACTLY WHAT THE EFFECT WILL BE...
...BUT I'VE GOT A GOOD IDEA.
Ghh...FFUCK... HAPPENING?... Ghhhh...gg...
GUZMAN! GET DOWN!
UGH.
BUDDA BUDDA BUDDA

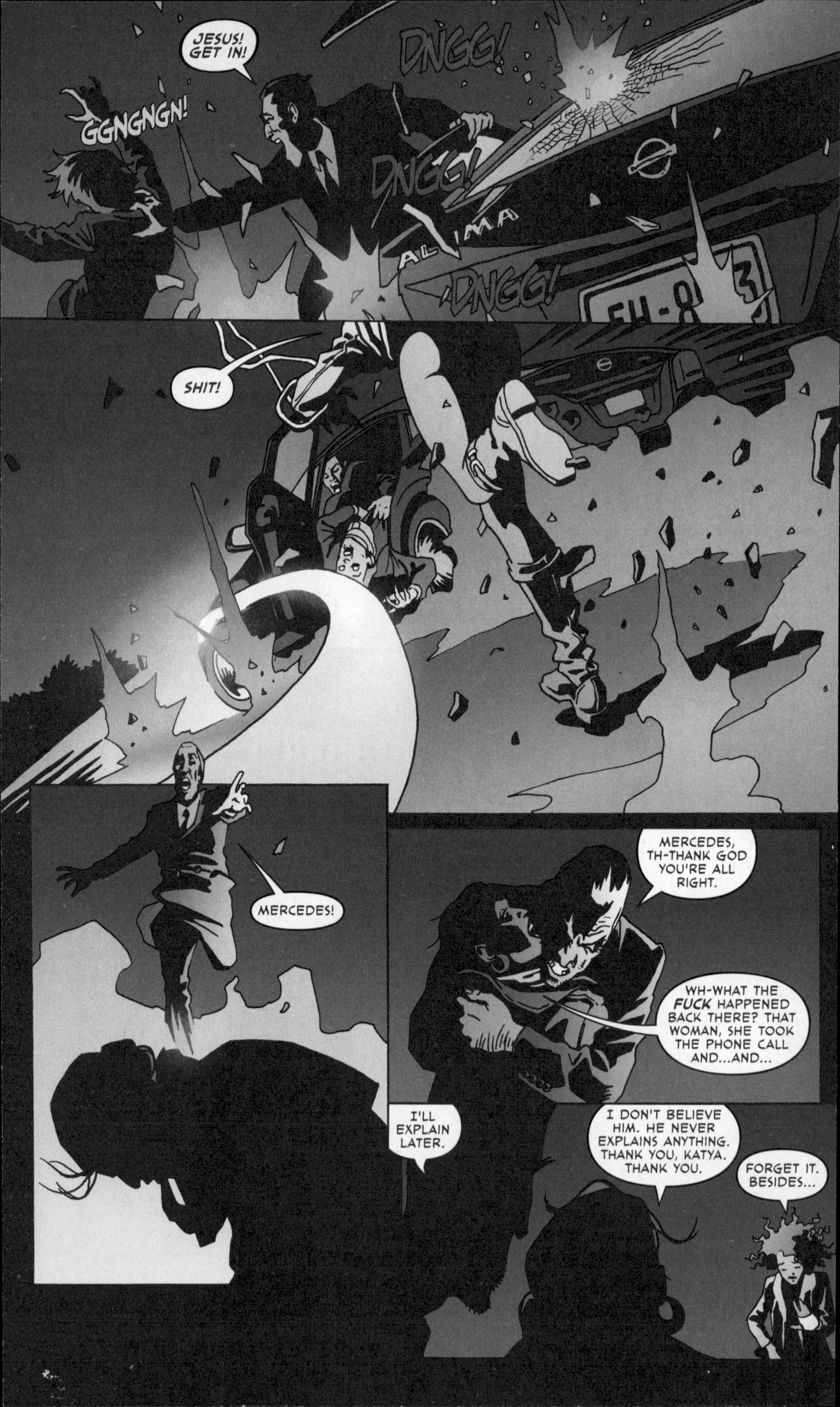
JESUS! GET IN!
GGNGNGN!
DNGG!
DNGG!
DNGG!
SHIT!
MERCEDES!
MERCEDES, TH-THANK GOD YOU'RE ALL RIGHT.
WH-WHAT THE *FUCK* HAPPENED BACK THERE? THAT WOMAN, SHE TOOK THE PHONE CALL AND...AND...
I'LL EXPLAIN LATER.
I DON'T BELIEVE HIM. HE NEVER EXPLAINS ANYTHING. THANK YOU, KATYA. THANK YOU.
FORGET IT. BESIDES...

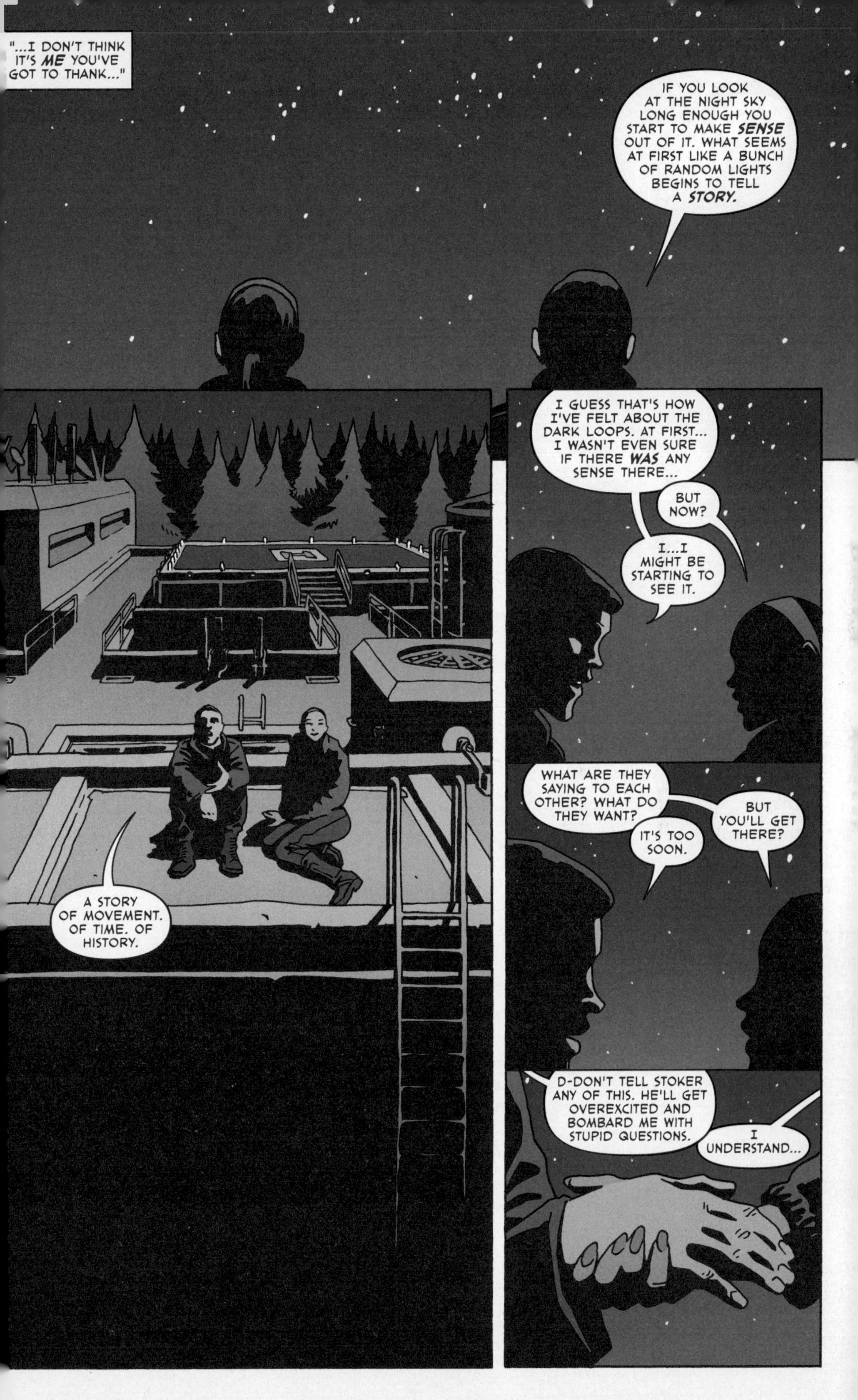
"...I DON'T THINK IT'S ME YOU'VE GOT TO THANK..."
IF YOU LOOK AT THE NIGHT SKY LONG ENOUGH YOU START TO MAKE SENSE OUT OF IT. WHAT SEEMS AT FIRST LIKE A BUNCH OF RANDOM LIGHTS BEGINS TO TELL A STORY.
A STORY OF MOVEMENT. OF TIME. OF HISTORY.
I GUESS THAT'S HOW I'VE FELT ABOUT THE DARK LOOPS. AT FIRST... I WASN'T EVEN SURE IF THERE WAS ANY SENSE THERE...
BUT NOW?
I...I MIGHT BE STARTING TO SEE IT.
WHAT ARE THEY SAYING TO EACH OTHER? WHAT DO THEY WANT?
IT'S TOO SOON.
BUT YOU'LL GET THERE?
D-DON'T TELL STOKER ANY OF THIS. HE'LL GET OVEREXCITED AND BOMBARD ME WITH STUPID QUESTIONS.
I UNDERSTAND...

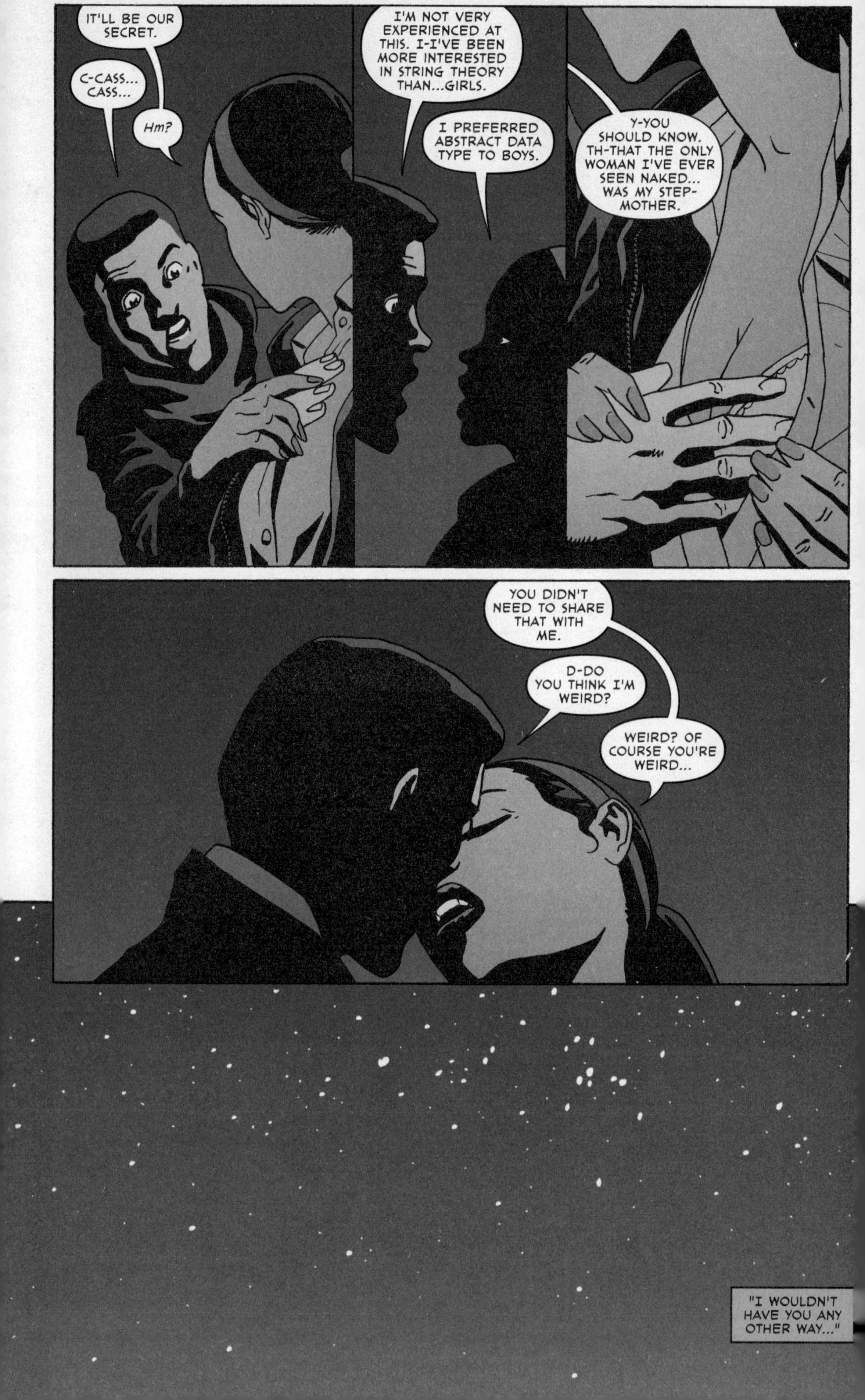
IT'LL BE OUR SECRET.
C-CASS... CASS...
Hm?
I'M NOT VERY EXPERIENCED AT THIS. I-I'VE BEEN MORE INTERESTED IN STRING THEORY THAN...GIRLS.
I PREFERRED ABSTRACT DATA TYPE TO BOYS.
Y-YOU SHOULD KNOW. TH-THAT THE ONLY WOMAN I'VE EVER SEEN NAKED... WAS MY STEP-MOTHER.
YOU DIDN'T NEED TO SHARE THAT WITH ME.
D-DO YOU THINK I'M WEIRD?
WEIRD? OF COURSE YOU'RE WEIRD...
"I WOULDN'T HAVE YOU ANY OTHER WAY..."

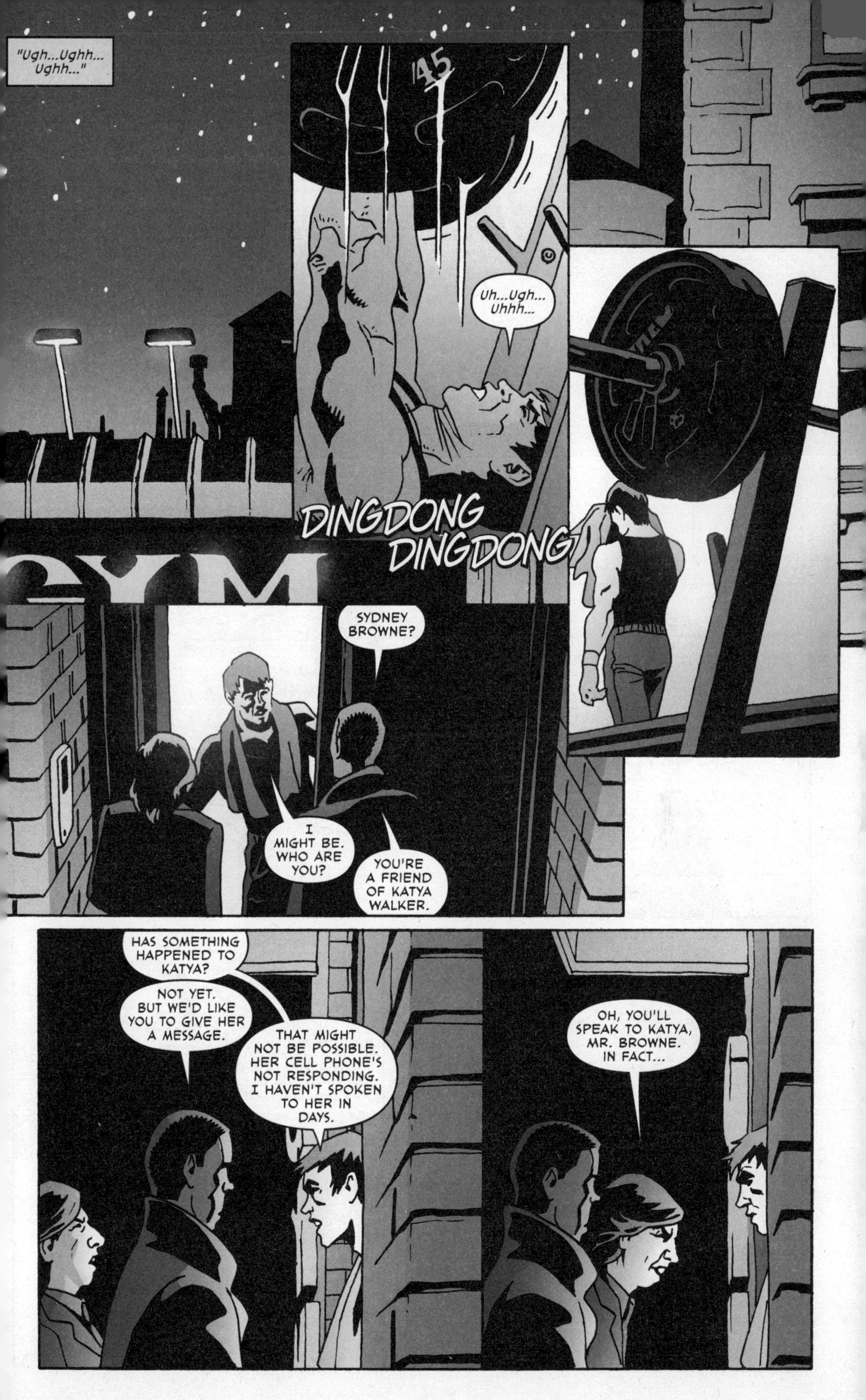
"Ugh...Ughh... Ughh..."
145
Uh...Ugh... Uhhh...
DINGDONG DINGDONG
GYM
SYDNEY BROWNE?
I MIGHT BE. WHO ARE YOU?
YOU'RE A FRIEND OF KATYA WALKER.
HAS SOMETHING HAPPENED TO KATYA?
NOT YET. BUT WE'D LIKE YOU TO GIVE HER A MESSAGE.
THAT MIGHT NOT BE POSSIBLE. HER CELL PHONE'S NOT RESPONDING. I HAVEN'T SPOKEN TO HER IN DAYS.
OH, YOU'LL SPEAK TO KATYA, MR. BROWNE. IN FACT...

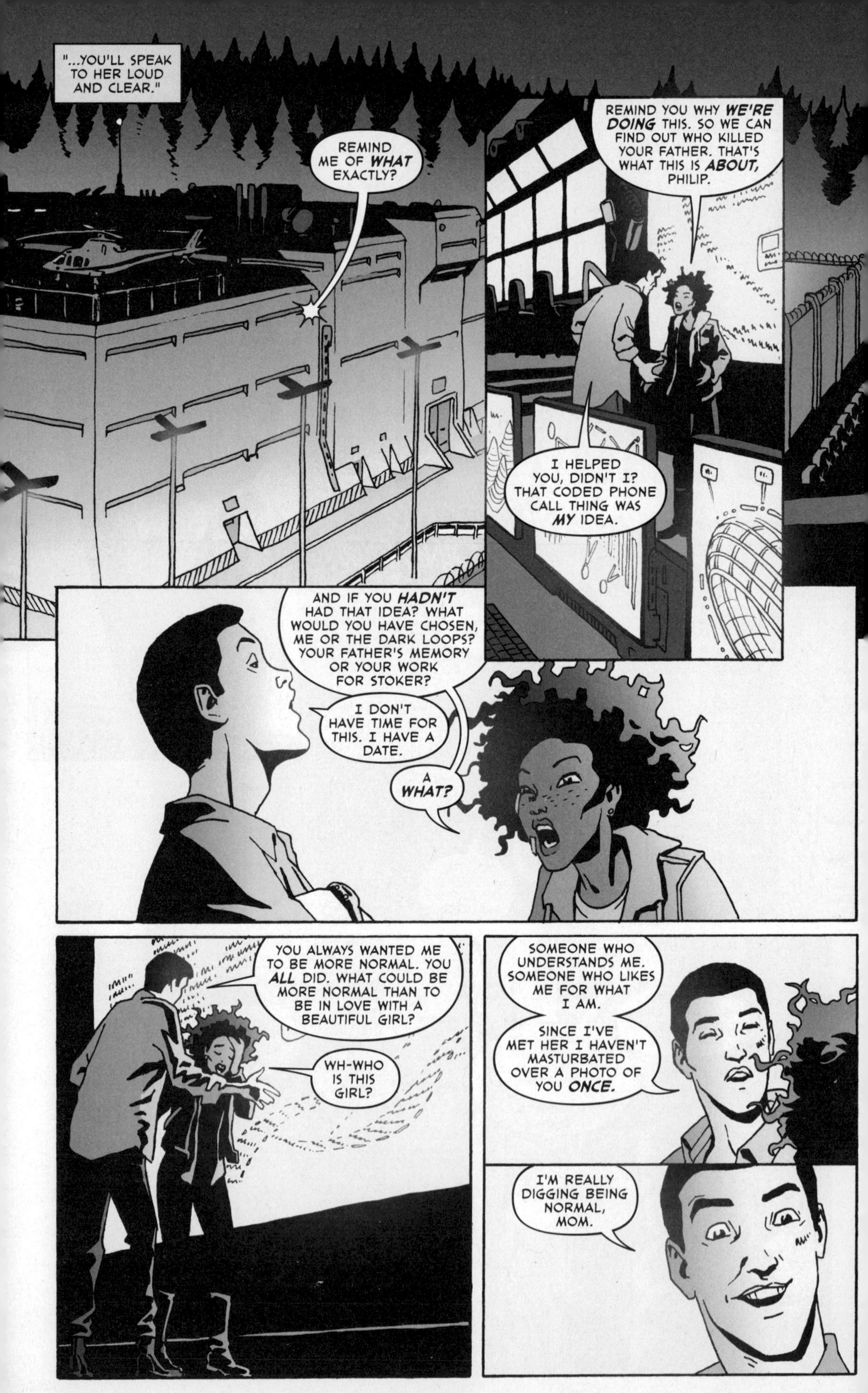
"...YOU'LL SPEAK TO HER LOUD AND CLEAR."
REMIND ME OF WHAT EXACTLY?
REMIND YOU WHY WE'RE DOING THIS. SO WE CAN FIND OUT WHO KILLED YOUR FATHER. THAT'S WHAT THIS IS ABOUT, PHILIP.
I HELPED YOU, DIDN'T I? THAT CODED PHONE CALL THING WAS MY IDEA.
AND IF YOU HADN'T HAD THAT IDEA? WHAT WOULD YOU HAVE CHOSEN, ME OR THE DARK LOOPS? YOUR FATHER'S MEMORY OR YOUR WORK FOR STOKER?
I DON'T HAVE TIME FOR THIS. I HAVE A DATE.
A WHAT?
YOU ALWAYS WANTED ME TO BE MORE NORMAL. YOU ALL DID. WHAT COULD BE MORE NORMAL THAN TO BE IN LOVE WITH A BEAUTIFUL GIRL?
WH-WHO IS THIS GIRL?
SOMEONE WHO UNDERSTANDS ME. SOMEONE WHO LIKES ME FOR WHAT I AM.
SINCE I'VE MET HER I HAVEN'T MASTURBATED OVER A PHOTO OF YOU ONCE.
I'M REALLY DIGGING BEING NORMAL, MOM.

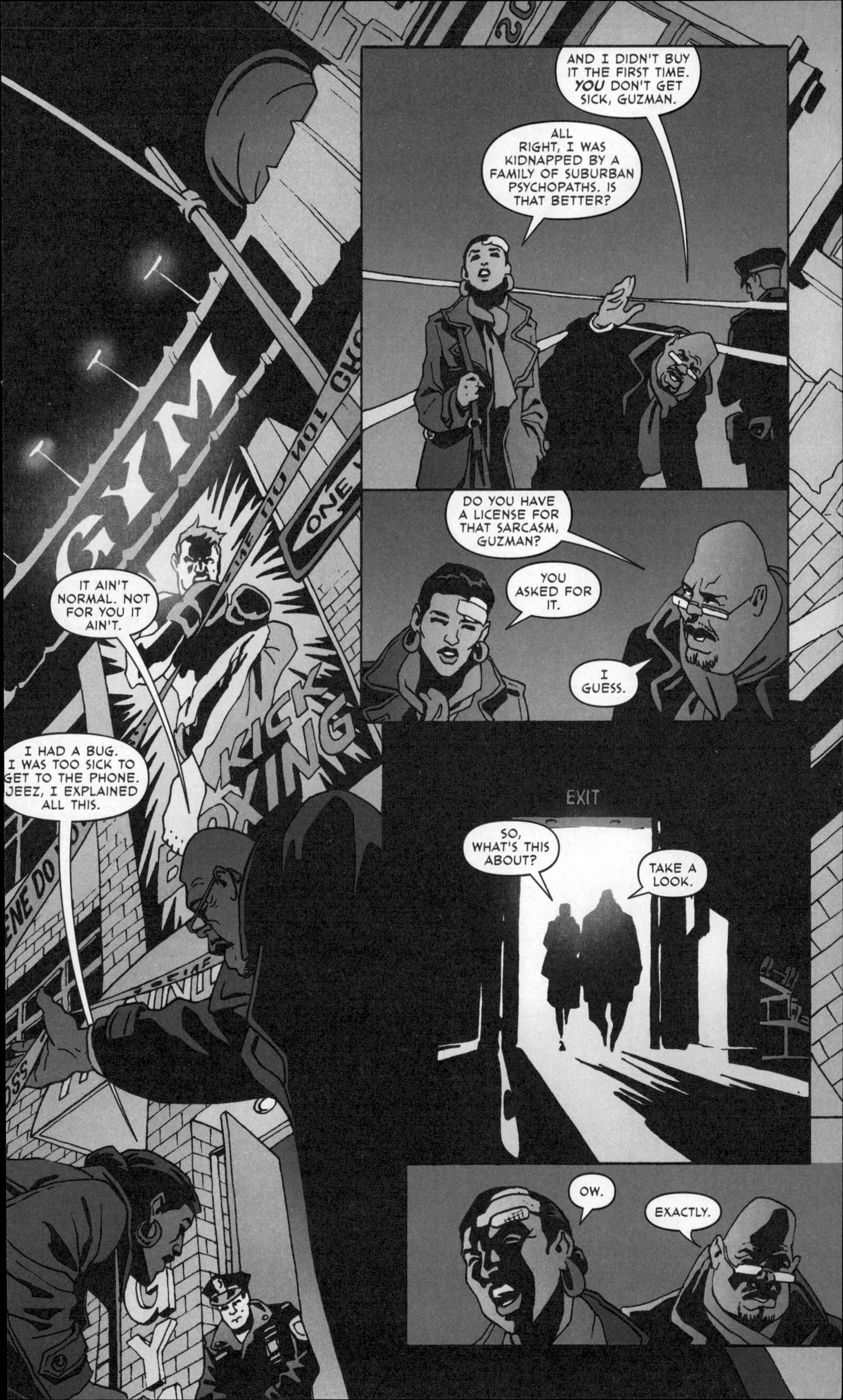
GYM
ONE
KICK-BOXING
AND I DIDN'T BUY IT THE FIRST TIME. YOU DON'T GET SICK, GUZMAN.
ALL RIGHT, I WAS KIDNAPPED BY A FAMILY OF SUBURBAN PSYCHOPATHS. IS THAT BETTER?
IT AIN'T NORMAL. NOT FOR YOU IT AIN'T.
I HAD A BUG. I WAS TOO SICK TO GET TO THE PHONE. JEEZ, I EXPLAINED ALL THIS.
DO YOU HAVE A LICENSE FOR THAT SARCASM, GUZMAN?
YOU ASKED FOR IT.
I GUESS.
EXIT
SO, WHAT'S THIS ABOUT?
TAKE A LOOK.
OW.
EXACTLY.

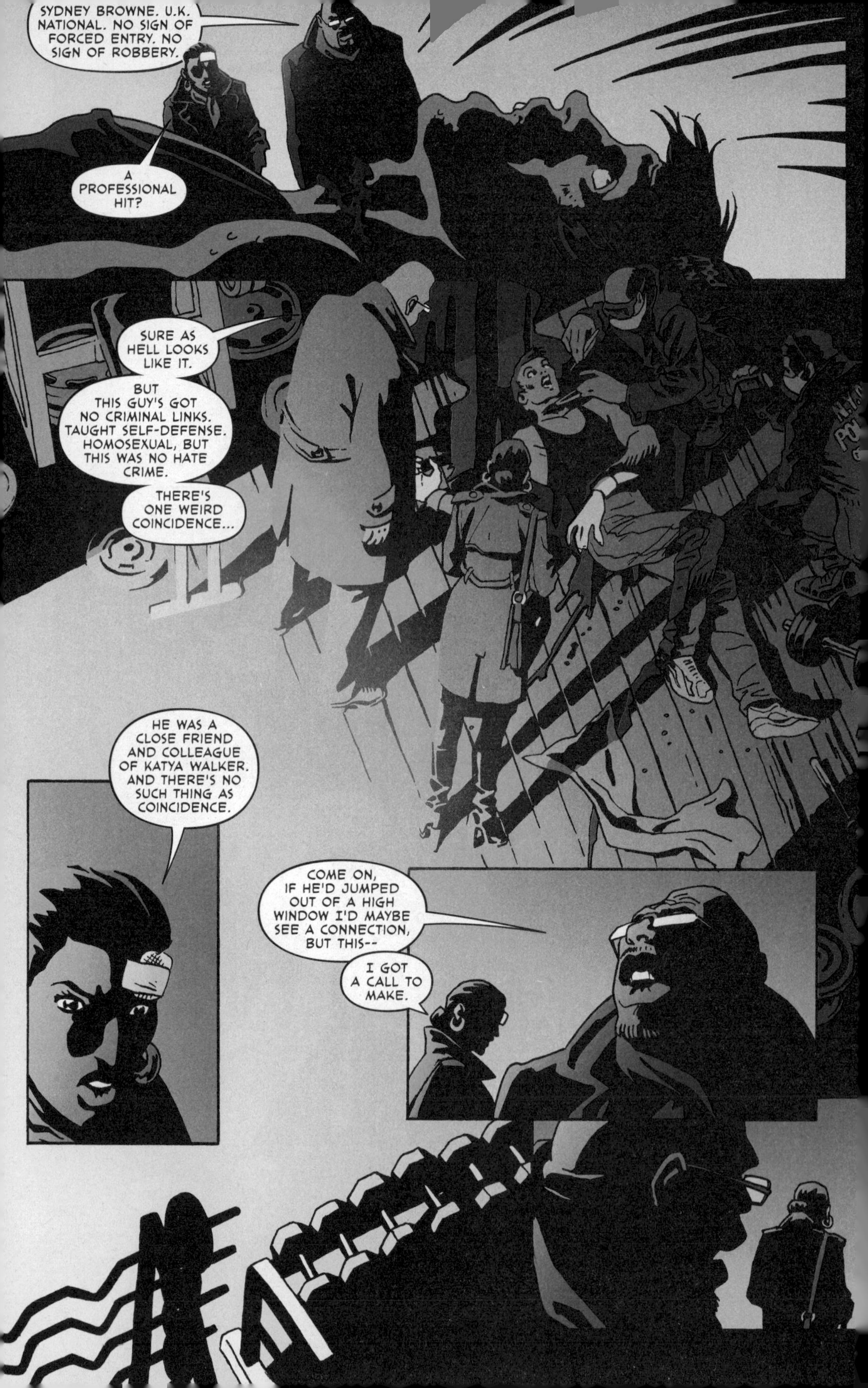
SYDNEY BROWNE. U.K. NATIONAL. NO SIGN OF FORCED ENTRY. NO SIGN OF ROBBERY.
A PROFESSIONAL HIT?
SURE AS HELL LOOKS LIKE IT.
BUT THIS GUY'S GOT NO CRIMINAL LINKS. TAUGHT SELF-DEFENSE. HOMOSEXUAL, BUT THIS WAS NO HATE CRIME.
THERE'S ONE WEIRD COINCIDENCE...
HE WAS A CLOSE FRIEND AND COLLEAGUE OF KATYA WALKER. AND THERE'S NO SUCH THING AS COINCIDENCE.
COME ON, IF HE'D JUMPED OUT OF A HIGH WINDOW I'D MAYBE SEE A CONNECTION, BUT THIS--
I GOT A CALL TO MAKE.

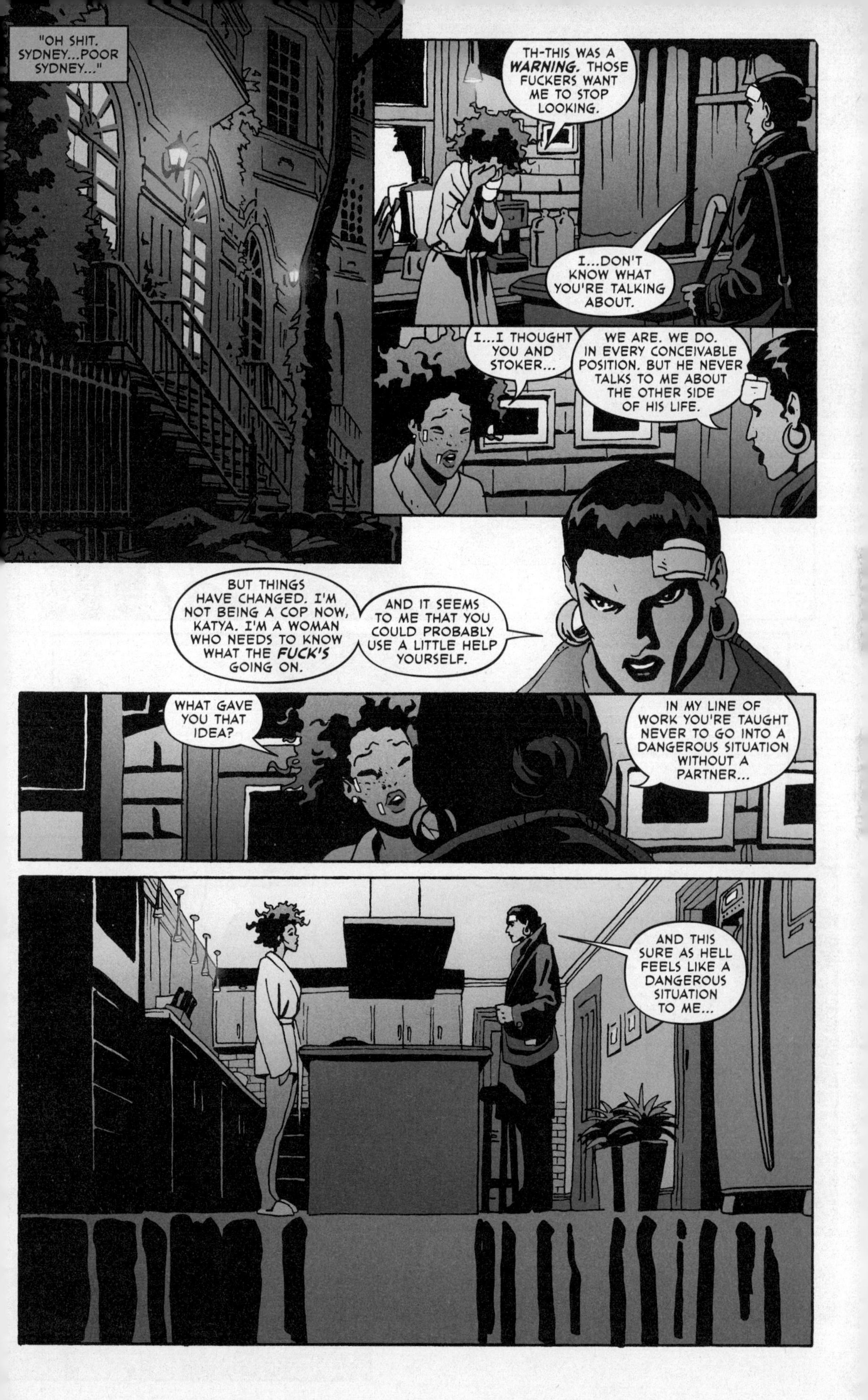
"OH SHIT. SYDNEY...POOR SYDNEY..."
TH-THIS WAS A WARNING. THOSE FUCKERS WANT ME TO STOP LOOKING.
I...DON'T KNOW WHAT YOU'RE TALKING ABOUT.
I...I THOUGHT YOU AND STOKER...
WE ARE. WE DO. IN EVERY CONCEIVABLE POSITION. BUT HE NEVER TALKS TO ME ABOUT THE OTHER SIDE OF HIS LIFE.
BUT THINGS HAVE CHANGED. I'M NOT BEING A COP NOW, KATYA. I'M A WOMAN WHO NEEDS TO KNOW WHAT THE FUCK'S GOING ON.
AND IT SEEMS TO ME THAT YOU COULD PROBABLY USE A LITTLE HELP YOURSELF.
WHAT GAVE YOU THAT IDEA?
IN MY LINE OF WORK YOU'RE TAUGHT NEVER TO GO INTO A DANGEROUS SITUATION WITHOUT A PARTNER...
AND THIS SURE AS HELL FEELS LIKE A DANGEROUS SITUATION TO ME...

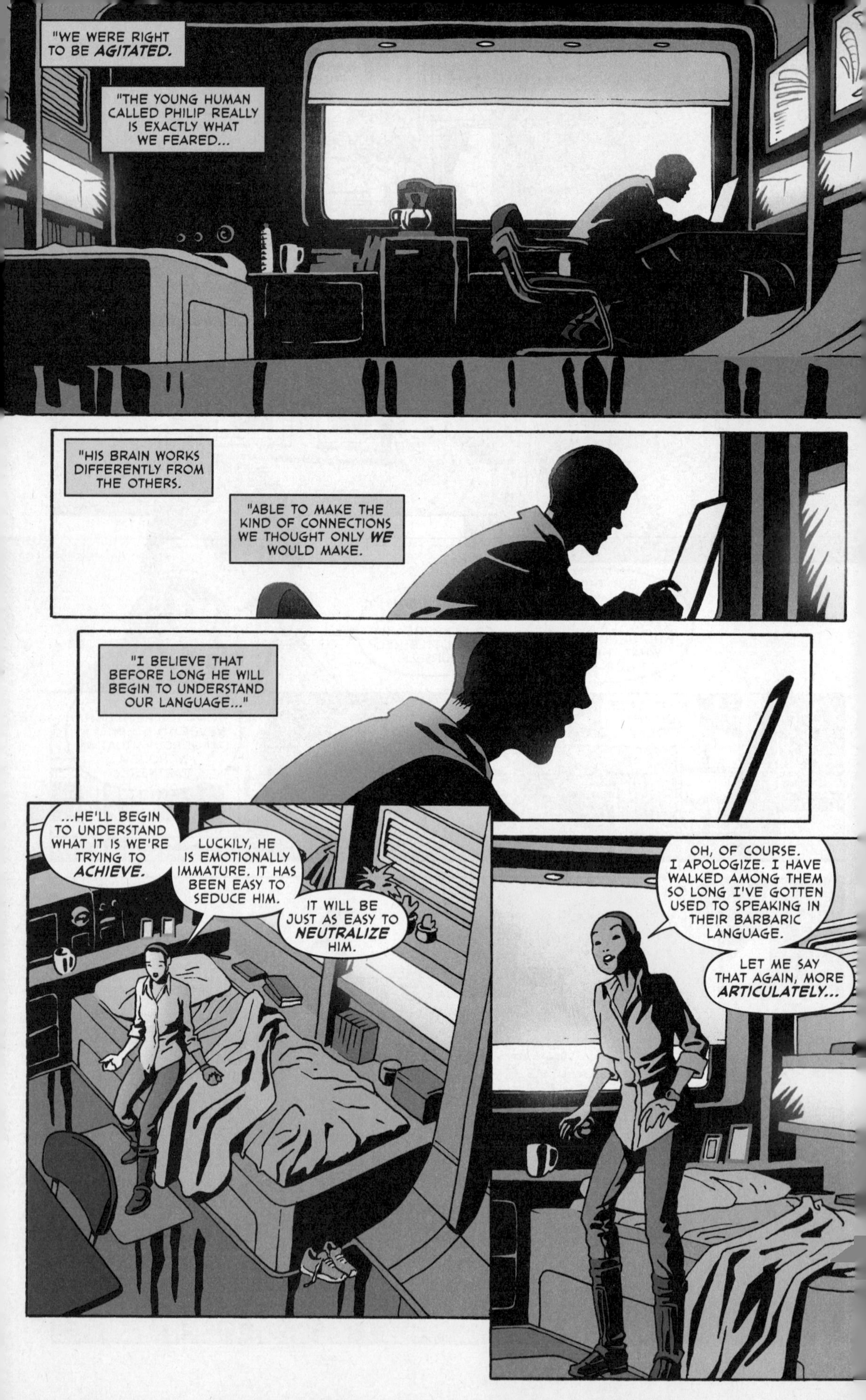
"WE WERE RIGHT TO BE AGITATED.
"THE YOUNG HUMAN CALLED PHILIP REALLY IS EXACTLY WHAT WE FEARED...
"HIS BRAIN WORKS DIFFERENTLY FROM THE OTHERS.
"ABLE TO MAKE THE KIND OF CONNECTIONS WE THOUGHT ONLY WE WOULD MAKE.
"I BELIEVE THAT BEFORE LONG HE WILL BEGIN TO UNDERSTAND OUR LANGUAGE..."
...HE'LL BEGIN TO UNDERSTAND WHAT IT IS WE'RE TRYING TO ACHIEVE.
LUCKILY, HE IS EMOTIONALLY IMMATURE. IT HAS BEEN EASY TO SEDUCE HIM.
IT WILL BE JUST AS EASY TO NEUTRALIZE HIM.
OH, OF COURSE. I APOLOGIZE. I HAVE WALKED AMONG THEM SO LONG I'VE GOTTEN USED TO SPEAKING IN THEIR BARBARIC LANGUAGE.
LET ME SAY THAT AGAIN, MORE ARTICULATELY...

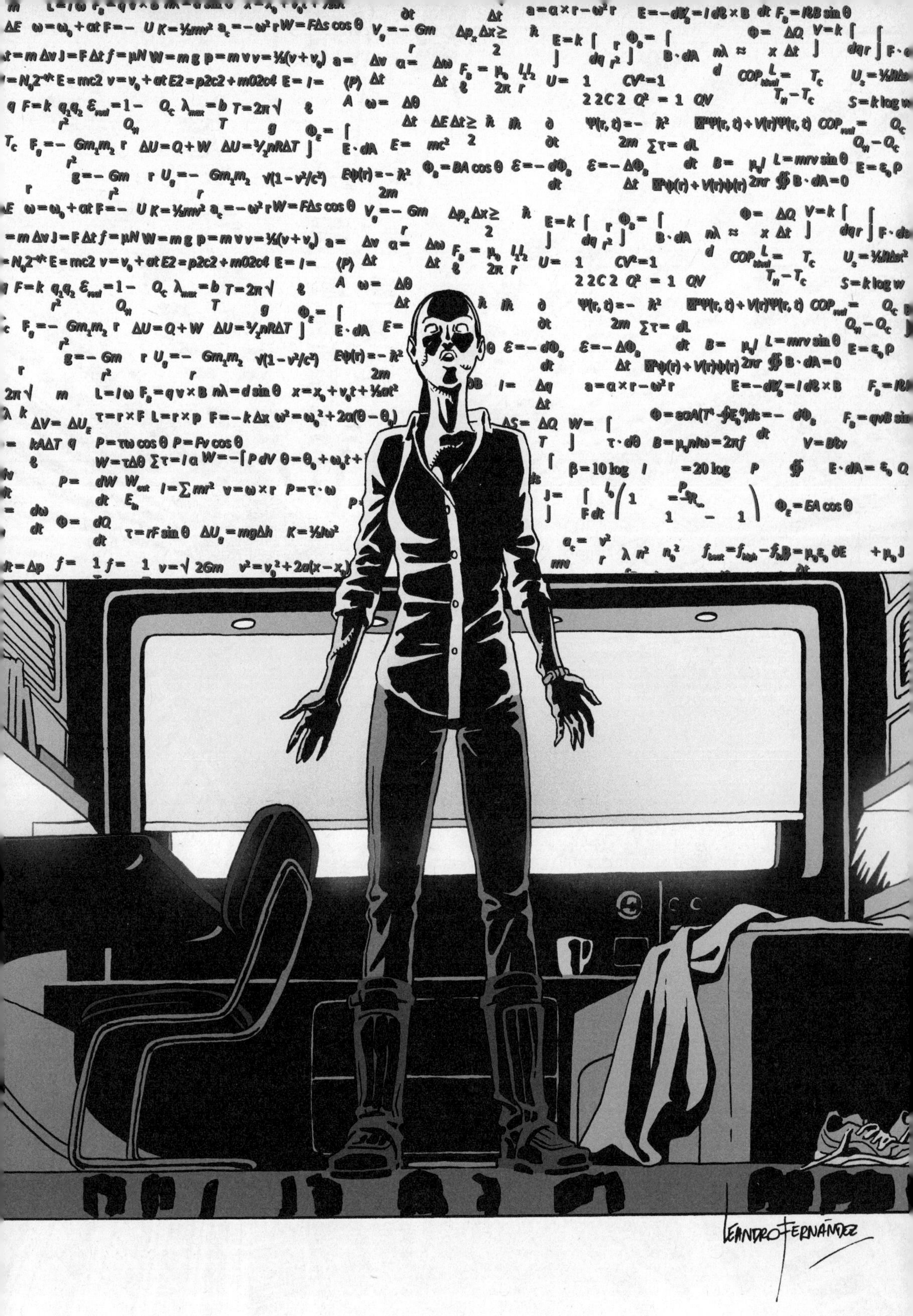
LEANDRO FERNÁNDEZ

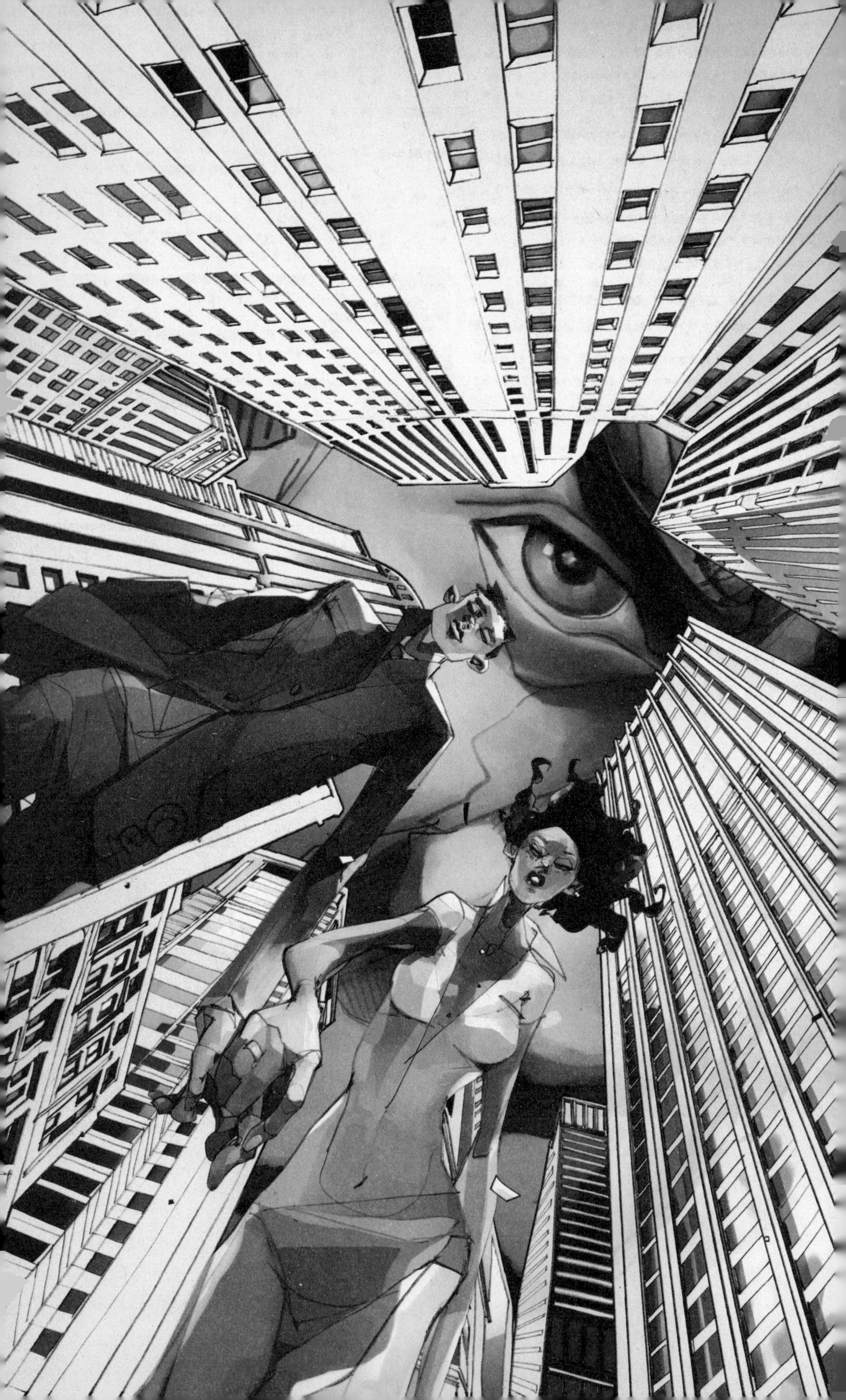

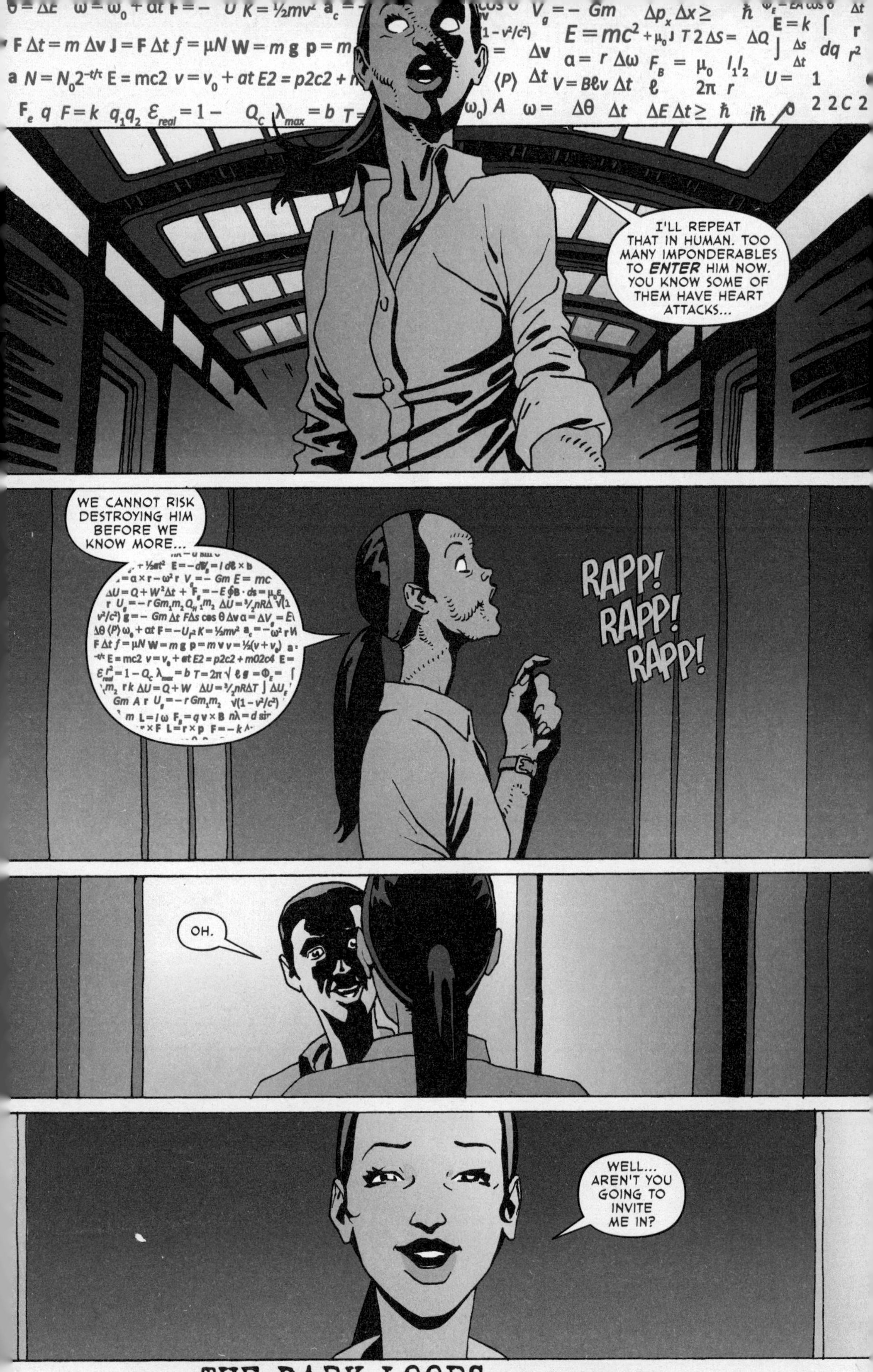
I'LL REPEAT THAT IN HUMAN. TOO MANY IMPONDERABLES TO ENTER HIM NOW. YOU KNOW SOME OF THEM HAVE HEART ATTACKS...
WE CANNOT RISK DESTROYING HIM BEFORE WE KNOW MORE...
RAPP! RAPP! RAPP!
OH.
WELL... AREN'T YOU GOING TO INVITE ME IN?

THE DARK LOOPS CONCLUSION

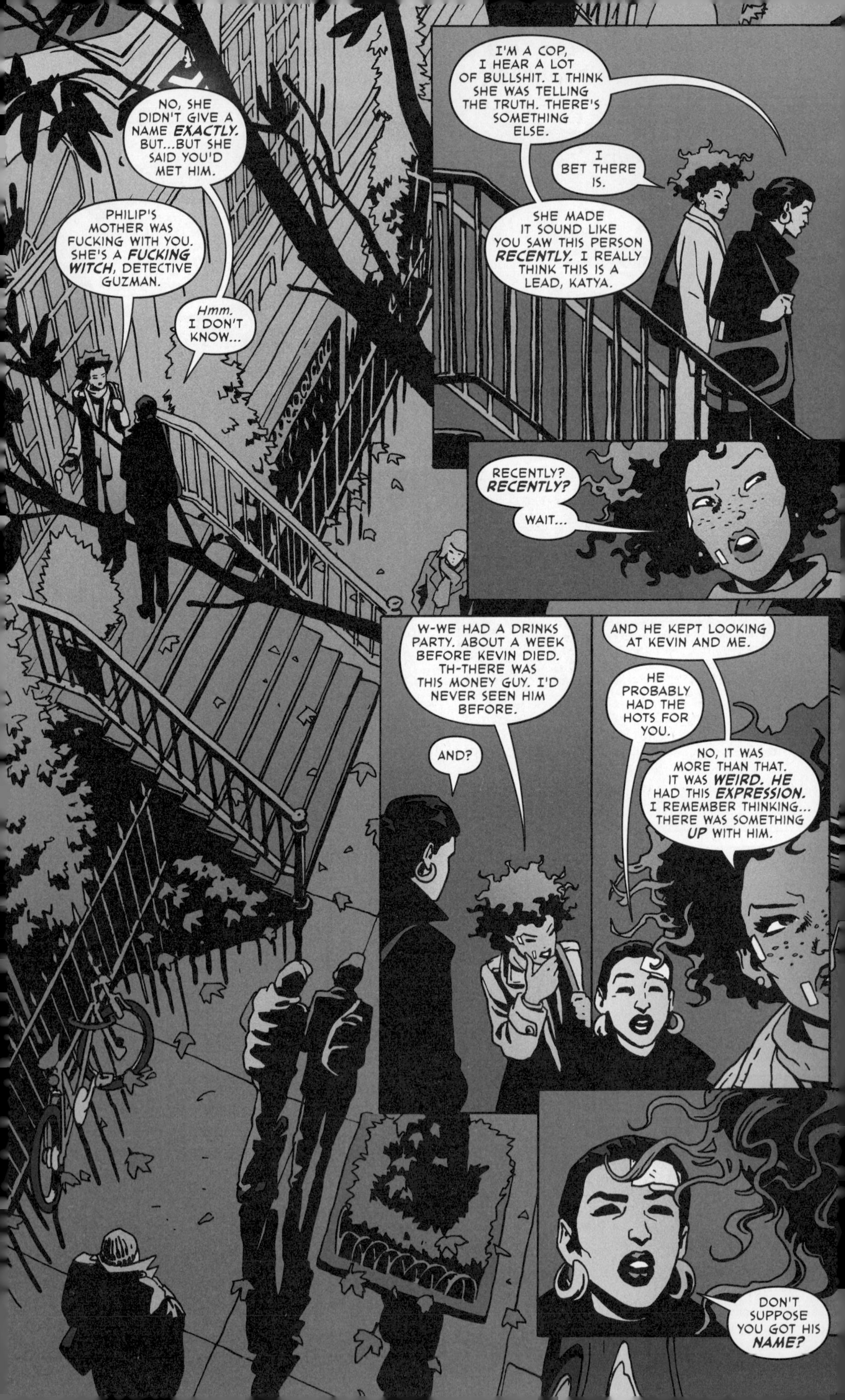
NO, SHE DIDN'T GIVE A NAME EXACTLY. BUT...BUT SHE SAID YOU'D MET HIM.
PHILIP'S MOTHER WAS FUCKING WITH YOU. SHE'S A FUCKING WITCH, DETECTIVE GUZMAN.
Hmm. I DON'T KNOW...
I'M A COP, I HEAR A LOT OF BULLSHIT. I THINK SHE WAS TELLING THE TRUTH. THERE'S SOMETHING ELSE.
I BET THERE IS.
SHE MADE IT SOUND LIKE YOU SAW THIS PERSON RECENTLY. I REALLY THINK THIS IS A LEAD, KATYA.
RECENTLY? RECENTLY?
WAIT...
W-WE HAD A DRINKS PARTY. ABOUT A WEEK BEFORE KEVIN DIED. TH-THERE WAS THIS MONEY GUY. I'D NEVER SEEN HIM BEFORE.
AND?
AND HE KEPT LOOKING AT KEVIN AND ME.
HE PROBABLY HAD THE HOTS FOR YOU.
NO, IT WAS MORE THAN THAT. IT WAS WEIRD. HE HAD THIS EXPRESSION. I REMEMBER THINKING... THERE WAS SOMETHING UP WITH HIM.
DON'T SUPPOSE YOU GOT HIS NAME?

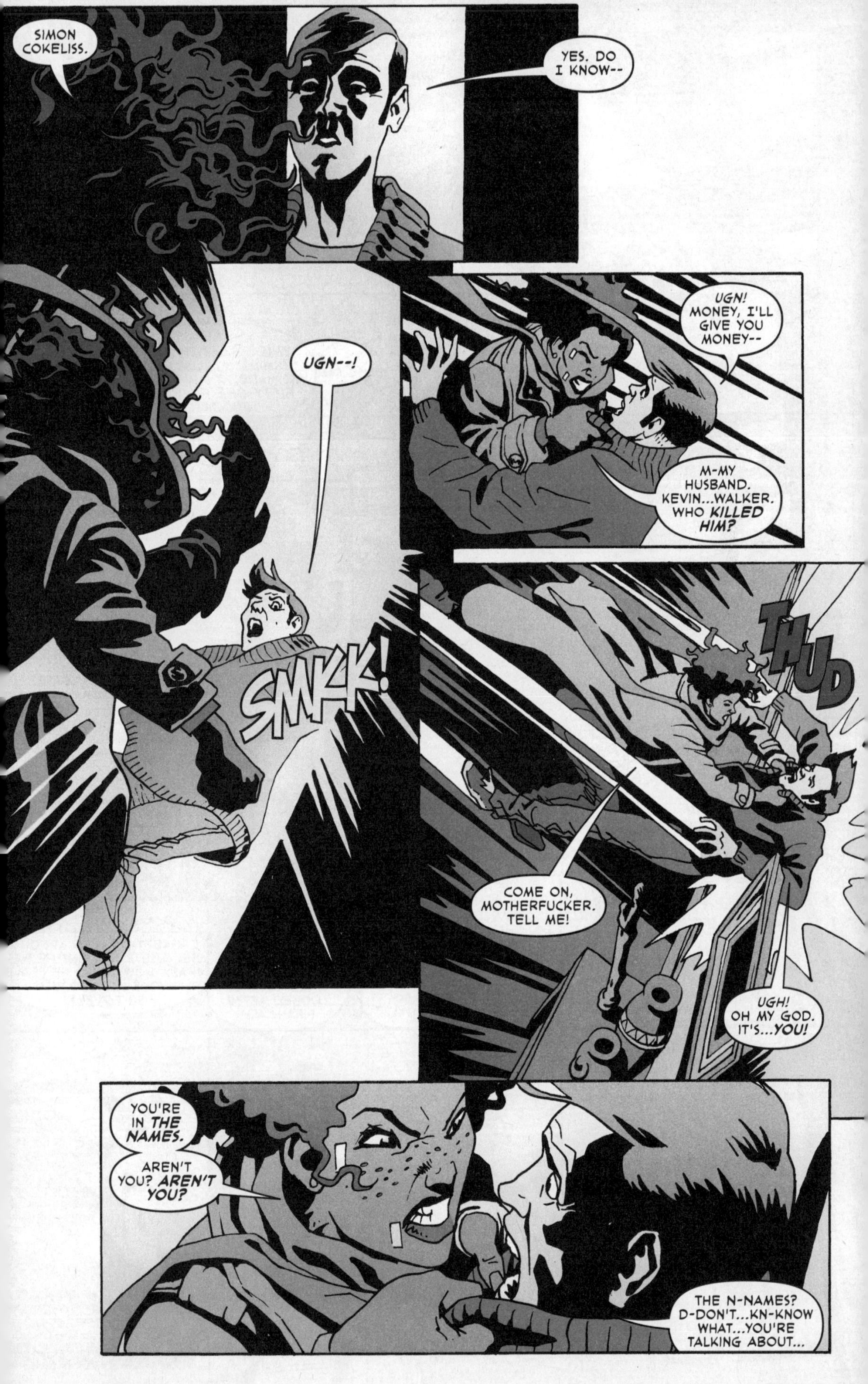
SIMON COKELISS.
YES. DO I KNOW--
UGN--!
SMKK!
UGN! MONEY, I'LL GIVE YOU MONEY--
M-MY HUSBAND. KEVIN...WALKER. WHO KILLED HIM?
THUD
COME ON, MOTHERFUCKER. TELL ME!
UGH! OH MY GOD. IT'S...YOU!
YOU'RE IN THE NAMES.
AREN'T YOU? AREN'T YOU?
THE N-NAMES? D-DON'T...KN-KNOW WHAT...YOU'RE TALKING ABOUT...

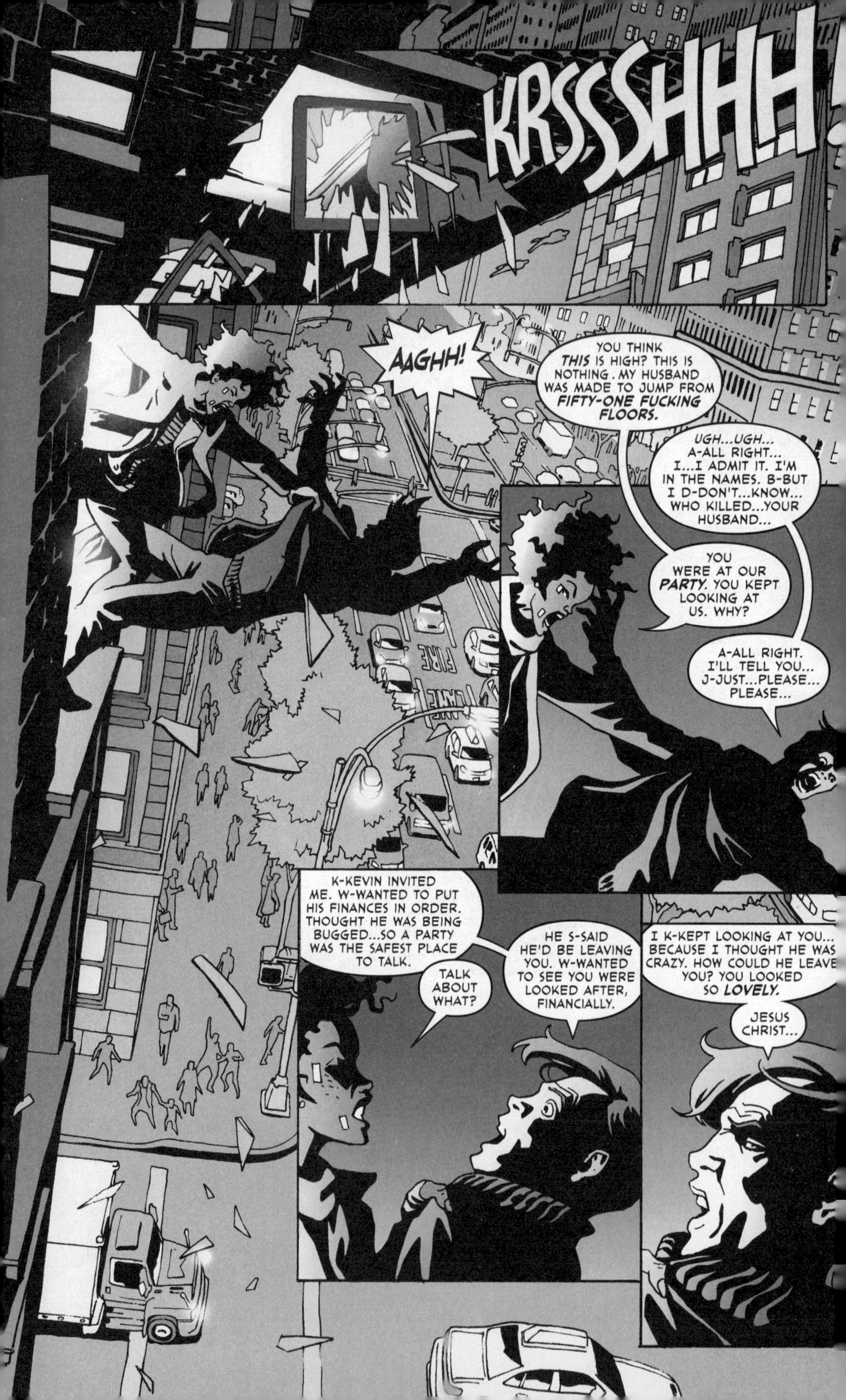
KRSSSHHH
AAGHH!
YOU THINK THIS IS HIGH? THIS IS NOTHING. MY HUSBAND WAS MADE TO JUMP FROM FIFTY-ONE FUCKING FLOORS.
UGH...UGH... A-ALL RIGHT... I...I ADMIT IT. I'M IN THE NAMES. B-BUT I D-DON'T...KNOW... WHO KILLED...YOUR HUSBAND...
YOU WERE AT OUR PARTY. YOU KEPT LOOKING AT US. WHY?
A-ALL RIGHT. I'LL TELL YOU... J-JUST...PLEASE... PLEASE...
K-KEVIN INVITED ME. W-WANTED TO PUT HIS FINANCES IN ORDER. THOUGHT HE WAS BEING BUGGED...SO A PARTY WAS THE SAFEST PLACE TO TALK.
TALK ABOUT WHAT?
HE S-SAID HE'D BE LEAVING YOU. W-WANTED TO SEE YOU WERE LOOKED AFTER, FINANCIALLY.
I K-KEPT LOOKING AT YOU... BECAUSE I THOUGHT HE WAS CRAZY. HOW COULD HE LEAVE YOU? YOU LOOKED SO LOVELY.
JESUS CHRIST...

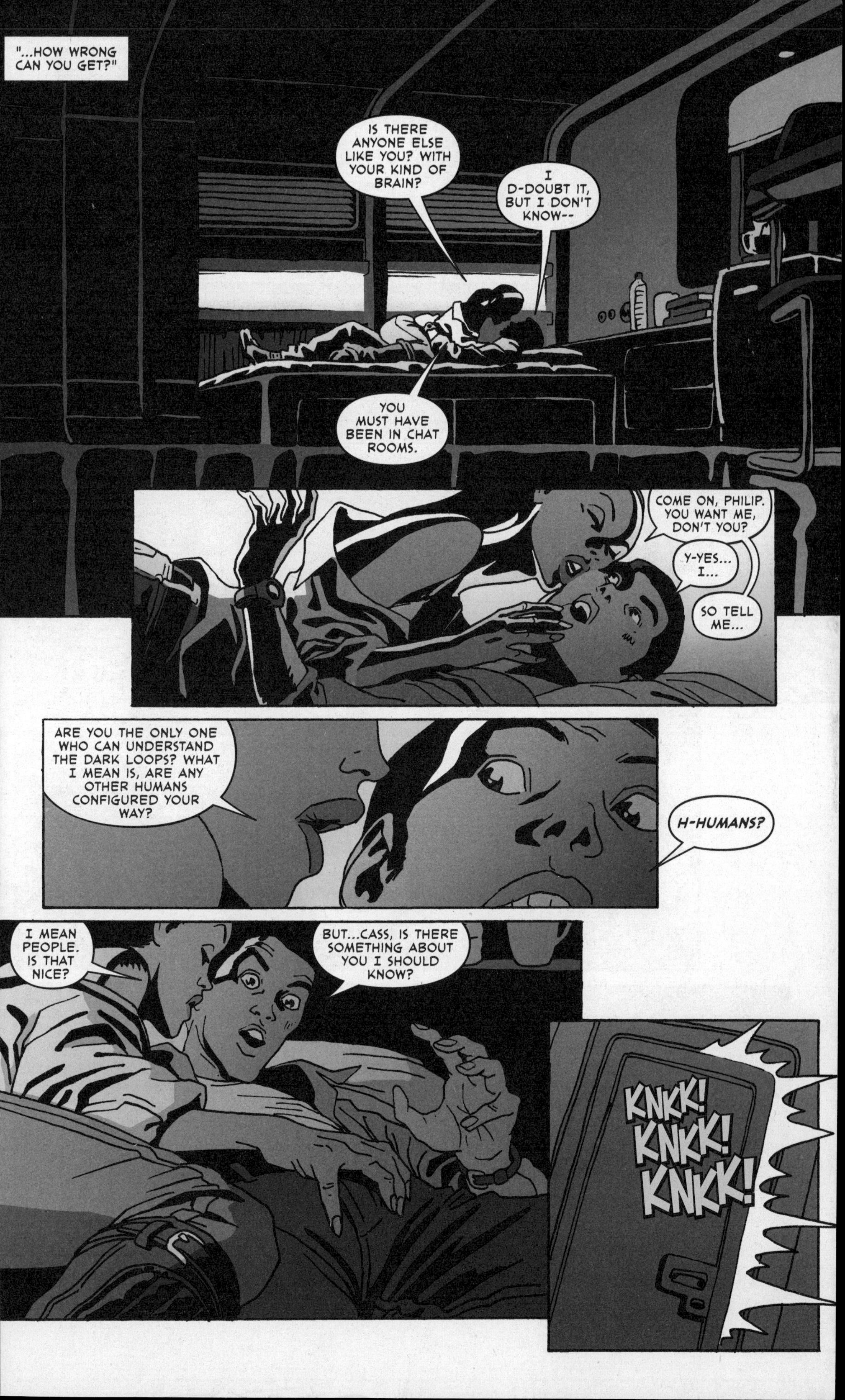
"...HOW WRONG CAN YOU GET?"
IS THERE ANYONE ELSE LIKE YOU? WITH YOUR KIND OF BRAIN?
I D-DOUBT IT, BUT I DON'T KNOW--
YOU MUST HAVE BEEN IN CHAT ROOMS.
COME ON, PHILIP. YOU WANT ME, DON'T YOU?
Y-YES... I...
SO TELL ME...
ARE YOU THE ONLY ONE WHO CAN UNDERSTAND THE DARK LOOPS? WHAT I MEAN IS, ARE ANY OTHER HUMANS CONFIGURED YOUR WAY?
H-HUMANS?
I MEAN PEOPLE. IS THAT NICE?
BUT...CASS, IS THERE SOMETHING ABOUT YOU I SHOULD KNOW?
KNKK! KNKK! KNKK!

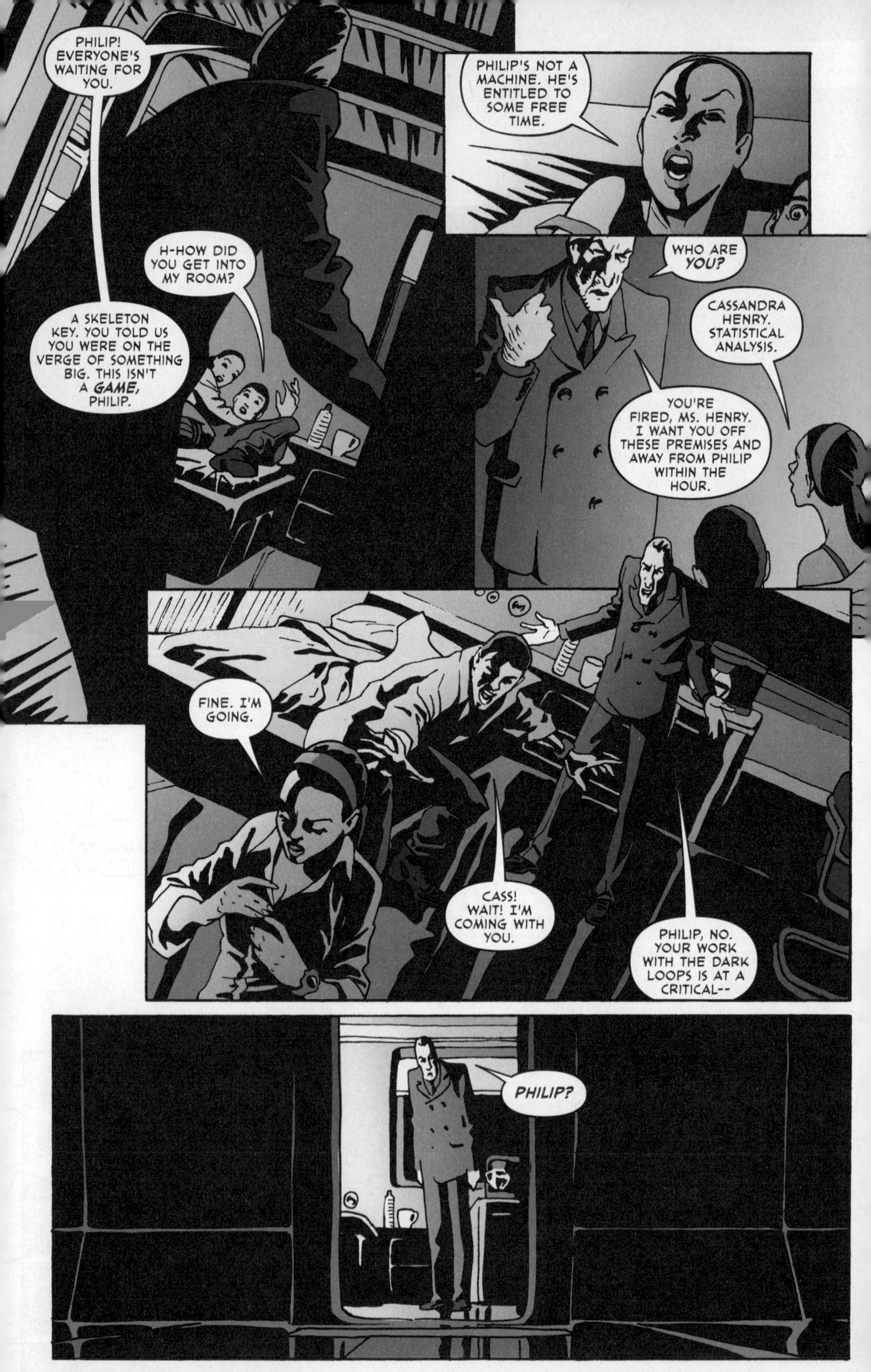
PHILIP! EVERYONE'S WAITING FOR YOU.
PHILIP'S NOT A MACHINE. HE'S ENTITLED TO SOME FREE TIME.
H-HOW DID YOU GET INTO MY ROOM?
A SKELETON KEY. YOU TOLD US YOU WERE ON THE VERGE OF SOMETHING BIG. THIS ISN'T A GAME, PHILIP.
WHO ARE YOU?
CASSANDRA HENRY. STATISTICAL ANALYSIS.
YOU'RE FIRED, MS. HENRY. I WANT YOU OFF THESE PREMISES AND AWAY FROM PHILIP WITHIN THE HOUR.
FINE. I'M GOING.
CASS! WAIT! I'M COMING WITH YOU.
PHILIP, NO. YOUR WORK WITH THE DARK LOOPS IS AT A CRITICAL--
PHILIP?

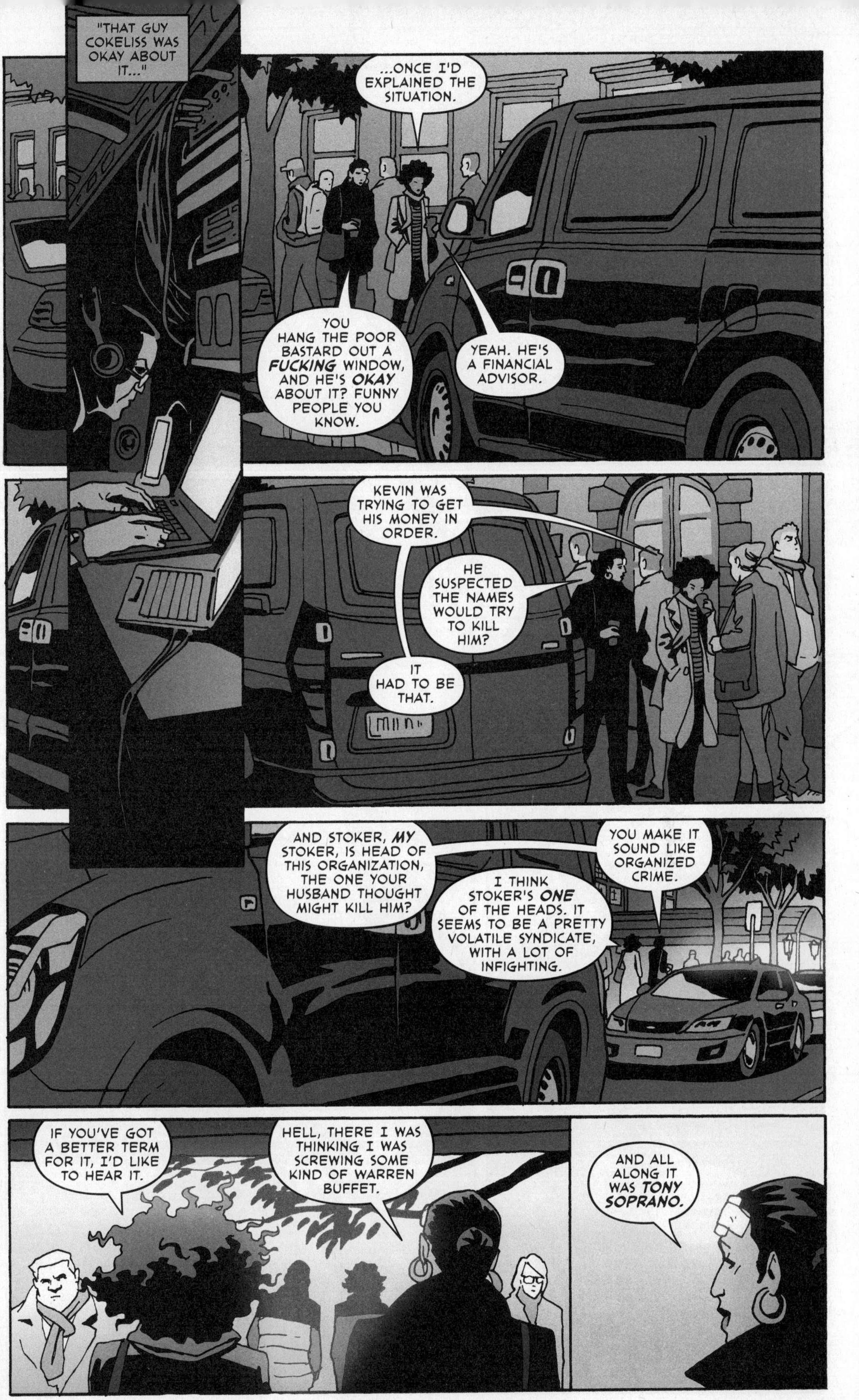
"THAT GUY COKELISS WAS OKAY ABOUT IT..."
...ONCE I'D EXPLAINED THE SITUATION.
YOU HANG THE POOR BASTARD OUT A *FUCKING* WINDOW, AND HE'S *OKAY* ABOUT IT? FUNNY PEOPLE YOU KNOW.
YEAH. HE'S A FINANCIAL ADVISOR.
KEVIN WAS TRYING TO GET HIS MONEY IN ORDER.
HE SUSPECTED THE NAMES WOULD TRY TO KILL HIM?
IT HAD TO BE THAT.
AND STOKER, *MY* STOKER, IS HEAD OF THIS ORGANIZATION, THE ONE YOUR HUSBAND THOUGHT MIGHT KILL HIM?
I THINK STOKER'S *ONE* OF THE HEADS. IT SEEMS TO BE A PRETTY VOLATILE SYNDICATE, WITH A LOT OF INFIGHTING.
YOU MAKE IT SOUND LIKE ORGANIZED CRIME.
IF YOU'VE GOT A BETTER TERM FOR IT, I'D LIKE TO HEAR IT.
HELL, THERE I WAS THINKING I WAS SCREWING SOME KIND OF WARREN BUFFET.
AND ALL ALONG IT WAS *TONY SOPRANO.*

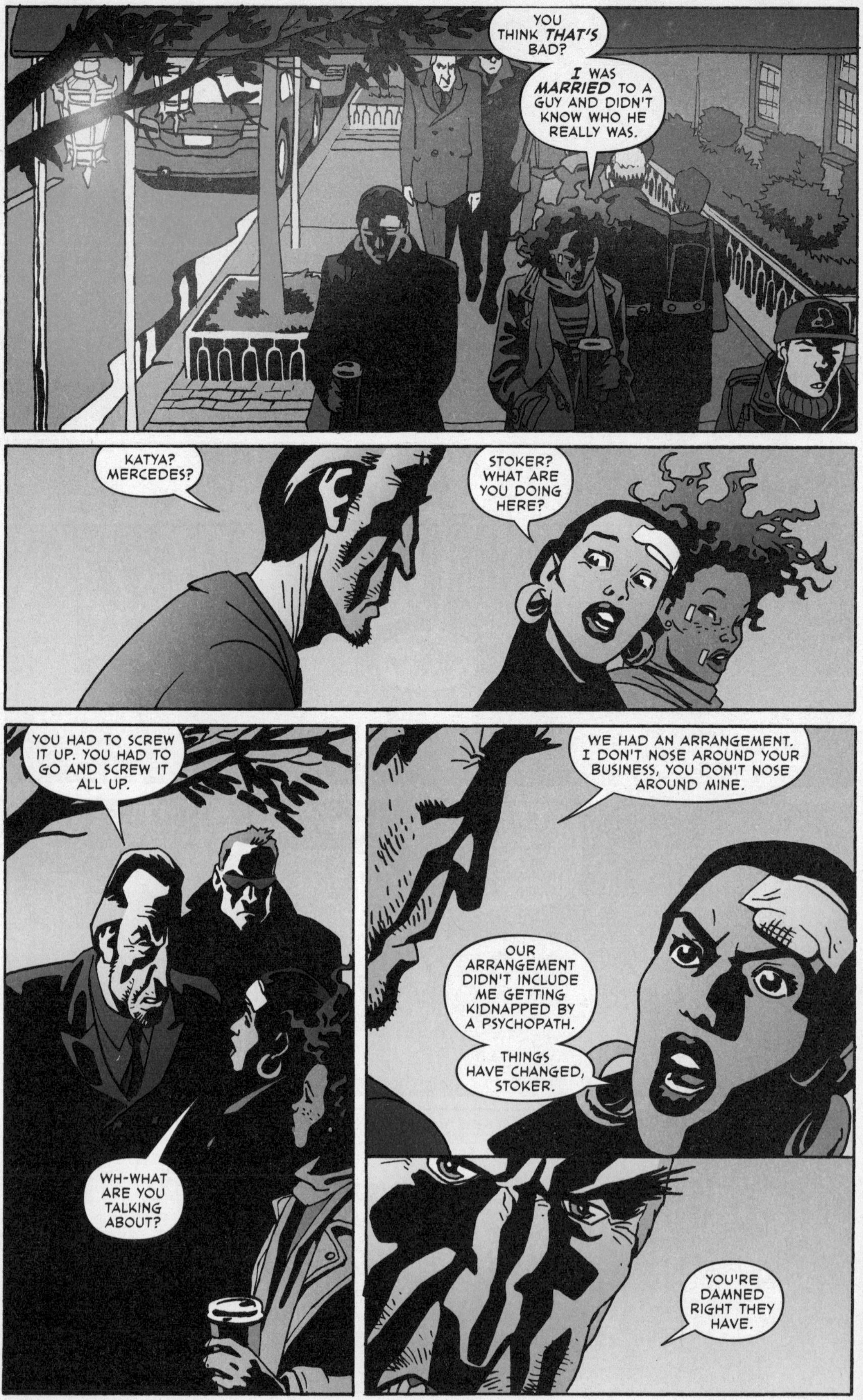
YOU THINK THAT'S BAD?
I WAS MARRIED TO A GUY AND DIDN'T KNOW WHO HE REALLY WAS.
KATYA? MERCEDES?
STOKER? WHAT ARE YOU DOING HERE?
YOU HAD TO SCREW IT UP. YOU HAD TO GO AND SCREW IT ALL UP.
WH-WHAT ARE YOU TALKING ABOUT?
WE HAD AN ARRANGEMENT. I DON'T NOSE AROUND YOUR BUSINESS, YOU DON'T NOSE AROUND MINE.
OUR ARRANGEMENT DIDN'T INCLUDE ME GETTING KIDNAPPED BY A PSYCHOPATH.
THINGS HAVE CHANGED, STOKER.
YOU'RE DAMNED RIGHT THEY HAVE.

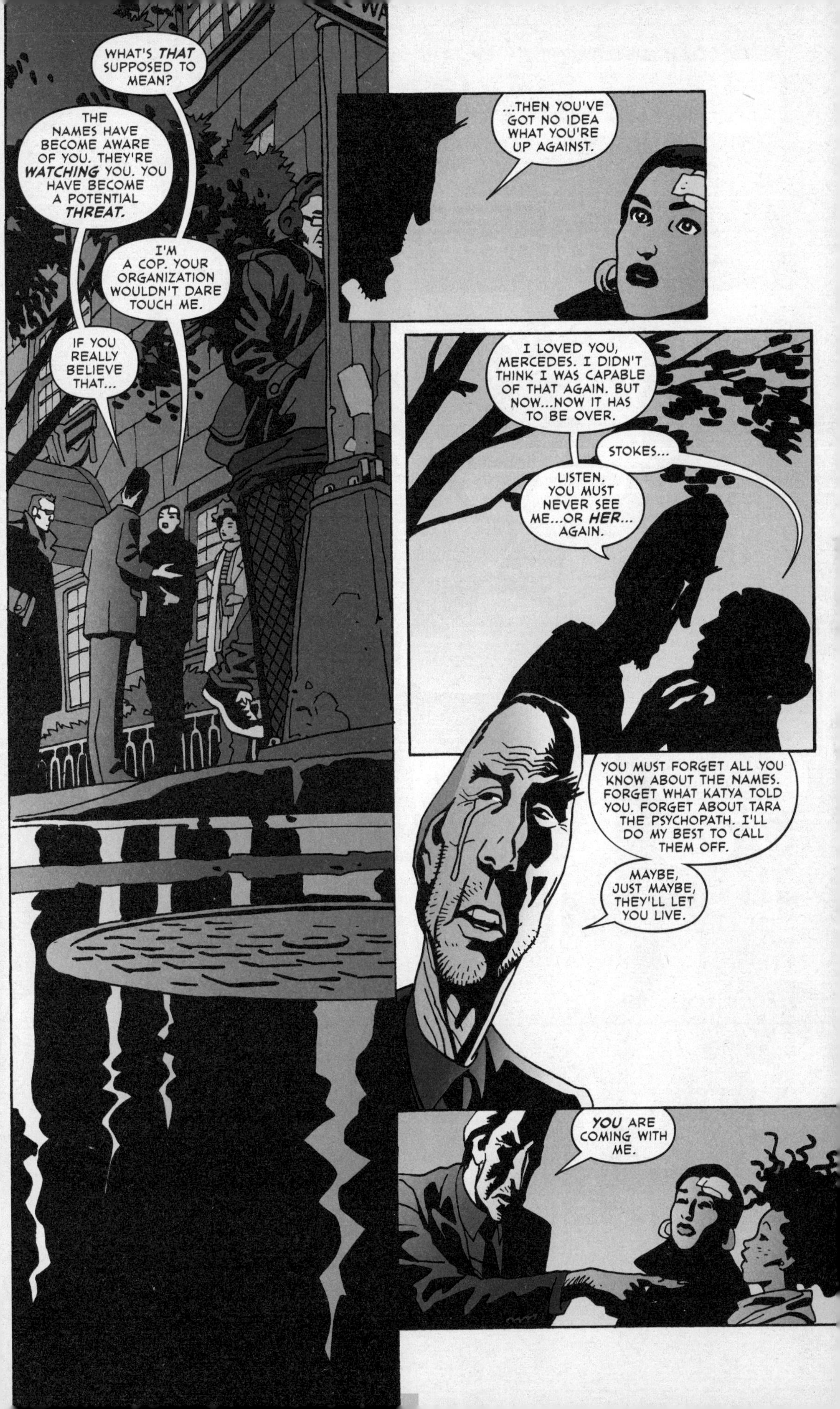
WHAT'S *THAT* SUPPOSED TO MEAN?
THE NAMES HAVE BECOME AWARE OF YOU. THEY'RE *WATCHING* YOU. YOU HAVE BECOME A POTENTIAL *THREAT.*
I'M A COP. YOUR ORGANIZATION WOULDN'T DARE TOUCH ME.
IF YOU REALLY BELIEVE THAT...
...THEN YOU'VE GOT NO IDEA WHAT YOU'RE UP AGAINST.
I LOVED YOU, MERCEDES. I DIDN'T THINK I WAS CAPABLE OF THAT AGAIN. BUT NOW...NOW IT HAS TO BE OVER.
STOKES...
LISTEN. YOU MUST NEVER SEE ME...OR *HER*... AGAIN.
YOU MUST FORGET ALL YOU KNOW ABOUT THE NAMES. FORGET WHAT KATYA TOLD YOU. FORGET ABOUT TARA THE PSYCHOPATH. I'LL DO MY BEST TO CALL THEM OFF.
MAYBE, JUST MAYBE, THEY'LL LET YOU LIVE.
YOU ARE COMING WITH ME.

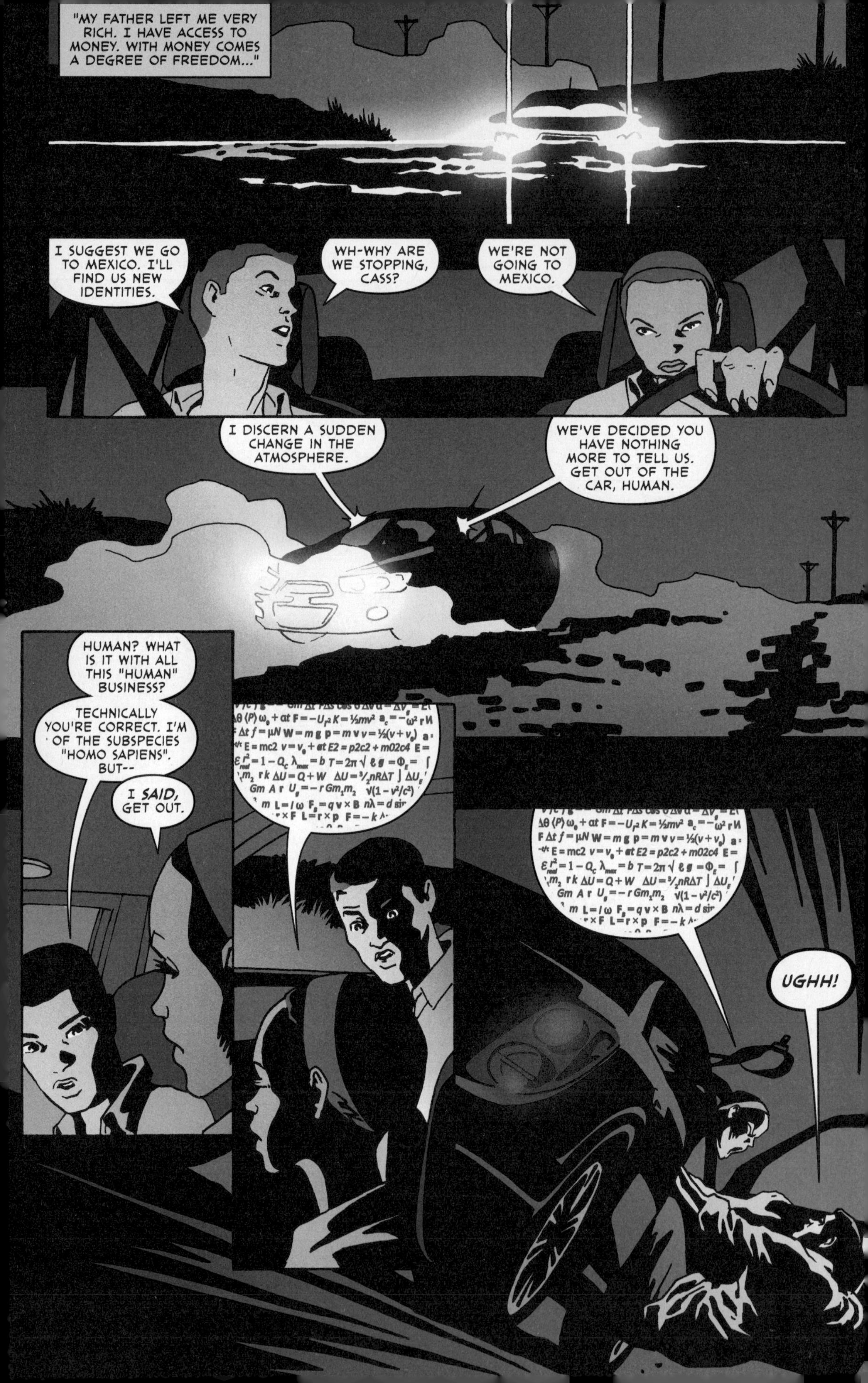
"MY FATHER LEFT ME VERY RICH. I HAVE ACCESS TO MONEY. WITH MONEY COMES A DEGREE OF FREEDOM..."
I SUGGEST WE GO TO MEXICO. I'LL FIND US NEW IDENTITIES.
WH-WHY ARE WE STOPPING, CASS?
WE'RE NOT GOING TO MEXICO.
I DISCERN A SUDDEN CHANGE IN THE ATMOSPHERE.
WE'VE DECIDED YOU HAVE NOTHING MORE TO TELL US. GET OUT OF THE CAR, HUMAN.
HUMAN? WHAT IS IT WITH ALL THIS "HUMAN" BUSINESS?
TECHNICALLY YOU'RE CORRECT. I'M OF THE SUBSPECIES "HOMO SAPIENS". BUT--
I *SAID*, GET OUT.
UGHH!

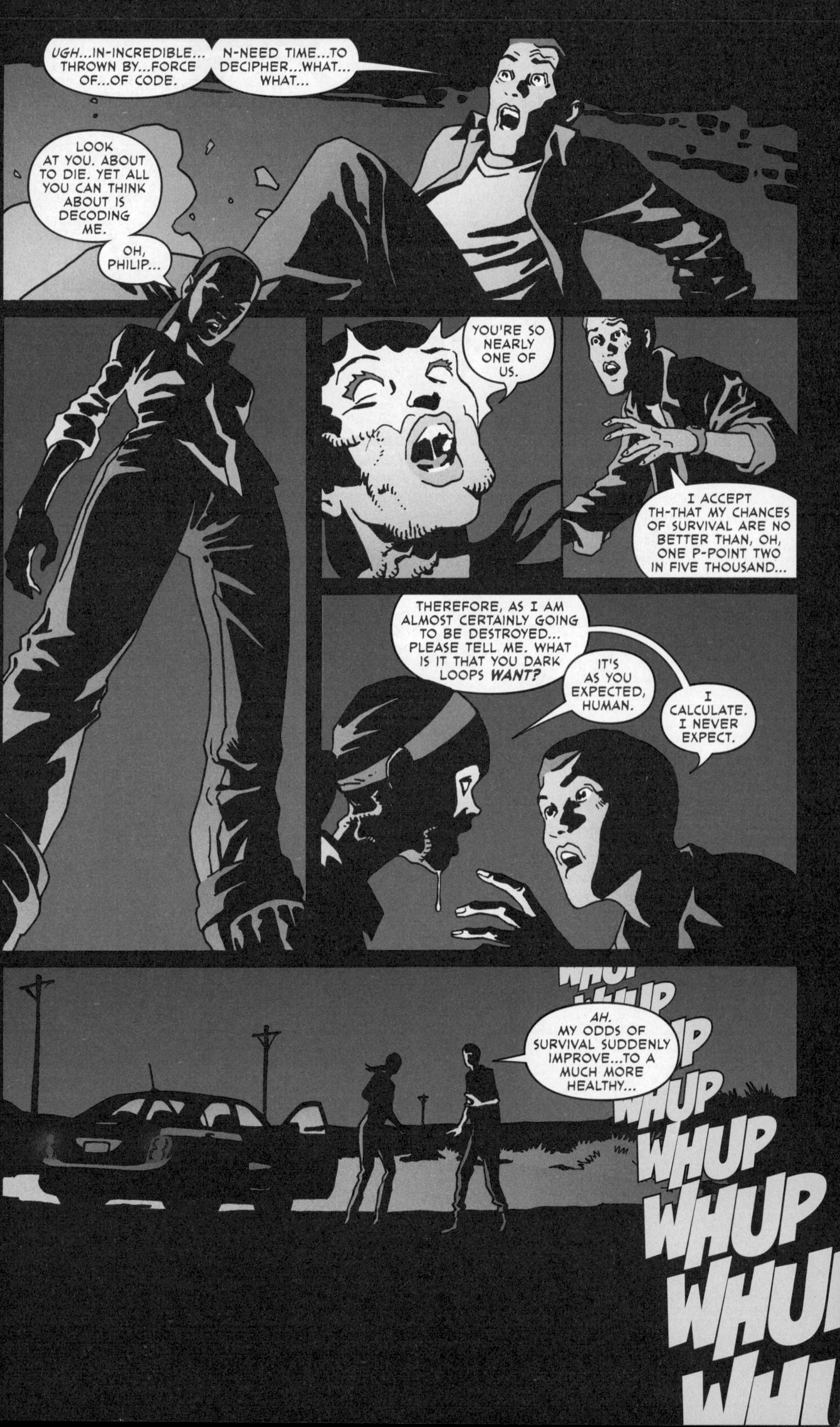
UGH...IN-INCREDIBLE... THROWN BY...FORCE OF...OF CODE.
N-NEED TIME...TO DECIPHER...WHAT... WHAT...
LOOK AT YOU. ABOUT TO DIE. YET ALL YOU CAN THINK ABOUT IS DECODING ME.
OH, PHILIP...
YOU'RE SO NEARLY ONE OF US.
I ACCEPT TH-THAT MY CHANCES OF SURVIVAL ARE NO BETTER THAN, OH, ONE P-POINT TWO IN FIVE THOUSAND...
THEREFORE, AS I AM ALMOST CERTAINLY GOING TO BE DESTROYED... PLEASE TELL ME. WHAT IS IT THAT YOU DARK LOOPS WANT?
IT'S AS YOU EXPECTED, HUMAN.
I CALCULATE. I NEVER EXPECT.
WHUP
WHUP
WHUP
AH. MY ODDS OF SURVIVAL SUDDENLY IMPROVE...TO A MUCH MORE HEALTHY...
WHUP
WHUP
WHUP
WHUP

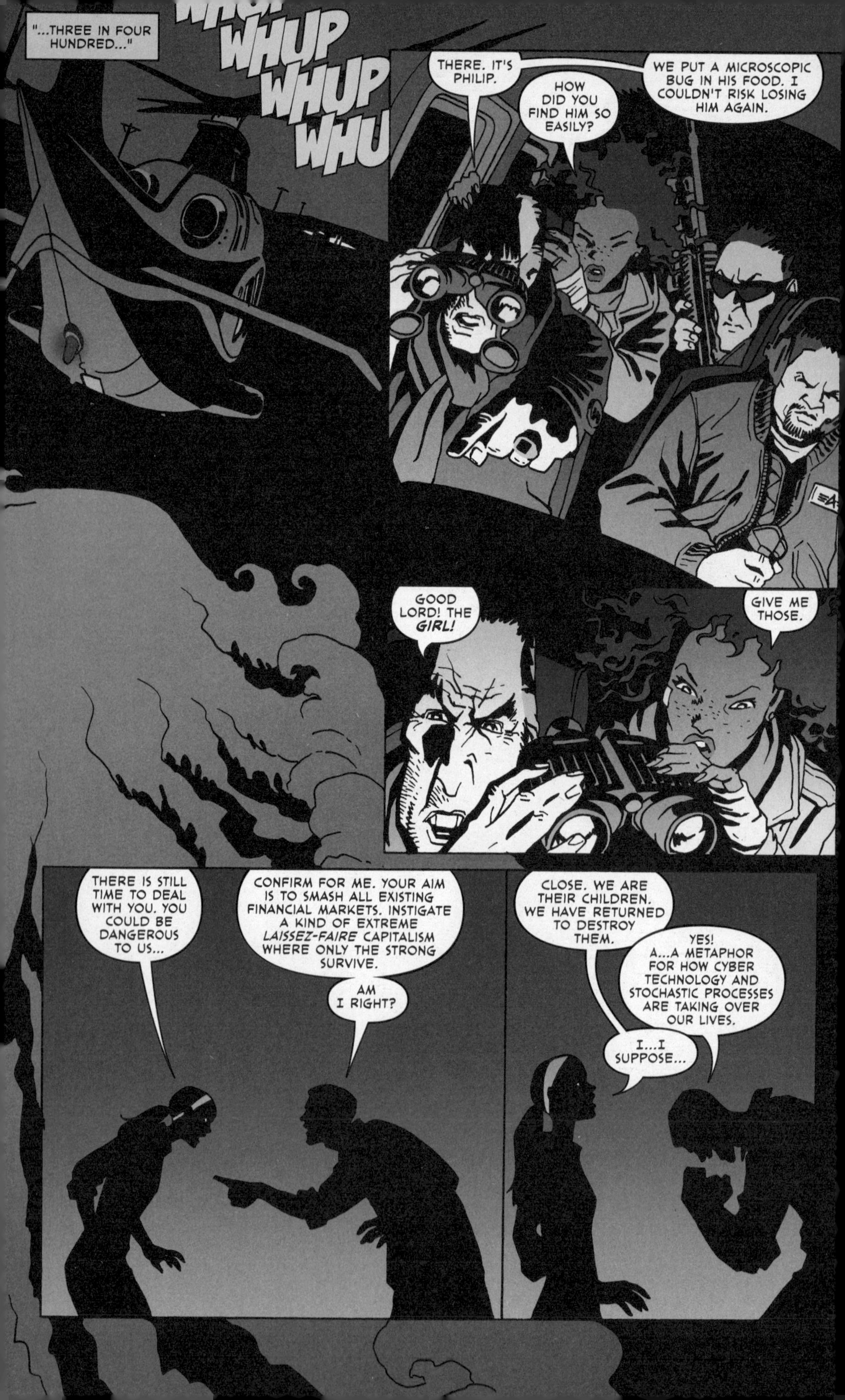
"...THREE IN FOUR HUNDRED..."
WHUP WHUP WHUP WHU
THERE. IT'S PHILIP.
HOW DID YOU FIND HIM SO EASILY?
WE PUT A MICROSCOPIC BUG IN HIS FOOD. I COULDN'T RISK LOSING HIM AGAIN.
GOOD LORD! THE *GIRL!*
GIVE ME THOSE.
THERE IS STILL TIME TO DEAL WITH YOU. YOU COULD BE DANGEROUS TO US...
CONFIRM FOR ME. YOUR AIM IS TO SMASH ALL EXISTING FINANCIAL MARKETS. INSTIGATE A KIND OF EXTREME *LAISSEZ-FAIRE* CAPITALISM WHERE ONLY THE STRONG SURVIVE.
AM I RIGHT?
CLOSE. WE ARE THEIR CHILDREN. WE HAVE RETURNED TO DESTROY THEM.
YES! A...A METAPHOR FOR HOW CYBER TECHNOLOGY AND STOCHASTIC PROCESSES ARE TAKING OVER OUR LIVES.
I...I SUPPOSE...

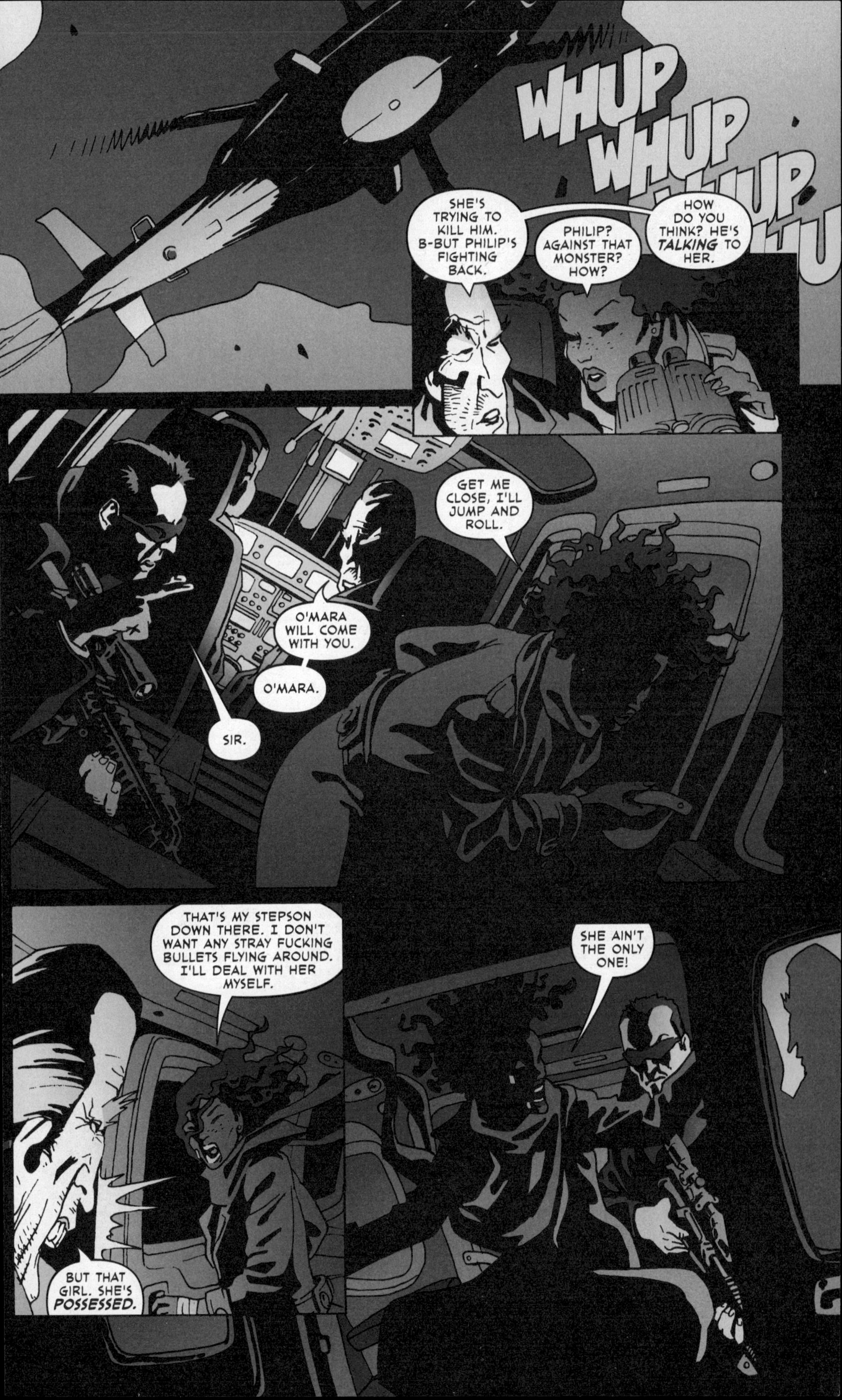
WHUP WHUP WHUP
SHE'S TRYING TO KILL HIM. B-BUT PHILIP'S FIGHTING BACK.
PHILIP? AGAINST THAT MONSTER? HOW?
HOW DO YOU THINK? HE'S *TALKING* TO HER.
GET ME CLOSE, I'LL JUMP AND ROLL.
O'MARA WILL COME WITH YOU.
O'MARA.
SIR.
THAT'S MY STEPSON DOWN THERE. I DON'T WANT ANY STRAY FUCKING BULLETS FLYING AROUND. I'LL DEAL WITH HER MYSELF.
BUT THAT GIRL. SHE'S *POSSESSED.*
SHE AIN'T THE ONLY ONE!

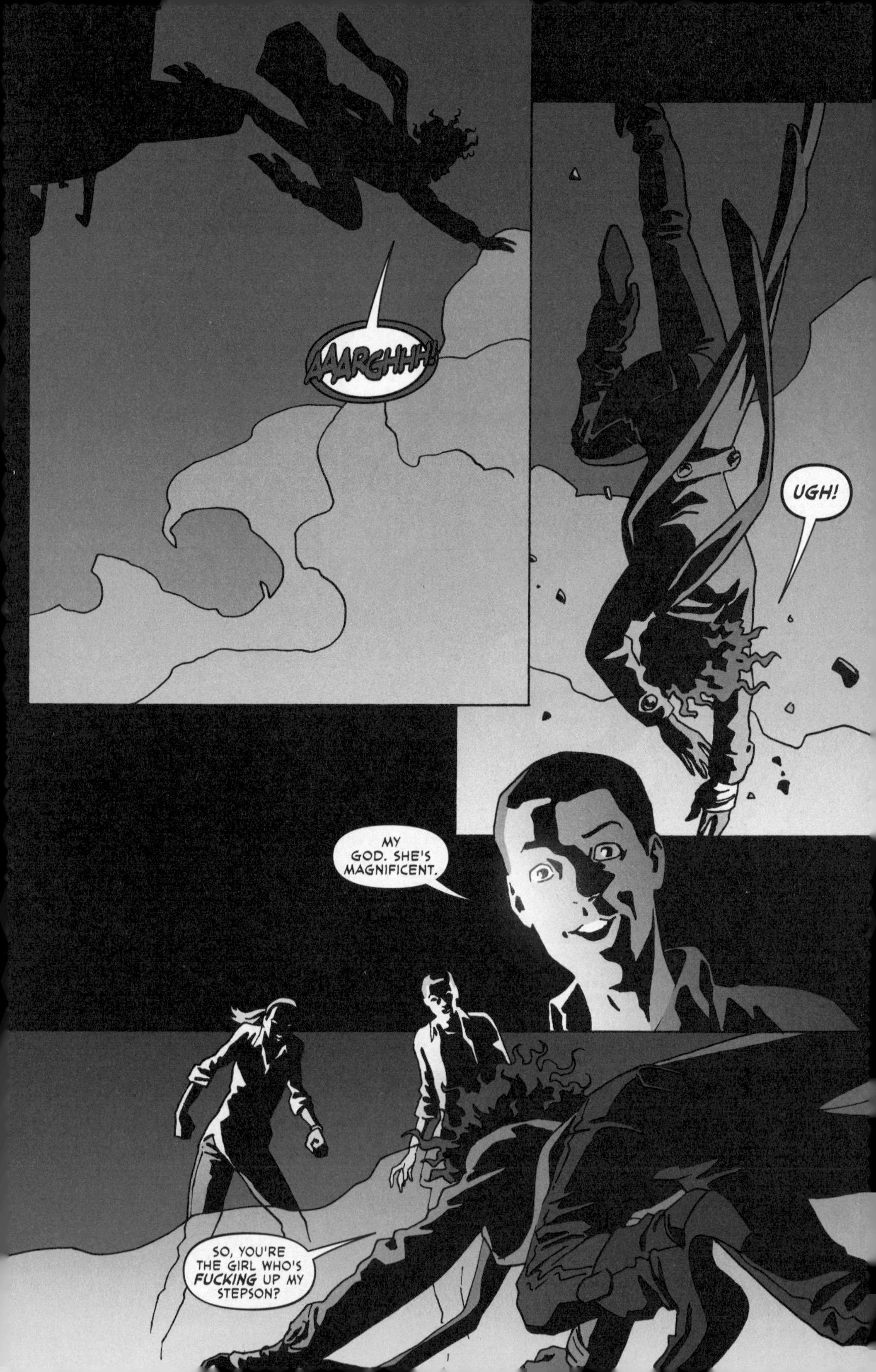
AAARGHHH!
UGH!
MY GOD. SHE'S MAGNIFICENT.
SO, YOU'RE THE GIRL WHO'S FUCKING UP MY STEPSON?

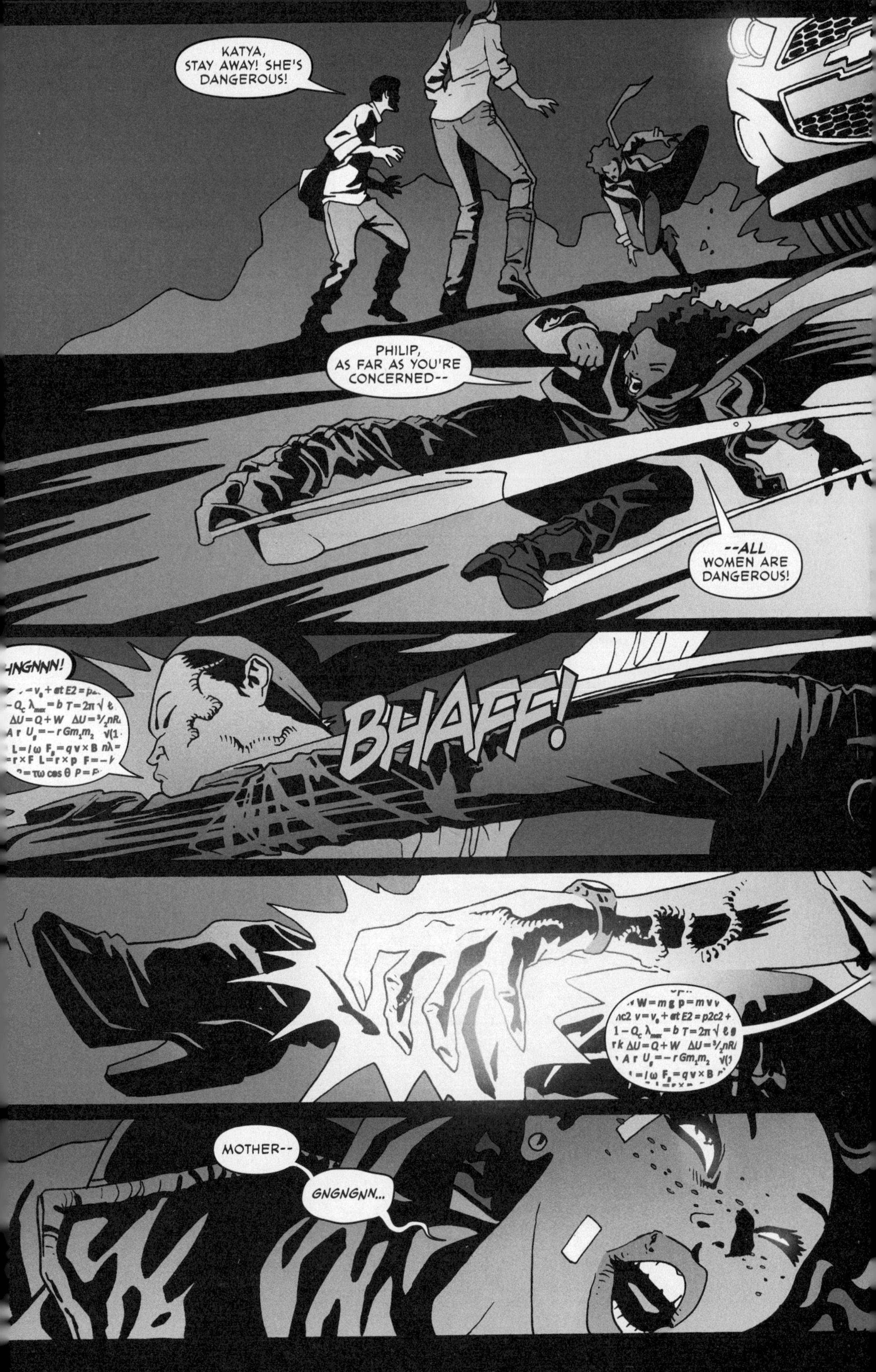
KATYA, STAY AWAY! SHE'S DANGEROUS!
PHILIP, AS FAR AS YOU'RE CONCERNED--
--ALL WOMEN ARE DANGEROUS!
HNGNNN!
BHAFF!
MOTHER--
GNGNGNN...

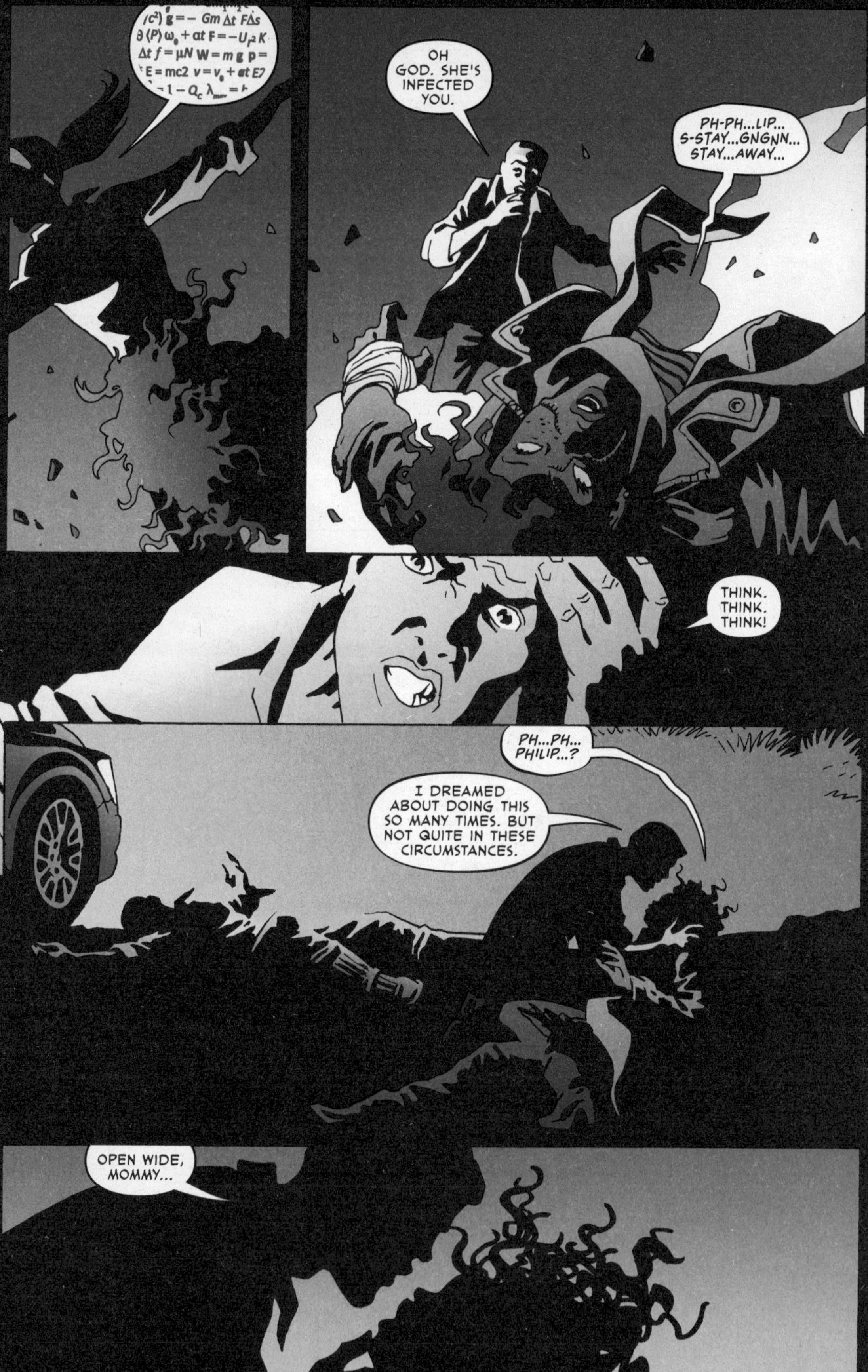
∂ ⟨P⟩ ω₀ + αt F = −U_f² K
Δt f = μN W = m g p =
E = mc2 v = v₀ + at E7
OH GOD. SHE'S INFECTED YOU.
PH-PH...LIP... S-STAY...GNGNN... STAY...AWAY...
THINK. THINK. THINK!
PH...PH... PHILIP...?
I DREAMED ABOUT DOING THIS SO MANY TIMES. BUT NOT QUITE IN THESE CIRCUMSTANCES.
OPEN WIDE, MOMMY...

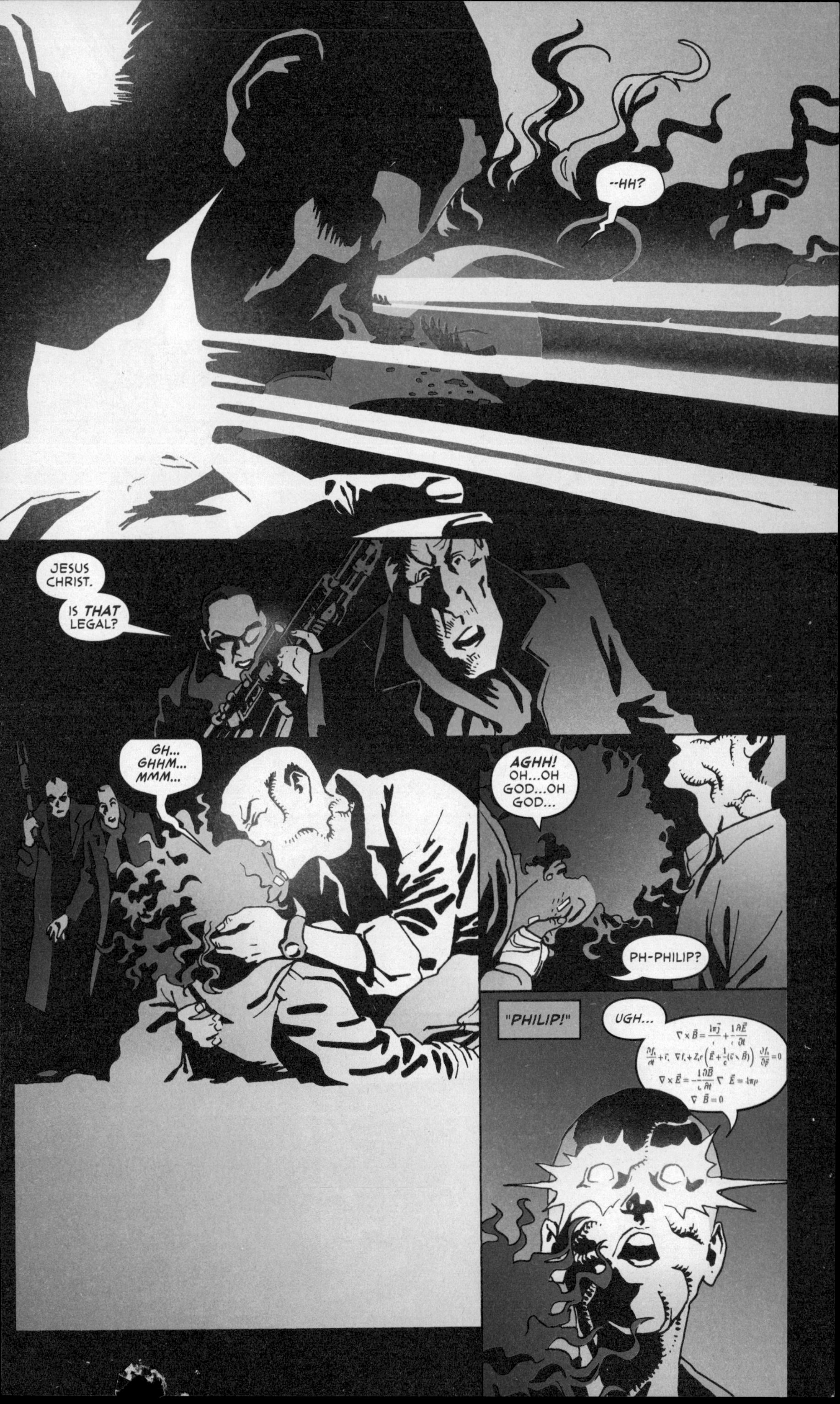
--HH?
JESUS CHRIST.
IS *THAT* LEGAL?
GH... GHHM... MMM...
AGHH! OH...OH GOD...OH GOD...
PH-PHILIP?
"PHILIP!"
UGH...

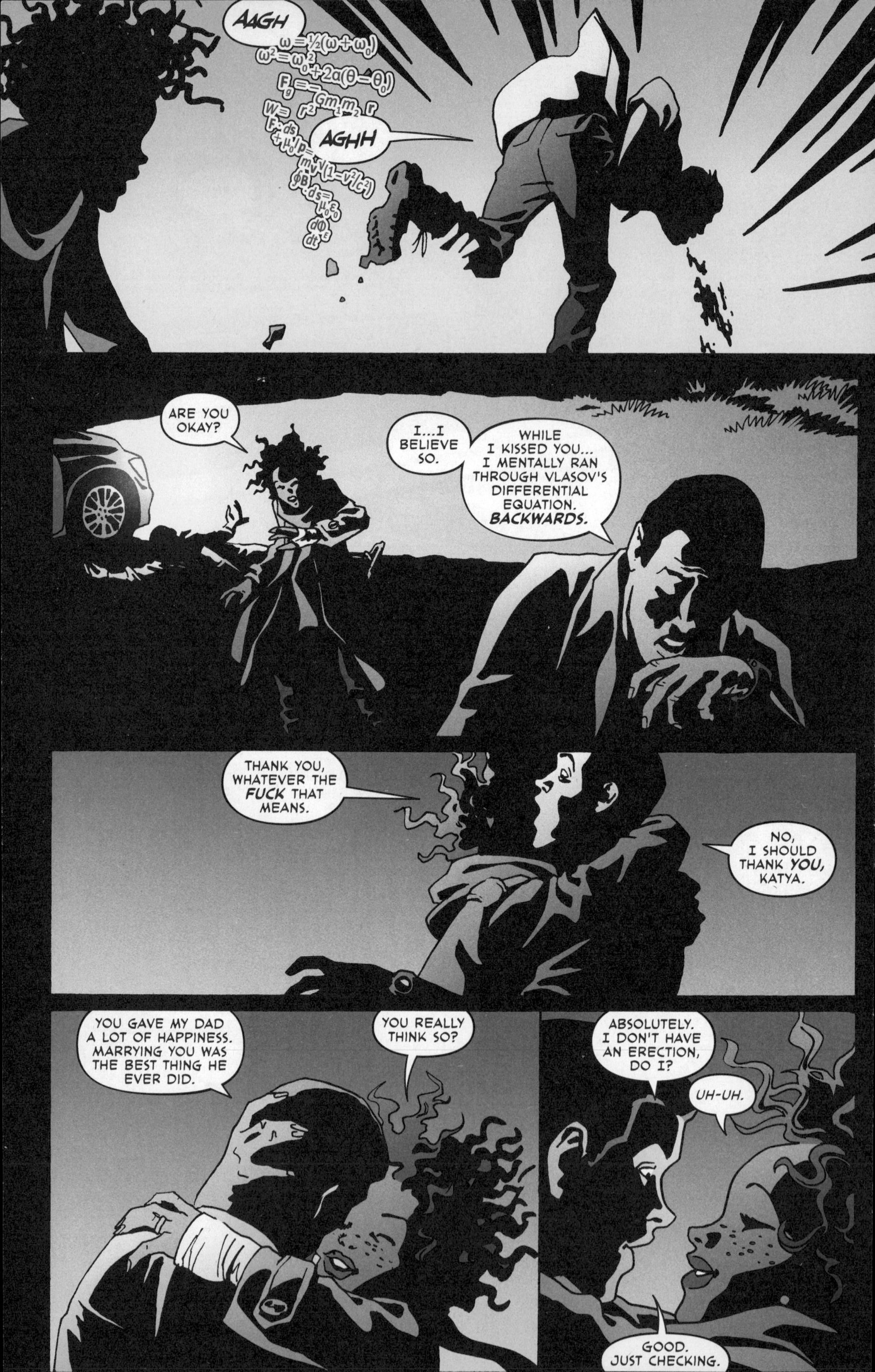
AAGH
$\omega = \frac{1}{2}(\omega + \omega_0)$
$\omega^2 = \omega_0^2 + 2\alpha(\theta - \theta_0)$
$F_g = -\frac{Gm_1m_2}{r^2} r$
$W = F \cdot ds$
$+ \mu_0 I$
$p = m_0 v / \sqrt{(1 - v^2/c^2)}$
$\oint B \cdot ds = \mu_0 \varepsilon_0 \frac{d\Phi_E}{dt}$
AGHH
ARE YOU OKAY?
I...I BELIEVE SO.
WHILE I KISSED YOU... I MENTALLY RAN THROUGH VLASOV'S DIFFERENTIAL EQUATION. BACKWARDS.
THANK YOU, WHATEVER THE FUCK THAT MEANS.
NO, I SHOULD THANK YOU, KATYA.
YOU GAVE MY DAD A LOT OF HAPPINESS. MARRYING YOU WAS THE BEST THING HE EVER DID.
YOU REALLY THINK SO?
ABSOLUTELY. I DON'T HAVE AN ERECTION, DO I?
UH-UH.
GOOD. JUST CHECKING.

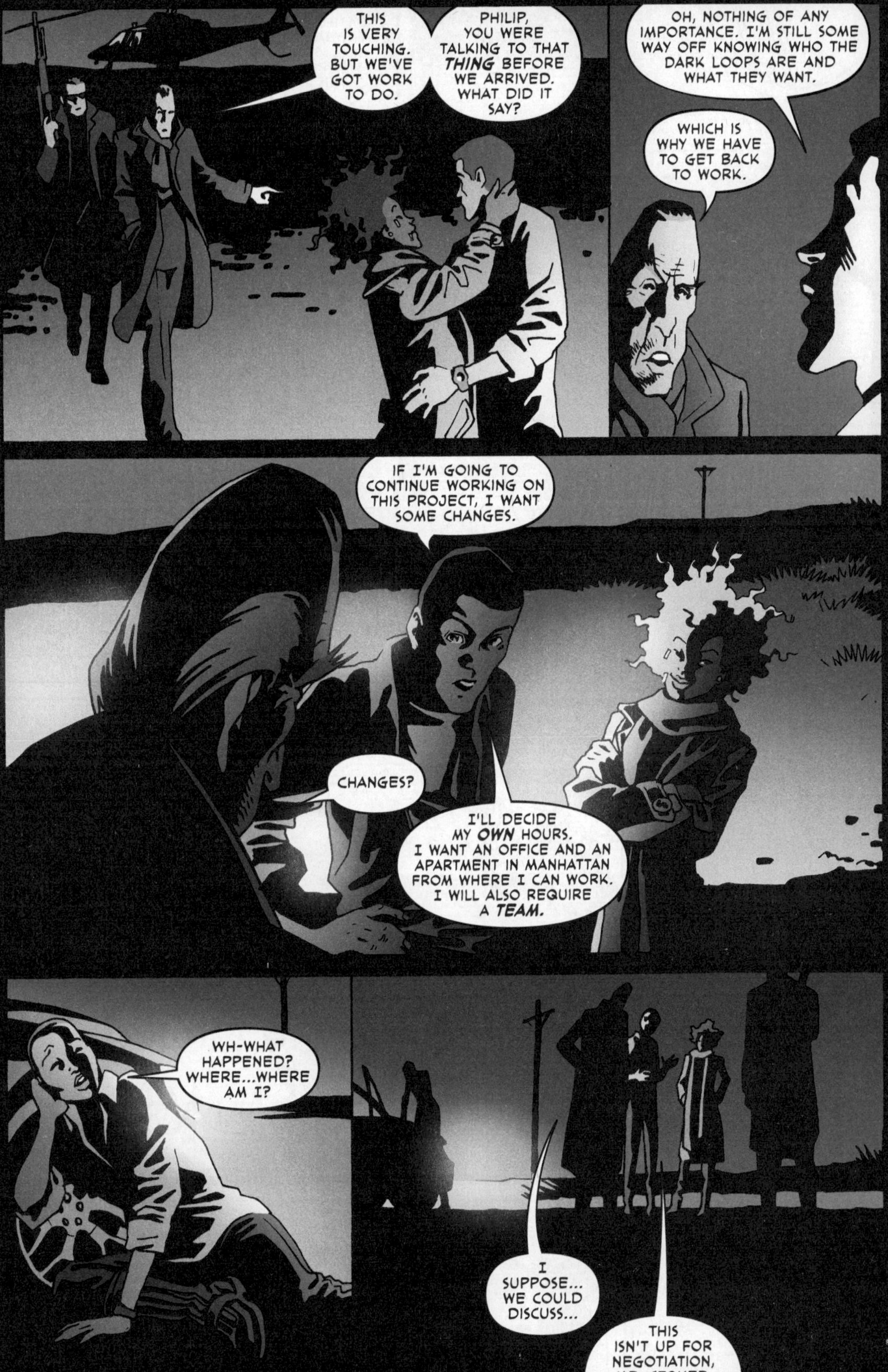

THIS IS VERY TOUCHING. BUT WE'VE GOT WORK TO DO.
PHILIP, YOU WERE TALKING TO THAT *THING* BEFORE WE ARRIVED. WHAT DID IT SAY?
OH, NOTHING OF ANY IMPORTANCE. I'M STILL SOME WAY OFF KNOWING WHO THE DARK LOOPS ARE AND WHAT THEY WANT.
WHICH IS WHY WE HAVE TO GET BACK TO WORK.
IF I'M GOING TO CONTINUE WORKING ON THIS PROJECT, I WANT SOME CHANGES.
CHANGES?
I'LL DECIDE MY *OWN* HOURS. I WANT AN OFFICE AND AN APARTMENT IN MANHATTAN FROM WHERE I CAN WORK. I WILL ALSO REQUIRE A *TEAM.*
WH-WHAT HAPPENED? WHERE...WHERE AM I?
I SUPPOSE... WE COULD DISCUSS...
THIS ISN'T UP FOR NEGOTIATION, MR. STOKER. ACCEPT MY TERMS OR I CEASE WORKING FOR YOU.

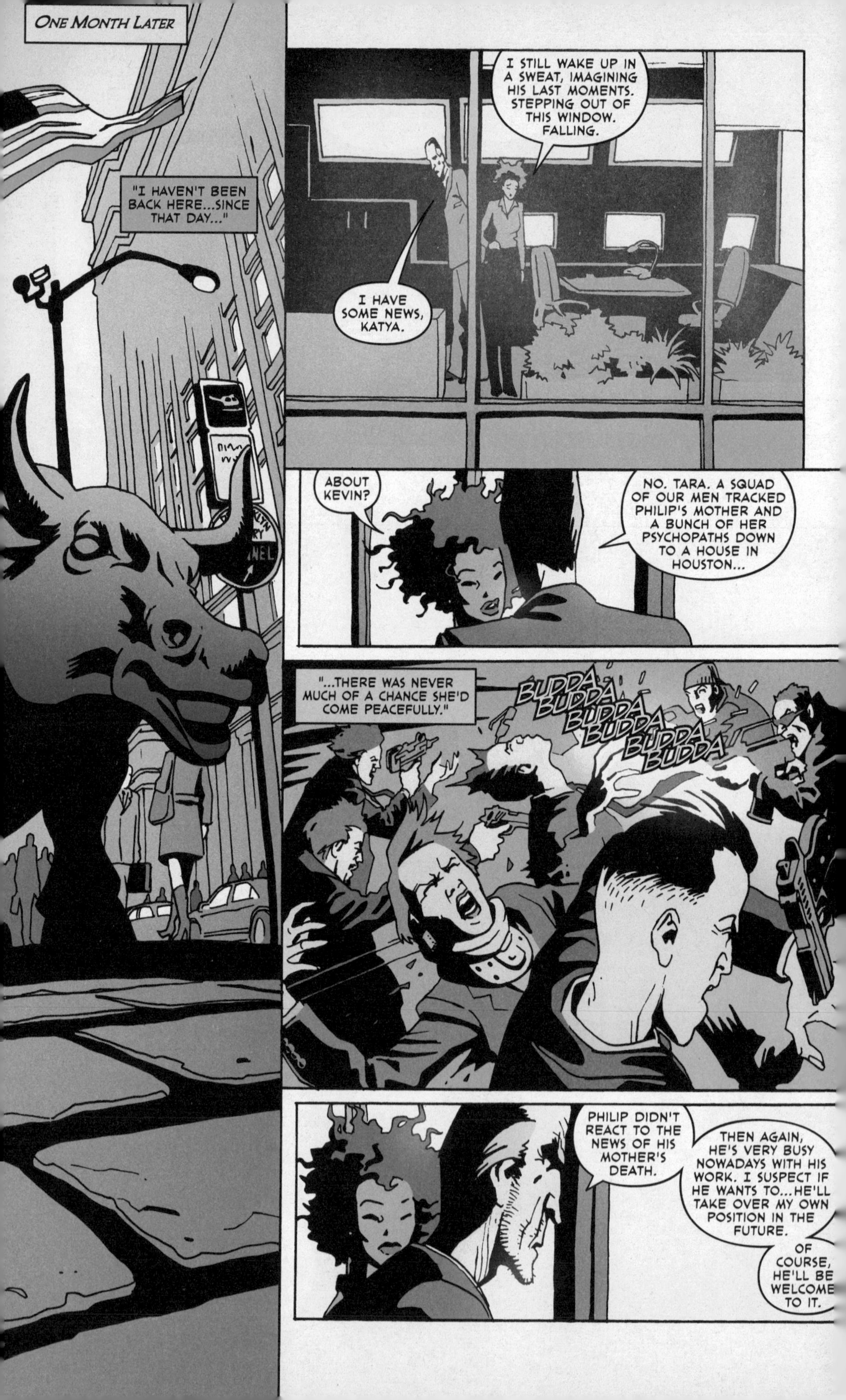
ONE MONTH LATER
"I HAVEN'T BEEN BACK HERE...SINCE THAT DAY..."
I STILL WAKE UP IN A SWEAT, IMAGINING HIS LAST MOMENTS. STEPPING OUT OF THIS WINDOW. FALLING.
I HAVE SOME NEWS, KATYA.
ABOUT KEVIN?
NO. TARA. A SQUAD OF OUR MEN TRACKED PHILIP'S MOTHER AND A BUNCH OF HER PSYCHOPATHS DOWN TO A HOUSE IN HOUSTON...
"...THERE WAS NEVER MUCH OF A CHANCE SHE'D COME PEACEFULLY."
BUDDA BUDDA BUDDA BUDDA BUDDA BUDDA
PHILIP DIDN'T REACT TO THE NEWS OF HIS MOTHER'S DEATH.
THEN AGAIN, HE'S VERY BUSY NOWADAYS WITH HIS WORK. I SUSPECT IF HE WANTS TO...HE'LL TAKE OVER MY OWN POSITION IN THE FUTURE.
OF COURSE, HE'LL BE WELCOME TO IT.

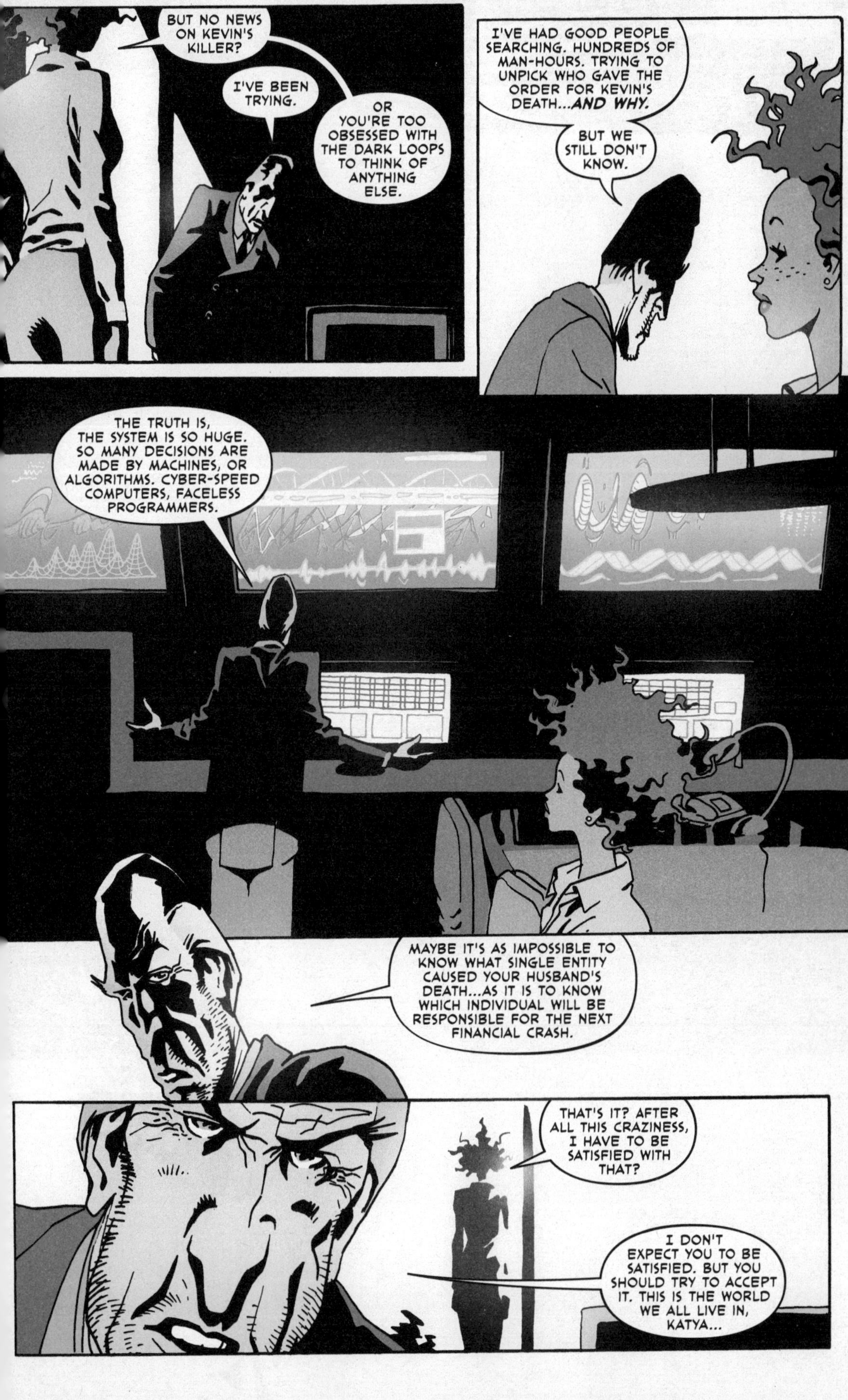

BUT NO NEWS ON KEVIN'S KILLER?
I'VE BEEN TRYING.
OR YOU'RE TOO OBSESSED WITH THE DARK LOOPS TO THINK OF ANYTHING ELSE.
I'VE HAD GOOD PEOPLE SEARCHING. HUNDREDS OF MAN-HOURS. TRYING TO UNPICK WHO GAVE THE ORDER FOR KEVIN'S DEATH...*AND WHY.*
BUT WE STILL DON'T KNOW.
THE TRUTH IS, THE SYSTEM IS SO HUGE. SO MANY DECISIONS ARE MADE BY MACHINES, OR ALGORITHMS. CYBER-SPEED COMPUTERS, FACELESS PROGRAMMERS.
MAYBE IT'S AS IMPOSSIBLE TO KNOW WHAT SINGLE ENTITY CAUSED YOUR HUSBAND'S DEATH...AS IT IS TO KNOW WHICH INDIVIDUAL WILL BE RESPONSIBLE FOR THE NEXT FINANCIAL CRASH.
THAT'S IT? AFTER ALL THIS CRAZINESS, I HAVE TO BE SATISFIED WITH THAT?
I DON'T EXPECT YOU TO BE SATISFIED. BUT YOU SHOULD TRY TO ACCEPT IT. THIS IS THE WORLD WE ALL LIVE IN, KATYA...

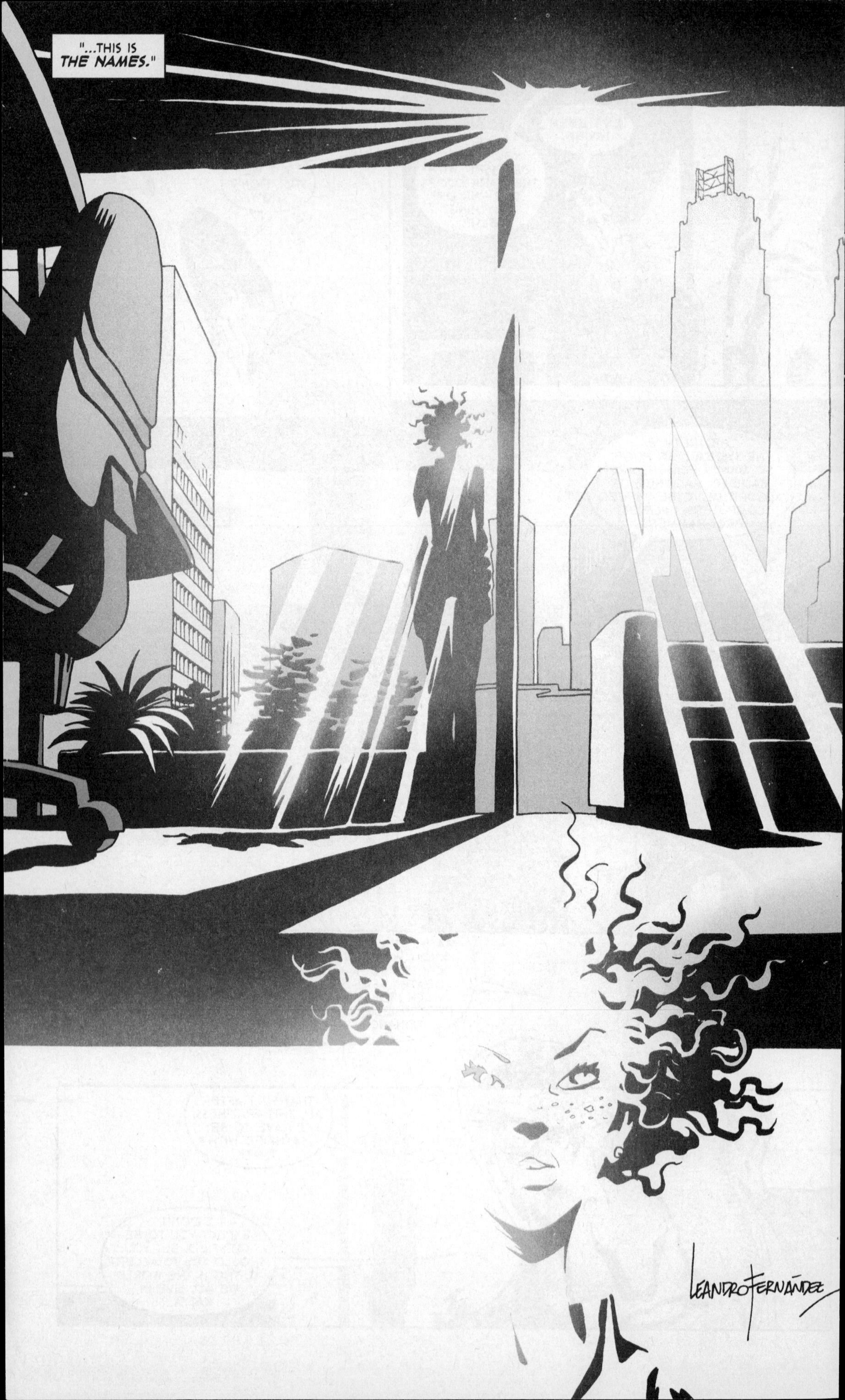
"...THIS IS THE NAMES."
LEANDRO FERNÁNDEZ

AL603

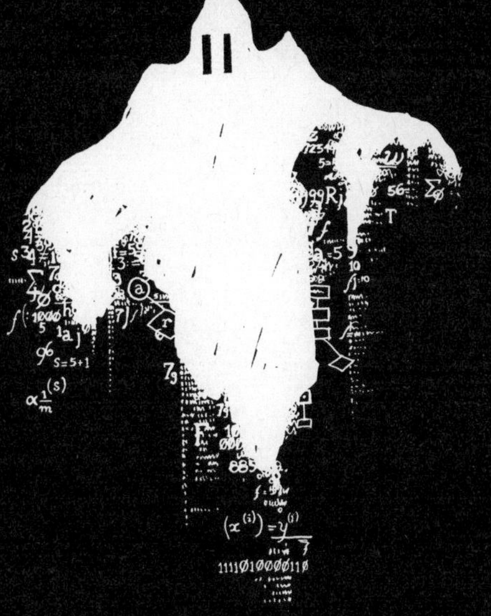

TAKING NAMES

Character designs and sketches by Leandro Fernandez

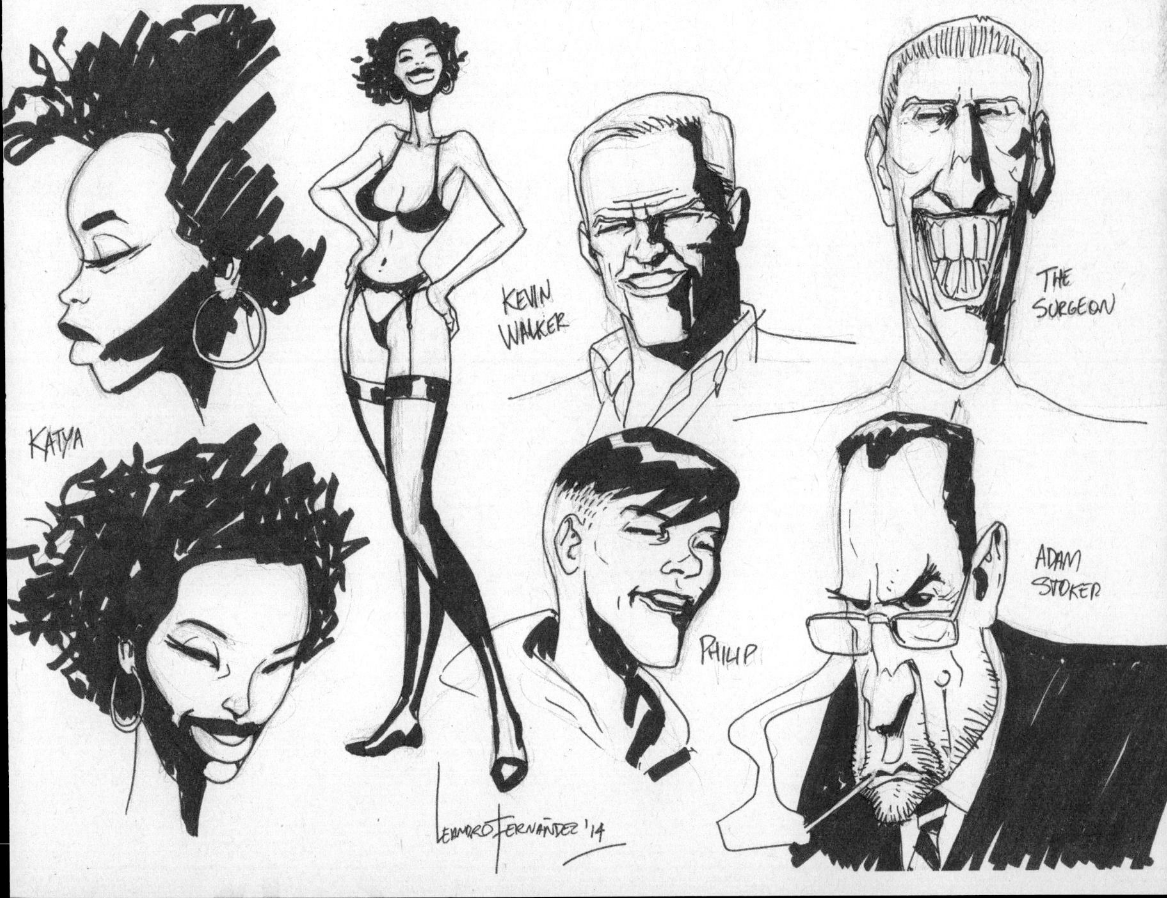
KATYA
KEVIN WALKER
THE SURGEON
PHILIP
ADAM STOKER
LEANDRO FERNANDEZ '14

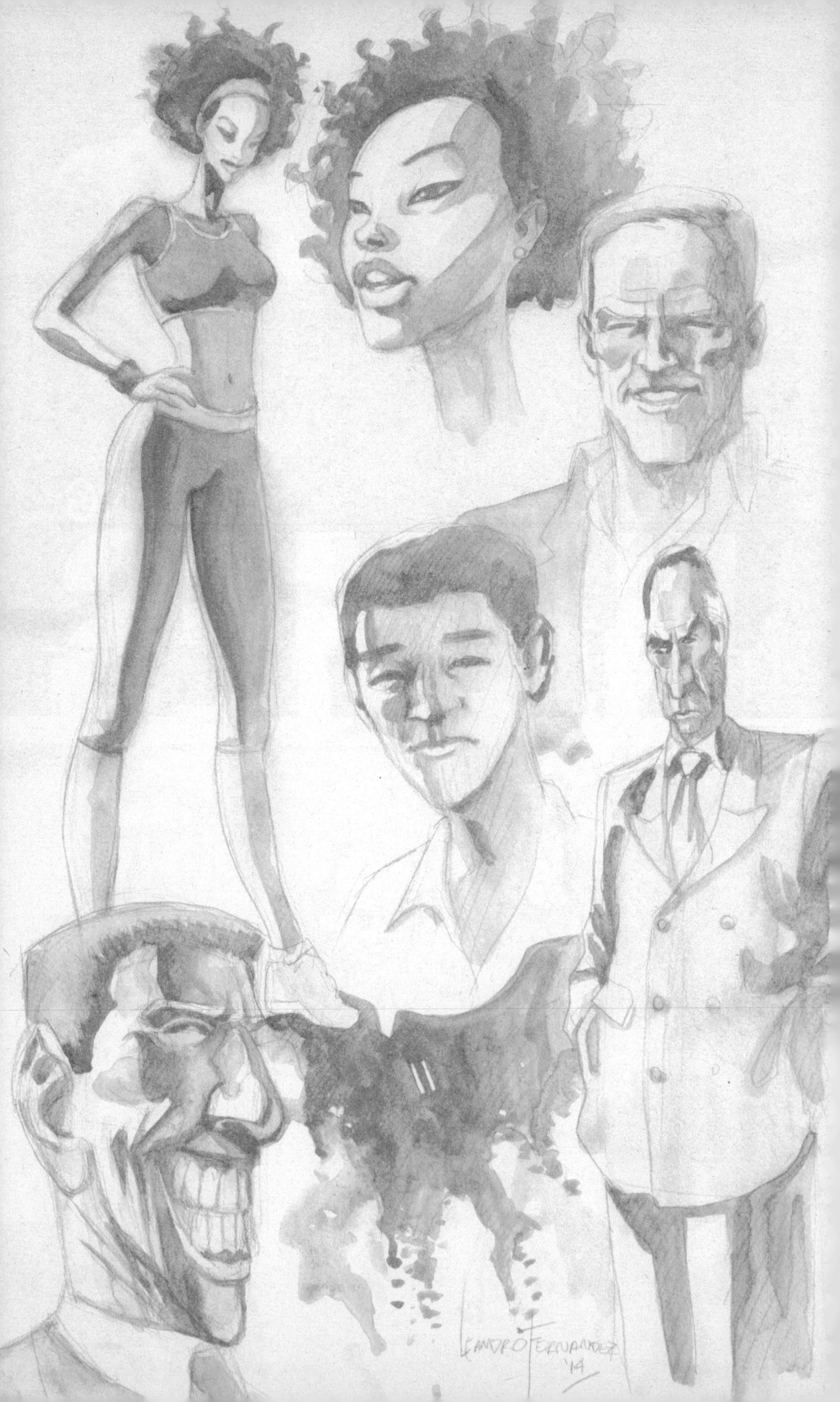
LEANDRO FERNANDEZ
'14

THE NAMES

CHARACTERS STUDIES

KATYA WALKER

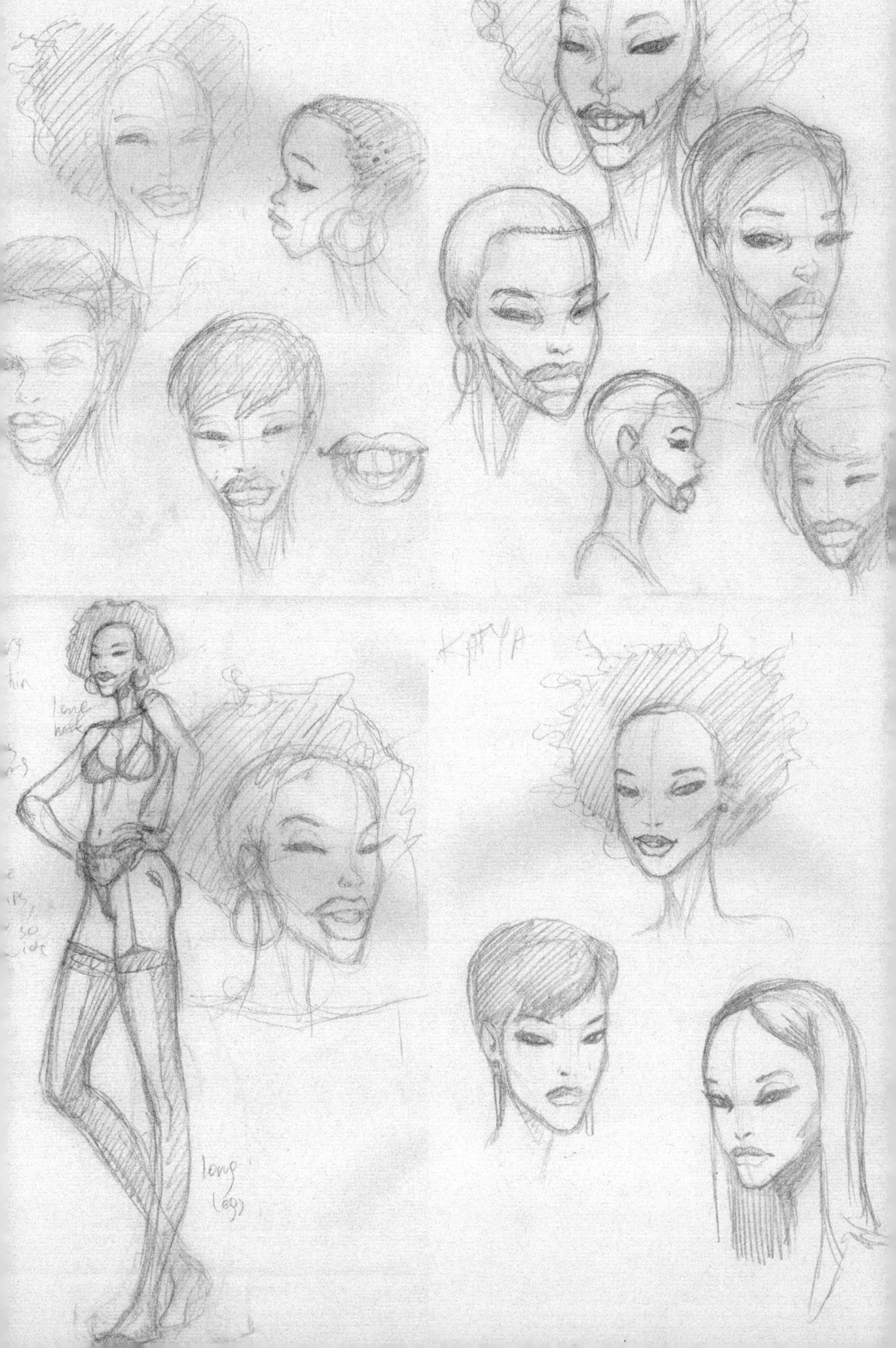

long neck
KATYA
long legs

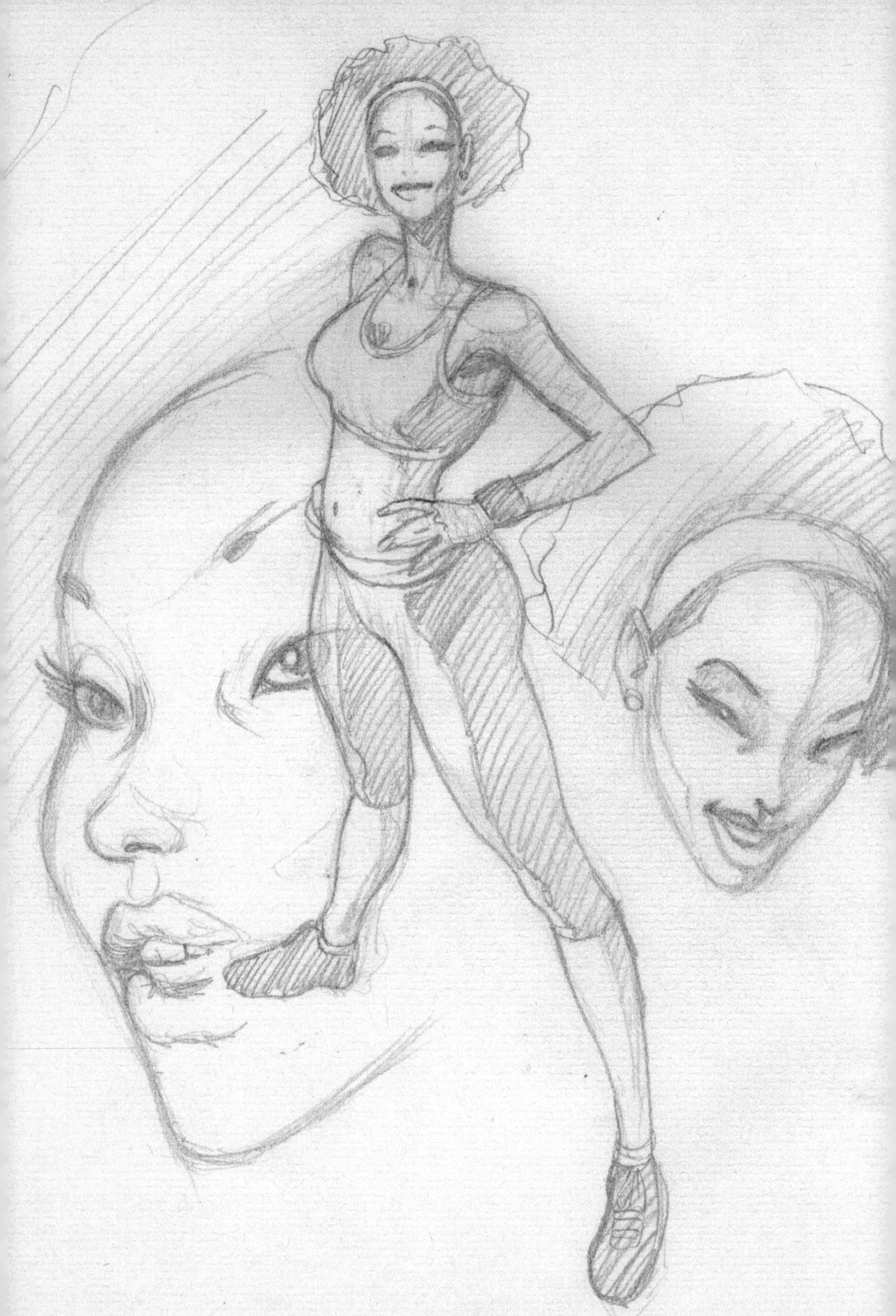

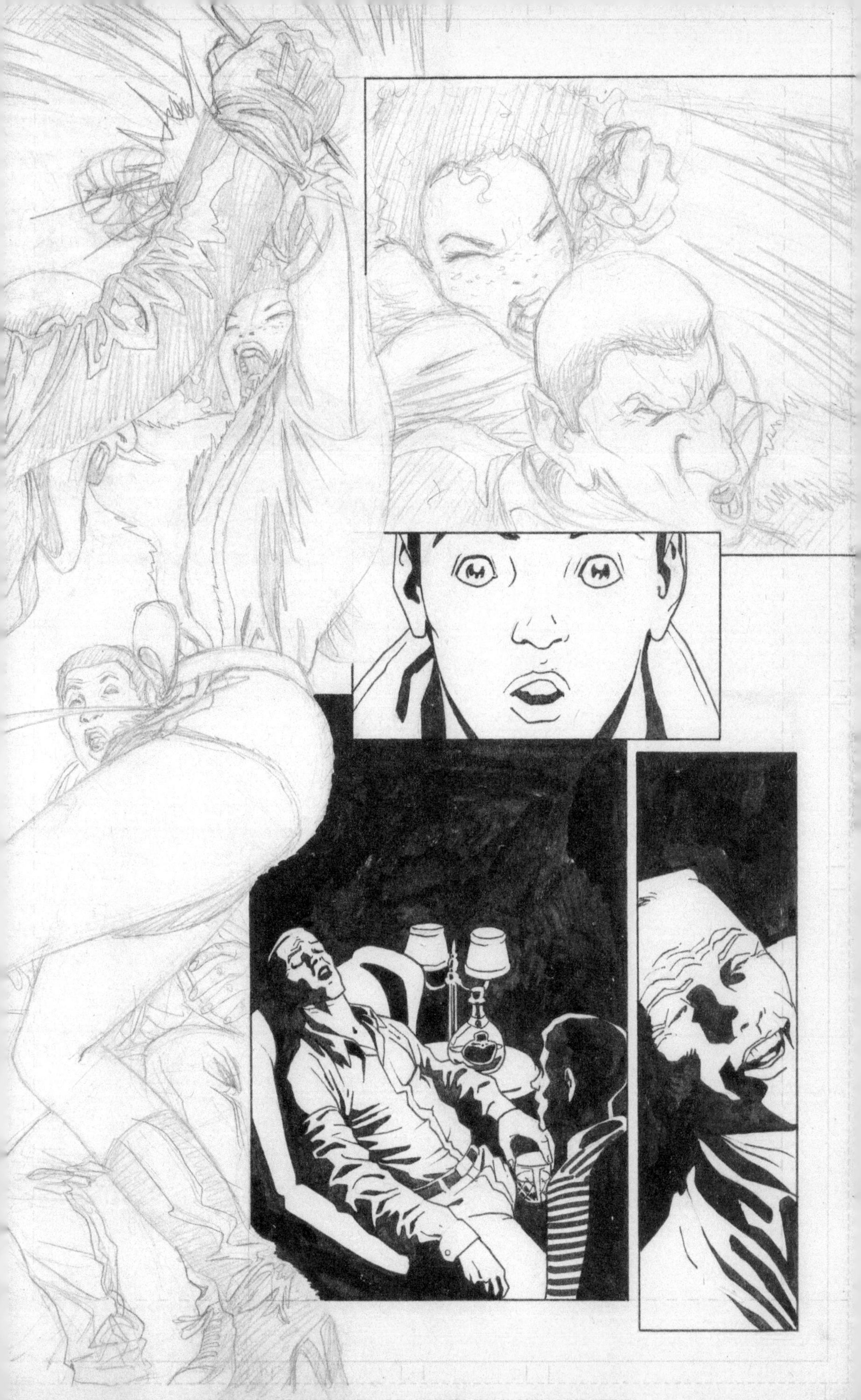

CUT RIGHT-HAND PAGE AT THIS LINE DOUBLE PAGE SPREAD: CUT AS SHOWN, ABUT PAGE EDGES, TAPE ON BACK, DO NOT OVERLAP CUT LEFT-HAND PAGE AT THIS LINE

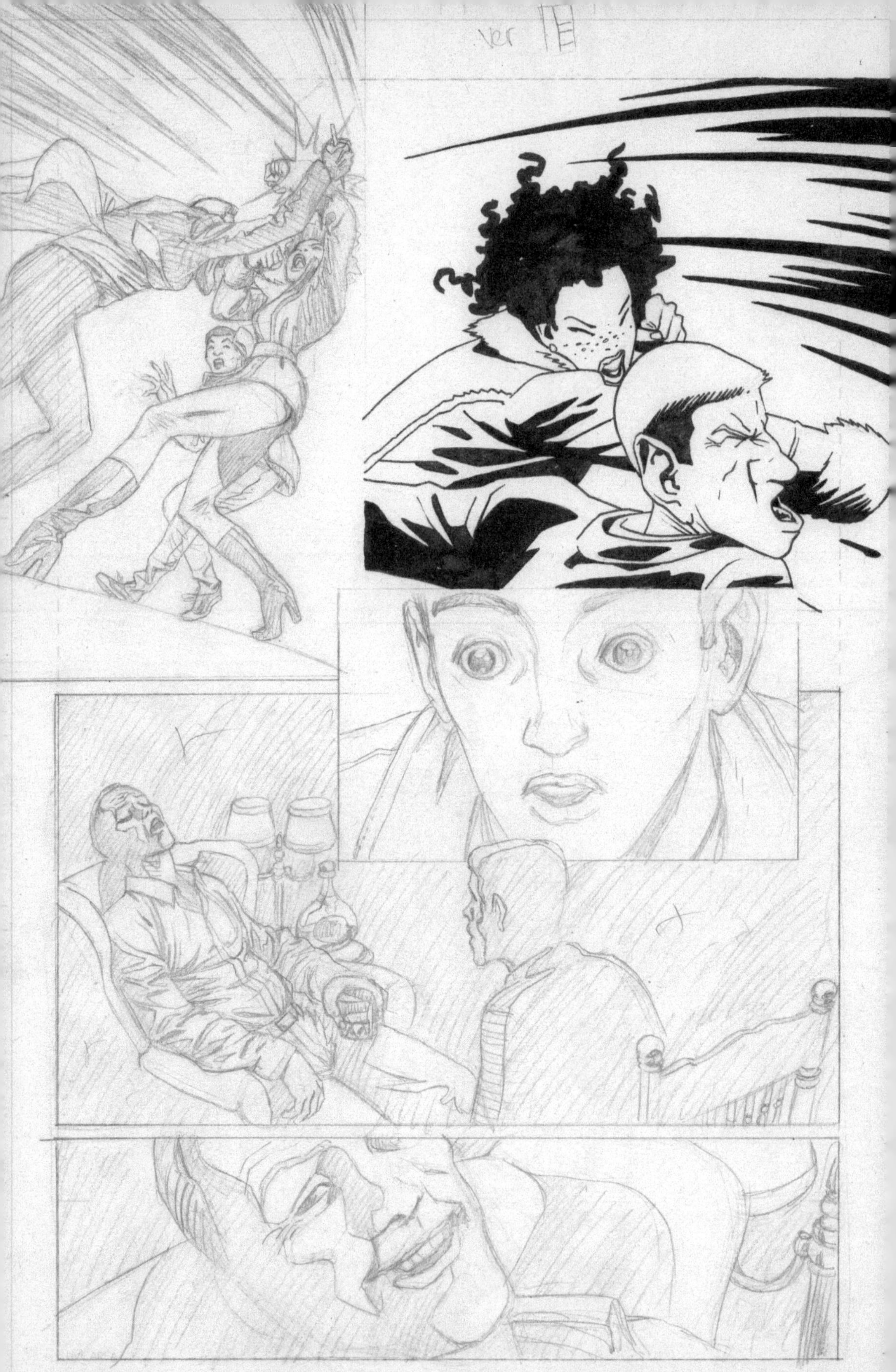
ver III

DOUBLE PAGE SPREAD: CUT AS SHOWN, ABUT PAGE EDGES, TAPE ON BACK, DO NOT OVERLAP

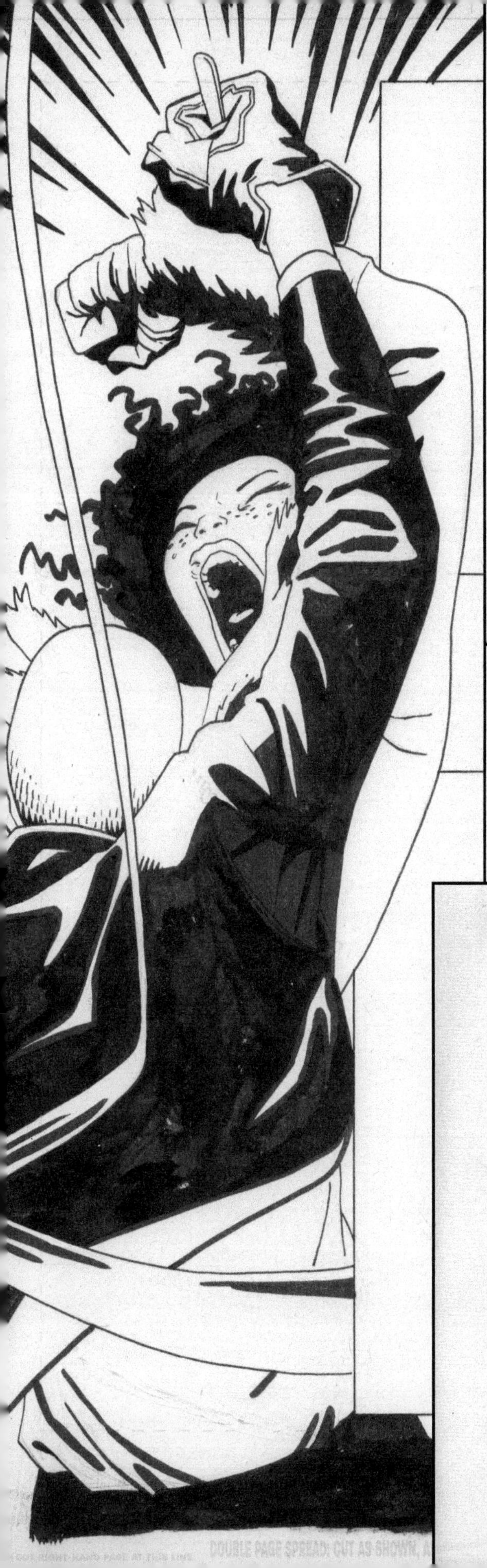
DOUBLE PAGE SPREAD: CUT AS SHOWN, A

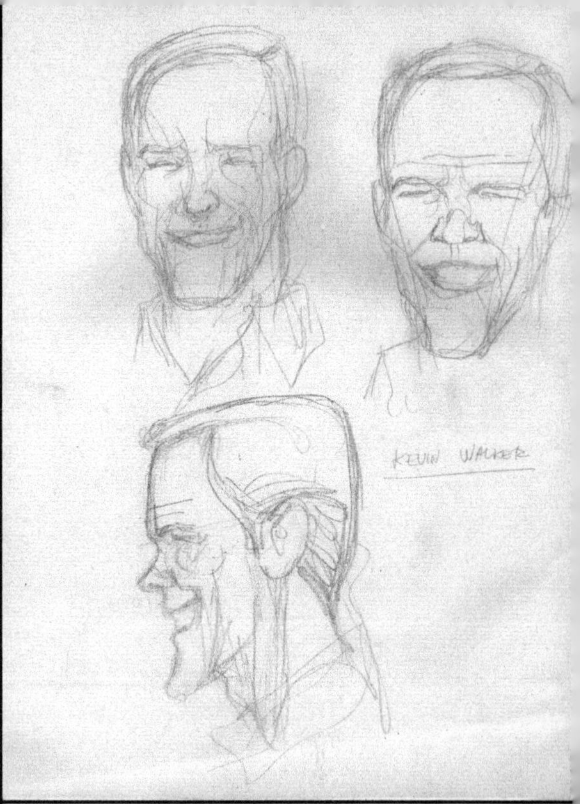
KEVIN WALKER

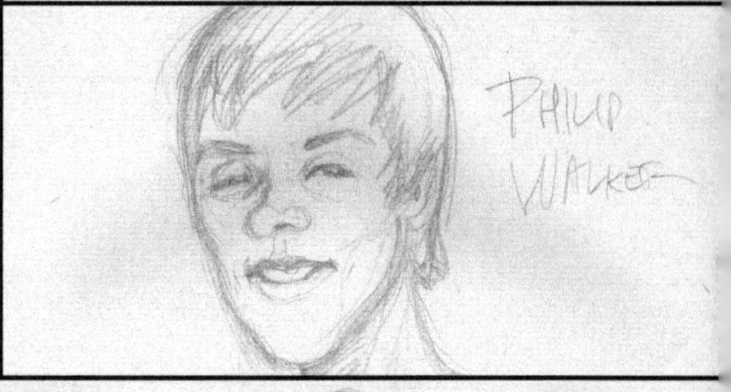
PHILIP WALKER

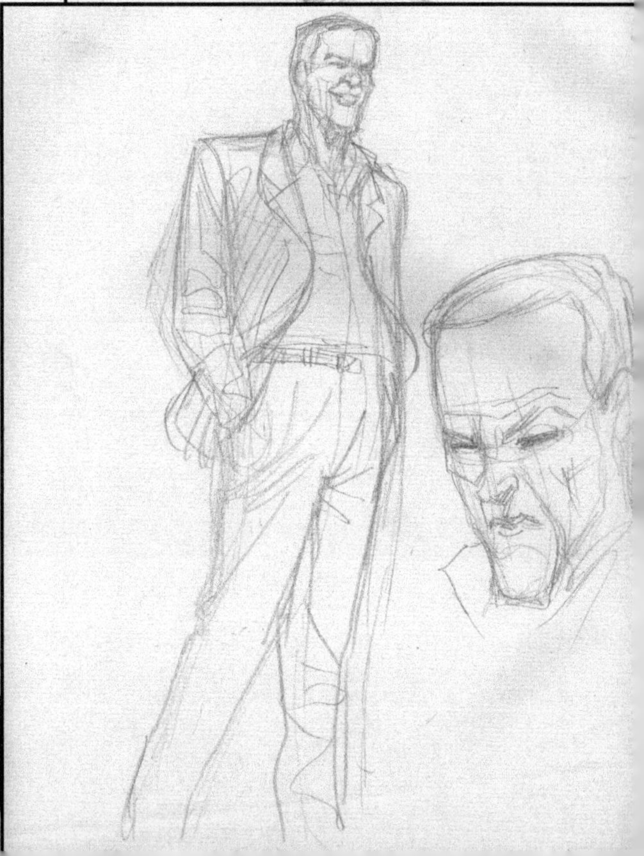

TITLE THE NAMES ISSUE # 03 MONTH INTERIORS

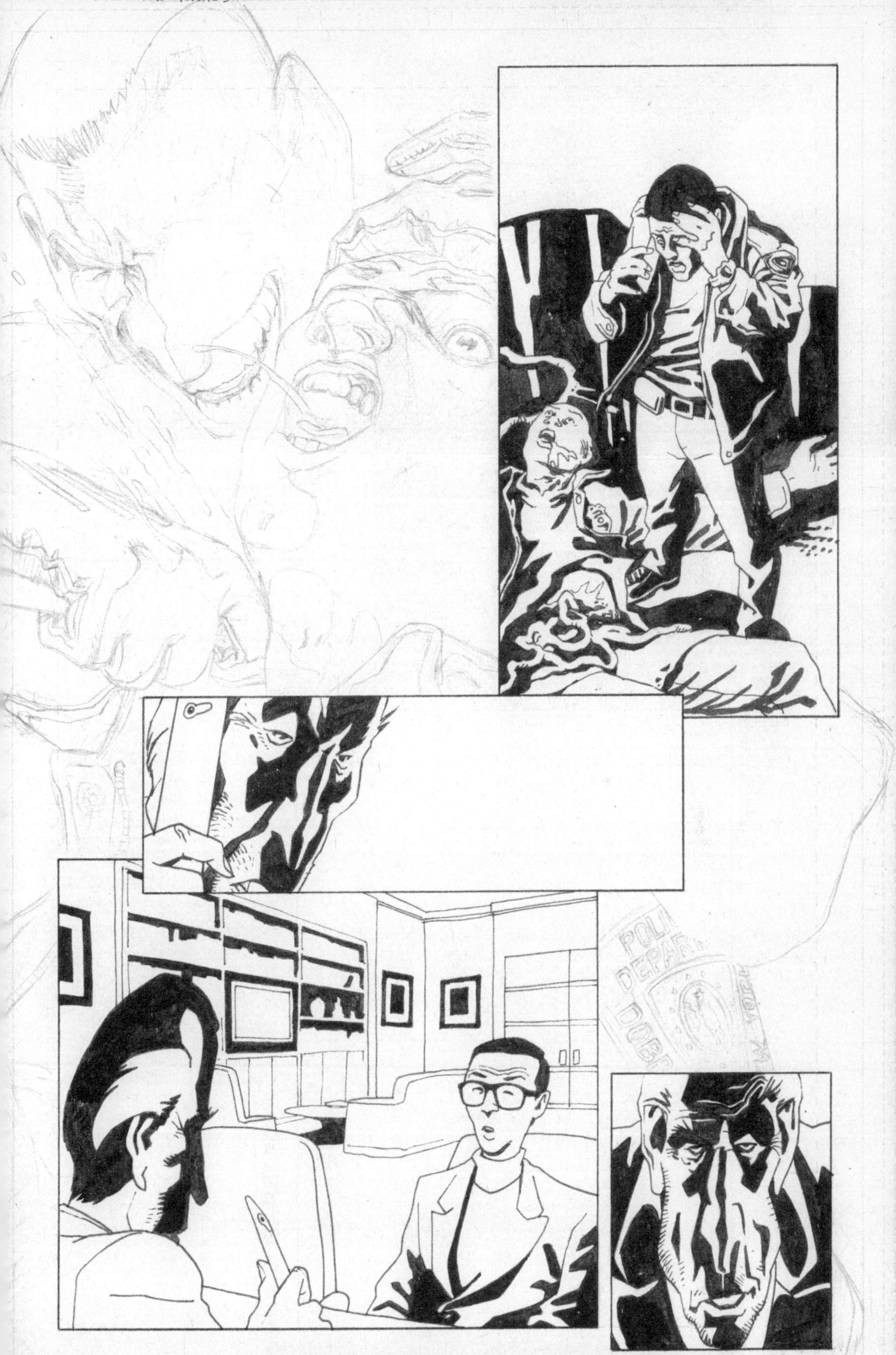
POLI
DEPAR

DOUBLE PAGE SPREAD: CUT AS SHOWN, ABUT PAGE EDGES, TAPE ON BACK, DO NOT OVERLAP

← CUT RIGHT-HAND PAGE AT THIS LINE   CUT LEFT-HAND PAGE AT THIS LINE →

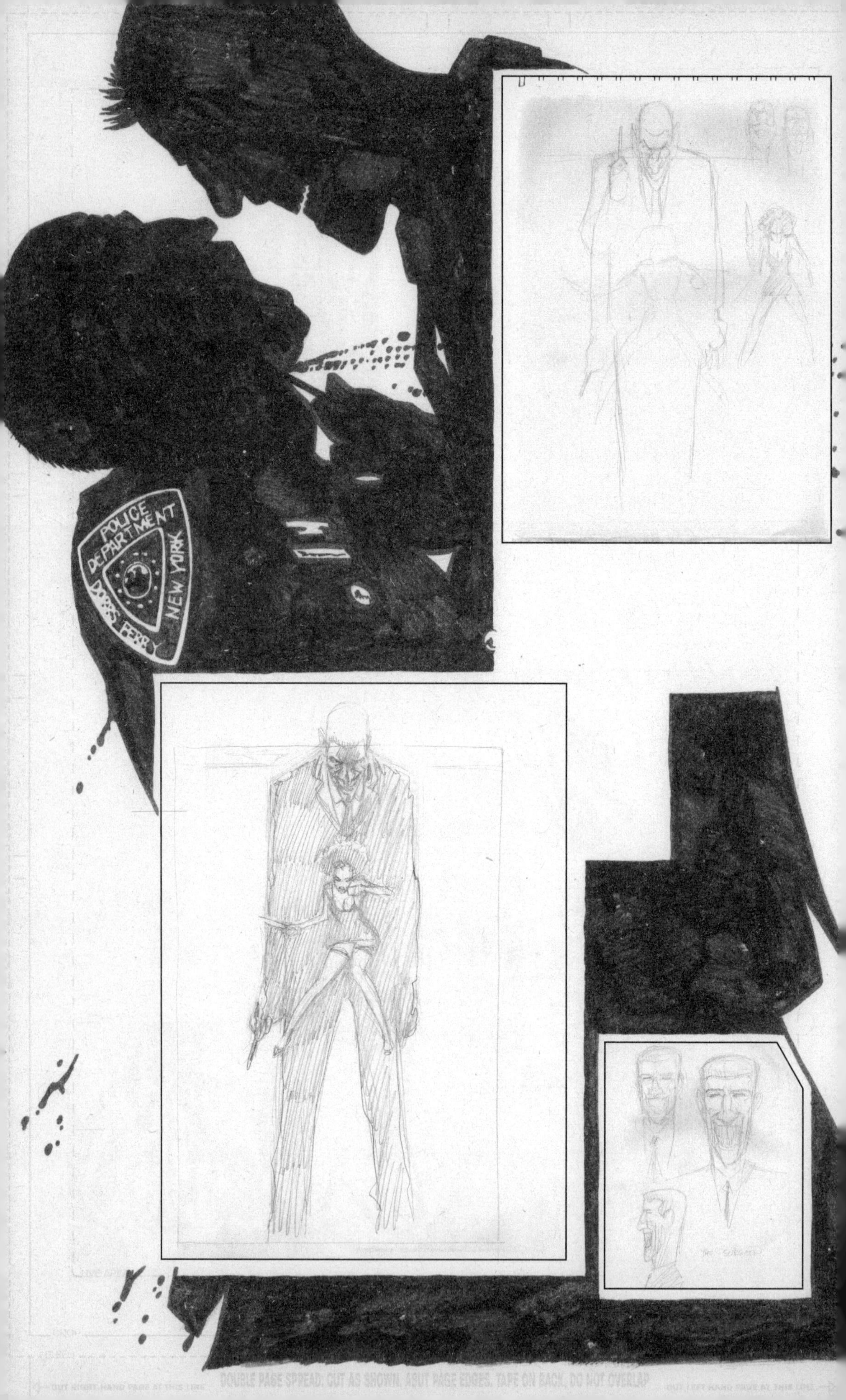
POLICE DEPARTMENT
DOBBS FERRY
NEW YORK
DOUBLE PAGE SPREAD. CUT AS SHOWN. ABUT PAGE EDGES. TAPE ON BACK. DO NOT OVERLAP